3/20

THE AGE OF THE WARRIOR

Also by Robert Fisk

The Point of No Return:
The Strike Which Broke the British in Ulster

In Time of War:
Ireland, Ulster and the Price of Neutrality 1939–45

Pity the Nation: Lebanon at War

The Great War for Civilisation:
The Conquest of the Middle East

THE AGE OF THE WARRIOR

SELECTED ESSAYS

ROBERT FISK

NATION
BOOKS

New York

Books published by Nation Books are available at
special discounts for bulk purchases in the United States by
corporations, institutions, and other organizations. For more
information, please contact the Special Markets Department at
the Perseus Books Group, 2300 Chestnut Street, Suite 200,
Philadelphia, PA 19103, or call (800) 810-4145, ext. 5000,
or e-mail special.markets@perseusbooks.com.

A CIP catalog record for this book
is available from the Library of Congress.
ISBN-13: 978-1-56858-403-4
LCCN: 2008929645

British ISBN: 978-0-00-727073-6
10 9 8 7 6 5 4 3 2 1

CONTENTS

ACKNOWLEDGEMENTS

My thanks for their help in the articles that make up this book go to Anas al-Abdeh, head of the Movement for Justice and Development in Syria; Taner Akçam, Turkish historian; Taiseer Alouni of al-Jazeera; Terry Anderson, former AP bureau chief in Beirut and the longest-held hostage in Lebanon; Vietnam veteran George W. Appenzeller; Laila al-Arian, daughter of Palestinian prisoner Sami al-Arian; the late Ane-Karine Arvesen, Norwegian diplomat; Armenian historian Peter Balakian; Dr Mona el-Baradei of Cairo University's politics department; Antoine Bechir of Beirut; Mohsen Bilal, former Syrian information minister; Andrea Bistrich for permission to quote from her letter to me on the death of her lover Christian Kleinert; ex-Mayor Willie Brown of San Francisco; Vincent Browne, Irish journalist; Pat and Alice Carey of Ireland; Tony Clifton, formerly of *Newsweek*; Denise Epstein, daughter of Irène Némirovsky; Norman Finkelstein of DePaul University, Chicago; my late parents, William and Peggy Fisk; diver Christian Francis of Enfeh, Lebanon; Jim Harland of Blyth, Northumberland; Seymour Hersh of the *New Yorker*; Marion Irvine, sister of Bill Cadman who was killed on Pan Am Flight 103 over Lockerbie; Adrien Jaulmes of *Le Figaro*; Walid and Nora Jumblatt of Lebanon; Dr Antony Loewenstein of Melbourne University; Syrian actor Ghassan Massoud; Samia Melki of Beirut; Peter Metcalfe for his superlative knowledge of T. E.

Lawrence; Captain Ramzi Najjar, formerly of Middle East Airlines; the British National Archives at Kew for permission to quote from Colonial Office papers on the Grand Mufti in Beirut; Dr Michael Noll of Valdosta State University, Georgia, USA; film-maker and journalist Nelofer Pazira; the late Mstislav Rostropovich; Michele Santoro, formerly of Italian television RAI 2; Dr David Shotter, formerly of Lancaster University classics department; Eric Stackhouse, for taking me to the *Titanic* cemetery in Halifax, Nova Scotia; Melanie Storoschuk, formerly of HarperCollins, Toronto; Perouz Taslakian of McGill University, Montreal; Stephen Williams for his translation of Dean Swift's epitaph; former Afghan refugee Mohamed Ziya. My thanks also to *Encyclopaedia Britannica* for permission to reproduce T. E. Lawrence's 1929 article 'Guerrilla'.

Finally, my immense gratitude, as always, goes to my Editor at *The Independent*, Simon Kelner, who allows me to be his Middle East Correspondent and to compile books at the same time (he also suffers me to tour the world lecturing – even when his man in Beirut phones in from São Paulo or Los Angeles!); to *The Independent* for permission to quote from my columns in the paper; to Louise Haines, my indefatigable editor at 4th Estate, and to Steve Cox, the sharpest 'reader' in the publishing industry. Very lastly, to Adrian Hamilton, my features editor at *The Independent*, who has never – ever – complained about anything I have written for him and whose help in collecting my writing over five years has been invaluable.

I have chosen to 'theme' the articles in this book in order to give them a coherence that a strict adherence to chronology would lose. A few have been cut to avoid repetition. Several errors of fact, which necessarily creep into journalism, have been corrected. But the opinions and predictions – those that proved to be true and those that turned out to be lamentably wrong – remain as they were originally printed. Only I am to blame, of course, for omissions or mistakes.

PREFACE

Iraq, I suspect, will come to define the world we live in, even for those of us who have never been within a thousand miles of its borders. The war's colossal loss in human life – primarily Iraqi, of course – and the lies that formed a bodyguard for our invasion troops in 2003 should inform our understanding of conflict for years to come. Weapons of mass destruction. Links to al-Qaeda and the crimes against humanity of 11 September 2001. We were fooled. Yet I sometimes believe that we wanted to be fooled – that we wish to be led to the slaughter by our masters, to race for the cliff-edge with the desperate enthusiasm of the suicide bomber, our instincts awakened by something that should have been buried at Hastings or Waterloo or Antietam or Berlin or even Da Nang. Do we need war? Do we need it the way we need air and love and children and safety? I wonder.

This is not a war book in the traditional sense. You will find the torn and shredded bodies of the Middle East in my two histories, of Lebanon and of the West's involvement in the region over the past century, a volume whose witness to suffering and pain caused me – during its writing – much distress; there is another to come, a companion volume that will take the reader down the road to perdition which is already being cut into the sand by our folly in Iraq and in Afghanistan and 'Palestine', in Lebanon and in Iran and in the dictatorships of the Muslim world.

The collection of articles in this book, most of them published in *The Independent* over the past five years, is therefore
angry rather than brutal, cynical rather than bloody. They
record, I suppose, a foreign correspondent's thoughts amid
war, a corner of the journalist's brain that usually goes unrecorded; the weekly need to write something at a right-angle
to the days gone by, the need to explore one's own anger as
well as the gentler, kinder moments in a life that has been
spent – let me speak bluntly – that has been used up and
squandered in watching human folly on a massive, unstoppable
scale.

Anger is a ferocious creature. Journalists are supposed to
avoid this nightmare animal, to observe this beast with 'objec-
tive' eyes. A reporter's supposed lack of 'bias' – which, I suspect,
is now the great sickness of our Western press and television
– has become the antidote to personal feeling, the excuse for
all of us to avoid the truth. Record the fury of a Palestinian
whose land has been taken from him by Israeli settlers – but
always refer to Israel's 'security needs' and its 'war on terror'.
If Americans are accused of 'torture', call it 'abuse'. If Israel
assassinates a Palestinian, call it a 'targeted killing'. If
Armenians lament their Holocaust of 1,500,000 souls in 1915,
remind readers that Turkey denies this all too real and fully
documented genocide. If Iraq has become a hell on earth for
its people, recall how awful Saddam was. If a dictator is on
our side, call him a 'strongman'. If he's our enemy, call him a
tyrant, or part of the 'axis of evil'. And above all else, use the
word 'terrorist'. Terror, terror, terror, terror, terror, terror, ter-
ror. Seven days a week.

That's the kind of anger that journalists are permitted to
deploy, the anger of righteousness and fear. It is the language
of our masters, the Bushes and Blairs and Browns, the Kinkels
and the Sarkozys and, of course, the Mubaraks and the King
Husseins and the Arabian kings and emirs and the Musharrafs

and, indeed, anyone – even the crazed Muammar Ghadafi of Libya – who signs up to the war of Good against Evil. For journalists, this has nothing to do with justice – which is all the people of the Middle East demand – and everything to do with avoidance. Ask 'how' and 'who' – but not 'why'. Source everything to officials: 'American officials', 'intelligence officials', 'official sources', anonymous policemen or army officers. Above all, show respect. For authority, for government, for power. And if those institutions charged with our protection abuse that power, then remind readers and listeners and viewers of the dangerous age in which we now live, the age of terror – which means that we must live in the Age of the Warrior, someone whose business and profession and vocation and mere existence is to destroy our enemies.

As Middle East Correspondent of *The Independent* of London, I endure a charmed but dangerous life. I travel to Iraq, Afghanistan, Syria, 'Palestine', Israel. I live in Lebanon. I have covered, over thirty-two years in the Middle East, eleven major wars, countless insurgencies and more massacres – more sheer bloody slaughter – than I care to count. And I have a newspaper, *The Independent*, which also encourages me to tell it how it is, to report not the clichés and blusterings of 'think tanks' and 'experts', but what I as a reporter see and believe. Each Saturday my editor, Simon Kelner, allows me to let rip in a column in which I can – like a journalist in paradise – swim in any direction in the sacred pool, examine any monster, visit any graveyard, talk to any murderer or friend, examine any document, write about any empire, look back even at the history of my own very ordinary English family in which my dad was a soldier in the First World War, in which his father was first mate on the giant tea clipper *Cutty Sark*. And I can say what I think.

It is a privilege and it is a trust – especially in a country, Britain, where the system of democracy has been so badly stained (principally by former prime minister Blair) that the press has come to play the role of parliamentary opposition – but it must be used, I think, with vigour and fury and cynicism, yes, and gentleness and, sometimes, with despair. This book therefore reflects my life as a journalist, largely over the past five years, but it also shows the need, I believe, to speak out against the fraud and injustice of a world in which consent has become automatic, in which criticism, however mild, is regarded as subversive. This is not my battle. I have colleagues who try to do what I try to do: to call our masters liars and mock their mendacity and their provable untruths and to bite them – hard – for the way in which they have damaged and soiled our world. I am not sure if history has a special integrity. But we should show an integrity towards the history which we are now creating in the hell–disaster of the Middle East.

I have sometimes strained the patience of my readers. Several have complained that they found my constant references to 'Lord Blair of Kut al-Amara' repetitive or childish. One of our *Independent* readers complained to the Editor, Simon Kelner, in October of 2007 that Fisk:

> should be more careful with his words. One thing I certainly cavil at is his snide reference to our current Prime Minister, whom he delights in calling Lord of Kut al-Amara. Not all his readers will understand his reference, but I do ... It was a terrible tragedy when it happened in the Great War, and even worse when the POWs had to march to Turkey. Surely Fisk must have read about it ...

Indeed, I had read of it. Kut al-Amara was the greatest British defeat at the hands of a Muslim army – the Ottoman Turks – in the First World War, a humiliating collapse of imperial power after Major-General Charles Townshend took 13,000 men up the banks of the Tigris in a vain attempt to reach

Baghdad. This comprehensive military disaster – Townshend was surrounded at Kut and watched his captive soldiers set out on a death march to Turkey – seemed to me to sum up both the arrogance with which Tony Blair took his country to war and the swamp in which our army found itself in Iraq. So Blair remains, for the most part, 'Lord Blair of Kut al-Amara' in these articles.* A columnist must sometimes write with a cartoonist's strokes.

Books occasionally write themselves. Reading the proofs, it became clear to me that my own journalism over the past five years has concentrated more and more on the sheer hypocrisy of the political–military–journalistic nexus of power which is deployed to fool us, to persuade us to follow policies which are contrary to our national interests and against all morality. Indeed, the use of power to terrorise us – to put more fear in our hearts than any 'terrorist' is capable of doing – seems to me to be one of the most frightening and damning characteristics of our age.

The blood of Iraqis flows through these pages, but *The Age of the Warrior* is neither a story of unrelieved carnage nor of unremitting journalistic rage. I examine the use and misuse of words, the influence of the cinema and of novels on our age, the need to create some form of beauty even amid war. You will meet my former Latin professor, the old boys of my English school, you will walk round the mass grave of the *Titanic*'s passengers in Canada and read the battle honours in the oldest church in Wellington, New Zealand, and you will sit beside Mstislav Rostropovich, the greatest cellist of his age, as he

---

* By extraordinary irony, Amara was the first city that British troops abandoned to insurgents. Under a 'gentleman's agreement' in 2006, UK forces were permitted a single afternoon patrol through the city in return for handing over power to armed tribal leaders. The British could thus claim they had not retreated, while at the same time giving up all responsibility for the tens of thousands of local inhabitants: a truly Blairite solution.

travels to a Beirut still ravaged by war, his 'wife' – his most precious musical instrument – strapped beside him in seat 1K. And you will meet again my soldier father Bill who bravely refused to execute a comrade in the First World War – an Australian who did indeed stand before a firing squad but who died, it now turns out, with an extraordinary secret in his heart.

Collections of this kind are bound to be a patchwork, but in this case I have found a meaning in the compilation. I have deliberately allowed some few repetitions to preserve the integrity of articles as they were originally published. But a journalist's life – however specialised – revolves around a theme. And in this case, my columns have returned, again and again, to the semantics of politics and war and the need to expose the needless mass suffering that we inflict on our fellow humans. Death, as usual, walks through these pages until, at the end, Denise Epstein – surviving daughter of that wonderful Jewish–French novelist Irène Némirovsky, who perished at Auschwitz – warns us of the 'dilution of memory'. It is this dilution, this wilful refusal to see and recognise cruelty, which will push us back into the inferno.

Beirut
February 2008

CHAPTER ONE

A firestorm coming

War is a paradox for journalists. Millions around the world are fascinated by the mass violence of war – from Shakespeare to Hollywood – and are obsessed with its drama, the cruel, simple choice it offers of triumph or defeat. Our Western statesmen – not one of whom has witnessed or participated in a real conflict and whose only experience of war comes from movies or television – are inspired by war and thus often invoke religion, or 'good and evil', to justify its brutality. If Shakespeare understood that human conflict was an atrocity, the history of the last century in the Middle East – leading irrevocably to the attacks of 11 September and thus the assault on Afghanistan and the preparations for an even more ambitious subjugation of Iraq – suggests that our politicians and our journalists are able to overcome this scruple. The peoples of the Middle East – though not their leaders – often seem to have a surer grasp of reality than those who make history, a superb irony since 'we' usually blame 'them' for the violence with which we are now all supposedly threatened.

Cry havoc and let slip the dogs of war

Poor old Bardolph. The common soldier, the Poor Bloody Infantry, the GI Joe of Agincourt, survives *Henry IV*, only to end up on the end of a rope after he's avoided filling up the breach at Harfleur with his corpse. Henry V is his undoing – in every sense of the word – when he robs a French church. He must be executed, hanged, 'pour encourager les autres'. 'Bardolph,' laments his friend Pistol to Fluellen, 'a soldier firm and sound of heart . . . hanged must' a be –

> A damned death!
> Let gallows gape for dog, let man go free,
> And let not hemp his wind-pipe suffocate:
> But Exeter hath given the doom of death . . .
> Therefore go speak, the duke will hear thy voice;
> And let not Bardolph's vital thread be cut . . .
> Speak, captain, for his life . . .

How many such military executions have been recorded in the past thirty years of Middle East history? For theft, for murder, for desertion, for treachery, for a momentary lapse of discipline. Captain Fluellen pleads the profoundly ugly Bardolph's cause – not with great enthusiasm, it has to be said – to Henry himself.

... I think the Duke hath lost never a man, but one that is like to be executed for robbing a church, one Bardolph, if your majesty know the man: his face is all bubukles and whelks, and knobs, and flames o' fire, and his lips blows at his nose ...

But the priggish Henry, a friend of Bardolph in his princely, drinking days (shades of another, later Prince Harry), will have none of it:

We would have all such offenders so cut off. And we give express charge that in our marches through the country there be nothing compell'd from the villages, nothing taken but paid for, none of the French upbraided or abused in disdainful language ...

In France, Eisenhower shot post-D-Day rapists in the US army. The SS hanged their deserters even as Berlin fell.

And I never pass the moment when Shakespeare's French king asks if Henry's army 'hath passed the river Somme' without drawing in my breath. Did some faint moment of Renaissance prescience touch the dramatist in 1599? But I have still to be convinced that Shakespeare saw war service in the army of Elizabeth. 'Say'st thou me so?' Pistol asks of a cringing French prisoner who does not speak English. 'Come hither, boy, ask me this slave in French/What is his name.' I heard an almost identical quotation in Baghdad, shorn of its sixteenth-century English, when a US Marine confronted an Iraqi soldier-demonstrator in 2003. 'Shut the fuck up,' he screamed at the Iraqi. Then he turned to his translator. 'What the fuck's he saying?' At the siege of Harfleur, the soldier Boy wishes he was far from battle – 'Would I were in an alehouse in London! I would give all my fame for a pot of ale, and safety' – and Henry's walk through his camp in disguise on the eve of Agincourt evokes some truly modern reflections on battle. The soldier Bates suggests to him that if the king had come on his own to Agincourt, he would be safely ransomed 'and a many poor men's lives saved'.

The equally distressed soldier Williams argues that if the English cause is doubtful, '. . . the king himself hath a heavy reckoning to make when all those legs and arms and heads, chopp'd off in a battle, shall join together at the latter day and cry all "We died at such a place" some swearing, some crying for a surgeon, some upon their wives left poor behind them, some upon the debts they owe, some upon their children rawly left . . .'

This bloody accounting would be familiar to any combat soldier, but Shakespeare could have heard these stories from the English who had been fighting on the Continent in the sixteenth century. I've seen those chopped-off legs and arms and heads on the battlefields of the Middle East, in southern Iraq in 1991 when the eviscerated corpses of Iraqi soldiers and refugee women and children were lying across the desert, their limbs afterwards torn apart by ravenous dogs. And I've talked to Serb soldiers who fought Bosnian Muslims in the battle for the Bihac pocket, men who were so short of water that they drank their own urine.

Similarly, Shakespeare's censorious Caesar Augustus contemplates Antony's pre-Cleopatran courage:

When thou once
Was beaten from Modena,
. . . at thy heel
Did famine follow, whom thou fought'st against,
. . . with patience more
Than savages could suffer. Thou didst drink
The stale of horses and the gilded puddle
Which beasts would cough at . . .

Yet Wilfred Owen's poetry on the 'pity of war' – his description, say, of the gassed soldier coughing his life away, the blood gargling 'from the froth-corrupted lungs' – has much greater immediacy. True, death was ever present in the life of any Tudor man or woman; the Plague that sometimes closed down the Globe Theatre, the hecatomb of child mortality, the overflowing, pestilent graveyards, united all mankind in the proximity of death. Understand death and you understand war, which is primarily about the extinction of human life rather than victory or defeat. And despite constant repetition, Hamlet's soliloquy over poor Yorick's skull remains a deeply disturbing contemplation of death:

> My gorge rises at it. Here hung those lips that I have kiss'd I know not how oft. Where be your gibes now, your gambols, your songs, your flashes of merriment that were wont to set the table on a roar? Not one now to mock your own grinning quite chapfall'n?

And here is Omar Khayyam's contemplation of a king's skull at Tus – near the modern-day Iranian city of Mashad – written more than 400 years before Shakespeare's Hamlet stood in the churchyard at Elsinore:

> I saw a bird alighted on the city walls of Tus
> Grasping in its claws Kaika'us's head:
> It was saying to that head, 'Shame! Shame!
> Where now the sound of the bells and the boom of the drum?'

The swiftness with which disease struck the living in previous centuries was truly murderous. And I have my own testimony of how quickly violent death can approach. Assaulted by a crowd of Afghans in a Pakistani border village in 2001

– their families had just been slaughtered in an American B-52 air raid on Kandahar – an ever-growing crowd of young men were banging stones on to my head, smashing my glasses into my face, cutting my skin open until I could smell my own blood. And, just for a moment, I caught sight of myself in the laminated side of a parked bus. I was crimson with blood, my face was bright red with the stuff and it was slopping down my shirt and on to my bag and my trousers and shoes; I was all gore from head to foot. And I distinctly remember, at that very moment – I suppose it was a subconscious attempt to give meaning to my own self-disgust – the fearful ravings of the insane Lady Macbeth as she contemplates the stabbing of King Duncan: '. . . who would have thought the old man to have had so much blood in him?'

Shakespeare would certainly have witnessed pain and suffering in daily London life. Executions were staged in public, not filmed secretly on mobile telephones. But who can contemplate Saddam's hanging – the old monster showing nobility as his Shi'ite executioners tell him he is going 'to hell' – without remembering 'that most disloyal traitor', the condemned Thane of Cawdor in *Macbeth*, of whom Malcolm was to remark that '. . . nothing in his life/Became him like the leaving it'? Indeed, Saddam's last response to his tormentors – 'to the hell that is Iraq?' – was truly Shakespearean.

How eerily does Saddam's shade haunt our modern reading of Shakespeare. 'Hang those that talk of fear!' must have echoed through many a Saddamite palace, where 'mouth-honour' had long ago become the custom, where – as the casualties grew through the long years of his eight-year conflict with Iran – a Ba'athist leader might be excused the Macbethian thought that he was 'in blood/Stepp'd in so far that, should I wade no more,/Returning were as tedious as go o'er'. The Iraqi dictator tried to draw loose inspiration from the *Epic of Gilgamesh* in his own feeble literary endeavours, an infantile novel which –

if David Damrosch is right – was the work of an Iraqi writer subsequently murdered by Saddam. Perhaps Auden best captures the nature of the beast:

> Perfection, of a kind, was what he was after,
> And the poetry he invented was easy to understand;
> He knew human folly like the back of his hand,
> And was greatly interested in armies and fleets . . .

In an age when we are supposed to believe in the 'War on Terror', we may quarry our way through Shakespeare's folios in search of Osama bin Laden and George W. Bush with all the enthusiasm of the mass murderer who prowls through Christian and Islamic scriptures in search of excuses for ethnic cleansing. Indeed, smiting the Hittites, Canaanites and Jebusites is not much different from smiting the Bosnians or the Rwandans or the Arabs or, indeed, the modern-day Israelis. And it's not difficult to find a parallel with Bush's disasters in Afghanistan and Iraq – and his apparent desire to erase these defeats with yet a new military adventure in Iran – in Henry IV's deathbed advice to his son, the future Henry V:

> . . . Therefore, my Harry,
> Be it thy course to busy giddy minds
> With foreign quarrels, that action, hence borne out,
> May waste the memory of the former days.

The wasteland and anarchy of Iraq in the aftermath of our illegal 2003 invasion is reflected in so many of Shakespeare's plays that one can move effortlessly between the tragedies and the histories to read of present-day civil war Baghdad. Here's the father, for example, on discovering that he has killed his own child in *Henry VI, Part III*:

> O, pity, God, this miserable age!
> What stratagems, how fell, how butcherly,
> Erroneous, mutinous and unnatural,
> This deadly quarrel daily doth beget!

Our treachery towards the Shi'ites and Kurds of Iraq in 1991 – when we encouraged them to rise up against Saddam and then allowed the butcher of Baghdad to destroy them – was set against the genuine cries for freedom that those doomed people uttered in the days before their betrayal. '. . . waving our red weapons o'er our heads,' as Brutus cried seconds after Julius Caesar's murder, 'Let's all cry, "Peace, freedom, and liberty".'

My own experience of war has changed my feelings towards many of Shakespeare's characters. The good guys in Shakespeare's plays have become ever less attractive, ever more portentous, ever more sinister as the years go by. Henry V seems more than ever a butcher. 'Now, herald, are the dead numb'red?' he asks.

> This note doth tell me of ten thousand French
> That in the field lie slain; of princes, in this number,
> And nobles bearing banners, there lie dead
> One hundred twenty-six; added to these,
> Of knights, esquires, and gallant gentlemen,
> Eight thousand and four hundred . . .

Henry is doing 'body counts'. When the herald presents another list – this time of the English dead – Henry reads off the names of Edward, Duke of York, the Earl of Suffolk, Sir Richard Kikely, Davy Gam, Esquire:

> None else of name; and of all other men
> But five and twenty. O God, thy arm was here . . .

Was ever known so great and little loss
On one part and on th'other?

This is pure Gulf War Part One, when General Norman Schwarzkopf was gloating at the disparate casualty figures – while claiming, of course, that he was 'not in the business of body counts' and while General Peter de la Billière was telling Britons to celebrate victory by ringing their church bells.

Shakespeare can still be used to remind ourselves of an earlier, 'safer' (if non-existent) world, a reassurance of our own ultimate survival. It was not by chance that Olivier's *Henry V* was filmed during the Second World War. The Bastard's final promise in *King John* is simple enough:

Come the three corners of the world in arms,
And we shall shock them. Naught shall make us rue,
If England to itself do rest but true.

But the true believers – the Osamas and Bushes – probably lie outside the history plays. The mad King Lear – betrayed by two of his daughters just as bin Laden felt he was betrayed by the Saudi royal family when they rejected his offer to free Kuwait from Iraqi occupation without American military assistance – shouts that he will 'do such things/What they are yet, I know not; but they shall be/The terrors of the earth.'

Lear, of course, was written in the immediate aftermath of the Gunpowder Plot, a 'terrorist' conspiracy with potential 11 September consequences. Similarly, the saintly Prospero in *The Tempest* contains both the self-righteousness and ruthlessness of bin Laden and the covert racism of Bush. When he sends Ariel to wreck the usurping King Alonso's ship on his island, the airy spirit returns with an account of his success which – despite his subsequent saving of lives – is of near Twin Towers dimensions:

> Now in the waist, the deck, in every cabin,
> I flam'd amazement. Sometime I'd divide,
> And burn in many places . . .
> Not a soul
> But felt a fever of the mad, and play'd
> Some tricks of desperation. All but mariners
> Plung'd in the foaming brine, and quit the vessel;
> Then all afire with me; the King's son, Ferdinand,
> With hair up-staring then like reeds, not hair
> Was the first man that leapt; cried "Hell is empty,
> And all the devils are here".

In almost the same year, John Donne was using equally terrifying imagery, of a 'fired ship' from which 'by no way/But drowning, could be rescued from the flame,/Some men leap'd forth . . .' Prospero's cruelty towards Caliban becomes more frightening each time I read of it, not least because *The Tempest* is one of four Shakespeare plays in which Muslims appear and because Caliban is himself an Arab, born of an Algerian mother.

'This damn'd witch Sycorax,/For mischiefs manifold, and sorceries terrible/To enter human hearing, from Argier/Thou know'st was banish'd . . .' Prospero tells us. 'This blue-ey'd hag was hither brought with child . . . /A freckl'd whelp, hag-born not honour'd with/A human shape.'

Caliban is the 'terrorist' on the island, first innocently nurtured by Prospero and then condemned to slavery after trying to rape Prospero's daughter, the colonial slave who turns against the fruits of civilisation that were offered him.

You taught me language, and my profit on't
Is, I know how to curse. The red plague rid you
For learning me your language!

Yet Caliban must 'obey' Prospero because 'his art is of such power'. Prospero may not have F-18s or bunker-busters, but Caliban is able to play out a familiar Western narrative; he teams up with the bad guys, offering his help to Trinculo – 'I'll show you the best springs; I'll pluck thee berries;/I'll fish for thee ...' – making the essential linkage between evil and terror that Bush vainly tried to claim between al-Qaeda and Saddam. Caliban is an animal, unworthy of pity, not honoured with a 'human shape'. Compare this with an article in the newspaper *USA Today*, in which a former American military officer, Ralph Peters – arguing that Washington should withdraw from Iraq because its people are no longer worthy of our Western sacrifice – refers to 'the comprehensive inability of the Arab world to progress in any sphere of organised human endeavor'.* Prospero, of course, prevails and Caliban survives to grovel to his colonial master: 'How fine my master is! I am afraid/He will chastise me/ ... I'll be wise hereafter,/And seek for grace ...' The war of terror has been won!

Shakespeare lived at a time when the largely Muslim Ottoman empire – then at its zenith of power – remained an existential if not a real threat for Europeans. The history plays are replete with these fears, albeit that they are also a product of propaganda on behalf of Elizabeth and, later, James. In *Henry IV, Part I*, the king is to set out on the Crusades:

As far as to the sepulchre of Christ ...
Forthwith a power of English shall we levy,
Whose arms were moulded in their mothers' womb

---

* *USA Today* 3 November 2006.

To chase these pagans in those holy fields
Over whose acres walked those blessed feet.

Rhetoric is no one's prerogative – compare King Henry V's pre-Agincourt speech with Saddam's prelude to the 'Mother of All Battles' where Prospero-like purity is espoused for the Arab 'side'. This is Saddam: 'Standing at one side of this confrontation are peoples and sincere leaders and rulers, and on the other are those who stole the rights of God and the tyrants who were renounced by God after they renounced all that was right, honourable, decent and solemn and strayed from the path of God until . . . they became obsessed by the devil from head to toe.'

Similar sentiments are espoused by Tamburlaine in Marlowe's play. Tamburlaine is the archetypal Muslim conqueror, the 'scourge of God' who found it passing brave to be a king, and ride in triumph through Persepolis.

But *Othello* remains the most obvious, tragic narrative of our Middle Eastern fears. He is a Muslim in the service of Venice – close neighbour to the Ottoman empire – and is sent to Cyprus to battle the Turkish fleet. He is a mercenary whose self-hatred contaminates the play and eventually leads to his own death. Racially abused by both Iago and Roderigo, he lives in a world where there are men whose heads supposedly grow beneath their shoulders, where he is black – most Arabs are not black, although Olivier faithfully followed this notion – and where, just before killing himself, he compares his terrible stabbing of Desdemona to the work of a 'base Indian' who:

> . . . threw a pearl away
> Richer than all his tribe; of one whose subdu'd eyes,
> . . . Drops tears as fast as the Arabian trees
> . . . Set you down this:

And say besides that in Aleppo once,
Where a malignant and a turban'd Turk
Beat a Venetian and traduc'd the state,
I took by the throat the circumcised dog,
And smote him thus.

That, I fear, is the dagger that we now feel in all our hearts.

The Independent Magazine, 30 March 2007

Flirting with the enemy

After the Second World War, Palestine was crumbling. Menachem Begin's Irgun had blown up British headquarters at the King David Hotel in Jerusalem, the British were executing Jewish 'terrorists', and the Jews had hanged two kidnapped British army sergeants. The Arabs were determined to destroy the future Jewish state of Israel. The old imperial mandate was in a state of incipient civil war. You have only to open Colonial Office file 537/2643 to understand why, in their moment of agony, the British toyed with the idea of negotiating with an Arab cleric whom they had, only two years earlier, tried to extradite as a war criminal.

Indeed, in 1941 Haj Amin al-Husseini, the Grand Mufti of Jerusalem, had been chatting to Hitler in Berlin, urging the Reich to prevent the departure of European Jews to Palestine; and two years later he had been helping to raise a Muslim SS battalion in Sarajevo to fight on the Russian front. Later on, in 1944 claiming ignorance of the Jewish Holocaust, he told the German foreign minister Ribbentrop that if Jews were to be 'removed' from Germany, 'it would be infinitely preferable to send them to other countries where they would find themselves under active control [*sic*], as for example, Poland . . .'

When he attempted to flee Germany in 1945, the French captured the Grand Mufti, but allowed him to escape to Egypt. In 1947 he turned up in Lebanon as leader of the Palestinian

Arabs, a powerful and influential voice that could pacify – or provoke – an Arab uprising against Britain in its last days of rule in Palestine. No wonder, then, that the old Colonial Office file was not released under the usual thirty-year rule, but kept secret for half a century. Its contents – astonishingly, they were overlooked by historians on their release last month – speak not only of hidden contacts between the Grand Mufti and British diplomats in Cairo, but also of imperial despair in Palestine and, most dramatically, of outrage at Jewish 'reprisals' against Arab civilians which constituted, according to the British High Commissioner, 'an offence to civilisation'. Indignation and fury permeate the file. So does defeat.

On 15 December 1947, Lieutenant General Sir Alan Cunningham sent a top-secret memorandum to the British colonial secretary Arthur Creech Jones, outlining the civil war in Palestine in fearful detail. 'Situation now is deteriorating,' he wrote,

> into a series of reprisals and counter-reprisals between Jews and Arabs, in which many innocent lives are being lost, the tempo of which may accelerate ... I have been considering what steps could be taken to mitigate this dangerous situation. As far as the Arabs are concerned it is undoubtedly a fact that word from the Mufti in the right quarter is probably now the only chance of inducing them to hold their hand until we have gone.

Haj Amin had arrived in newly independent Lebanon in early October 1947, and the British Legation in Beirut immediately set out to discover how much freedom he would be given. The Grand Mufti's sudden appearance, the legation noted, had not surprised the Lebanese prime minister, Riad Solh,* but the

---

* Lebanon's first post-independence prime minister. He was assassinated in 1951.

Lebanese insisted that 'a member of the Sûreté' was in constant attendance on Haj Amin, that his activities would be 'controlled and restricted' by the Lebanese and that he 'would not be allowed to indulge in any activities directed against British interests'. As our diplomats in Beirut were well aware, however, the British Middle East Office in Cairo had already made contact with the man whom Britain and the Allied Forces Command in Europe regarded as a war criminal.

On 29 September, our man in Cairo had sent a secret note to the Foreign Office enclosing the report of an interview with the Mufti from 'an unimpeachable source'. The carefully typed notes – presumably from a British intelligence officer – portray a man who realised that disaster faced the Arabs of Palestine. The Mufti refused to contemplate the partition of Palestine into Jewish and Arab states. 'He was not bargaining with the Zionists about a possession in dispute,' says the report. 'Palestine, including Jaffa and the Negev, belonged to the Arabs, and he did not recognise the right of anyone to "offer" them what was theirs as a condition of consent to partition. 'It was like a robber trying to make conditions on which he would return stolen property.' Besides, Haj Amin said, 'no form of partition . . . would finally satisfy the Zionists. Whatever they got would merely be a springboard from which to leap on more.'

The Grand Mufti, who had supported the Arab revolt against British rule in the Thirties and had subsequently sought refuge in Iraq after a pro-German coup, then lectured his interviewee in words that must have taken the Briton's breath away. 'Put yourselves in the Arabs' place,' Haj Amin advised. 'Remember yourselves in 1940. Did you ever think of offering the Germans part of Britain on condition that they let you alone in the rest? Of course not, and you never would.' The answer to partition or a federal Palestine was 'NO, categorically NO.' Jews would have the same rights as Arabs in a Palestinian nation 'but the Arabs would never agree to any bestowal on

the Zionists of political power or privilege that put them above
. . . the Palestinian state government'.

There was no reason why Arabs and the British should not
cooperate, Haj Amin said. But common interests 'should not
deceive the British into thinking that any Arab leader would
weaken where Palestine was concerned . . . Palestinian Arab
enmity towards the British was purely political – they hated
the policy that had founded . . . the Zionist national home.' If
Britain did not support Zionist claims to Palestine, and rejected
partition, 'she would gain Arab friendship in a moment'.
But if the British continued their support, 'they could never
hope for Arab co-operation, for the Arabs would then be
co-operating in bringing about their own destruction'.

Then, in words which have an ironic historical resonance,
the Grand Mufti talked of the future. 'He did not fear the Jews,
their Stern, Irgun, Haganah [gangs]. The Arabs might lose at
first, they would have many losses, but in the end they must
win.' The Zionists 'will eventually crumble into nothing, and
he did not fear the result, unless of course Britain or America
. . . intervened, and even then the Arabs would fight and the
Arab world would be perpetually hostile'. When his British
visitor suggested that the Arabs might do better to accept part
of Palestine rather than risk losing all, Haj Amin replied: 'Who
are we? A handful of exiles. Nothing. But we shall never give
in or surrender our principles no matter what bribe is offered.'

Should the British talk directly to Haj Amin? As fighting
continued in Palestine, the British Legation in Beirut reported
to the Foreign Office on 27 November that Haj Amin 'no
longer regards us as Arab Public Enemy No 1'. But 'if a decision
unfavourable to the Arabs is reached at the United Nations . . .
it is probable that the ex-Mufti [sic] will be exposed to pressure
from his extremist followers . . . Contact even of a most infor-
mal sort with British officials might serve as a safety valve.'
The British memorandum, marked 'Secret', adds that although

Haj Amin's 'dubious past renders the prospect of even un-official contact with him distasteful', it could not be denied 'that he enjoys very considerable prestige and influence and he may still play a part in the future government of Palestine'. The Mufti had 'learnt a lesson through backing the wrong side in the last war,' and 'advantage might be taken of his anti-Communist leanings'.

Riad Solh, the Lebanese prime minister, had already offered to arrange a meeting between the Mufti and a Beirut-based British diplomat called Evans, over cups of tea – Evans had been 'non-committal' to the idea – but 'I think it would be all to the good for a member of my staff to see him occasionally,' the Legation head wrote. It would now pay the British 'hand over fist' to exert any influence to avoid a wholesale clash with Palestinian Arabs. Meeting the Mufti as 'an individual' would not mean 'that His Majesty's Government had abandoned their principles or condoned the Mufti's misguided [sic] past . . . if . . . he has had a change of heart, mild and discreet contacts with the British might give him a chance to prove it. If the leopard is still the same we shall soon find the spots under his henna.'

Beneath this eloquent letter, the British diplomat added in his own hand the damning remark that the US assistant military attaché in Lebanon had already paid a visit to the Mufti. By mid-December, General Cunningham was pleading from Jerusalem for pressure on Haj Amin 'to get him to dissuade local Arabs from further violence . . . while we are still here'. But, the High Commissioner noted, 'it is clear that we cannot approach the Arabs without taking parallel action against the Jews. We are, of course, doing all we can to point out to Jews the unmitigated folly of their actions which can only end in future bitterness which may well in the end mean disaster for their new State.' Jewish claims that their actions were carried out by 'dissident groups' had proved to be untrue and 'it can be seen that the Jews have inflicted many more casualties on the Arabs than the reverse. Practically all [Jewish] attacks have been against buses or in civilian centres.' In a remarkable moment of anger, Cunningham concluded that 'we have never at any time on the slightest excuse escaped vociferous and hysterical accusations by Jews that we were a people who were prone to brutal reprisals. Now they [the Jews] have themselves come out with reprisals of a kind which would not have crossed the mind of any soldier here, and which are an offence to civilisation.'

Cunningham's plea for discussions with the Mufti was forwarded to the Foreign Office. Within days, however, the Legation in Beirut was ordered to make no contact with Haj Amin. British MPs had long demanded his trial for war crimes, and our ally King Abdullah of Jordan – the late King Hussein's grandfather – hated the Mufti. The British departed from Palestine in disgrace, leaving Arab and Jew to fight for the land. Three-quarters of a million Palestinians fled or were expelled from their homes. The Arabs did not eventually win, as Haj Amin had predicted, and the Israeli state did not end in disaster as Cunningham suggested it might. Israeli spokesmen regularly condemn the Mufti for his flirtation with Nazism, and have sought to demonise the Palestinians with his name. But recent research suggests that he was an Arab nationalist rather than a national socialist – his fairest biographer is a former Israeli military governor of the occupied West Bank.*

The Mufti died in Beirut in 1974, ignored and largely forgotten even in Lebanon. Among the mourners at his funeral was Yasser Arafat.

The Independent, 20 February 1999

---

* Zvi Elpeleg, *The Grand Mufti: Haj Amin al-Husseini, Founder of the Palestinian National Movement* (London, Frank Cass, 1993).

'Thank you, Mr Clinton, for the kind words'

In August, 1998, following attacks on the US embassies in Nairobi and Dar es-Salaam and at the height of the scandal over his affair with intern Monica Lewinski, President Bill Clinton launched a cruise missile attack on Sudan and on a base in Afghanistan at which Osama bin Laden was supposed to be living. In Khartoum, the missiles destroyed a factory which the Americans claimed was producing chemical warfare components. They later admitted that it was manufacturing medicine for Sudan's deprived population. Several al-Qaeda supporters – including two British citizens – were killed in the Afghan raid. But bin Laden was not there.

If there is one thing that enrages the Arab world about the United States government – apart from its betrayal of the principles of the peace process, its unconditional support for Israel, its enthusiasm for sanctions that are killing thousands of Iraqi civilians and its continued presence in Saudi Arabia – it is the administration's habit of telling Arabs how much it loves them.

Before every air strike, the President assures his future victims how much he admires them. Ronald Reagan told the Libyan people that America regarded them as friends – then he unleashed his bombers on Tripoli and Benghazi. George Bush waffled on about Iraq's history as the birthplace of civilis-

ation and America's friendship for ordinary Iraqis – before
bombing every town and city in Iraq. And this week, as his
missiles had just left their ships in the Red Sea and the Arabian
Gulf, there was Bill Clinton telling the people of the Middle
East that Islam was one of the world's great religions.

As my Beirut grocer put it to me yesterday – his smile as
crooked as his message – 'it's good of Mr Clinton to tell me
about my religion. It's always nice to be informed that religion
doesn't condone murder. Thank you, Mr Clinton.' My grocer
was not being polite. Clinton's admonition from the White
House – 'no religion condones the murder of innocent men,
women and children' – came across in the Middle East as
patronising as well as insulting, coming as it did from a man
who is embroiled in a sex scandal. 'That filthy man' is how he
was called by an Egyptian over the phone to me yesterday,
although the Arabs have not grasped the complexities of Mr
Clinton's adventures with Miss Lewinsky (mercifully, there is
no word for 'oral sex' in Arabic).

What was immediately grasped in the region yesterday, however, was the ease with which the Americans could once again
choose an enemy without disclosing any evidence for his guilt
and then turn journalists and television commentators into
their cheerleaders. 'I was so sickened by the constant use of the
word "terrorism" that I turned to French radio,' a Palestinian
acquaintance told me at midday. 'And what happened? All I
heard in French was "*terroristes, terroristes, terroristes*".' He was
right. Almost all the reporting out of America was based on
the accuracy of the 'compelling evidence' – so "compelling"
that we haven't been vouchsafed a clue as to what it is – that
links Osama bin Laden to the ferocious bombings in Kenya
and Tanzania. Several times yesterday, I had to interrupt live
radio interviews to point out that the journalists in London
and Washington were adopting the US government's claims
without question.

The plots in which bin Laden is now supposed to have been involved, according to the Americans, are now taking on *Gone with the Wind* proportions. Bin Laden, we are told, was behind not only the US embassy bombings, but also the earlier bombing of US troops in Dhahran, anti-government violence in Egypt, the 1993 New York bombing of the World Trade Center, and now – wait for it – an attempt to kill the Pope. Is this really conceivable? The fact that all this was taken at face value by so many reporters probably says as much about the state of journalism as it does about American paranoia.

The use of the word 'terrorist' – Arabs who murder the innocent are always 'terrorists' but Israeli killers who slaughter twenty-nine Palestinians in a Hebron mosque or assassinate their prime minister, Yitzhak Rabin, are called 'extremists' – is only part of the problem. 'Terrorist' is a word that avoids all meaning. The who and the how are of essential importance. But the 'why' is something the West usually prefers to avoid. Not once yesterday – not in a single press statement, press conference or interview – did a US leader or diplomat explain why the enemies of America hate America. Why is bin Laden so angry with the United States? Why – not just who and how – but why did anyone commit the terrible atrocities in Africa?

Clearly, someone blew up the US embassies in Nairobi and Dar es-Salaam. They may have been suicide bombers, but they must have known that they were slaughtering the innocent. Their deeds were wicked. But they were not, as one US diplomat called them, mindless. Whether or not bin Laden was involved, there was a reason for these dreadful deeds. And the reason almost certainly lies with US policy – or lack of policy – towards the Middle East. 'How can America protect its embassies?' a US radio station asked me last week. When I suggested it could adopt fairer policies in the region, I was admonished for not answering a question about 'terrorism'.

For what really lies at the root of Arab reaction to the US

attacks on Sudan and Afghanistan is that they come when America's word has never been so low; when the Arab sense of betrayal has never been greater. America's continued military presence in Saudi Arabia, its refusal to bring Israel to heel as it continues to build Jewish settlements on Arab land in violation of the Oslo agreement, its almost lip-smacking agreement to continue sanctions which are clearly culling the civilian population of Iraq; Arab fury at this catastrophe is one reason why a normally compassionate people responded with so little sympathy to the bombing of the US embassies. After all this, being lectured by Mr Clinton and then bombed by him was like getting a kick in the teeth from a man who has already stabbed you in the back.

Bin Laden or not, it is a fair and fearful bet that the embassy bombings were organised by – or at the least involved – Arabs. And the culprits should be found and brought to justice. But Cruise missiles do not represent due process, as Mr Clinton knows all too well. Talk of a massive 'international terrorist conspiracy' is as exotic as the perennial Arab belief in the 'international Zionist conspiracy'. Bin Laden is protected in Afghanistan by the Taliban. But the Taliban are paid, armed and inspired by Saudi Arabia. And Saudi Arabia is supposed to be America's best friend in the Gulf, so close an ally that US troops are still stationed there (which is, of course, bin Laden's grouse). Could it be that powerful people in Saudi Arabia, a fundamentalist and undemocratic state if ever there was one, support bin Laden and share his desire for a 'jihad' against America? This is one question the Americans should be asking.

Bin Laden himself was obsessed for many months with the massacre of Lebanese civilians by the Israelis at the UN base at Qana in southern Lebanon in April 1996. Why had Clinton not condemned this 'terrorist act', he asked. (In fact, Bill Clinton called it a 'tragedy', as if it was some form of natural disaster – the Israelis said it was a 'mistake' but the UN concluded it wasn't). Why had the perpetrators not been brought to justice, bin Laden wanted to know? It is odd now to compare bin Laden's words with those of Bill Clinton just forty-eight hours ago. They talked much the same language. And now their language has grown far more ferocious. 'The United States wants peace, not conflict,' Clinton said. He is likely to find little peace in the Middle East for the rest of his presidency.

The Independent, 22 August 1998

Brace yourself for Part Two of the War for Civilisation

It needed my old Irish journalist colleague Vincent Browne to point out the obvious to me. With a headache as big as Afghanistan, reading through a thousand newspaper reports on the supposed 'aftermath' of the Afghan war, I'd become drugged by the lies. Afghan women were free at last, 'our' peacekeeping force was on its way, the Taliban were crushed. Anti-American demonstrations in Pakistan had collapsed – we'll forget my little brush with some real Afghans there a couple of weeks ago. Al-Qaeda was being 'smoked out' of its cave. Osama bin Laden was – well, not captured or even dead; but – well, the Americans had a videotape, incomprehensible to every Arab I've met, which 'proves' that our latest monster planned the crimes against humanity in New York and Washington.

So it needed Vincent, breathing like a steam engine as he always does when he's angry, to point to the papers in Gemma's, my favourite Dublin newsagents. 'What in Christ's sake is going on, Bob?' he asked. 'Have you seen the headlines of all this shite?' and he pulled *Newsweek* from the shelf. The headline: 'After The Evil'. 'What is this biblical bollocks?' Vincent asked me. Osama bin Laden's overgrained, videotaped face stared from the cover of the magazine, a dark, devilish image from Dante's circles of hell. When he captured Berlin, Stalin announced that his troops had entered 'the lair of the fascist beast'. But the Second World War has nothing on this.

So let's do a 'story-so-far'. After Arab mass-murderers crashed four hijacked aircraft into the World Trade Center, the Pentagon and Pennsylvania, a crime against humanity which cost more than 4,000 innocent lives, President Bush announced a crusade for infinite 'justice' – later downgraded to infinite freedom – and bombed Afghanistan. Using the gunmen and murderers of the discredited Northern Alliance to destroy the gunmen and murderers of the discredited Taliban, the Americans bombed bin Laden's cave fortresses and killed hundreds of Afghan and Arab fighters, not including the prisoners executed after the Anglo–US–Northern Alliance suppression of the Mazar prison revolt.

The production of the bin Laden videotape – utterly convincing evidence of his guilt to the international press, largely, if wilfully, ignored by the Muslim world – helped to obscure the fact that Mr Evil seemed to have disappeared. It also helped to airbrush a few other facts away. We could forget that US air strikes, according to statistics compiled by a New Hampshire university professor, have now killed more innocent Afghans than the hijackers killed Westerners and others in the World Trade Center.* We could forget that Mullah Omar, the mysterious leader of the Taliban, has also got away. We could ignore the fact that, save for a few brave female souls, almost all Afghan women continued to wear the burqa. We could certainly close our eyes to the massive preponderance of Northern Alliance killers represented in the new UN-supported, pro-Western government in Kabul. We could clap our hands when a mere fifty Royal Marines arrived in Afghanistan this weekend to support a UN-mandated British-led 'peace' force of only a

---

* Professor Marc W. Herold, 'A Dossier on Civilian Victims of United States Aerial Bombing of Afghanistan: A Comprehensive Accounting' (Revised March 2002). (*http://www.cursor.org/stories/civiliandeaths.htm*)

few thousand men who will need the Kabul government's permission to operate in the city and which, in numbers, will come to about one-third of the complement of the British army destroyed in the Kabul Gorge in 1842. The 'peace' force thinks it will have to defend humanitarian aid convoys from robbers and dissident Taliban. In fact, it will have to fight off the Northern Alliance mafia and drug-growers and warlords, as well as the vicious guerrillas sent out to strike them by bin Laden's survivors. If nothing else, the Taliban made the roads and villages of Afghanistan safe for Afghans and foreigners alike. Now, you can scarcely drive from Kabul to Jalalabad.

Presumably, the CIA will let us pay the Alliance mobsters for their war in Afghanistan. One of the untold stories of this conflict is the huge amount of money handed out to militia leaders to persuade them to fight for the US. When Taliban members changed sides for an Alliance payment of $250,000 and then attacked their benefactors, we all dwelt on their treachery. None of us asked how the Alliance – which didn't have enough money to pay for bullets a few weeks earlier – could throw a quarter of a million bucks at the Taliban in the middle of a fire-fight. Nor how the Pashtun tribal leaders of Kandahar province are now riding around in brand-new four-wheel-drives with thousands of dollars to hand out to their gunmen. I wasn't surprised to read that a Somali warlord is now offering his cash-for-hire services to the US for the next round of the War for Civilisation.

Fortunately for us, the civilian victims of America's B-52s will remain unknown in their newly dug graves. Even before the war ended, around 3,700 of them – not counting Mullah Omar's and bin Laden's gunmen – had been ripped to pieces in our War for Civilisation. A few scattered signs of discontent – the crowd that assaulted me two weeks ago, for example, outraged at the killing of their families – can be quickly erased from the record.

It is obviously perverse to note that I haven't met a single ordinary Muslim or, indeed, many Westerners – Pakistani, Afghan, Arab, British, French, American – who actually believe all this guff. Let's just remember that the new Kabul government is as committed to support 'Islam, democracy, pluralism [*sic*] and social justice' as George W. Bush is to Good and the Destruction of Evil. Roll on next year, and don't worry about bin Laden – he may be back just in time to participate in Part Two of the War for Civilisation.

The Independent, 22 December 2001

By the autumn of 2007, thousands of Western troops had been fought to a standstill outside Kandahar by a resurgent Taliban. Hamid Karzai's Afghan 'government' controlled little more than its own ministries in Kabul as dozens of suicide bombers assaulted, Iraq-style, his forces and those of his Western allies.

The pit of desperation

A few days ago, Crown Prince Abdullah of Saudi Arabia* called upon the 'conscience' of the American people to help the Palestinians. The Emir of Qatar went one step further in self-abasement. The Arabs, he said – and he apologised for using the word – had to 'beg' the United States to use its influence on the Israelis. Truly, when such words are uttered, it is the very pit of Arab desperation. Beg? Conscience? Washington may still turn down Ariel Sharon's request to break all relations with Yasser Arafat, but President Bush has long ago forgotten his 'vision' of a Palestinian state – produced when he needed Arab acquiescence in the bombardment of Afghanistan but swiftly buried once it had served its purpose – and Arafat's role now is to remember his job: to protect Israel from his own people.

From his office in Ramallah, surrounded by Israeli tanks, Arafat fantasises about his derring-do during Israel's 1982 siege of West Beirut, but it is diffficult to underestimate the degree of shame with which many Palestinians now regard him. Last Christmas, Arafat insisted that he would march to Bethlehem to attend church services. But when the Israelis refused him permission, he merely appeared on Palestinian television and preposterously claimed that Israel's refusal was a 'crime' and

* Now King Abdullah of Saudi Arabia.

an act of 'terrorism'. Why, the Arabic daily *Al Quds al-Arabi* asked, was there no explanation for this 'bizarre and incomprehensible' performance by Arafat? Why did he not march out of Ramallah with the Christian clerics who had come to give their support until physically stopped by Israeli troops in front of the television cameras? The more he talks about Israel's 'terrorism', the less we examine his own record of corruption, cronyism and brutality.

In the meantime, Israel's own mythmaking goes on apace. In New York, Shimon Peres announces the presence of Iranian Revolutionary Guards in Lebanon and the arrival of 8,000 long-range missiles for Hizballah; now there hasn't been an Iranian militiaman in Lebanon for fifteen years, and the 'new' missiles don't exist* – but this nonsense is reported in the US media without the slightest attempt to check the facts. The latest whopper came from Sharon.† He regretted, he said, that he had not 'liquidated' Arafat during the 1982 siege of Beirut, but there had been an agreement not to do so. This is rubbish; during the siege, Israeli jets five times bombed the buildings in which Sharon, then Israel's defence minister, believed Arafat to be hiding, on two occasions destroying whole apartment blocks – along, of course, with all the civilians living in them – only minutes after Arafat had left. Again, Sharon's untrue version of history was reported in the American press as fact.

Indeed, all the participants in the Middle East conflict are now engaged in a game of self-deception, a massive and fraudulent attempt to avoid any examination of the critical issues that lie behind the tragedy. The Saudis want to appeal to America's 'conscience', not because they are upset at Arafat's

---

* By 2006, however, mythmaking had become reality: the Hizballah then had many more than 8,000 rockets in Lebanon.
† Israeli prime minister Ariel Sharon suffered a massive stroke on 4 January 2006 and was still on life support in February 2008.

predicament but because fifteen of the 11 September hijackers were themselves Saudis. Sharon's attempt to join in the 'war against terror' – the manufacturing of non-existent Iranian enemies in Lebanon, for example, along with some very real enemies in the West Bank and Gaza – is a blatant attempt to ensure American support for his crushing of the Palestinian intifada and for the continuation of Israel's colonisation of Palestinian land.

Similarly, Mr Bush's messianic claim that he is fighting 'evil' – 'evil' now apparently being a fully-fledged nation-state – and that America's al-Qaeda enemies hate America because they are 'against democracy' is poppycock. Most of America's Muslim enemies don't know what democracy is – they have certainly never enjoyed it – and their deeds, which are indeed wicked, have motives. Mr Bush knows – and certainly his secretary of state, Colin Powell, does – that there is an intimate link between the crimes against humanity of 11 September and the Middle East. After all, the killers were all Arabs, they wrote and spoke Arabic, they came from Saudi Arabia, Egypt and Lebanon. This much we are allowed to reflect upon.

But the moment anyone takes the next logical step and looks at the Arab world itself, we tread on forbidden territory. For any analysis of the current Middle East will encounter injustice and violence and death, often the result – directly or indirectly – of the policies of the United States and its regional allies (Arab as well as Israeli). At this point, all discussion must cease. Because if America's own involvement in the region – its unconditional support for Israel, its acquiescence in the Jewish colonisation of Arab land, the sanctions against Iraq that have killed so many tens of thousands of children – and the very lack of that democracy that Bush thinks is under attack suggest that America's own actions might have something to do with the rage and fury that generated the mass murders of 11 September, then we are on very dangerous territory indeed.

And oddly, the Arab regimes go along with all this. The Arab people do not – they know full well what lies behind the dreadful deeds of 11 September – but the leadership has to pretend ignorance. It supports the 'war on terrorism' and then asks – begs – America to recognise a difference between 'terrorism' and 'national resistance'. The Saudis wilfully ignore the implications of their own citizens' involvement, howling instead about a 'Jewish conspiracy' against Saudi Arabia. Arafat says he supports the 'war on terrorism' and then – let us not kid ourselves – permits his acolytes to try a gun-running operation on the *Karine A*.* And Sharon, hopelessly unable to protect his people from the cruel Palestinian suicide bombers, concentrates on presenting the intifada as 'world terror' rather than the nationalist uprising that it represents. After all, if it's about nationalism, it's also about Israeli occupation and, like American policy in the region, that is not to be discussed.

At the end of next month, the Arab presidents and princes are to hold a summit in Beirut. They will issue ringing declarations of support for the Palestinians and almost equally earnest support for a war against 'terrorism'. They cannot criticise US policy, however outrageous they believe it to be, because they are almost all beholden to it. So they will appeal again to America's conscience. And they will do what the Emir of Qatar did a few days ago. They will beg. And they will get nothing.

The Independent, 14 February 2002

At the March 2002 Arab summit in Beirut, Saudi Arabia offered Israel recognition by the Arab states, including peace agreements and normalisation, in return for an Israeli withdrawal from all Arab territories occupied in the 1967 war, a 'just solution' to the

---

* The *Karine A*, a 4,000-ton freighter, was stopped at sea by the Israeli navy on 3 January 2002. Israel claimed that it was carrying 50 tons of weapons for Arafat's Palestinian Authority in Gaza.

Palestinian refugee problem and recognition of a sovereign and independent Palestinian state in the West Bank and Gaza. Israel rejected the proposal. Washington showed no interest.

The lies leaders tell when they want to go to war

In the aftermath of the 9/11 assaults on the US, Israel tried to bind its continuing colonial war with Yasser Arafat's Palestinians into the same narrative. Israeli diplomats referred to Arafat – transmogrified from 'super-terrorist' to 'super-statesman' under the Oslo agreement – as 'our bin Laden' in the hope that Americans would see Israel's conflict with its colonised Arabs as part of the same battle against 'terrorism' that George W. Bush thought he was fighting.

How much longer can Ariel Sharon pretend that he's fighting in the 'war against terror'? How much longer are we supposed to believe this nonsense? How much longer can the Americans remain so gutlessly silent in the face of a vicious conflict which is coming close to obscuring the crimes against humanity of 11 September? Terror, terror, terror. Like a punctuation mark, the word infects every Israeli speech, every American speech, almost every newspaper article. When will someone admit the truth: that the Israelis and Palestinians are engaged in a dirty colonial war which will leave both sides shamed and humiliated?

Just listen to what Sharon has been saying in the past twenty-four hours. 'Arafat is an enemy. He decided on a strategy of terror and formed a coalition of terror.' That's pretty much what President Bush said about Osama bin Laden. But what

on earth does it mean? That Arafat is actually sending off the
suicide bombers, choosing the target, the amount of explosives? If he was, then surely Sharon would have sent his death
squads after the Palestinian leader months ago. After all,
Sharon's killers have managed to murder dozens of Palestinian
gunmen already, including occasional women and children
who get in the way.

The real problem with Arafat is that he has a lot in common
with Sharon: old, ruthless and cynical; both men have come
to despise each other. Sharon believes that the Palestinians can
be broken by military power. He doesn't realise what the rest
of the world learned during Sharon's own 1982 siege of Beirut:
that the Arabs are no longer afraid. Once a people lose their
fear, they cannot be re-inoculated with fear. Once the suicide
bomber is loose, the war cannot be won. And Arafat knows
this. No, of course he doesn't send the bombers off on their
cruel missions to restaurants and supermarkets. But he does
know that every suicide bombing destroys Sharon's credibility
and proves that the Israeli leader's promises of security are
false. Arafat is well aware that the ferocious bombers are serving his purpose – however much he may condemn them in
public.

But he – like Sharon – also believes his enemies can be
broken by fire. He thinks that the Israelis can be frightened
into withdrawing from the West Bank and Gaza and East
Jerusalem. Ultimately, the Israelis probably will have to give
up their occupation. But the Jews of Israel are not going to
run or submit to an endless war of attrition. Even if Sharon is
voted out of power – a prospect for which many Israelis pray
– the next Israeli prime minister is not going to negotiate out
of fear of the suicide bomber.

Thus the rhetoric becomes ever more revolting. Hamas calls
its Jewish enemies 'the sons of pigs and monkeys', while Israeli
leaders have variously bestialised their enemies as 'serpents',

'crocodiles', 'beasts' and 'cockroaches'. Now we have an Israeli officer – according to the Israeli daily *Ma'ariv* – advising his men to study the tactics adopted by the Nazis in the Second World War. 'If our job is to seize a densely packed refugee camp or take over the Nablus casbah, and if this job is given to an [Israeli] officer to carry out without casualties on both sides, he must before all else analyse and bring together the lessons of past battles, even – shocking though this might appear – to analyse how the German army operated in the Warsaw ghetto.'

Pardon? What on earth does this mean? Does this account for the numbers marked by the Israelis on the hands and foreheads of Palestinian prisoners earlier this month? Does this mean that an Israeli soldier is now to regard the Palestinians as subhumans – which is exactly how the Nazis regarded the trapped and desperate Jews of the Warsaw ghetto in 1944?

Yet from Washington comes only silence. And silence, in law, gives consent. Should we be surprised? After all, the US is now making the rules as it goes along. Prisoners can be called 'illegal combatants' and brought to Guantanamo Bay with their mouths taped for semi-secret trials. The Afghan war is declared a victory – and then suddenly explodes again. Now we are told there will be other 'fronts' in Afghanistan, a spring offensive by 'terrorists'. Washington has also said that its intelligence agencies – the heroes who failed to discover the 11 September plot – have proof (undisclosed, of course) that Arafat has 'a new alliance' with Iran, which brings the Palestinians into the 'axis of evil'.

Is there no one to challenge this stuff? Just over a week ago, CIA director George Tenet announced that Iraq had links with al-Qaeda. 'Contacts and linkages' have been established, he told us. And that's what the headlines said. But then Tenet continued by saying that the mutual antipathy of al-Qaeda and Iraq towards America and Saudi Arabia 'suggests that tactical cooperation between them is possible'. 'Suggests?' 'Possible?' Is that what Mr Tenet calls proof?

But now everyone is cashing in on the 'war against terror'. When Macedonian cops gun down seven Arabs, they announce that they are participating in the global 'war on terror'. When Russians massacre Chechens, they are now prosecuting the 'war on terror'. When Israel fires at Arafat's headquarters, it says it is participating in the 'war on terror'. Must we all be hijacked into America's dangerous self-absorption with the crimes of 11 September? Must this vile war between Palestinians and Israelis be distorted in so dishonest a way?

The Independent, 30 March 2002

George Tenet resigned as CIA director on 3 June 2004, to be replaced by former Soviet analyst Robert Gates, who had joined the intelligence organisation while still a student at Indiana University.

'You are not welcome'

President George W. Bush addressed the German Bundestag on 23 May 2002.

So now Osama bin Laden is Hitler. And Saddam Hussein is Hitler. And George Bush is fighting the Nazis. Not since Menachem Begin fantasised to President Reagan that he felt he was attacking Hitler in Berlin – his Israeli army was actually besieging Beirut, killing thousands of civilians, 'Hitler' being the pathetic Arafat – have we had to listen to claptrap like this. But the fact that we Europeans had to do so in the Bundestag on Thursday – and, for the most part, in respectful silence – was extraordinary. Must we, forever, live under the shadow of a war that was fought and won before most of us were born? Do we have to live forever with living, diminutive politicians playing Churchill (Thatcher and, of course, Blair) or Roosevelt? 'He's a dictator who gassed his own people,' Bush reminded us of Saddam Hussein for the two thousandth time, omitting as always to mention that the Kurds whom Saddam viciously gassed were fighting for Iran and that the United States, at the time, was on Saddam's side.

But there is a much more serious side to this. Mr Bush is hoping to corner the Russian president, Vladimir Putin, into a new policy of threatening Iran. He wants the Russians to lean on the northern bit of the 'axis of evil', the infantile phrase which he still trots out to the masses. More and more, indeed, Bush's rhetoric sounds like the crazed videotapes of bin Laden. And still he tries to lie about the motives for the crimes against humanity of 11 September. Yet again, in the Bundestag, he insisted that the West's enemies hated 'justice and democracy', even though most of America's Muslim enemies wouldn't know what democracy was.

In the United States, the Bush administration is busy terrorising Americans. There will be nuclear attacks, bombs in high-rise apartment blocks, on the Brooklyn bridge, men with exploding belts – note how carefully the ruthless Palestinian war against Israeli colonisation of the West Bank is being strapped to America's ever weirder 'war on terror' – and yet more aircraft suiciders. If you read the words of President Bush, Vice President Dick Cheney and the ridiculous 'national security adviser', Condoleezza Rice, over the past three days, you'll find they've issued more threats against Americans than bin Laden. But let's get to the point. The growing evidence that Israel's policies are America's policies in the Middle East – or, more accurately, vice versa – is now being played out for real in statements from Congress and on American television. First, we have the chairman of the US Senate Foreign Relations Committee announcing that Hizballah – the Lebanese guerrilla force that drove Israel's demoralised army out of Lebanon in the year 2000 – is planning attacks in the US. After that, we had an American television network 'revealing' that Hizballah, Hamas and al-Qaeda have held a secret meeting in Lebanon to plot attacks on the US.

American journalists insist on quoting 'sources' but there was, of course, no sourcing for this balderdash, which is now repeated *ad nauseam* in the American media. Then take the 'Syrian Accountability Act' that was introduced into the US Senate by Israel's friends on 18 April. This includes the falsity uttered earlier by Israel's foreign minister, Shimon Peres, that

Iranian Revolutionary Guards 'operate freely' on the southern Lebanese border. And I repeat: there haven't been Iranian Revolutionary Guards in Lebanon – let alone the south of the country – for fifteen years. So why is this lie repeated yet again?

Iran is under threat. Lebanon is under threat. Syria is under threat – its 'terrorism' status has been heightened by the State Department – and so is Iraq. But Ariel Sharon, the Israeli prime minister held personally responsible by Israel's own inquiry for the Sabra and Chatila massacre of 1,700 Palestinians in Beirut in 1982, is – according to Mr Bush – 'a man of peace'. How much further can this go? A long way, I fear. The anti-American feeling throughout the Middle East is palpable. Arab newspaper editorials don't come near to expressing public opinion. In Damascus, Majida Tabbaa has become famous as the lady who threw the US consul Roberto Powers out of her husband's downtown restaurant on 7 April. 'I went over to him,' she said, 'and told him, "Mr Roberto, tell your George Bush that all of you are not welcome – please get out".' Across the Arab world, boycotts of American goods have begun in earnest.

How much longer can this go on? America praises Pakistani president Musharraf for his support in the 'war on terror', but remains silent when he arranges a dictatorial 'referendum' to keep him in power. America's enemies, remember, hate the US for its 'democracy'. So is General Musharraf going to feel the heat? Forget it. My guess is that Pakistan's importance in the famous 'war on terror' – or 'war for civilisation' as, we should remember, it was originally called – is far more important. If Pakistan and India go to war, I'll wager a lot that Washington will come down for undemocratic Pakistan against democratic India.

Now here's pause for thought. Abdelrahman al-Rashed writes in the international Arabic daily *Asharq al-Awsat* that if anyone had said prior to 11 September that Arabs were plotting a vast scheme to murder thousands of Americans in the US, no one would have believed them. 'We would have charged that this was an attempt to incite the American people against Arabs and Muslims,' he wrote. And rightly so. But Arabs did commit the crimes against humanity of 11 September. And many Arabs greatly fear that we have yet to see the encore from the same organisation. In the meantime, Mr Bush goes on to do exactly what his enemies want: to provoke Muslims and Arabs, to praise their enemies and demonise their countries, to bomb and starve Iraq and give uncritical support to Israel and maintain his support for the dictators of the Middle East.

Each morning now, I awake beside the Mediterranean in Beirut with a feeling of great foreboding. There is a firestorm coming. And we are blissfully ignoring its arrival; indeed, we are provoking it.

The Independent, 25 May 2002

Be very afraid: Bush Productions is preparing to go into action

I have always been a sucker for wide-screen epics. Ever since my dad took me to see *Quo Vadis* – which ends with centurion Robert Taylor heading off to his execution with his bride on his arm – I've been on the movie roller-coaster. My dad didn't make a great distinction between the big pictures and B-movies; he managed to squeeze *Hercules Unchained* in between *Ben Hur* and *Spartacus*. But the extraordinary suspension of disbelief provided by the cinema carried me right through to *Titanic*, *Pearl Harbor* and *Gladiator*. Awful they may be. Spectacular they are.

Yet the important thing, as my dad used to tell me, was to remember that the cinema did not really imitate reality. Newly converted Christian centurions did not go so blithely to their deaths, nor did love reign supreme on the *Titanic*. The fighter pilots of Pearl Harbor did not perform so heroically, nor did wicked Roman emperors die so young. From John Wayne's *The Green Berets*, war films have lied to us about life and death. After the crimes against humanity in New York and Washington last September, I suppose it was inevitable that the Pentagon and the CIA would call on Hollywood for ideas – yes, the movie boys actually did go to Washington to do a little synergy with the local princes of darkness. But when Vice President Cheney and Secretary of Defense Rumsfeld turned up together for the premiere of *Black Hawk Down*, I began to get worried.

After all, if the Bush administration is so keen on war, it better work out the difference between Hollywood and the real thing. Yet what we've been getting is a movie version of reality, a work of fiction to justify the prospect of 'war without end'. It started, of course, with all the drivel about 'crusades' and 'war against terror' and 'war against evil', the now famous 'they hate us because we are a democracy', the 'axis of evil' and most recently – it would be outlandishly funny if this trash hadn't come from the Rand Corporation – the 'kernel of evil'. The latter, by the way, is supposed to be Saudi Arabia, but it might just as well have been Iran, Iraq, Syria or anywhere west of the Pecos. Along with this tosh, history is being falsified. Even a crime movie supplies a motive for the crime, but after 11 September Bush Productions would allow no motives to be discussed. The identity and religion of the perpetrators was permissible information: they were Arabs, Muslims. But the moment any of us suggested glancing towards the area from which these Arabs came – an area rich in injustice, oppression, occupation and UN-sanctioned child death – we were subjected to a campaign of calumny.

As Bush's regional enemies grew in number to include not just al-Qaeda but Iraq and Iran and their allies, a fabric of stories began to be woven. Last June, for example, we had Donald Rumsfeld spinning tales about Iran. At a press conference in Qatar – these lies can be spun, please note, just as well in the Arab world as in the West – Rumsfeld told us that Iranians 'are engaging in terrorist activities and transporting people down through Damascus and into the Bekaa Valley. They have harboured al-Qaeda and served as a facilitator for the movement of al-Qaeda out of Afghanistan down through Iran.' Now the implication of all this is that al-Qaeda men were being funnelled into Lebanon with the help of Iran and Syria. Yet we know that Iran, far from 'transporting' al-Qaeda men to Syria, has been packing them off to Saudi Arabia for imprisonment and possible death. We know that the Syrians have locked up an important al-Qaeda official. The Americans have since acknowledged all this. And, save for ten Lebanese men hiding in a Palestinian camp – who may have no contact with al-Qaeda – there isn't a single Osama bin Laden follower in Lebanon.*

So Hizballah had to be lined up for attack. The *Washington Post* did the trick with the following last month: 'The Lebanon-based Hezbollah organisation, one of the world's most formidable terrorist groups, is increasingly teaming up with al-Qa'ida on logistics and training for terrorist operations, according to US and European intelligence officials and terrorism experts.' This tomfoolery was abetted by Steven Simon, who once worked for the US National Security Council and who announced that 'there's a convergence of objectives. There's something in the *zeitgeist* that is pretty well established now.' Except, of course – *zeitgeist* notwithstanding – it is simply untrue. The *Washington Post* had already lined up the Palestinians as America's enemies – again, 'terrorism experts' were the source of this story – by telling its readers in May that 'the sheer number of suicide belt-bombers attacking Israel this spring has increased fear among terrorism experts that the tactic will be exported to the United States.'

A similar theme was originally used to set up Saddam Hussein as an al-Qaeda ally. Back in March, George Tenet, the CIA director, stated that Baghdad 'has also had contacts with al-Qaeda', although he somewhat diluted this bald statement by adding that 'the two sides' mutual antipathy toward the

---

* Five years later, there would be: the al-Qaeda-inspired 'Fatah al-Islam' group opened an offensive on 20 May 2007 from the Nahr el-Bared Palestinian refugee camp in northern Lebanon against Lebanese government troops. It took the national army three months to crush the insurgents – who included Saudis, Yemenis and Syrians – at a cost of 300 dead, 158 of them soldiers. Forty civilians also died in the fighting.

United States and the Saudi royal family suggests that tactical cooperation between them is possible.' Note the discrepancy here between 'has also had contacts' and 'is possible'. On the West Bank, Rumsfeld has already talked about the 'so-called occupied' territories, a step down from William Safire's outrageous column in the *New York Times* last March in which he admonished us not to call the occupied territories occupied. 'To call them "occupied" reveals a prejudice against Israel's right to what were supposed to be "secure and defensible" borders,' he wrote. Now we have Condoleezza Rice, President Bush's National Security Adviser, telling us that 'Arafat is somebody who failed to lead when he had a chance. Ehud Barak gave him a terrific opportunity to lead. And what did they get in return? Arafat started the second intifada instead and rejected that offered hand of friendship.'

Now it's true that Ms Rice's knowledge of the Middle East gets dimmer by the week, but this palpable falsification is now the Washington 'line'. No mention, you'll note, that Arafat was supposed to 'lead' by accepting Israeli sovereignty over all of Jerusalem, no mention of a 'right of return' for a single refugee, of the settlements built illegally outside east Jerusalem, of the ten-mile-wide Israeli buffer zone round 'Palestine', of scarcely 46 per cent of the 22 per cent of Palestine under negotiation to be given to Palestinians.

It's not difficult to see what's going on. It's not just al-Qaeda who are the 'enemy'. It's Iraq, Syria, Lebanon, Palestine, Saudi Arabia. Bush Productions are setting up the Arab world. We are being prepared for a wide-screen epic, a spectacle supported by Hollywood fiction and a plot of lies. Alas, my dad is no longer with us to remind them all that cinema does not imitate reality, that war films lie about life and death.

The Independent, 17 August 2002

'Our guys may kick them around a little . . .'

I think I'm getting the picture. North Korea breaks all its nuclear agreements with the United States, throws out UN inspectors and sets off to make a bomb a year, and President Bush says it's 'a diplomatic issue'. Iraq hands over a 12,000-page account of its weapons production and allows UN inspectors to roam all over the country, and – after they've found not a jam-jar of dangerous chemicals in 230 raids – President Bush announces that Iraq is a threat to America, has not disarmed and may have to be invaded. So that's it, then.

How, readers keep asking me in the most eloquent of letters, does he get away with it? Indeed, how does Tony Blair get away with it? Not long ago in the House of Commons, our dear prime minister was announcing in his usual schoolmasterly tones – the ones used on particularly inattentive or dim boys in class – that Saddam's factories of mass destruction were 'up [pause] and running [pause] now'. But the Dear Leader in Pyongyang does have factories that are up [pause] and running [pause] now. And Tony Blair is silent.

Why do we tolerate this? Why do Americans? Over the past few days there has been just the smallest of hints that the American media – the biggest and most culpable backer of the White House's campaign of mendacity – has been, ever so timidly, asking a few questions. Months after *The Independent* first began to draw its readers' attention to Donald Rumsfeld's chummy personal visits to Saddam in Baghdad at the height of Iraq's use of poison gas against Iran in 1983, the *Washington Post* has at last decided to tell its own readers a bit of what was going on. Reporter Michael Dobbs included the usual weasel clauses ('opinions differ among Middle East experts ... whether Washington could have done more to stop the flow to Baghdad of technology for building weapons of mass destruction'), but the thrust is there: we created the monster and Mr Rumsfeld played his part in doing so.

But no American – or British – newspaper has dared to investigate another, almost equally dangerous, relationship that the present US administration is forging behind our backs: with the military-supported regime in Algeria. For ten years now, one of the world's dirtiest wars has been fought out in this country, supposedly between 'Islamists' and 'security forces', in which almost 200,000 people – mostly civilians – have been killed. But over the past five years there has been growing evidence that elements of those same security forces were involved in some of the bloodiest massacres, including the throat-cutting of babies. *The Independent* has published the most detailed reports of Algerian police torture and of the extrajudicial executions of women as well as men. Yet the US, as part of its obscene 'war on terror', has cosied up to the Algerian regime. It is helping to rearm Algeria's army and promised more assistance. William Burns, the US assistant secretary of state for the Middle East, announced that Washington 'has much to learn from Algeria on ways to fight terrorism'.

And he's right. The Algerian security forces can instruct the Americans on how to make a male or female prisoner believe that they are going to suffocate. The method – US personnel can find the experts in this particular torture technique work-ing in the basement of the Châteauneuf police station in central Algiers – is to cover the trussed-up victim's mouth with a rag and then soak it with cleaning fluid.* The prisoner slowly suffocates. There's also the usual nail-pulling and the usual wires attached to penises and vaginas and – I'll always remember the eyewitness description – the rape of an old woman in a police station, from which she emerged, covered in blood, urging other prisoners to resist.

Some of the witnesses to these abominations were Algerian police officers who had sought sanctuary in London. But rest assured, Mr Burns is right, America has much to learn from the Algerians. Already, for example – don't ask why this never reached the newspapers – the Algerian army chief of staff has been warmly welcomed at Nato's southern command headquarters at Naples. And the Americans are learning. A national security official attached to the CIA divulged last month that when it came to prisoners, 'Our guys may kick them around a little in the adrenaline of the immediate aftermath'. Another US 'national security' official announced that 'pain control in wounded patients is a very subjective thing'. But let's be fair. The Americans may have learned this wickedness from the Algerians. They could just as well have learned it from the Taliban.

Meanwhile, inside the US, the profiling of Muslims goes on apace. On 17 November, thousands of Iranians, Iraqis, Syrians, Libyans, Afghans, Bahrainis, Eritreans, Lebanese, Moroccans, Omanis, Qataris, Somalis, Tunisians, Yemenis and Emiratis turned up at federal offices to be fingerprinted. The *New York Times* – the most chicken of all the American papers in covering the post-9/11 story – revealed (only in paragraph 5 of its report, of course) that 'over the past week, agency officials . . . have handcuffed and detained hundreds of men who showed

---

* The Americans, of course, did subsequently adopt – and use – a suffocation torture technique called 'waterboarding', during which the (usually Arab Muslim) prisoner is almost drowned before being 'saved' from death by his captors.

up to be finger-printed. In some cases the men had expired student or work visas; in other cases, the men could not provide adequate documentation of their immigration status.' In Los Angeles, the cops ran out of plastic handcuffs as they herded men off to the lockup. Of the 1,000 men arrested without trial or charges after 11 September, many were native-born Americans.

Indeed, many Americans don't even know what the chilling acronym of the 'US Patriot Act' even stands for. 'Patriot' is not a reference to patriotism. The name stands for the 'United and Strengthening America by Providing Appropriate Tools Required to Intercept and Obstruct Terrorism Act'. America's $200 m 'Total Awareness Program' will permit the US government to monitor citizens' e-mail and internet activity and collect data on the movement of all Americans. And although we have not been told about this by our journalists, the US administration is now pestering European governments for the contents of their own citizens' data files. The most recent – and most preposterous – of these claims came in a US demand for access to the computer records of the French national airline, Air France, so that it could 'profile' thousands of its passengers. All this is beyond the wildest dreams of Saddam and the Dear Leader Kim.

The new rules even worm their way into academia. Take the friendly little university of Purdue in Indiana, where I lectured a few weeks ago. With federal funds, it's now setting up an 'Institute for Homeland Security', whose eighteen 'experts' will include executives from Boeing and Hewlett-Packard and US Defense and State Department officials, to organise 'research programmes' around 'critical mission areas'. What, I wonder, are these areas to be? Surely nothing to do with injustice in the Middle East, the Arab–Israeli conflict or the presence of thousands of US troops on Muslim lands. After all, it was Richard Perle, the most sinister of George Bush's pro-Israeli advisers, who stated last year that 'terrorism must be decontextualised'.

Meanwhile, we are – on that very basis – ploughing on to war in Iraq, which has oil, but avoiding war in Korea, which does not have oil. And our leaders are getting away with it. In doing so, we are threatening the innocent, torturing our prisoners and 'learning' from men who should be in the dock for war crimes. This, then, is our true memorial to the men and women so cruelly murdered in the crimes against humanity of 11 September 2001.

The Independent, 4 January 2003

The wind from the East

I was sitting on the floor of an old concrete house in the suburbs of Amman this week, stuffing into my mouth vast heaps of lamb and boiled rice soaked in melted butter. The elderly, bearded, robed men from Maan – the most Islamist and disobedient city in Jordan – sat around me, plunging their hands into the meat and soaked rice, urging me to eat more and more of the great pile until I felt constrained to point out that we Brits had eaten so much of the Middle East these past hundred years that we were no longer hungry. There was a muttering of prayers until an old man replied. 'The Americans eat us now,' he said.

Through the open door, where rain splashed on the paving stones, a sharp wind howled in from the east, from the Jordanian and Iraqi deserts. Every man in the room believed President Bush wanted Iraqi oil. Indeed, every Arab I've met in the past six months believes that this – and this alone – explains his enthusiasm for invading Iraq. Many Israelis think the same. So do I. Once an American regime is installed in Baghdad, our oil companies will have access to 112 billion barrels of oil. With unproven reserves, we might actually end up controlling almost a quarter of the world's total reserves. And this forthcoming war isn't about oil?

The US Department of Energy announced at the beginning of this month that by 2025, US oil imports will account for perhaps 70 per cent of total US domestic demand. (It was 55 per cent two years ago.) As Michael Renner of the Worldwatch Institute put it bleakly this week, 'US oil deposits are increasingly depleted, and many other non-Opec fields are beginning to run dry. The bulk of future supplies will have to come from the Gulf region.' No wonder the whole Bush energy policy is based on the increasing consumption of oil. Some 70 per cent of the world's proven oil reserves are in the Middle East. And this forthcoming war isn't about oil?

Take a look at the statistics on the ratio of reserve to oil production – the number of years that reserves of oil will last at current production rates – compiled by Jeremy Rifkin in *Hydrogen Economy*. In the US, where more than 60 per cent of the recoverable oil has already been produced, the ratio is just 10 years, as it is in Norway. In Canada, it is 8:1. In Iran, it is 53:1, in Saudi Arabia 55:1, in the United Arab Emirates 75:1. In Kuwait, it's 116:1. But in Iraq it's 526:1. And this forthcoming war isn't about oil?

Even if Donald Rumsfeld's hearty handshake with Saddam Hussein in 1983 didn't show how little the present master of the Pentagon cares about human rights or crimes against humanity, along comes Joost Hilterman's analysis of what was really going on in the Pentagon back in the late 1980s. Hilterman, who is preparing a book on the US and Iraq, has dug through piles of declassified US government documents, only to discover that after Saddam gassed 6,800 Kurdish Iraqis at Halabja (that's well over twice the total of the World Trade Center dead of 11 September 2001) the Pentagon set out to defend Saddam by partially blaming Iran for the atrocity. A newly declassified State Department document proves that the idea was dreamed up by the Pentagon – who had all along backed Saddam – and states that US diplomats received instructions to push the line of Iran's culpability, but not to discuss details. No details, of course, because the story was a lie.

This, remember, followed five years after US National Security Decision Directive 114 – concluded in 1983, the same year as Rumsfeld's friendly visit to Baghdad – gave formal sanction to billions of dollars in loan guarantees and other credits to Baghdad. And this forthcoming war is about human rights?

Back in 1997, in the years of the Clinton administration, Rumsfeld, Dick Cheney and a bunch of other right-wing men – most involved in the oil business – created the Project for the New American Century, a lobby group demanding 'regime change' in Iraq. In a 1998 letter to President Clinton, they called for the removal of Saddam from power. In a letter to Newt Gingrich, who was then Speaker of the House, they wrote that 'we should establish and maintain a strong US military presence in the region, and be prepared to use that force to protect our vital interests in the Gulf – and, if necessary, to help remove Saddam from power'. The signatories of one or both letters included Rumsfeld, Paul Wolfowitz, now Rumsfeld's Pentagon deputy, John Bolton, now undersecretary of state for arms control, and Richard Armitage, Colin Powell's under-secretary at the State Department – who called last year for America to take up its 'blood debt' with the Lebanese Hizballah. They also included Richard Perle, a former assistant secretary of defence, currently chairman of the defence science board, and Zalmay Khalilzad, the former Unocal Corporation oil industry consultant who became US special envoy to Afghanistan – where Unocal once tried to cut a deal with the Taliban for a gas pipeline across Afghan territory – and who now, miracle of miracles, has been appointed a special Bush official for Iraq.

The signatories also included our old friend Elliott Abrams, one of the most pro-Sharon of pro-Israeli US officials, who was convicted for his part in the Iran–Contra scandal. Abrams it was who compared Israeli prime minister Ariel Sharon to Winston Churchill. So this forthcoming war – the whole shooting match, along with that concern for 'vital interests' (i.e. oil) in the Gulf – was concocted five years ago, by men like Cheney and Khalilzad who were oil men to their manicured fingertips.

In fact, I'm getting heartily sick of hearing the Second World War being dug up yet again to justify another killing field. It's not long ago that Bush was happy to be portrayed as Churchill standing up to the appeasement of the no-war-in-Iraq brigade. In fact, Bush's whole strategy with the odious and Stalinist-style Korean regime – the 'excellent' talks which US diplomats insist they are having with the Dear Leader's Korea which very definitely does have weapons of mass destruction – reeks of the worst kind of Chamberlain-like appeasement. Even though Saddam and Bush deserve each other, Saddam is not Hitler. And Bush is certainly no Churchill. But now we are told that the UN inspectors have found what might be the vital evidence to go to war: eleven empty chemical warheads that just may be twenty years old.

The world went to war eighty-eight years ago because an archduke was assassinated in Sarajevo. The world went to war sixty-three years ago because a Nazi dictator invaded Poland. But for eleven empty warheads? Give me oil any day. Even the old men sitting around the feast of mutton and rice would agree with that.

The Independent, 18 January 2003

CHAPTER TWO

Publish and be damned?
Or stay silent?

The Armenian genocide of 1915 – the systematic murder of one and a half million Christian Armenians by the Ottoman Turks during the First World War – was one of the most terrible atrocities visited upon humanity in the twentieth century. Yet modern-day Turkey is permitted by its Western allies – who fully acknowledged these crimes against humanity at the time – to deny that this Holocaust ever took place. To our peril – and our shame – we refuse to condemn the Ottoman Turks for what proved to be the testing ground for Hitler's destruction of European Jewry in the Second World War. Little did I realise, when I first researched the Armenian genocide, that my own writing would become entangled in Turkey's refusal to acknowledge history.

So let me denounce genocide from the dock

This has been a bad week for Holocaust deniers. I'm talking about those who wilfully lie about the 1915 genocide of Armenian Christians by the Ottoman Turks. On Thursday, France's lower house of parliament approved a bill making it a crime to deny that Armenians suffered genocide. And within an hour, Turkey's most celebrated writer, Orhan Pamuk – only recently cleared by a Turkish court of insulting 'Turkishness' by telling a Swiss newspaper that nobody in Turkey dared mention the Armenian massacres – won the Nobel Prize for Literature. In the mass graves below the deserts of Syria and beneath the soil of southern Turkey, a few souls may have been comforted.

While Turkey continues to blather on about its innocence – the systematic killing of hundreds of thousands of male Armenians and of their gang-raped women is supposed to be the sad result of 'civil war' – Armenian historians such as Vahakn Dadrian continue to unearth new evidence of the premeditated Holocaust (and, yes, it will deserve its capital H, since it was the direct precursor of the Jewish Holocaust, some of whose Nazi architects were in Turkey in 1915) with all the energy of a gravedigger.

Armenian victims were killed with daggers, swords, hammers and axes to save ammunition. Massive drowning operations were carried out in the Black Sea and the Euphrates

river – mostly of women and children, so many that the
Euphrates became clogged with corpses and changed its course
for up to half a mile. But Dadrian, who speaks and reads
Turkish fluently, has now discovered that tens of thousands of
Armenians were also burned alive in haylofts. He has produced
an affidavit presented to the Turkish court martial that briefly
pursued the Turkish mass murderers after the First World
War, a document written by General Mehmet Vehip Pasha,
commander of the Turkish Third Army. He testified that when
he visited the Armenian village of Chourig (it means 'little
water' in Armenian) he found all the houses packed with
burned human skeletons, so tightly packed that all were standing upright. 'In all the history of Islam,' General Vehip wrote,
'it is not possible to find any parallel to such savagery.'

The Armenian Holocaust, now so 'unmentionable' in
Turkey, was no secret to the country's population in 1918.
Millions of Muslim Turks had witnessed the mass deportation
of Armenians three years earlier – a few, with infinite courage,
protected Armenian neighbours and friends at the risk of the
lives of their own Muslim families – and on 19 October 1918
Ahmed Riza, the elected president of the Turkish senate and a
former supporter of the Young Turk leaders who committed
the genocide, stated in his inaugural speech: 'Let's face it, we
Turks savagely [*vahshiane* in Turkish] killed off the Armenians.'
Dadrian has detailed how two parallel sets of orders were
issued, Nazi-style, by Turkish interior minister Talat Pasha.
One set solicitously ordered the provision of bread, olives and
protection for Armenian deportees; but a parallel set instructed
Turkish officials to 'proceed with your mission' as soon as
the deportee convoys were far enough away from population
centres for there to be few witnesses to murder. As Turkish
senator Reshid Akif Pasha testified on 19 November 1918:
'The "mission" in the circular was: to attack the convoys and
massacre the population ... I am ashamed as a Muslim, I

am ashamed as an Ottoman statesman. What a stain on the reputation of the Ottoman Empire, these criminal people . . .'

How extraordinary that Turkish dignitaries could speak such truths in 1918, could fully admit in their own parliament to the genocide of the Armenians and could read editorials in Turkish newspapers of the great crimes committed against this Christian people. Yet how much more extraordinary that their successors today maintain that all of this is a myth, that anyone who says in present-day Istanbul what the men of 1918 admitted can find themselves facing prosecution under the notorious Law 301 for 'defaming' Turkey.

I'm not sure that Holocaust deniers – of the anti-Armenian or anti-Semitic variety – should be taken to court for their rantings. David Irving is a particularly unpleasant 'martyr' for freedom of speech and I am not at all certain that Bernard Lewis's one-franc fine by a French court for denying the Armenian genocide in a November 1993 *Le Monde* article did anything more than give publicity to an elderly historian whose work deteriorates with the years.

But it's gratifying to find that French president Jacques Chirac and his interior minister Nicolas Sarkozy have both announced that Turkey will have to recognise the Armenian deaths as genocide before it is allowed to join the European Union. True, France has a powerful half-million-strong Armenian community. And, typically, no such courage has been demonstrated by Lord Blair of Kut al-Amara, nor by the EU itself, which gutlessly and childishly commented that the new French bill, if passed by the senate in Paris, will 'prohibit dialogue' which is necessary for reconciliation between Turkey and modern-day Armenia. What is the subtext of this, I wonder? No more talk of the Jewish Holocaust lest we hinder 'reconciliation' between Germany and the Jews of Europe?

But, suddenly, last week, those Armenian mass graves opened up before my own eyes. Next month my Turkish publishers are producing my book, *The Great War for Civilisation*, in the Turkish language, complete with its long chapter on the Armenian genocide entitled 'The First Holocaust'. On Thursday, I received a fax from Agora Books in Istanbul. Their lawyers, it said, believed it 'very likely that they will be sued under Law 301' – which forbids the defaming of Turkey and which right-wing lawyers tried to use against Pamuk – but that, as a foreigner, I would be 'out of reach'. However, if I wished, I could apply to the court to be included in any Turkish trial. Personally, I doubt if the Holocaust deniers of Turkey will dare to touch us. But, if they try, it will be an honour to stand in the dock with my Turkish publishers, to denounce a genocide which even Mustafa Kemal Ataturk, founder of the modern Turkish state, condemned.

The Independent, 14 October 2006

You're talking nonsense, Mr Ambassador

A letter from the Turkish ambassador to the Court of St James arrived for me a few days ago, one of those missives that send a shudder through the human soul. 'You allege that an Armenian "genocide" took place in Eastern Anatolia in 1915,' His Excellency Mr Akin Alptuna told me. 'I believe you have some misconceptions about those events . . .'

Oh indeedydoody, I have. I am under the totally mistaken conception that hundreds of thousands of Armenians were cruelly and deliberately done to death by their Turkish Ottoman masters in 1915, that the men were shot and knifed while their womenfolk were raped and eviscerated and cremated and starved on death marches and their children butchered. I have met a few of the survivors – liars to a man and woman, if the Turkish ambassador to Britain is to be believed – and I have seen the photographs taken of the victims by a brave German photographer called Armen Wegner whose pictures must now, I suppose, be consigned to the waste bins. So must the archives of all those diplomats who courageously catalogued the mass murders inflicted upon Turkey's Christian population on the orders of the gang of nationalists who ran the Ottoman government in 1915.

What would have been our reaction if the ambassador of Germany had written a note to the same effect? 'You allege that a "Jewish genocide" took place in Eastern Europe between

1939 and 1945 ... I believe you have some misconceptions about those events ...' Of course, the moment such a letter became public, the ambassador of Germany would be condemned by the Foreign Office, our man in Berlin would – even the pusillanimous Blair might rise to the occasion – be withdrawn for consultations and the European Union would debate whether sanctions should be placed upon Germany.

But Mr Alptuna need have no such worries. His country is not a member of the European Union – it merely wishes to be – and it was Mr Blair's craven administration that for many months tried to prevent Armenian participation in Britain's Holocaust Day. Amid this chicanery, there are a few shining bright lights and I should say at once that Mr Alptuna's letter is a grotesque representation of the views of a growing number of Turkish citizens, a few of whom I have the honour to know, who are convinced that the story of the great evil visited upon the Armenians must be told in their country. So why, oh why, I ask myself, are Mr Alptuna and his colleagues in Paris and Beirut and other cities still peddling this nonsense?

In Lebanon, for example, the Turkish embassy has sent a 'communiqué' to the local French-language *L'Orient-Le Jour* newspaper, referring to the 'soi-disant [so-called] Armenian genocide' and asking why the modern state of Armenia will not respond to the Turkish call for a joint historical study to 'examine the events' of 1915. In fact, the Armenian president, Robert Kotcharian, will not respond to such an invitation for the same reason that the world's Jewish community would not respond to the call for a similar examination of the Jewish Holocaust from the Iranian president – because an unprecedented international crime was committed, the mere questioning of which would be an insult to the millions of victims who perished.

But the Turkish appeals are artfully concocted. In Beirut, they recall the Allied catastrophe at Gallipoli in 1915 when

British, French, Australian and New Zealand troops suffered massive casualties at the hands of the Turkish army. In all – including Turkish soldiers – up to a quarter of a million men perished in the Dardanelles. The Turkish embassy in Beirut rightly states that the belligerent nations of Gallipoli have transformed these hostilities into gestures of reconciliation, friendship and mutual respect. A good try. But the bloodbath of Gallipoli did not involve the planned murder of hundreds of thousands of British, French, Australian, New Zealand – and Turkish – women and children.

But now for the bright lights. A group of 'righteous Turks' are challenging their government's dishonest account of the 1915 genocide: Ahmet Insel, Baskin Oran, Halil Berktay, Hrant Dink,* Ragip Zarakolu and others claim that the 'democratic process' in Turkey will 'chip away at the darkness' and they seek help from Armenians in doing so. Yet even they will refer only to the 1915 'disaster', the 'tragedy' and the 'agony' of the Armenians. Dr Fatma Goçek of the university of Michigan is among the bravest of those Turkish-born academics who are fighting to confront the Ottoman Empire's terror against the Armenians. Yet she, too, objects to the use of the word genocide – though she acknowledges its accuracy – on the grounds that it has become 'politicised' and thus hinders research.

I have some sympathy with this argument. Why make the job of honest Turks more difficult when these good men and women are taking on the might of Turkish nationalism? The problem is that other, more disreputable folk are demanding the same deletion. Mr Alptuna writes to me – with awesome disingenuousness – that Armenians 'have failed to submit any irrefutable evidence to support their allegations of genocide'. And he goes on to say that 'genocide, as you are well aware, has a quite specific legal definition' in the UN's 1948 Conven-

* Hrant Dink's fate is recorded in the next pages.

tion. But Mr Alptuna is himself well aware – though he does not say so, of course – that the definition of genocide was set out by Raphael Lemkin, a Jew, in specific reference to the wholesale mass slaughter of the Armenians.

And all the while, new diplomatic archives are opening in the West which reveal the smell of death – Armenian death – in their pages. I quote here, for example, from the newly discovered account of Denmark's minister in Turkey during the First World War. 'The Turks are vigorously carrying through their cruel intention, to exterminate the Armenian people,' Carl Wandel wrote on 3 July 1915. The bishop of Karput was ordered to leave Aleppo within forty-eight hours 'and it has later been learned that this Bishop and all the clergy that accompanied him have been killed between Diyarbekir and Urfa at a place where approximately 1,700 Armenian families have suffered the same fate . . . In Angora . . . approximately 6,000 men . . . have been shot on the road. Even here in Constantinople [Istanbul], Armenians are being abducted and sent to Asia . . .'

There is much, much more. Yet now here is Mr Alptuna in his letter to me: 'In fact, the Armenians living outside Eastern Armenia including Istanbul . . . were excluded from deportation.' Somebody here is not telling the truth. The late Mr Wandel of Copenhagen? Or the Turkish ambassador to the Court of St James?

The Independent, 20 May 2006

Armenia's 1,500,001st genocide victim

Hrant Dink became the 1,500,001st victim of the Armenian genocide yesterday. An educated and generous journalist and academic – editor of the weekly Turkish–Armenian newspaper *Agos* – he tried to create a dialogue between the two nations to reach a common narrative of the twentieth century's first Holocaust. And he paid the price: two bullets shot into his head and two into his body by an assassin in the streets of Istanbul yesterday afternoon. It was not only a frightful blow to Turkey's surviving Armenian community but a shattering reversal to Turkey's hope of joining the European Union, a visionary proposal already endangered by the country's broken relations with Cyprus and its refusal to acknowledge the genocide for what it was: the deliberate mass killing of an entire race of Christian people by the country's Ottoman Turkish government in 1915. Winston Churchill was among the first to call it a holocaust, but to this day the Turkish authorities deny such a definition, ignoring documents which Turkey's own historians have unearthed to prove the government's genocidal intent.

The 53-year-old journalist, who had two children, was murdered at the door of his newspaper. Just over a year ago, he was convicted under Turkey's notorious Law 301 of 'anti-Turkishness', a charge he strenuously denied even after he received a six-month suspended sentence from an Istanbul court. The EU has demanded that Turkey repeal the law under which the country also tried to imprison Nobel Prize-winning novelist Orhan Pamuk. At the time of his trial, Dink appeared on Turkish television in tears. 'I'm living together with Turks in this country,' he said then. 'And I'm in complete solidarity with them. I don't think I could live with an identity of having insulted them in this country.'

It is a stunning irony that Dink, in one of his articles, had accused his fellow Armenians of allowing their enmity towards the Turks for the genocide to develop to the point where it had a 'poisoning effect on your blood' – and that the court took the article out of context and claimed he was referring to Turkish blood as poisonous. Dink told news agency reporters in 2005 that his case had arisen from a question on what he felt when, at primary school, he had to take a traditional Turkish oath: 'I am a Turk, I am honest, I am hard-working.' In his defence, Dink said: 'I said that I was a Turkish citizen but an Armenian and that even though I was honest and hard-working, I was not a Turk, I was an Armenian.' He did not like a line in the Turkish national anthem that refers to 'my heroic race'. He did not like singing that line, he said, 'because I was against using the word "race", which leads to discrimination'.

Pamuk had earlier faced a court for talking about the 1915 genocide in a Swiss magazine. Leading Turkish publishers say that there is now an incendiary atmosphere in Turkey towards all writers who want to tell the truth about the genocide, when vast areas of Turkish Armenia were 'cleansed' of their Christian populations.

The Independent, 20 January 2007

Sneaking a book out in silence

Stand by for a quotation to take your breath away. It's from a letter from my Istanbul publishers, who are chickening out of publishing the Turkish-language edition of my book *The Great War for Civilisation*. The reason is a chapter entitled 'The First Holocaust', which records the Armenian genocide. It is, I hasten to add, only one chapter in my book about the Middle East, but the fears of my Turkish friends were being expressed even before the Armenian-Turkish journalist Hrant Dink was so cruelly murdered outside his Istanbul office in January. And when you read the following, from their message to my London publishers HarperCollins, remember it is written by a citizen of a country that seriously wishes to enter the European Union. Since I do not speak Turkish, I am in no position to criticise the occasional lapses in Mr Osman's otherwise excellent English.

We would like to denote that the political situation in Turkey concerning several issues such as Armenian and Kurdish Problems, Cyprus issue, European Union etc do not improve, conversely getting worser and worser due to the escalating nationalist upheaval that has reached its apex with the Nobel Prize of Orhan Pamuk and the political disagreements with the EU. Most probably, this political atmosphere will be effective until the coming presidency elections of April 2007 . . . Therefore we would like to undertake the publication quietly, which means there will be no press campaign for Mr Fisk's book. Thus, our request from [for] Mr Fisk is to show his support to us if any trial [is] . . . held against his book. We hope that Mr Fisk and HarperCollins can understand our reservations.

I can. Here is a publisher in a country negotiating for EU membership for whom Armenian history, the Kurds, Cyprus (unmentioned in my book) – even Turkey's bid to join the EU – is reason enough to sneak my book out in silence. When in the history of bookselling, I ask myself, has any publisher tried to avoid publicity for his book? Well, I can give you an example. When Taner Akçam's magnificent *A Shameful Act: The Armenian Genocide and the Question of Turkish Responsibility* was first published in Turkish – it uses Ottoman Turkish state documents and contemporary Turkish statements to prove that the genocide was a terrifying historical fact – the Turkish historian experienced an almost identical reaction. His work was published 'quietly' in Turkey – and without a single book review.

Now I'm not entirely unsympathetic with my Turkish publishers. It is one thing for me to rage and roar about their pusillanimity. But I live in Beirut, not in Istanbul. And after Hrant Dink's foul murder, I'm in no position to lecture my colleagues in Turkey to stand up to the racism that killed Dink. While I'm sipping my morning coffee on the Beirut Corniche, Mr Osman could be assaulted in the former capital of the Ottoman Empire. But there's a problem nonetheless. My Turkish publishers want to bring my book out like illicit pornography – but still have me standing with them in the dock if right-wing lawyers bring charges under Law 301!

I understand, as they write in their own letter, that they do not want to be forced to take political sides in the 'nonsensical collision between nationalists and neo-liberals', but I fear that the roots of this problem go deeper. The sinister photograph of the Turkish police guards standing proudly next to Dink's alleged murderer after his arrest shows just what we are up against here. Yet still our own Western reporters won't come clean about the Ottoman Empire's foul actions in 1915. When, for example, Reuters sent a reporter, Gareth Jones, off to the Turkish city of Trabzon – where Dink's supposed killer lived – he quoted the city's governor as saying that Dink's murder was related to 'social problems linked to fast urbanisation'. A 'strong gun culture and the fiery character of the people' might be to blame.

I wonder why Reuters didn't mention a much more direct and terrible link between Trabzon and the Armenians. For in 1915, the Turkish authorities of the city herded thousands of Armenian women and children on to boats and set off into the Black Sea – the details are contained in an original Ottoman document unearthed by Akçam – where they were 'thrown off to drown'. Historians may like to know that the man in charge of these murder boats was called Niyazi Effendi. No doubt he had a 'fiery character'.

Yet still this denial goes on. The Associated Press this week ran a story from Ankara in which its reporter, Selçan Hacaoglu, repeated the same old mantra about there being a 'bitter dispute' between Armenia and Turkey over the 1915 slaughter, in which Turkey 'vehemently denies that the killings were genocide'. When will the Associated Press wake up and cut this cowardly nonsense from its reports? Would the AP insert in all its references to the equally real and horrific murder of 6 million European Jews that right-wing Holocaust negationists 'vehemently deny' that there was a genocide?

But real history will win. Last October, according to local newspaper reports, villagers of Kuru in eastern Turkey were digging a grave for one of their relatives when they came across a cave containing the skulls and bones of around forty people – almost certainly the remains of 150 Armenians from the town of Oguz who were murdered in Kuru on 14 June 1915. The local Turkish gendarmerie turned up to examine the cave last year, sealed its entrance and ordered villagers not to speak of what they found. But there are hundreds of other Kurus in Turkey and their bones, too, will return to haunt us all. Publishing books 'quietly' will not save us.

The Independent, 17 March 2007

'A conflict of interest'

I despise the internet. It's irresponsible, and often a net of hate. And I don't have time for Blogopops. But here's a tale of two gutless newspapers which explains why more and more people are Googling rather than turning pages.

First the *Los Angeles Times*. Last year, reporter Mark Arax was assigned a routine story on the Armenian genocide. His report focused on divisions within the local Jewish community over whether to call the genocide a genocide. The Israeli government and its new Nobel Prize-winning president, Shimon Peres – anxious to keep cosy relations with modern Turkey – have adopted Istanbul's mendacious version of events. However, many Jews, both inside and outside Israel, have bravely insisted that they do constitute a genocide, indeed the very precursor to the later Nazi Holocaust of 6 million Jews.

Yet Arax's genocide report was killed on the orders of managing editor Douglas Frantz because the reporter had a 'position on the issue' and 'a conflict of interest'. Readers will already have guessed that Arax is an Armenian-American. His sin, it seems, was that way back in 2005 he and five other writers wrote a formal memo to *LA Times* editors reminding them that the paper's style rules meant that the Armenian genocide was to be called just that – not 'alleged genocide'. Frantz, however, described the old memo as a 'petition' and apparently accused Arax of landing the assignment by dealing with a Washington editor who was also an Armenian.

The story was reassigned to Washington reporter Rich Simon, who concentrated on Turkey's attempt to block Congress from recognising the Armenian slaughter – and whose story ran under the headline 'Genocide Resolution Still Far From Certain'. *LA Times* executives then went all coy, declining interviews, although Frantz admitted in a blog (of course) that he had 'put a hold' on Arax's story because of concerns that the reporter 'had expressed personal views about the topic in a public manner . . .' Ho ho.

Truth can be dangerous for the *LA Times*. Even more so, it seems, when the managing editor himself – Frantz, no less – once worked for the *New York Times*, where he referred to the Armenian massacres as, yes, an 'alleged' genocide. Frantz, it turns out, joined the *LA Times* as its Istanbul correspondent. Well, Arax has since left the *LA Times* after a settlement which forestalled a lawsuit against the paper for defamation and discrimination. His employers heaped praise upon his work while Frantz has just left the paper to become Middle East correspondent of the *Wall Street Journal* based in – of course, you guessed it – Istanbul.

But now let's go north of the border, to the *Toronto Globe and Mail*, which assigned columnist Jan Wong to investigate a college murder in Montreal last September. Wong is not a greatly loved reporter. A third-generation Canadian, she moved to China during Mao's 'cultural revolution' and, in her own words, 'snitched on class enemies and did my best to be a good little Maoist'. She later wrote a 'Lunch With' series for the *Globe* in which she acted all sympathetic to interviewee guests to catch them out. 'When they relax, that's when their guard is down,' she told a college newspaper. 'It's a trick, but it's legit.' Yuk!

Wong's take on the Montreal Dawson College shooting,

however, was more serious. She compared the killer to a half-Algerian Muslim who murdered fourteen women in another Montreal college shooting in 1989 and to a Russian immigrant who killed four university colleagues in Montreal in 1992. 'In all three cases,' she wrote, 'the perpetrator was not "pure laine", the argot for a "pure" francophone. Elsewhere, to talk of racial purity is repugnant. Not in Quebec.' Painfully true, I'm afraid. Parisians, who speak real French, would never use such an expression – *pure laine* translates literally as 'pure wool' but means 'authentic' – but some Montrealers do. Wong, however, had touched a red-hot electric wire in 'multicultural' Canada. Prime Minister Stephen Harper complained. 'Grossly irresponsible,' said the man who enthusiastically continued the policy of sending Canadian troops on their suicidal mission to Afghanistan.

The French-Canadian newspaper *Le Devoir* – can you imagine a British paper selling a single copy if it called itself 'Duty'? – published a cartoon of Wong with exaggerated Chinese slanted eyes. Definitely not *pure laine* for *Le Devoir*. The hate mail was even more to the point. Some contained excrement. But then the *Globe and Mail* ran for cover. Its editor-in-chief, Edward Greenspon, wrote a cowardly column in which he claimed that the offending paragraphs 'should have been removed' from Wong's story. 'We regret that we allowed these words to get into a reported [*sic*] article,' he sniffled. There had been a breakdown in what he hilariously called 'the editorial quality control process'.

Now I happen to know a bit about the *Globe*'s 'quality control process'. Some time ago I discovered that the paper had reprinted an article of mine from *The Independent* about the Armenian genocide. But they had tampered with it, altering my word 'genocide' to read 'tragedy'. *The Independent*'s subscribers promise to make no changes to our reports. But when our syndication folk contacted the *Globe*, they discovered that the Canadian paper had simply stolen the article. They were made to pay a penalty fee. But as for the censorship of the word 'genocide', a female executive explained to *The Independent* that nothing could be done because the editor responsible had 'since left the *Globe and Mail*'.

It's the same old story, isn't it? Censor then whinge, then cut and run. No wonder the bloggers are winning.

The Independent, 21 July 2007

This column provoked a blizzard of mail from Québécois (French-Canadians), accusing me of calling them racists, misunderstanding their minority status, demeaning their French-language paper Le Devoir *(whose Middle East coverage I had praised in earlier articles) and abusing them for not speaking 'proper' French. The fact that the purpose of 'Conflict of Interest' was to condemn the gutlessness of English-language newspapers somehow got lost along the way.*

Bravery, tears and broken dreams

There is nothing so infinitely sad – so pitiful and yet so courageous – as a people who yearn to return to a land forever
denied them; the Poles to Brest Litovsk, the Germans to Silesia,
the Palestinians to that part of Palestine that is now Israel.
When a people claim to have settled again in their ancestral
lands – the Israelis, for example, at the cost of 'cleansing'
750,000 Arabs who had perfectly legitimate rights to their
homes – the world becomes misty-eyed. But could any nation
be more miserably bereft than one which sees, each day, the
towering symbol of its own land in the hands of another?

Mount Ararat will never return to Armenia – not to the
rump state which the Soviets created in 1920 after the genocide
– and its presence to the west of the capital, Yerevan, is a
desperate, awful, permanent reminder of wrongs unrighted,
atrocities unacknowledged, dreams never to be fulfilled. I
watched Ararat all last week, cloud-shuffled in the morning,
blue-hazed through the afternoon, ominous, oppressive, inspiring, magnificent, ludicrous in a way – for the freedom
which it encourages can never be used to snatch it back from
the Turks – capable of inspiring the loftiest verse and the most
execrable commercialism.

There is a long-established Ararat cognac factory in Yerevan,
Ararat gift shops – largely tatty affairs of ghastly local art and
far too many models of Armenian churches – and even the

Marriott Ararat Hotel, which is more than a rung up from the old Armenia Two Hotel where I stayed fifteen years ago, an ex-Soviet Intourist joint whose chief properties included the all-night rustling of cockroach armies between the plaster and the wallpaper beside my pillow.

Back in the Stalinist 1930s, the architect Aleksander Tamanian built an almost fascistic triumphal arch at one side of Republic Square through which the heights of Ararat, bathed in eternal snow, would forever be framed to remind Armenians of their mountain of tears. But the individualism of the descendants of Tigran the Great, whose empire stretched from the Caspian to Beirut, resisted even Stalin's oppression. Yeghishe Charents, one of the nation's favourite poets – a famous philanderer who apparently sought the Kremlin's favours – produced a now famous poem called 'The Message'. Its praise of Uncle Joe might grind the average set of teeth down to the gum; it included the following: 'A new light shone on the world./Who brought this sun?/ ... It is only this sunlight/ Which for centuries will stay alive.' And more of the same.

Undiscovered by the Kremlin's censors for many months, however, Charents had used the first letter of each line to frame a quite different 'message', which read: 'O Armenian people, your only salvation is in the power of your unity.' Like the distant Mount Ararat, it was a brave, hopeless symbol, as doomed as it was impressive. Charents was 'disappeared' by the NKVD in 1937 after being denounced by Tamanian – now hard at work building Yerevan's new Stalinist opera house – the moment Charents's schoolboy prank was spotted. Then Tamanian fell from the roof of his still unfinished opera house, and even today Armenians – with their Arab-like desire to believe in 'the plot' – ask the obvious questions. Did the architect throw himself to his death in remorse? Or was he pushed?

Plots live on in the country that enjoyed only two years of post-genocide independence until its 1991 'freedom' from the decaying Soviet Union. Its drearily re-elected prime minister, Serzh Sargsian, permits 'neutral' opposition but no real political debate – serious opponents would have their parties and newspapers closed down – and he recently told the local press that 'the economy is more important than democracy'. Not surprising, I suppose, when the corrupt first president of free Armenia, Ter-Petrosian, is rumoured to be plotting a comeback. Sargsian even tried to throw the American Radio Liberty/ Free Europe station out of Armenia – though I suppose that's not necessarily an undemocratic gesture.

Nonetheless, interviewed by Vartan Makarian on an Armenian TV show this week, I found it a bit hard to take when Vartan suggested that my Turkish publisher's fear of bringing out my book on the Middle East was a symbol of Turkey's 'lack of democratisation'. What about Armenia's pliant press, I asked? And why was it that present-day Armenia seemed to protest much less about the twentieth century's first Holocaust than the millions of Armenians in the diaspora, in the US, Canada, France, Britain, even Turkish intellectuals in Turkey itself? The TV production crew burst into laughter behind their glass screen. Guests on Armenian television are supposed to answer questions, not ask them. Long live the Soviet Union.

But you have to hand it to the journalists of Yerevan. Each August they all go on holiday. At the same time. Yup. Every editor, reporter, book reviewer, columnist and printer packs up for the month and heads off to Lake Sevan or Karabakh for what is still called, Soviet-style, a 'rest'. 'We wish all our readers a happy rest-time and we'll be back on August 17th,' the newspaper *Margin* announced this week. And that was that. No poet may die, no Patriotic War hero expire, no minister may speak, no man may be imprisoned, lest his passing or his words or incarceration disappear from written history. I encourage the management of *The Independent* to consider this idea; if only we had operated such a system during the rule of the late Tony Blair . . . But no doubt a civil servant would have e-mailed him that this was a 'good time' to announce bad news.

In any event, a gloomy portrait of the poet–martyr Charents now adorns Armenia's 1,000-dram note and Tamanian's massive arch still dominates Republic Square. But the dying Soviet Union constructed high-rise buildings beyond the arch and so today, Ararat – like Charents – has been 'disappeared', obliterated behind the grey walls of post-Stalinist construction, the final indignity to such cloud-topped, vain hopes of return. Better by far to sip an Ararat cognac at the Marriott Ararat Hotel from which, at least, Noah's old monster can still be seen.

The Independent, 4 August 2007

A holocaust denier in the White House

How are the mighty fallen! President George W. Bush, the Crusader king who would draw the sword against the forces of Darkness and Evil, he who said there was only 'them or us', who would carry on, he claimed, an eternal conflict against 'world terror' on our behalf; he turns out, well, to be a wimp. A clutch of Turkish generals and a multi-million-dollar public relations campaign on behalf of Turkish Holocaust deniers have transformed the lion into a lamb. No, not even a lamb – for this animal is, by its nature, a symbol of innocence – but into a household mouse, a diminutive little creature which, seen from afar, can even be confused with a rat. Am I going too far? I think not.

The 'story so far' is familiar enough. There are photographs, diplomatic reports, original Ottoman documentation, the process of an entire post-First World War Ottoman trial, Winston Churchill and Lloyd George and a massive report by the British Foreign Office in 1915 and 1916 to prove that it is all true. Even movie film is now emerging – real archive footage taken by Western military cameramen in the First World War – to show that the first Holocaust of the twentieth century, perpetrated in front of German officers who would later perfect its methods in their extermination of 6 million Jews, was as real as its pitifully few Armenian survivors still claim.

But the Turks won't let us say this. They have blackmailed

the Western powers – including our own British government, and now even the United States – to kowtow to their shameless denials. These (and I weary that we must repeat them, because every news agency and government does just that through fear of Ankara's fury) include the canard that the Armenians died in a 'civil war', that they were anyway collaborating with Turkey's Russian enemies, that fewer Armenians were killed than have been claimed, that as many Turkish Muslims were murdered as Armenians. And now President Bush and the United States Congress have gone along with these lies. There was, briefly, a historic moment for Bush to walk tall after the US House Foreign Relations Committee voted last month to condemn the mass slaughter of Armenians as an act of genocide. Ancient Armenian-American survivors gathered at a House panel to listen to the debate. But as soon as Turkey's fossilised generals started to threaten Bush, I knew he would give in.

Listen, first, to General Yasar Buyukanit, chief of the Turkish armed forces, in an interview with the newspaper *Milliyet*. The passage of the House resolution, he whinged, was 'sad and sorrowful' in view of the 'strong links' Turkey maintained with its NATO partners. And if this resolution was passed by the full House of Representatives, then 'our military relations with the US would never be as they were in the past . . . The US, in that respect, has shot itself in the foot.'

Now listen to Mr Bush as he snaps to attention before the Turkish general staff. 'We all deeply regret the tragic suffering of the Armenian people . . . But this resolution is not the right response to these historic mass killings. Its passage would do great harm to our relations with a key ally in NATO and in the global war on terror.' I loved the last bit about the 'global war on terror'. Nobody – save for the Jews of Europe – has suffered 'terror' more than the benighted Armenians of Turkey in 1915. But that NATO should matter more than the integrity of history – that NATO might one day prove to be so

important that the Bushes of this world might have to equivo-
cate over the Jewish Holocaust to placate a militarily resurgent
Germany – beggars belief.

Among those men who should hold their heads in shame
are those who claim they are winning the war in Iraq. They
include the increasingly disoriented General David Petraeus,
US commander in Iraq, and the increasingly delusionary US
ambassador to Baghdad, Ryan Crocker, both of whom warned
that full passage of the Armenian genocide bill would 'harm
the war effort in Iraq'. And make no mistake, there are big
bucks behind this disgusting piece of Holocaust denial. Former
Representative Robert L. Livingston, a Louisiana Republican,
has already picked up $12 million from the Turks for his
company, the Livingston Group, for two previously successful
attempts to pervert the cause of moral justice and smother
genocide congressional resolutions. He personally escorted
Turkish officials to Capitol Hill to threaten US congressmen.
They got the point. If the resolution went ahead, Turkey would
bar US access to the Incirlik air base through which passed
much of the 70 per cent of American air supplies to Iraq which
transit Turkey. In the real world, this is called blackmail –
which was why Bush was bound to cave in. Defense Secretary
Robert Gates was even more craven – although he obviously
cared nothing for the details of history. Petraeus and Crocker,
he said, 'believe clearly that access to the airfields and to the
roads and so on in Turkey would be very much put at risk if
this resolution passes . . .'

How terrible an irony did Gates utter. For it is these very
'roads and so on' down which walked the hundreds of thousands of Armenians on their 1915 death marches. Many were
forced aboard cattle trains which took them to their deaths.
One of the railway lines on which they travelled ran due east
of Adana – a great collection point for the doomed Christians
of western Armenia – and the first station on the line was

called Incirlik, the very same Incirlik which now houses the huge air base which Mr Bush is so frightened of losing. Had the genocide which Bush refuses to acknowledge not taken place – as the Turks claim – the Americans would be asking the *Armenians* for permission to use Incirlik. There is still alive – in Sussex if anyone cares to see her – an ageing Armenian survivor from that region who recalls the Ottoman Turkish gendarmes setting fire to a pile of living Armenian babies on the road close to Adana. These are the same 'roads and so on' which so concern the gutless Mr Gates.

But fear not. If Turkey has frightened the boots off Bush, he's still ready to rattle the cage of the all-powerful Persians. People should be interested in preventing Iran from acquiring the knowledge to make nuclear weapons if they're 'interested in preventing World War Three', he has warned us. What piffle. Bush can't even summon up the courage to tell the truth about World War One. Who would have thought that the leader of the Western world – he who would protect us against 'world terror' – would turn out to be the David Irving of the White House?

The Independent, 10 November 2007

CHAPTER THREE

Words, words, words . . .

The misuse and manipulation of language – the worthless semantics of journalists and politicians and even academics – is becoming ever more frequent and ever more dangerous. It's not just the clichés we are taught to use when we are cub reporters, nor the banal language of our pseudo-statesmen nor the secretive language of anthropologists; nor the politically 'correct' message of advertisers, company executives and diplomats. In the Middle East, our weasel words can be lethal, especially when they are subtly intended to define the 'good guys' from the 'bad guys', to undermine the humanity of one race of people at the expense of another. Our journalism is already biased – the initial response of French writers and intellectuals to the 1967 Middle East war is proof enough of this – without resorting to subterranean words that 'key in' our prejudice. Perhaps we now 'experience' language rather than listen to it. Over the years, I have more and more studied the Babel of lies that we produce, and the few – the pitifully few – writers who believe, like Victor Klemperer, in 'the truth of language'.

Hack blasts local rags

I was seventeen when I first arrived in Newcastle upon Tyne. It was a city of heavy, black, nineteenth-century buildings, a spider's web of iron bridges and smouldering steam locomotives, the air thick with coal smoke and red haze from the steel works at Consett. The news editor of the *Evening Chronicle*, John Brownlee, did his best to cheer me up. 'You'll be in our Blyth office, Bob, a bustling little coal town on the coast with plenty of life and lots of news.' Brownlee was in estate-agent mode. Blyth was a down-at-heel collier harbour, smothered in the dust of doomed mines and a thousand coal fires. The slagheaps glowed red at night, the dying shipyards were bankrupt, pools of vomit lay splashed over the pavements outside the Blyth and Tyne and two dozen other pubs and clubs every Sunday morning. Even in summer, a kind of North Sea mildew settled over the town, a damp, cold cloth mixed with coal smoke that smothered all who lived there.

I was homesick and lonely and I was paid £17.50 a week, a third of which I handed over to Mrs Hamilton, my landlady at 82 Middleton Street, where I slept in a room 7 ft in length and just 5 ft wide with a single tiny gas fire. When I came home one day I found the Gas Board asking my landlady why there was no money in the meter; I had to explain that I didn't earn enough to pay for the heating. So I spent all evening in front of the fire in the rotting old back-to-back *Chronicle* office in Seaforth Street, then walked home through the smoke at midnight and cowered under my blankets for warmth. I used to read history books on Sunday afternoons, wrapped in a heavy overcoat, sitting in the overgrown Victorian beach garden near the port.

But there were stories. I shared my digs with the gloriously named Captain Fortune, deputy harbour-master of Blyth, whose moment of glory arrived when a Cold War Polish fishing-fleet put into port during a storm. And stayed. And stayed. When Fortune boarded the first trawler to demand its immediate departure, the Polish captain slapped him round the face with a massive, sharp-finned fish. I warned readers that the Victorian wooden staithes from which freight trains would unload coal into the colliers were in danger of collapse. I staggered through feet of water deep under the Tyne to watch two teams of miners hack their way through to each other in the first stage of what was to be Newcastle's first under-river motorway. I catalogued the massive overspending on Blyth's spanking new power station. I recorded the classical learning of the Blyth town clerk as he used quotations from mythology to defeat motorway extension objectors. The Golden Fleece was on his tongue. When the council failed, its plans were – of course – 'put on ice'.

And I covered the courts. Some cases were truly pathetic. There was the mother whose son, a Morpeth male nurse, died hanging from the back of his hospital bedroom door; she wailed outside the court as officials gently explained to her that her son had stood on a pile of books with a noose round his neck to 'stimulate sexual glands'. The books had slid apart and the boy had been left choking to death on the door. Then there was the teenager arrested for stealing a toaster from his grandparents. They wanted him imprisoned. His real 'crime', it quickly turned out, was that he was homosexual – 'indecency with a male' was our journalistic cliché – and he was swiftly remanded. On his way out, he made a pass at the most senior policeman in all Blyth.

And we wrote in clichés. Always clichés. When the police were seeking a hit-and-run driver, they either 'spread their net' or 'narrowed their search' or 'stepped up their hunt'. Company directors were 'bosses', scientists were invariably 'boffins', officials were always 'chiefs', storm-battered ships inevitably 'limped' into port. Suicides were always tragic, brides always beautiful, angry councillors were 'hopping mad' and protesting villagers would always 'take to the streets'. Those who discovered bodies were 'horror-struck' or 'mystified'; the latter applied to the construction gang building a new Blyth bypass who excavated dozens of corpses – all in their Victorian Sunday best – and thought they'd discovered a mass murder before realising they were digging up an old cemetery. Needless to say, Tory election candidates always 'lashed out' at the sitting Labour MP, Eddie Blythe.

They actually taught us to write like this. There was a whole Thomson Newspapers school of journalism in Newcastle which I and my fellow 'cub' reporters from other *Chronicle* district offices were ordered to attend once a week – much to the disgust of my senior reporter in Blyth, Jim Harland, a Sean Connery lookalike with a reservoir of immense kindness and – for really stupid reporters – volcanic anger. 'You learn journalism on the job, not listening to that bunch of wankers,' Harland once told me. But sure enough, every Thursday morning, I'd arrive in Newcastle on a pre-war double-decker bus from Blyth – the interior filled with a suffocating fog of blue cigarette smoke – wolf down an egg sandwich at the aptly named Rumbling Tum café and endure hours of shorthand, legal advice and clichés.

The best stories could be told in 400 words, we were told. All the facts in the first para, plenty of punchy lines, equal time to all parties in a dispute and a good 'kicker'. No anger, no passion, no suggestion that there was right or wrong. I was reminded of Joe Friday in *Dragnet*. 'Just the facts, Ma'am, just the facts,' he'd yell at the broads. We were given 'story-lines'. Write the intro to the following: a retired soldier – who once took part in the Normandy landings – was blaming the local council because his wife had disappeared after seeing a ghost in her council-supplied house. Answer: 'A mystified D-Day vet lashed out at council chiefs last night after his terrified wife fled "phantoms" in their council home.' Anything that moved away from this rubric, that suggested a more subtle, nuanced approach – perhaps the old soldier was suffering from shell-shock or his wife was mentally ill or perhaps the ghosts were real – was wiped out. Our Thomson 'trainers' quickly decided that a reporter called Simon Winchester would never make the grade. He was too imaginative, too thoughtful, too critical in his approach. Simon, of course, went on to become the best *Guardian* correspondent in Belfast. We were supposed to write stories the readers would easily 'understand'. Readers were in a hurry, tired, often not well educated, we were taught. Having talked for hours to miners and part-time shipyard workers and firemen and cops and landladies, I didn't think our readers were that dumb. I thought they might like something more than our clichés. But not according to the journalism teachers. We had to have 'key' words. Lash out. Bosses. Phantoms. Chiefs. Terrified.

Yes, we had to be 'trained'. I still remember the guffaws of our 'Stop Press' printer in the Blyth office when he read my report of a launching in the local shipyard by the wife of the chairman of the Central Electricity Generating Board. 'Mrs Smith smashed the Champagne against the hull of the vessel,' I had written, 'and the workers cheered as she slid down the slipway.' Then there was the Tory election candidate who, in my interview, 'smiled as he spoke of his many and varied pastimes'. Harland collapsed. 'You're a fucking innocent, Bob,' he screamed. 'What do you think our readers will make of "many and varied pastimes"?'

But I also remember what the *Chronicle* didn't say. My reference to the weeping mother outside the Morpeth coroner's inquest was cut from the story. The tale of Captain Fortune's fish never made it – the paper needed a quote from the long-departed Polish trawler captain to 'balance' the story. My report on the dangerous state of Blyth staithes was followed by a formal apology to the National Coal Board – inserted by *Chronicle* editors without any reference to me – to the effect that the wooden pier met all safety standards. A wolfish smile crossed my face weeks later when a roar of splintering wood and exploding steam shook the Blyth office. A tank engine – its driver mercifully unhurt – had crashed down through the flimsy old pit-props and settled precariously on the edge of the dock. We reported it straight – no reference to my previous story, nor to the grovelling apology we had carried only weeks earlier.

I had nothing against the *Chron*. When Liverpool University offered me a place to read English, the editors cheerfully accepted my resignation and wished me luck in my studies. When Liverpool then unforgivably decided that – without O-level maths – they couldn't after all give me the promised place, John Brownlee equally cheerfully offered me my job back. Then when Lancaster University gave me a real undergraduate place, Brownlee sent me off again with his best wishes. He later wrote me a stunning reference for the *Sunday Express* which impressed its late, irascible editor, John Junor. Harland overrode my desire to stay on the paper. 'Don't be a fucking eejit,' the coal miner's son solemnly told me. 'Go do your studies, Bob, and get a degree.'

Which is what I did. Within months, I was studying linguistics and reading Noam Chomsky and learning, thanks to David Craig's English lectures on Dickens, of the social devastation which the Industrial Revolution had spread across northern England, indeed across the very area where I had been a cub reporter. The decaying mines, the growing unemployment, the doomed shipyards – even the rotten wood of the Blyth staithes – suddenly made sense. But I had to go to university to understand this. Journalism was about history. But not in the *Chron*.

And in the end, it was this thought – the idea that language and history shape our lives – that lured me back this month to the north-east of England. I had a suspicion that the language we were forced to write as trainee reporters all those years ago had somehow imprisoned us, that we had been schooled to mould the world and ourselves in clichés, that for the most part this would define our lives, destroy our anger and imagination, make us loyal to our betters, to governments, to authority. For some reason, I had become possessed of the belief that the blame for our failure as journalists to report the Middle East with any sense of moral passion or indignation lay in the way that we as journalists were trained.

When I returned, a cold, heavy rain was falling across Blyth. The old harbour was a dark, mud-sided, empty lagoon. There were no more shipyards. The mines had closed – all but one pit up the coast – and the power station, glowering through the murk on the other side of the river, had been decommissioned. At the end of Middleton Street, the newsagent – grills on the windows, damp stains covering the ceiling – told me Blyth was still dying. 'Fourteen per cent unemployment, thirty-four drug deaths in four years,' he said. 'No future.' I bought the *Chronicle*. The wooden staithes had disappeared. So had the railway. The beach garden where I used to read was still there, its curved stone balustrade broken and collapsing into the sand.

I knocked on the door of number 82. My landlady, Mrs Hamilton, was long gone. The couple who now lived there allowed me to climb the stairs, turn right at the top and push open the little cubby-hole where I slept almost forty years ago. Seven-by-five. I hadn't got the measurements wrong. There were bookshelves in the room now, newly painted, centrally heated, the old gas-pipe concealed within the wall. The room where I had eaten my bacon breakfasts – Mrs Hamilton provided full board – contained a magnificent marble fireplace which I could not remember. The new owners of number 82 were – they were the first to proclaim the fact and I saw the proof on the living room table – *Independent* readers. They never bought the *Chronicle*. Was there, I wondered, a message here?

In the car, the rain guttering down the windscreen, the same old grey streets shimmering through the glass, I opened the *Chronicle*. Nothing had changed. All that follows came from one single issue. 'Bosses leading a management buyout of stricken shipyard Cammell Laird say a £2 m damages claim from former workers could scupper the bid.' Key words: Bosses. Stricken. Scupper. Bid. 'A pair of high-flyers will be winging their way to France for the most gruelling cycle race in the world.' Key words: High-flyers. Gruelling. 'A mum of three who lured a teenage girl babysitter into a seedy sex session with a stranger she met through an internet chatroom has failed in her bid to cut her jail term.' Lured. Seedy. Bid. 'Jet-away MPs have been condemned for heading off on foreign jaunts rather than holidaying in the North-east to help the region's ailing tourist industry.' Sympathetic though I was to the MPs as I glanced at the weather grizzling down outside my car, I got the message: Jet-away. Jaunts. Ailing. 'Police hunting the murderer of Sara Cameron have spread their net abroad.' Yes, almost forty years since I'd been writing this crap, the cops were still 'spreading their net' and – I had little doubt – would soon be 'narrowing their search' or 'stepping up' their hunt for Sara's killer. It was left to the successor of the old weekly *Blyth News* – now a free-sheet with the immortal title of the *News Post Leader* – to tell me that 'plans to build a housing estate on scrubland in Blyth Valley have been put on ice . . .'

I drove to Morpeth to see the old magistrates court, and Gateshead, and back and forth over the Tyne bridges where I once had my picture taken in a waistcoat, and I found that the Rumbling Tum was now part of an underground bus station, that the slag-heaps had been largely 'greened', that the smoke had gone. Yes, that great, greasy, wet smoke that I breathed day and night – even in my unheated bedroom – had vanished. Perhaps smokeless coal and gas has its advantages. Or, as I grimly thought, perhaps there's nothing left to burn.

Jim Harland was leaning over his front wall when I drove up. Plumper, a little jowled, eyes sharp as coals, Sean Connery features still in evidence, along with his tongue. 'You're the man who missed the story in Blyth port on your day off,' he growled. The sun had come out. He had set up the annual town fair and today – deus ex machina – was town fair day. There was a fire engine and pin-bowling and pop-singing and dancing by a team of overweight cuties in old US army uni-forms – I'm still puzzling the meaning of that one – and a ball-in-the-tub throwing session (which Fisk lost) and an awful lot of very tough-looking mums and dads with sallow faces and sad smiles and, I thought, a life of great hardship behind them. Blyth, Harland told me, was becoming a great dormitory town for Newcastle. Pity they'd torn up the railway. But the sleeping bit I could well understand.

Harland is a big man, 'Big Jim Harland' we used to call him – he went on in later years to work for the *Mirror*, then the BBC – and he propelled me towards the Federation Club where pints moved like quicksilver around a room where huge ex-miners and ex-shipyard men kept winning all kinds of bingo games. I had never seen so many £5 notes. Life had been good to Harland and his wife Rosemary and we walked back to his home – just across from my old 'digs' – for lunch. 'Space was the problem for us in journalism, Bob,' he said. 'I was taught at sixteen that you had to economise on space. We couldn't write "Mrs S, who was 23 years old", I had to write "23-year-old Mrs S". But if we said what we thought, well, we'd have called that bias. We could say "this is what I saw" but not "this is what I feel I saw". The journalists who trained us were regional journalists – and they taught us what they knew, the way they had been trained.'

But slowly, as Rosemary made the lunch in the kitchen, Harland revealed more about Blyth. He thought Margaret Thatcher and Arthur Scargill had done most harm to the town. But he knew much that I had not known when I worked there. The town clerk who had been such a classical scholar – he had lived near my digs but was now long dead – had been on the make. The police chief – the man who was the target of the gay man in the court but now also dead – had been in the habit of ringing up landlords in the early hours of the morning for a drink, forcing them to open their pubs at 6 a.m. for the local, newly off-duty, cops. 'No, we didn't write this,' Harland said. 'These people fed us. They'd help us. The policeman who'd want an early morning drink would also tip us off on stories. We had to talk to everyone, the town clerk, the police, the fire brigade . . . Then there was child abuse. There was a lot of it here. A terrible thing. But the social services wouldn't talk to us. They said all their enquiries were confidential, that we didn't have the right to know what they had learnt. And so child abuse went on. I only realised the state of things when a cricketer I knew made a comment about his daughters and I realised it was a common thing. But we accept the "privacy" of the social services. And in court, we reported "indecency with a minor". Those were the words we used.'

I asked about the Middle East. Did Harland think that perhaps our 'training' had caused us to fail when we journalists were faced not with local government disputes or coroners' courts but with a great historical tragedy? 'I've never covered a story that was a great tragedy like the Middle East,' he said. 'I can see the problem, yes. How do you make the journalism here stretch to the journalism there?' He had made the point precisely.

For out in the Middle East, more and more journalists, each with their local reporting experience, their 'training', their journalism schools – the American version even more banal than the English ones – are using clichés and tired adjectives to obscure reality. Turn on your television tonight or read tomorrow's agency reports and we are told of the 'cycle of violence' – no side taken there – of 'clashes' (in which the identities of victim and killer are obscured) or of 'the fears of Israeli security chiefs'. Note how the word 'security' is always linked to the word 'Israel'. And how 'chiefs' has made the grade from Blyth to Palestine. And just as the police chief in Blyth would tip us off on a story, so Israelis – to a much lesser extent Palestinians – tip us off on stories. No one wants to rock the boat, to be controversial. Why write about the Blyth staithes if we're going to carry a Coal Board denial? Why write about the outrageous nature of Israel's killing of stone-throwing children if we're going to get outraged letters to the editor?

Much better to stick to clichés. Arab 'terrorists' threaten Israel. Israeli 'security chiefs' warn Arafat. Can Arafat 'control' his own people, we asked when the Israelis asked the same question. Yet when a Jewish settlers' group killed two Palestinian civilian men and a baby, we did not ask if Sharon could control his own people. Since the Palestinians had not asked that question, we did not ask it. We were silent that time round. Over five days in the North-east and on the long drive back to London, I listened to the radio news. Two Israelis had been killed by a Palestinian suicide bomber at Binyamina. The

Israelis 'struck back' at the Palestinians, killing four guerrillas in a 'targeted' killing. 'Targeted' was Israel's word. In other words, death squads. But that wasn't what the BBC said. When the Israeli settlers murdered the three Palestinians – including the baby – the Israeli police were reported as 'narrowing their search' for the killers.

Never the why. Only the what. We reported the closure of Blyth's mines. But we rarely asked why the mines had to die. We watched Blyth decay. We reported its death. In my cub reporter days, we watched its last moments as a coal-and-ship city. But we didn't scratch the black, caked soot off the walls of Newcastle and ask why Britain's prime ministers allowed the centre of the Industrial Revolution to go to the grave. Harland agreed that there was a culture of 'accepting' authority. We didn't challenge the police or the council – or the social services. They may not have been our friends. But we needed them. We respected them, in an odd sort of way. They were the 'chiefs', the 'bosses'. And now we rarely challenge friendly governments. We can (and should) attack Arafat's corrupt dictatorship in Palestine. But Israeli wrongdoing has to be 'balanced' with quotations from Israel's 'security chiefs'. The off-the-record briefing from the council clerk or the police chief has become the off-the-record briefing from the Foreign Office. Look how we responded to Nato's wartime Kosovo briefings. How we accepted. How we parroted the words.

I'm glad the *Chron* exists. It was good to me. So was Big Jim Harland. He made me understand the need for accuracy. 'Say what you like later,' he once told me. 'But for Christ's sake, get it right.' But our conversation this month left me with much to think about. What was it he said to me before lunch? 'If we'd said what we thought, well, we'd have called that bias.' And no doubt one day, we'll find those reporters who so blithely accepted Nato's briefings and Israel's line on the Palestinians 'revealing' the truth. Like the rotten borough and the crooked cop and the sinister abuse of children in Blyth, they'll all one day be ready to tell us what they really knew. Only it will be a bit late to make any difference.

The Independent Magazine, 4 August 2001

We should have listened to Bin Laden

I belong to that generation of undergraduates who cut their teeth on linguistics. Lancaster University in its second year of existence – Class of '67, if I'm not mistaken – was as innovative as it was a bit odd. 'Digs' were on the Morecambe seafront, lectures in a converted chapel, and tutorials in an old linen factory. But the books we studied invariably included the immensely boring Zelig Harris and the stunningly brilliant Noam Chomsky.

Less famous then than now, he it was who introduced me to the 'foregrounded element'. 'Foregrounded' is when someone places words in such an order that a new meaning is attached to them or deliberately leaves out a word that we might expect. The big bad man emphasises the meanness of the man. But the bad big man makes us think of size. 'Big' has been 'fore-grounded'. Real linguists won't like the above definition but journalists, I fear, sometimes have to distort in order to make plain. Presidents too, it seems. Because I did a little linguistic analysis on George W. Bush's Fort Bragg address to Americans on 28 June – and came up with some pretty strange results. First, of course, was his use of the words 'terrorism' and 'terror' thirty-three times. More interesting was the way in which he deployed these massed ranks of terrorists. If you divided his speech up into eight parts, 'terrorists' or 'terror' popped up eight times in the first, eight times in the second, three times in the third, nine in the fourth, two in the fifth, none at all in the sixth, a measly three in the seventh and again none at all in the eighth.

The columns in which 'terror' disappeared were full of different clichés. Challenge, a good constitution (an Iraqi one, of course), a chance to vote, a free society, certain truths (I won't insult you by telling you where that was snitched from), defending our freedom, flying the flag, great turning points in the story of freedom, prevail (one of Churchill's favourite words) and no higher call. Put through Chomsky's machine, Bush's speech begins by frightening the audience to death with terrorism and finishes triumphantly by rousing them to patriotic confidence in their country's future victory. It wasn't actually a speech at all. It was a movie script, a screenplay. The bad guys are really bad but they're going to get their comeuppance because the good guys are going to win.

Other elements of the Bush speech were, of course, woefully dishonest. It's a bit much for Bush to claim that 'terrorists' want to 'topple governments' when the only guys who've been doing that – in Afghanistan and Iraq – were, ahem, ahem, the Americans. There are plenty of references to the evil nature of 'the enemy' – tyranny and oppression, remnants, the old order – and a weird new version of the Iraqi–11 September lie. Instead of Saddam's non-existent alliance with al-Qaeda, we now have the claim from Bush that the Iraqi 'terrorists who kill innocent men, women and children on the streets of Baghdad are followers of the same murderous ideology that took the lives of our citizens' on 11 September 2001. Whoops! It's no longer the Saddam regime that was involved in these attacks, it seems; it's now the post-Saddam insurgents who are part of the same gang.

It's strange that for a White House that writes screenplays, the words of Osama bin Laden appear so uninteresting. Whenever bin Laden speaks, no one bothers to read through his speech. The questions are always: Was it him? Is he alive? Where is he? Never: What did he say? There are real perils in this. Bin Laden, who hated Saddam – he told me this himself, in person – made a call to his followers to fight alongside an Iraqi force which included Saddam's Iraqi Baathist 'Socialists'. This was the moment when Iraq's future guerrilla army fused with the future suicide bombers, the message that would create the detonation that would engulf the West in Iraq. And we didn't even notice. The US 'experts' waffled about whether bin Laden was alive – not what he said. For once, Bush got it right – but he was too late. Always, as they say, read the text.

Take George Tenet, the CIA Ernest Borgnine lookalike who sat behind Colin Powell at the UN when the US secretary of state was uttering all those lies about weapons of mass destruction in February of 2003. It now turns out that George is mightily upset with the White House. He didn't refer to evidence of WMD as a 'slam dunk', he says. He was talking about the ability of the US government to persuade the American people to go to war based on these lies. In other words, he wasn't lying to the American president. He was only lying to the American people.

I was struck by all this last month when I came across one of Tony Blair's lies in my local Beirut paper. Sandwiched beneath a headline which read 'Saudi reforms lose momentum' – surely one of the more extraordinarily unnecessary stories in the Arab press – it quoted our dear prime minister as saying that he was very angry that a review committee had prevented him from deporting two Algerians because their government represented a 'different political system'. The 'foregrounded' element, of course, is the word 'different'. This is the word that contains the lie. For the reason the committee declined to return these men to their country was not – as Blair well knew – because Algeria possesses a 'different' political system but because the Algerian 'system' allows it to torture its prisoners.

I have myself interviewed Algerian policemen and women who have become perverted by their witness of torture: one policewoman told me how she now loves horror films because they remind her of the repulsive torture she had to watch at the Châteauneuf police station in Algiers – where prisoners had water pumped into their anuses until they died. I still remember the spiteful and abusive letter that the Algerian ambassador to London wrote to *The Independent*, sneering at Saida Kheroui, whose foot was broken under torture. She was a 'terrorist', this man announced. This is the 'different' political system that Blair was referring to. Ms Kheroui, by the way, never emerged from prison. She was murdered by her torturers.

Blair knows that the Algerian security forces rape women to death. So how does he dare lie about the 'different' political system which allows police officers to rape women? We Europeans now make a habit of lying about this. Take the Belgian government. It deported Bouasria Ben Othman to Algeria on 15 July 1996 on the grounds that he would not be in danger if he was returned to his country. He died in police custody at Moustaganem. A 'different' political system indeed.

And now I have before me Blair's repulsive 'goodbye' speech to the British people, uttered at Sedgefield. Putting the country first didn't mean 'doing the right thing according to conventional wisdom' (Chomsky foregrounded element: conventional) or the 'prevailing consensus' (Chomsky foregrounded element: prevailing). It meant 'what you genuinely believe to be right' (Chomsky foregrounded element: genuinely). Lord Blair of Kut al-Amara wanted to stand 'shoulder to shoulder' with Britain's oldest ally, which he assumed to be the United States. (It is actually Portugal, but no matter.) 'I did so out of belief,' he told us. Foregrounded element: belief. Am I alone in being repulsed by this? 'Politics may be the art of the possible [foregrounded element: may] but, at least in life, give the impossible a go.' What does this mean? Is Blair adopting saint-hood as a means to an end? 'Hand on heart, I did what I thought was right.' Excuse me? Is that Blair's message to the families of all those dead soldiers – and to the families of all those thousands of dead Iraqis? It has been an 'honour' to 'serve' Britain, this man tells us. What gall.

Yes, I must acknowledge Northern Ireland. If only Blair had kept to this achievement. If only he had accepted that his role was to end 800 years of the Anglo–Irish conflict. But no. He wanted to be our Saviour – and he allowed George Bush to do such things as Oliver Cromwell would find quite normal. Torture. Murder. Rape.

My dad used to call people like Blair a 'twerp' which, I think, meant a pregnant earwig. But Blair is not a twerp. I very much fear he is a vicious little man. And I can only recall Cromwell's statement to the Rump Parliament in 1653, repeated – with such wisdom – by Leo Amery to Chamberlain in 1940: 'You have sat too long here for any good you have been doing. Depart, I say, and let us have done with you. In the name of God, go.'

The Independent, 2 July 2005 and 19 May 2007

After a decade in power, Tony Blair resigned as British prime minister on 27 June 2007 to become 'peace' envoy to the Middle East, an irony not lost on Arabs who blame both Blair and George W. Bush for the disastrous invasion of Iraq in 2003 and the greatest suffering inflicted on Muslims since Saddam Hussein began his own Western-supported eight-year war against Iran in 1980.

The jargon disease

I once received an invitation to lecture at 'The University of Excellence'. I forget where this particular academy was located – Jordan, I think – but I recall very clearly that the suggested subject of my talk was as incomprehensible to me as it would, no doubt, have been to any audience. Invitation rejected. Only this week I received another request, this time to join 'ethics practitioners' to 'share evidence-based practices on dealing with current ethical practices' around the world. What on earth does this mean? Why do people write like this?

The word 'excellence', of course, has long ago been devalued by the corporate world – its favourite expression has long been 'Quality and Excellence', invariably accompanied by a 'mission statement', that claim to self-importance dreamed up by Robin Cook when foreign secretary (swiftly ditched when he decided to go on selling jets to Indonesia) and thereafter by every export company and amateur newspaper in the world.

There is something repulsive about this vocabulary, an aggressive language of superiority in which 'key players' can 'interact' with each other, can 'impact' society, 'outsource' their business or 'downsize' the number of their employees. They need 'feedback' and 'input'. They 'think outside the box' or 'push the envelope'. They have a 'work space', not a desk. They need 'personal space' – they need to be left alone – and sometimes they need 'time and space', a commodity much in

demand when marriages are failing. These lies and obfus-
cations are infuriating. 'Downsizing' employees means firing
them; 'outsourcing' means hiring someone else to do your
dirty work. 'Feedback' means 'response', 'input' means 'advice'.
'Thinking outside the box' means, does it not, to be
'imaginative'?

Being a 'key player' is a form of self-aggrandisement – which
is why I never agree to be a 'key speaker', especially if this
means participation in a 'workshop'. To me a workshop means
what it says. When I was at school, the workshop was a carpen-
try shop wherein generations of teachers vainly tried to teach
Fisk how to make a wooden chair or table that did not collapse
the moment it was completed. But today, a 'workshop' –
though we mustn't say so – is a group of tiresome academics
yakking in the secret language of anthropology or talking about
'cultural sensitivity' or 'core issues' or 'tropes'. Presumably
these are the same folk who invented the UN's own humani-
tarian-speak. Of the latter, my favourite is the label awarded
to any desperate refugee who is prepared (for a pittance) to
persuade their fellow victims to abide by the UN's wishes – to
abandon their tents and return to their dangerous, war-ravaged
homes. These luckless advisers are referred to by the UN as
'social animators'.

It is a disease, this language, caught by one of our own New
Labour ministers on the BBC last week when he talked about
'environmental externalities'. Presumably, this meant 'the
weather'. Similarly, an architect I know warned his client of
the effect of the 'aggressive saline environment' on a house
built near the sea. If this advice seems obscure, we might be
'conflicted' about it – who, I ask myself, invented the false
transitive verb? – or, worse still, 'stressed'. In northern Iraq in
1991, I was once ordered by a humanitarian worker from the
'International Rescue Committee' to leave the only room I
could find in the wrecked town of Zakho because it had been

booked for her fellow workers – who were very 'stressed'. Poor
souls, I thought. They were stressed, 'stressed out', trying – no
doubt – to 'come to terms' with their predicament, attempting
to 'cope'.

This is the language of therapy, in which frauds, liars and
cheats are always trying to escape. Thus President Clinton's
spokesman claimed after his admission of his affair with
Monica Lewinsky that he was 'seeking closure'. Like so many
mendacious politicians, Clinton felt – as Prime Minister Blair
will no doubt feel about his bloodbath in Iraq once he leaves
No. 10 – the need to 'move on'. In the same way, our psycho-
babble masters and mistresses – yes, there is a semantic problem there, too, isn't there? – announce after wars that it is a
time for 'healing', the same prescription doled out to families
which are 'dysfunctional', who live in a 'dystopian' world. Yes,
dystopian is a perfectly good word – it is the opposite of
utopian – but like 'perceive' and 'perception' (words once much
loved by Jonathan Dimbleby), they have become fashionable
because they appear enigmatic.

Some newly popular phrases, such as 'tipping point' – used
about Middle East conflicts when the bad guys are about to
lose – or 'big picture' – when moralists have to be reminded
of the greater good – are merely fashionable. Others are simply
odd. I always mixed up 'bonding' with 'bondage' and 'quality
time' with a popular assortment of toffees. I used to think that
'increase' was a perfectly acceptable word until I discovered
that in the military sex-speak of the Pentagon, Iraq would
endure a 'spike' of violence until a 'surge' of extra troops
arrived in Baghdad.

All this is different, of course, from the non-sexual 'no-
brainers' with which we now have to 'cope' – 'author' for
'authoress', for example, 'actor' for 'actress' – or the fearful
linguistic lengths we must go to in order to avoid offence to
Londoners who speak Cockney: as we all know – though only

those of us, of course, who come from the Home Counties –
these people speak 'Estuary' English. It's like those poor Americans in Detroit who, in fear and trepidation, avoided wishing
me a happy Christmas last year. 'Happy Holiday!' they
chorused until I roared 'Happy Christmas' back. In Beirut, by
the way, we all wish each other 'Happy Christmas' and 'Happy
Eid', whether our friends are Muslim or Christian. Is this really
of 'majority importance', as an Irish television producer once
asked a colleague of a news event?

I fear it is. For we are not using words any more. We are
utilising them, speaking for effect rather than meaning, for
escape. We are becoming – as the *New Yorker* now describes
children who don't care if they watch films on the cinema
screen or on their mobile phones – 'platform agnostic'. What,
Polonius asked his lord, was he reading? 'Words, words, words,'
Hamlet replied. If only . . .

The Independent, 13 January 2007

Poisonous academics and
their claptrap of exclusion

That great anthropological sage Michael Gilsenan – whose
Lords of the Lebanese Marshes once almost started a small civil
war in northern Lebanon – turned up this week to lecture at
that equally great bastion of learning, the American University
of Beirut, founded, as it happens, by Quakers during the nineteenth-century Lebanese Christian–Druze conflict. Gilsenan's
subject was abstruse enough: Arab migration to what our
Foreign Office still calls 'the Far East'. Most of these migrants,
it transpired, came from Arabia, especially the mountainous
Hadramaut district of Yemen. Under British rule, they pros-
pered, bought land, left inheritances and, once established,
wealthy Arab women also took their place in this new world,
even involving themselves in legal disputes.

All very fascinating. But once questions were invited from
the floor, Gilsenan was asked about 'matrilineal' issues in colonial Singapore. I closed my eyes. 'Matrilineal' doesn't exist in
my dictionary. Nor is it likely to. It is part of the secret language
of academe – especially of anthropology – and it is a turn-off.
We poor dunces should keep our noses out of this high-falutin'
stuff. That, I think, is the message. I recall a student raging to
me about her anthropology professor who constantly used
words like 'emic' and 'etic' – to this day, I have no idea what
they mean; readers are invited to reply – in an attempt to
mystify her discipline.

Keep Out, these words say to us. This Is Something You Are Not Clever Enough to Understand. A French professor put it to me quite bluntly this week. 'If we don't dress up what we want to say in this silly language,' she announced, 'we are told we are being journalists.' Well, well, I can quite see the problem. It's good against evil, us or them, university scholarship or dirty journalism. It's a new and dangerous phenomenon I'm talking about, a language of exclusion that must have grown up in universities over the past twenty years; after all, any non-university-educated man or woman can pick up an academic treatise or PhD thesis written in the 1920s or 30s and – however Hegelian the subject – fully understand its meaning. No longer.

About three years ago, I received a good example of this from Marc Gopin, visiting associate professor of international diplomacy at the Fletcher School of Tufts University and a visiting scholar in the programme on negotiation at Harvard. I received his latest book for review, a tome called *Holy War, Holy Peace: How Religion Can Bring Peace to the Middle East.* A promising title, you might think. Well, think again. For within pages, I was being bushwhacked by 'metaphorical constructs' and 'universalist mythic constructs' and 'romanticised, amoral constructs of culture' and 'fundamental dialogic immediacy' and 'prosocial tendencies'. Here is another cracker: 'The Abrahamic myth of a loving Patriarch and a loving God who care for a special people has created a home and a meaning system for millions of human beings.' Come again? Meaning system? The author grew up, he says, 'in a self-consciously exilic spirituality'. He talks about the 'interplay' of 'political and mythic interdependencies' and the 'ubiquitous human psychological process of othering'. He wants to 'problematise' intervention at 'elite' levels. A rabbi – whom I immediately felt sorry for – was 'awash in paradoxicality', which apparently proved that 'cognitive dissonance is good for intractable conflicts'. Well, you could have fooled me. There was more: 'dialogic injuries', 'cultural envelope', 'family psychodynamics', 'the rich texture of hermeneutic possibility', 'porous barriers of spiritual identity' and, of course, my old favourite, 'social intercourse'. 'Dialectic apologetics' makes an appearance, alongside 'persecutorial othering' and lots of other 'otherings', including a reference to 'pious transformation of old cognitive constructs as an end to othering: remythification'.

What is interesting is that when Professor Gopin chose to send a letter to President Clinton, which he prints in his book, he wrote in perfectly comprehensible English – indeed, he even got a reply from the old scallywag. The good professor was suggesting that private meetings between Jewish and Islamic leaders should become public under Clinton's leadership and produce 'a powerful new force for pursuing peace'. No 'constructs' here, you note. No 'otherings' or 'meaning systems' or 'paradoxicalities'. Because Gopin obviously knew that his academic claptrap wouldn't have got much further than the White House mail room.

So why this preposterous academic language? There's a clue when Gopin compares 'dress and behaviour codes in the Pentagon' to 'very complex speech and behaviour codes in academia'. Yes, university folk have to be complex, don't they? They have to speak in a language which others – journalists, perhaps? – simply would not understand. To enter this unique circle of brain-heavy men and women, all must learn its secret language lest interlopers manage to sneak through the door. It may be that all this came about as a protective shield against political interference in academe, an attempt to make teaching so impenetrable that no MP, congressman or senator could ever make accusations of political bias in class – on the grounds that they wouldn't have the slightest idea what the lecturer was talking about.

But I think it is about snobbishness. I recall a lady professor at George Mason University, complaining that 'most people' – she was referring to truck-drivers, Amtrak crews, bellhops and anyone else who didn't oppose the Iraq war – 'had so little information'. Well, I wasn't surprised. University teachers – especially in the States – are great at 'networking' each other but hopeless at communicating with most of the rest of the world, including those who collect their rubbish, deliver their laundry and serve up their hash browns. After lecturing at another university in the States, I was asked by a member of the audience how universities could have more influence in the community. I said that they must stop using what I called 'the poisonous language of academia'. At which there was an outburst of clapping from the students and total silence from the university staff who were present and who greeted this remark with scowls.

No, I'm not saying all teachers speak like this. There is no secret language in the work of Edward Said or Avi Shlaim or Martin Gilbert or Noam Chomsky. But it's growing and it's getting worse, and I suspect only students can now rebel against it. The merest hint of 'emics' and 'constructs' or 'hermeneutic possibilities' and they should walk out of class, shouting Winston Churchill's famous retort: 'This is English up with which I will not put.'

The Independent, 14 May 2005

Soft words – hard questions

When I worked at *The Times* – in the free, pre-Murdoch days – I enjoyed life as Middle East correspondent under the leadership of a bearded foreign news editor called Ivan Barnes. This brilliant, immensely humorous man – happily still with us – was a connoisseur of weasel words, get-out clauses and semantic humbug, and one of his favourite questions was this: What do you think of a man who begins each statement with the words, 'To be completely frank and open with you'? You can see his point. 'If someone promises to be frank with you – completely frank, mark you – then what is he being the rest of the time?' Barnes would ask. 'As for completely...' On balance, I agree that the key word is 'completely'. It reeks of 100 per cent, of totality, of black and white. It is also, I notice, one of Blair's favourite words – along with 'absolutely'. Blair is always being completely and absolutely honest with us. He is always absolutely convinced he was right to invade Iraq (even when the rest of the world completely realises the opposite). He is always completely and absolutely certain of his own integrity. I call this the 'Ho-ho' factor.

So all the Fisk radar warnings went off this week when Blair told us that 'we have got to address the completely false sense of grievance against the West' felt by Muslims. Completely. Muslims' 'sense of grievance' – fury might be a better word – is 'completely' false. Is it? We are screwing up Afghanistan, destroying tens of thousands of lives in Iraq, and America now has a military presence in Turkey, Uzbekistan, Kazakhstan, Afghanistan, Iraq, Jordan, Egypt, Algeria, Qatar, Bahrain, Kuwait, Yemen and Oman – and Muslim grievance is 'completely' false. No, look at Blair's statement again. He doesn't suggest there is even a grievance. It is a false 'sense' of grievance. Anyone who understands mendacity knows exactly what Blair comprehends all too well: that Muslims do have a 'sense' of grievance and that it is not false at all.

It's odd, though, how folk think they can get away with this stuff. Take my old chum Professor Alan Dershowitz, who announced on the evening of 11 September 2001 that I was a 'dangerous man' because I asked the question 'why' about the international crimes against humanity in the United States. This week, in an article in *The Independent*, Dershowitz was at it again. I especially enjoyed his description of a standard US military torture, 'waterboarding'. He described it as 'a technique that produces a near-drowning experience'. Ho ho. You bet it does. He says that this is torture. But why the word 'technique'? Why does it 'produce' an 'experience'? Actually, the experience is one of drowning, not 'near-drowning' – that's the point of this vile practice.

I love these key phrases which are littered throughout Dershowitz's article, so soft and gentle: 'the nature of permissible interrogation', 'questionable means', 'latitude' (as in 'should more latitude be afforded to interrogators in the preventive [*sic*] context'), 'sometimes excessive efforts' and so on. All this, mark you, is premised on one totally misleading statement. 'Weapons of mass destruction in the hands of suicide terrorists with no fear of death and no home address have rendered useless the deterrent threat of massive retaliation.' True – if such people existed. But there simply hasn't been any suicide terrorist with a weapon of mass destruction – not ever. Like the weapons of mass destruction in Iraq – which were also, I recall, going to be handed over to suicide terrorists – they don't exist. What Dershowitz is actually trying to do is change the laws so that we can torture legally when faced by this mythical beast, a creature that is in fact intended to instil fear in us (and thus persuade us to go along with another round of 'waterboarding').

The whole torture fandango gathers weasel words like moss. Take a reference in the *Wall Street Journal* last month to torture as 'aggressive interrogation techniques'. 'Technique' again, please note. I suppose that's what you can claim the US soldier was applying when he last year stuffed an Iraqi general upside down inside a sleeping bag, sat on his chest and killed him. Take Agim Çeku, the brutal KLA leader who has popped up as Kosovo's prime minister, but who is still wanted for war crimes by Belgrade. The *Financial Times* did a wonderful portrait of him just over a week ago in which he was described as 'slim and youthful . . . Mr Çeku, 44, exudes an effortless authority born of long experience as a military commander'. Ho ho. You bet he does.

Chris Hitchens got in on the act last month when he tried to explain why the slaughter of twenty-four Iraqi civilians at Haditha didn't mean a return to the days of My Lai massacres. So here we go. 'Unjust though the assumption may prove to be, let us imagine that on November 19th, 2005, US Marines of Kilo company did indeed crack up and cut loose in Haditha . . .' Get it? Their comrade had just been killed by insurgents. So the Americans may have 'cracked up' and 'cut loose'. Later, Hitchens describes the massacre at Haditha as 'a white-hot few minutes', and later still he talks of a 'coalition soldier who relieves his rage by discharging a clip'. A few seconds later and he is going on about the 'alleged rampage'. Rampage! Ho ho. The point, of course, is that it takes much more than a 'clip' of ammunition to kill twenty-four civilians. And it takes a long time – not a 'few' minutes – to go from room to room, amid the shrieking children who are being slaughtered and the women trying to protect themselves from murder, to blast that many people to death. Some 'rampage'.

So what does it take to run the earth these days? Effortless authority, I suppose. A little bit of 'excess', plenty of 'technique' and a mere clip of ammunition. Completely and absolutely.

The Independent, 8 July 2006

The pen, the telex, the phone and the despised e-mail

The laptop has done bad things to us. I've spent the past year writing a history of the Middle East which has proved to me – quite apart from the folly of man – that the computer has not necessarily helped our writing or our research into the sins of our fathers. As a journalist who still refuses to use e-mail – forcing people to write real letters cuts down the amount of ungrammatical and often abusive messages we receive – I would say that, wouldn't I? But, along with a researcher, I've ploughed through 328,000 documents in my library for my book – my reporter's notebooks, newspapers, magazines, clippings, government statements, letters, photocopies of First World War archives and photographs – and I cannot escape the fact that the laptop has helped to destroy my files, my memories and, indeed, my handwriting. My notebooks of the Lebanese civil war in the late 1970s are written in a graceful easy-to-read script, a pale blue fountain pen moving in a stately way across the page. My notes of the 2003 American invasion of Iraq are illegible – except to myself – because I cannot keep pace with the speed of the laptop. I no longer write words, I have discovered. I represent them – that is to say I draw their likeness, which I cannot read but which I must *construe* when transcribing them. I should add at once that this very article is being handwritten on an Air France jet from Beirut and even now, as I write, I find I am skipping letters, words, and expressions because I know what I want to say – but it is no longer there on the page.

What a relief to go back to my reports on the 1979–80 Soviet invasion of Afghanistan. They were punched out on telex machines – those wonderful clunkers that perforated tapes – even though, today, the wafer-thin paper falls to pieces in my hands. I remember a Kabul post office official using a welding iron to cement the H back on to his machine – Conor O'Clery of the *Irish Times* is my witness – but I have every memorandum and every report I sent to my then employers at *The Times*.

Today, we use telephones – or e-mails, which are easy to delete – but my telexed messages to London in those terrible years of war, just as in the 1980–88 Iran–Iraq conflict, tell their own tale. When I was filing reports from Cairo or Riyadh, a foreign desk 'blooper' – a last paragraph cut, an inelegantly phrased headline – was easy for a foreign correspondent to forgive. But emerging from Iran's front lines at Fao – guns, shellfire and corpses – I found it difficult to see a dropped comma as anything but an act of treachery by *The Times*. Pity the poor foreign desk. And the correspondent. Of course, there are ridiculous moments in this historical 'search for truth'. My researcher, after only three days of work, could not understand why she constantly felt hungry at mid-morning – until we realised that between 1976 and 1990, the only way I catalogued my flights around the Middle East was by noting the desti-nation and date on my airline lunch menus. Three days of foie gras, caviar and champagne was too much for my brave friend to read. For my part, I did not, for many weeks, understand the deep depression in which I would go to bed – or wake – after hours of writing.

The answer was simple: the written notebooks and telex tapes – taken together – became an archive of humanity's suffering, of torture and despair. As a journalist, you can catalogue this daily, go back to your hotel and forget and start again next day. But when I put the telex tape and the notebooks together, they became a dreadful, utterly convincing testimony of inhumanity. Telexed copy dies out in my files in the late 1980s and computer records suddenly arrive. But they don't work. While I always kept a 'hard copy' of my reports for *The Independent*, I assumed that the blessed internet would preserve the prose which I had supposedly hammered out on the anvil of literature. Not so. Many websites contain only those pieces of 'fiskery' which their owners approved of; others, however legal, simply missed out reports that seemed unemotional. I am always amused by the number of institutions which telephone me in Beirut each week to check on quotations, dates or facts. Google cannot help them. They assume – usually correctly – that the Fisk Memorial Library (all on paper) can. And they are right. I have discovered other, equally discredited, 'facts'. For years I have been describing the meeting that *Newsweek*'s Tony Clifton had with Saddam Hussein in the late 1970s, in which he was driven by Saddam himself – after telling the Great Leader that some Iraqis might not like him – into the centre of Baghdad. 'Ask anyone here if they love their President,' Saddam Hussein told Clifton. I reported this in *The Independent*. I have my files. But Clifton told me last year that this was not correct. He had indeed interviewed Saddam Hussein – but the Iraqi president had merely laughed at Clifton's question and told him to talk to any Iraqis he wished. He never drove him into town. Ouch.

The first US proconsul to Iraq, retired general Jay Garner, spent much of his time deriding Saddam Hussein. But my researcher dug up an interview I had with Garner – when he was protecting the Kurds of northern Iraq in 1991 – in which he repeatedly stressed how the West must 'respect' Saddam's government and Iraq's 'sovereign territory'. My researcher's attacks on Google failed to discover this remarkable story.

Thank God for my notes. I'm not a Luddite. I do remember pounding some Churchillian prose on to telex tape in the luxurious lobby of the Damascus Sheraton Hotel – which had an indoor pond – after a mind-numbingly boring Arab summit. I also recall looking up – and seeing my paper tape literally floating away across the Sheraton's artificial lake.

E-mails, we are now told, will revive the art of the historian. I doubt it. It is easy to delete e-mails and – if governments are generous enough to keep them for archivists – historians will need a well-paid army of researchers to prowl through this ocean. In other words, historians will need to be rich in order to write.

The Independent, 5 February 2005

The forgotten art of handwriting

My father always complained about my handwriting. His almost copperplate accountant's script was measured, careful, full of lots of little squiggles which I noticed he also used in his long-ago King's Liverpool Regiment 12th Battalion war diary, written in the 1918 trenches when he was nineteen years old. My writing was sloppy by comparison and still gets worse.

So it was a relief to visit the Musée des Lettres et Manuscrits in Paris the other day to find that the great and the good also wrote in frustration and fury and sadness and – often – almost illegibly. I was greatly struck by Napoleon's script, a dogged, soldier's hand but sometimes signed merely 'Nap'. Churchill sometimes drew pigs on his letters to his wife. The great artists enjoyed covering their letters in pictures – Jean Cocteau, I notice, often adorned his letters with astonished faces. Matisse wrote to Martin Fabiani in March of 1943 with a sketch of a girl reading a newspaper. Gauguin once illustrated a missive with a drawing of a huge tube of paint at the bottom of the page. Handwriting is supposed to betray character – mine is scrappy, uneven and hurried – but I noticed that Catherine de Medici's script sometimes sloped unevenly and Robespierre's could be almost illegible.

I find something painfully human about reading the letters of long-dead heroes, their often pitiful attempts at humour, their mock-schoolboy touch, travelling badly over time. On

13 November 1930, Aircraftsman Shaw (Lawrence of Arabia) wrote to an American anthropologist, Henry Field – who died in 1986 – arranging to discuss Arab affairs in Plymouth. His letter, I notice, is in a simple, childish hand, his 'I's curled on top of each other, the letters of each word neatly joined.

> Dear Mr Field, I hope you are colossally rich, so that the cost of coming all the way to this misery of Plymouth (the last or first town of England, according to your hemisphere) will mean nothing to you. I'm a fraud, as regards both the Middle East and archaeology. Years ago I haunted both, and got fairly expert but the war overdosed me, and nine years ago I relapsed comfortably into the ranks of our Air Force, and have had no interests outside it since. Nine years is long enough to make me out of date but not long enough to make my views quaint and interestingly archaic. I have forgotten all I knew, too.

Poor Lawrence, forever demeaning himself. I thought at first he described himself as a 'friend' of the Middle East but alas it is indeed 'fraud' and his letter goes on to advise Mr Field to spot him in the crowd at the station. 'Look out for a small and aged creature in a slaty-blue uniform with brass buttons: like an RAC scout or tram driver, perhaps, only smaller and shabbier.'

In the French museum, there's now a *Titanic* exhibition with a terrifying telegram, recording the death of Thomas Stead, one of the greatest journalists of his time. It expresses – in the compact, official handwriting of the clerk – with 'deep regret' that there was 'no hope whatsoever' of finding Stead among the survivors. 'No hope' is always a killer – but the addition of that word 'whatsoever', with its awful finality, must have left the telegram's recipient in silence. Then there's Helen Churchill Condee's account of the sinking, a survivor's notes written shortly after the tragedy in sometimes surprisingly short paragraphs, as if the ship was submerging again in her memory as she wrote.

> I was in my bathroom ready for a stinging hot bath.
>   The music of the engines was beating and singing, rhythm and harmony.
>   Then the shock came.
>   Ararat's moment with the Ark stuck fast on top of it, was the mental image. The impact was below me. It toppled me over. We had struck the top of a mountain in the sea, a mountain never before discovered. It must be so.
>   With the door of the cabin thrown open two or three things were sinister, a silence absolute, a brilliance of light as in a ballroom, and an utter absence of human presence ...

In later pages, Condee's handwriting begins to slide about and she makes corrections with her fountain pen as she describes, from her lifeboat, the end of the *Titanic*.

> The only space of deck slopes high towards the stern and on this diminished point huddle the close pack awaiting death with the transcendent courage and grief that had been theirs for the last two hours.
>   I await the end transfixed. It is inevitable. May God delay it. No, may He in mercy hasten it.
>   At last the end of the world ...

Condee has underlined the E of 'end' and the W of 'world'.

> Over the waters only a heavy moan as of one being from whom ultimate agony forces a single sound.

Condee originally wrote 'final agony' but later substituted 'ultimate agony', as a composer might choose a different bar to end his tragic opera. Condee was only twelve years old when the *Titanic* went down, a year younger than my father, upon whose thirteenth birthday it sank. Their handwriting is eerily similar, the same squiggles and fanciful Ts, as if it was necessary to embroider the very words she was writing.

I suppose the laptop has brought all that to an end. I rarely ever receive handwritten letters – though occasionally one is produced on a faithful typewriter. Now our imagination flies at web-speed. And it's just as well my father can't see my handwriting today . . .

The Independent, 7 July 2007

'Believe it or not!'

When I was a schoolboy, I loved a column which regularly appeared in British papers called 'Ripley's Believe It or Not!' In a single rectangular box filled with naively drawn illustrations, Ripley – Bob Ripley – would try to astonish his readers with amazing facts: 'Believe It or Not, in California, an entire museum is dedicated to candy dispensers . . . Believe It or Not, a County Kerry man possesses an orange that is 25 years old . . . Believe It or Not, a weather researcher had his ashes scattered on the eve of Hurricane Danielle 400 miles off the coast of Miami, Florida.' Etc., etc., etc. Incredibly, Ripley's column lives on, and there is even a collection of 'Ripley Believe It or Not' museums in the United States.

The problem, of course, is that these are all extraordinary facts that will not offend anyone. There are no suicide bombers in Ripley, no Israeli air strikes ('Believe It or Not, 17,000 Lebanese and Palestinians, most of them civilians, were killed in Israel's 1982 invasion of Lebanon'), no major casualty tolls ('Believe It or Not, up to 650,000 Iraqis died in the four years following the 2003 Anglo-American invasion of Iraq'). See what I mean? Just a bit too close to the bone (or bones).

But I was reminded of dear old Ripley when I was prowling through the articles marking the anniversary of the 1967 Arab–Israeli war. Memoirs there have been aplenty, but I think only the French press – in the shape of *Le Monde Diplomatique* –

was prepared to confront a bit of 'Believe It or Not'. It recalled vividly – and shamefully – how the world's newspapers covered the story of Egypt's 'aggression' against Israel. In reality – Believe It or Not – it was Israel which attacked Egypt after Nasser closed the straits of Tiran and ordered UN troops out of Sinai and Gaza following his vituperative threats to destroy Israel. 'The Egyptians attack Israel,' *France-Soir* told its readers on 5 June 1967, a whopper so big that it later amended its headline to 'It's Middle East War!'

Quite so. Next day, the socialist *Le Populaire* headlined its story 'Attacked on all sides, Israel resists victoriously'. On the same day, *Le Figaro* carried an article announcing that 'the victory of the army of David is one of the greatest of all time'. Believe It or Not, the Second World War – which might be counted one of the greatest of all time – had ended only twenty-two years earlier. Johnny Hallyday, France's deathless pop star, sang for 50,000 French supporters of Israel – for whom solidarity was expressed in the French press by Serge Gainsbourg, Juliette Gréco, Yves Montand, Simone Signoret, Valéry Giscard d'Estaing and François Mitterrand. Believe It or Not – and you can believe it – Mitterrand once received the coveted Francisque medal from Pétain's Vichy collaborationists.

Only the president of France, General de Gaulle, moved into political isolation by telling a press conference several months later that Israel 'is organising, on the territories which it has taken, an occupation which cannot work without oppression, repression and expulsions – and if there appears resistance to this, it will in turn be called "terrorism"'. This accurate prophecy earned reproof from the *Nouvel Observateur* – to the effect that 'Gaullist France has no friends; it has only interests'. And Believe It or Not, with the exception of one small Christian paper, there was in the entire French press one missing word: Palestinians.

I owe it to the academic Anicet Mobé Fansiama to remind me this week that – Believe It or Not – Congolese troops from Belgium's immensely wealthy African colony scored enormous victories over Italian troops in Africa during the Second World War, capturing 15,000 prisoners, including nine generals. Called 'the Public Force' – a name which happily excluded the fact that these heroes were black Congolese – the army mobilised 13,000 soldiers and civilians to fight Vichy French colonies in Africa and deployed in the Middle East – where they were positioned to defend Palestine – as well as in Somalia, Madagascar, India and Burma. Vast numbers of British and American troops passed through the Congo as its wealth was transferred to the war chests of the United States and Britain. A US base was built at Kinshasa to move oil to Allied troops fighting in the Middle East.

But – Believe It or Not – when Congolese trade unions, whose members were requisitioned to perform hard labour inside Belgium's colony by carrying agricultural and industrial goods and military equipment, often on their backs, demanded higher salaries, the Belgian authorities confronted their demonstrations with rifle fire, shooting down fifty of their men. At least 3,000 political prisoners were deported for hard labour to a remote district of Congo. Thus were those who gave their blood for Allied victory repaid. Or rather not repaid. The 4 billion Belgian francs which was owed back to the Congo – about £500m in today's money – was never handed over. Believe It or Not.

So let's relax and return to Ripley reality and yes, there are new Ripleys:

Believe It or Not, Russell Parsons of Hurricane, West Virginia, has his funeral and cremation instructions tattooed on his arm! ... Believe It or Not, in April 2007 a group of animal lovers paid nearly $3,400 to buy 300 lobsters from a Maine fish market

– then set them free back into the ocean! . . . Believe It or Not, in a hospital waiting room, 70 per cent of people suffer from broken bones, 75 per cent are fatigued, 80 per cent have fevers. What percentage of people must have all four ailments?

Believe It or Not, I don't know. And oh yes, 'Geta, Emperor of Rome AD 189–212, insisted upon alternative meals. A typical menu: partridge (perdix), peacock (pavo), leek (porrum), beans (phaseoli), peach (persica), plum (pruna) and melon (pepone).'

I guess after that, you just have to throw up.

The Independent, 9 June 2007

Murder is murder is murder . . .

What on earth has happened to our reporting of the Middle East? George Orwell would have loved a Reuters dispatch from the West Bank city of Hebron last Wednesday. 'Undercover Israeli soldiers,' the world's most famous news agency reported, 'shot dead a member of Yasser Arafat's Fatah faction yesterday in what Palestinians called an assassination.' The key phrase, of course, was 'what Palestinians called an assassination'. Any sane reader would conclude immediately that Imad Abu Sneiheh, who was shot in the head, chest, stomach and legs by ten bullets fired by Israeli 'agents', had been murdered, let alone assassinated. But no. Reuters, like all the big agencies and television companies reporting the tragedy of the Palestinian–Israeli conflict, no longer calls murder by its name.

Back in the days of apartheid, no one minced their words when South African death squads gunned down militant opponents. They talked about murder and assassination. They still do when Latin American killers murder their political opponents. I've yet to find a newspaper that shrinks from reporting the 'murder' – or at the least 'assassination' – of IRA or UDA gangsters in Belfast. But not when the Israelis do the murdering. For when Israelis kill, they do not murder or assassinate, according to Reuters or CNN or the most recent convert to this flabby journalism, the BBC. Israelis perpetrate something which is only 'called' an assassination by

Palestinians. When Israelis are involved, our moral compass, our ability to report the truth, dries up.

Over the years, even CNN began to realise that 'terrorist' used about only one set of antagonists was racist as well as biased. When a television reporter used this word about the Palestinian who so wickedly bombed the Jerusalem pizzeria last week, he was roundly attacked by one of his colleagues for falling below journalistic standards. Rightly so. But in reality our reporting is getting worse, not better. Editors around the world are requesting their journalists to be ever softer, ever more mealy-mouthed in their reporting of any incident which might upset Israel. One sure way of spotting Israel's responsibility for a killing is the word 'crossfire'. Mohamed al-Dura, the little Palestinian boy shot dead by Israeli troops in Gaza last year, became a symbol of the Palestinian 'intifada'. Journalists investigating the boy's death, including *The Independent*'s Jerusalem correspondent, were in no doubt that the bullets which hit him were Israeli (albeit that the soldiers involved may not have seen him). Yet after a bogus Israeli military inquiry denounced in the Knesset by an Israeli member of parliament, all the major Western picture agencies placed captions on the photo for future subscribers. Yes, you've guessed it, the captions said he was killed in 'crossfire'.

Wars have always produced their verbal trickeries, their antiseptic phrases and hygienic metaphors, from 'collateral damage' to 'degrading the enemy'. The Palestinian–Israeli conflict has produced a unique crop. The Israeli siege of a city has become a 'closure', the legal border between Israel and the occupied territories has become the 'seam line', collaborators for the Israelis are 'co-operators', Israeli-occupied land has become 'disputed', Jewish settlements built illegally on Arab land have become 'neighbourhoods' – nice, folksy places which are invariably attacked by Palestinian 'militants'. And when suicide bombers strike – 'terrorists' to the Israelis, of course –

the Palestinians call them 'martyrs'. Oddest of all is Israel's creepy expression for its own extrajudicial murders: 'targeted killings'. If a dark humour exists in any of this dangerous nonsense, I must admit that Israel has found a real cracker in its expression for Palestinians who blow themselves to bits while making bombs: they die, so the Israelis say, from 'work accidents'.

But it's not the words Israelis and Palestinians use about each other that concern me. It's our journalistic submission to these words. Just over a week ago, I wrote in *The Independent* that the BBC had bowed to Israeli diplomatic pressure to drop the word 'assassination' for the murder of Palestinians in favour of Israel's own weird expression, 'targeted killings'. I was subsequently taken to task by Malcolm Downing, the BBC assignments editor, who decreed this new usage. I was one-sided, biased and misleading, he said; the BBC merely regarded 'assassination' as a word that should apply to 'high-ranking political or religious figures'. But the most important aspect of Mr Downing's reply was his total failure to make any reference to the point of my article: the BBC's specific recommended choice of words for Israel's murders: 'targeted attacks'. The BBC didn't invent that phrase. The Israelis did. I don't for a moment believe Mr Downing realises what he did. His colleagues regard him as a professional friend. But he has to realise that by telling his reporters to use 'targeted killings', he is perpetrating not only a journalistic error but a factual inaccuracy. So far, seventeen totally innocent civilians including two small children have been killed in Israel's state-sponsored assassinations. So the killings are at the least very badly 'targeted'. And I can't help recalling that when the BBC's own Jill Dando was shot dead on her doorstep, there was no doubt that she was killed by a man who had deliberately 'targeted' her. But that's not what the BBC said. They called it murder. And it was.

Within the past week, CNN, the news agencies and the BBC have all been chipping away at the truth once more. When the Jewish settlement at Gilo was attacked by Palestinian gunmen at Beit Jalla, it once more became a 'Jewish neighbourhood' on 'disputed' land even though most of the land, far from being in 'dispute', legally belongs to the Palestinian people of Beit Jalla ('Gilo' being the Hebrew for 'Jalla'). But viewers and readers were not told of this. When the next state-sponsored assassination of a Palestinian Hamas member took place, a television journalist – BBC this time – was reduced to telling us that his killing was 'regarded by the Israelis as a targeted killing but which the Palestinians regard as an assassination'. You could see the problem. Deeply troubled by the Israeli version, the BBC man had to 'balance' it with the Palestinian version, like a sports reporter unwilling to blame either side for a foul. So just watch out for the following key words about the Middle East in television reporting over the next few days: 'targeted killings', 'neighbourhood', 'disputed', 'terrorist', 'clash' and 'crossfire'. Then ask yourself why they are being used. I'm all for truth about both sides. I'm all for using the word 'terrorism' providing it's used about both sides' terrorists. I'm sick of hearing Palestinians talking about men who blow kids to bits as 'martyrs'. Murder is murder is murder. But where the lives of men and women are concerned, must we be treated by television and agency reporters to a commentary on the level of a football match?

The Independent, 18 August 2001

Ah, Mary, you poor diddums

Behold Mary Robinson, former president of Ireland, former UN High Commissioner for Human Rights, would-be graduation commencement speaker at Emory University in the United States. She has made a big mistake. She dared to criticise Israel. She suggested – horror of horrors – that 'the root cause of the Arab–Israeli conflict is the occupation'. Now whoah there a moment, Mary! 'Occupation'? Isn't that a little bit anti-Israeli? Are you really suggesting that the military occupation of the West Bank and Gaza Strip by Israel, its use of extrajudicial executions against Palestinian gunmen, the Israeli gunning down of schoolboy stone-throwers, the wholesale theft of Arab land to build homes for Jews, is in some way wrong?

Maybe I misheard you. Sure I did. Because your response to these scurrilous libels, to these slurs upon your right to free speech, to these slanderous attacks on your integrity, was a pussy-cat's whimper. You were 'very hurt and dismayed'. It is, you told the *Irish Times*, 'distressing that allegations are being made that are completely unfounded'. You should have threatened your accusers with legal action. When I warn those who claim in their vicious postcards that my mother was Eichmann's daughter that they will receive a solicitor's letter – Peggy Fisk was in the RAF in the Second World War, but no matter – they fall silent at once.

But no, you are 'hurt'. You are 'dismayed'. And you allow Professor Kenneth Stein of Emory University to announce that he is 'troubled by the apparent absence of due diligence on the part of decision makers who invited her [Mary Robinson] to speak'. I love the 'due diligence' bit. But seriously, how can you allow this twisted version of your integrity to go unpunished?

Dismayed. Ah, Mary, you poor diddums.

I tried to check the spelling of 'diddums' in *Webster's*, America's inspiring, foremost dictionary. No luck. But then, what's the point when *Webster's Third New International Dictionary* defines 'anti-Semitism' as 'opposition to Zionism: sympathy with opponents of the state of Israel'. So if you or I suggest – or, indeed, if poor wee Mary suggests – that the Palestinians are getting a raw deal under Israeli occupation, then we are 'anti-Semitic'. It is only fair, of course, to quote the pitiful response of the *Webster's* official publicist, Mr Arthur Bicknell, who was asked to account for this grotesque definition. 'Our job,' he responded, 'is to accurately reflect English as it is actually being used. We don't make judgement calls; we're not political.' Even more hysterically funny and revolting, he says that the dictionary's editors tabulate 'citational evidence' about anti-Semitism published in 'carefully written prose-like books and magazines'. Preposterous as it is, this Janus-like remark is worthy of the hollowest of laughs.

Even the Malaprops of American English are now on their knees to those who will censor critics of Israel's Middle East policy off the air. And I mean 'off the air'. I've just received a justifiably outraged note from Bathsheba Ratskoff, a producer and editor at the American Media Education Foundation (MEF), who says that their new documentary on 'the shutting-down of debate around the Israeli–Palestinian conflict' – in reality a film about Israel's public relations outfits in America – has been targeted by the 'Jewish Action Task Force'. The

movie *Peace, Propaganda and the Promised Land* was to be
shown at the Boston Museum of Fine Arts.

So what happened? The 'JATF' demanded an apology to the
Jewish community and a 'pledge [for] greater sensitivity when
tackling Israel and the Middle East conflict in the future'. JATF
members 'may want to consider threatening to cancel their
memberships and to withhold contributions'. And in due
course, a certain Susan Longhenry of the Museum of Fine Arts
wrote a creepy letter to Sut Jhally of the MEF, referring to
the concerns of 'many members of the Boston community' –
otherwise, of course, unidentified – suggesting a rescheduled
screening (because the original screening would have fallen on
the Jewish Sabbath) and a discussion that would have allowed
critics to condemn the film. The letter ended by stating – and
here I urge you to learn the weasel words of power – that
'we have gone to great lengths to avoid cancelling altogether
screenings of this film; however, if you are not able to support
the revised approach, then I'm afraid we'll have no choice but
to do just that'.

Does Ms Longhenry want to be a mouse? Or does she want
to have the verb 'to longhenry' appear in *Webster's*? Or at least
in the Oxford? Fear not, Ms Longhenry's boss overrode her
silly letter. For the moment, at least.

But where does this end? Last Sunday, I was invited to talk
on Irish television's TV3 lunchtime programme about Iraq,
and President Bush's support for Sharon's new wall on the
West Bank. Towards the end of the programme, Tom Cooney,
a law lecturer at University College, Dublin, suddenly claimed
that I had called Israeli army units a 'rabble' (absolutely correct
– they are) and that I reported they had committed a massacre
in Jenin in 2002.

I did not say they committed a massacre. But I should
have. A subsequent investigation showed that Israeli troops
had knowingly shot down innocent civilians, killed a female

nurse and driven a vehicle over a paraplegic in a wheelchair. 'Blood libel!' Cooney screamed. TV3 immediately – and correctly – dissociated themselves from this libel. Again, I noted the involvement of an eminent university – UCD is one of the finest academic institutions in Ireland and I can only hope that Cooney exercises a greater academic discipline with his young students than he did on TV3 – in this slander. And of course, I got the message. Shut up. Don't criticise Israel.

So let me end on a positive note. Just as Bathsheba is a Jewish American, British Jews are also prominent in an organisation called Deir Yassin Remembered, which commemorates the massacre of Arab Palestinians by Jewish militiamen outside Jerusalem in 1948. This year they remembered the Arab victims of that massacre – 9 April – on the same day that Christians commemorated Good Friday. The day also marked the fourth day of the eight-day Jewish Passover. It also fell on the anniversary of the 1945 execution by the Nazis of Pastor Dietrich Bonhoeffer at Flossenburg concentration camp. Jewish liberation 3,000 years ago, the death of a Palestinian Jew 2,000 years ago, the death of a German Christian fifty-nine years ago and the massacre of more than 100 Palestinian men, women and children fifty-six years ago. Alas, Deir Yassin Remembered does not receive the publicity it merits. *Webster's* dictionary would meretriciously brand its supporters 'anti-Semitic', and 'many members of the Boston community' would no doubt object. 'Blood libel,' UCD's eminent law lecturer would scream. We must wait to hear what UCD thinks. But let us not be 'hurt' or 'dismayed'. Let's just keep on telling it how it is. Isn't that what American journalism school was meant to teach us?

The Independent, 24 April 2004

'A very edgy situation'

You've got to fight. It's the only conclusion I can draw as I see the renewed erosion of our freedom to discuss the Middle East. The most recent example – and the most shameful – is the cowardly decision of the New York Theater Workshop to cancel the Royal Court's splendid production of *My Name Is Rachel Corrie*. It's the story – in her own words and e-mails – of the brave young American woman who travelled to Gaza to protect innocent Palestinians and who in March 2003 stood in front of an Israeli bulldozer in an attempt to prevent the driver from destroying a Palestinian home. The bulldozer drove over her and then reversed and crushed her a second time. 'My back is broken,' she said before she died.

An American heroine, Rachel earned no brownie points from the Bush administration which bangs on about courage and freedom from oppression every few minutes. Rachel's was the wrong sort of courage and she was defending the freedom of the wrong people. But when I read that James Nicola, the New York Theater Workshop's 'artistic director' – his title really should be in quotation marks – had decided to 'postpone' the play 'indefinitely' because (reader, hold your breath) 'in our pre-production planning and our talking around and listening in our communities [*sic*] in New York, what we heard was that after Ariel Sharon's illness and the election of Hamas . . . we had a very edgy situation', I didn't know whether to laugh or cry.

So let's confront this tomfoolery. Down in Australia, my old mate Antony Loewenstein, a journalist and academic, is having an equally vile time. He has completed a critical book on the Israel/Palestine conflict for Melbourne University Publishing and Jewish communities in Australia are trying to have it censored out of existence before it appears in August. Last year, Federal Labour MP Michael Danby, who like Loewenstein is Jewish, wrote a letter to the Australian *Jewish News* demanding that Loewenstein's publishers should 'drop this whole disgusting project'. The book, he said, would be 'an attack on the mainstream Australian Jewish community'. Now the powerful New South Wales Jewish Board of Deputies has weighed in against Loewenstein and efforts are under way to deprive him of his place on the board of Macquarie University's Centre for Middle East and North African Studies.*

A one-off bit of skulduggery on Israel's behalf? Not so. A letter arrived for me last week from Israeli-American Barbara Goldscheider, whose novel *Naqba: The Catastrophe: The Palestinian–Israeli Conflict* has just been published. She has been attacked, she told me, 'merely because I chose an Arabic title to my novel on the conflict . . . My brother-in-law has broken his relationship with me before he even read the book . . . From members of my "Orthodox" Jewish congregation in Bangor [Maine], I received a phone call from an irate "friend" sputtering . . . out: "Don't you know the Arabs want to destroy Israel?" '

A talk on her new novel scheduled to take place last month at a conservative synagogue was cancelled 'due to the uproar about my novel'. A Boston professor has thankfully written to Goldscheider with what I regard as bloody good advice.

---

* The pro-Israel lobby failed. Loewenstein's book *My Israel Question* was published to great critical acclaim and he retained his place on the university board.

'There's a vicious campaign out there,' he said. 'Don't cave in.'
But what do you do when a publisher – or an 'artistic director'
– caves in? I found out for myself not long ago when the
Military History Society of Ireland asked permission to reprint
a paper I had published some years ago on a battle between
the Irish Army's UN battalion in southern Lebanon and Israel's
proxy – and brutal – Lebanese militia, the so-called 'South
Lebanon Army', whose psychotic commander was a cashiered
Lebanese army major called Saad Haddad. In the paper, I
mentioned how an Israeli major called Haim extorted money
from the inhabitants of the south Lebanese village of Haris
and revealed the code name of an Israeli agent – 'Abu Shawki'
– who was present at the murder of two Irish soldiers.

I had published these details many times, both in my own
newspaper and in my previous book on the Lebanon war, *Pity
the Nation*. Major Haddad died of cancer more than ten years
ago. I actually met Haim in the early 1980s as he emerged
from a meeting with the mayor of Haris from whom he
demanded money to pay Israel's cruel militiamen – the UN
was also present and recorded his threats – while 'Abu Shawki',
whom the Irish police would like to interview, later tried to
arrest me in Tyre – and immediately freed me – when I told
him I knew that he was a witness to the murder of the two
Irish soldiers.

So what was I supposed to do when I received the following
letter from ex-Brigadier General Patrick Purcell of the Irish
Army? 'Unfortunately we have been forced to withdraw [your]
article in view of a letter from our publisher Irish Academic
Press. It is clear from our contract that [our] Society would be
responsible in the event of a libel action.' The enclosed letter
from publisher Frank Cass advised that his lawyer had 'cau-
tioned' him because I had described Haddad as 'psychotic',
named the blackmailing Israeli major and named the Israeli
agent present at the two murders. It's interesting that Frank

Cass's lawyer believes it is possible to libel a man (Haddad) who has been dead for more than a decade, even more so that he should think that publishing a military code name would prompt this rascal to expose his real identity in a court of law. As for Major Haim, he remains on UN files as the man who tried – and apparently succeeded – to force the people of southern Lebanon to cough up the cash to pay for their own oppressors.

And the moral of all this? Well obviously, don't contribute articles to the Military History Society of Ireland. But more to the point, I'd better remember what I wrote in this newspaper just over six years ago, that 'the degree of abuse and outright threats now being directed at anyone . . . who dares to criticise Israel . . . is fast reaching McCarthyite proportions. The attempt to force the media to obey Israel's rules is . . . international.' And growing, I should now add.

The Independent, 11 March 2006

'Abu Henry': what diplomats can get up to

'Abu Henry' says we may have to remain in Afghanistan for decades to protect Afghans from the Taliban. Our ambassador in Kabul – Sir Sherard Cowper-Coles, KCMG, LVO, to be precise – apparently sees no contradiction in this extraordinary prediction.

The Taliban are themselves mostly Afghans, and the idea that the British army is in Afghanistan to protect the locals from each other is a truly colonial proposition. It's what we said about the Northern Irish in 1969. Anyway, I thought we destroyed the Taliban in 2001. Wasn't that the idea at the time? Isn't that what Blair said back then?

Abu Henry – and I am indebted to one of the Saudi government's house magazines for telling me that this is how he 'is affectionately called by his Saudi friends' – left Riyadh in some haste, a 'surprise' as he put it, since he expected to spend another year there. And presumably, he has not been able to take the Cowper-Coles family's pet falcons – Nour and Alwaleed – with him to Kabul. But before he left, Abu Henry had some warm praise for the notoriously third-rate intelligence services in the kingdom. 'I've been hugely impressed by the way in which the Saudi Arabian authorities have tackled and contained what was a serious terrorist threat,' he announced. 'They've shrunk the pool of support for terrorism . . .'

No word, of course, of the Saudis' habit of chopping off the heads of 'criminals' after grotesquely unfair trials. In an unprecedented year for executions, the kingdom's swordsmen – the job is sometimes passed on father to son as was once the case with British hangmen – managed to hack off 100 heads by the middle of this month. But then again, you'd have to avoid any such references when British investment in Saudi Arabia is worth at least £6 billion. That, no doubt, is one reason why Abu Henry boasted to his Saudi friends – according to the same government magazine – that in Riyadh 'we've been proud of our visa policy, where 95 per cent of Saudis applying for a visa before 9 am on a workday obtain their visas by 2 pm the same working day'. Phew. Now that is something. The Saudis, you may remember, provided fifteen of the nineteen killers of 11 September 2001; quite a record for a little kingdom, and one which in other circumstances – had the murderers been from Chad, say, or Mali – would not have been rewarded with quite so generous a visa policy.

And no word from Abu Henry, of course, about that other little matter of the alleged bribery of Saudi officials by the British BAE Systems arms group. Here, however, there is much more to say – courtesy, I admit at once, of a delightfully written article by Michael Peel in the *Financial Times* last February. In the paper, Peel describes how Robert Wardle, director of the Serious Fraud Office, had 'much to ponder' after three London meetings with Cowper-Coles, 'Britain's urbane ambassador to Saudi Arabia'. Mr Wardle, it seems, was 'coming around to the view' that he might have to scrap his inquiry since it could damage 'national security'. Wardle told Peel that 'the matter was difficult and really I found it very helpful to have, as it were, the ambassador flesh out the position. It helped my understanding of the risks and very much helped me to make my decision to discontinue the investigation.'

Abu Henry, it seems, 'told how the probe might cause

Riyadh to cancel security and intelligence co-operation, potentially depriving London of access to vital surveillance of terror
suspects during the haj pilgrimage to Mecca . . . The ambassador had even suggested [that] persisting with the SFO probe
could endanger lives in Britain.' According to a person 'closely
involved in the events', wrote Peel – and I suspect the 'person'
was probably Wardle – Cowper-Coles 'didn't overelaborate,
but he spelt out in very clear terms, in specifics, what he
believed the consequences would be . . . including that people
could die'. Two days later, the bribery investigation was
scrapped. So no wonder the Saudis affectionately called him
'Abu Henry'.

Given some of his remarks during a recent visit to Oxford,
however, Abu Henry must himself have been surprised that
he could persuade Blair of the wisdom of dumping that all-
important bribery investigation. Among academics, he did not
hide his cynicism about our former prime minister, complaining that despite exhaustive Foreign Office briefing notes
and proposed speeches, Blair scarcely seemed to read them
and sometimes used only a single line from their contents.

But then again, I guess that's what diplomacy is all about,
persuading here, pleading there, trying to get what you want
by a few off-the-record comments to officials of the Serious
Fraud Office, even to journalists I have no doubt. Indeed, I
remember way back in the late 1970s – when I was Middle
East correspondent for *The Times* – how a British diplomat in
Cairo tried to persuade me to fire my local 'stringer', an Egyptian Coptic woman who also worked as a correspondent for
the Associated Press and who provided a competent coverage
of the country when I was in Beirut. 'She isn't much good,' he
said, and suggested I hire a young Englishwoman whom he
knew and who – so I later heard – had close contacts in the
Foreign Office. I refused this spooky proposal. Indeed, I told
The Times that I thought it was outrageous that a British

diplomat should have tried to engineer the sacking of our part-timer in Cairo. *The Times*'s foreign editor agreed.

But it just shows what diplomats can get up to.

And the name of that young British diplomat in Cairo back in the late 1970s?

Why, Sherard Cowper-Coles, of course.

The Independent, 30 June 2007

A lesson from the Holocaust

At a second-hand book stall in the Rue Monsieur le Prince in Paris a few days ago, I came across the second volume of Victor Klemperer's diaries.* The first volume, recounting his relentless, horrifying degradation as a German Jew in the first eight years of Hitler's rule – from 1933 to 1941 – I had bought in Pakistan just before America's 2001 bombardment of Afghanistan. It was a strange experience – while sipping tea amid the relics of the Raj, roses struggling across the lawn beside me, an old British military cemetery at the end of the road – to read of Klemperer's efforts to survive in Dresden with his wife Eva as the Nazis closed in on his Jewish neighbours. Even more intriguing was to find that the infinitely heroic Klemperer, a cousin of the great conductor, showed immense compassion for the Palestinian Arabs of the 1930s who feared that they would lose their homeland to a Jewish state.

'I cannot help myself,' Klemperer writes on 2 November 1933, nine months after Hitler became chancellor of Germany. 'I sympathise with the Arabs who are in revolt [in Palestine], whose land is being "bought". A Red Indian fate, says Eva.' Even more devastating is Klemperer's critique of Zionism –

---

* The diaries of Victor Klemperer, businessman, journalist, professor of literature and Holocaust survivor, were published in two volumes in 1998 (Random House, New York). He died in 1960, aged seventy-eight.

which he does not ameliorate even after Hitler's persecution of the Jews of Europe begins. 'To me,' he writes in June of 1934, 'the Zionists, who want to go back to the Jewish state of AD 70 . . . are just as offensive as the Nazis. With their nosing after blood, their ancient "cultural roots", their partly canting, partly obtuse winding back of the world they are altogether a match for the National Socialists . . .'

Yet Klemperer's day-by-day account of the Holocaust, the cruelty of the local Dresden Gestapo, the suicide of Jews as they are ordered to join the transports east, his early knowledge of Auschwitz – Klemperer got word of this most infamous of extermination camps as early as March 1942, although he did not realise the scale of the mass murders there until the closing months of the war – fill one with rage that anyone could today still deny the reality of the Jewish genocide. Reading these diaries as the RER train takes me out to Charles de Gaulle airport – through the 1930s art deco architecture of Drancy station where French Jews were taken by their own police force before transportation to Auschwitz – I wish President Ahmadinejad of Iran could travel with me. For Ahmadinejad it was who suggested that the Jewish Holocaust was a 'myth', who ostentatiously called for a conference – in Tehran, of course – to find out the truth about the genocide of 6 million Jews, which any sane historian acknowledges to be one of the terrible realities of the twentieth century, along, of course, with the Armenian Holocaust of 1915.

The best reply to Ahmadinejad's childish nonsense came from ex-President Khatami of Iran, the only honourable Middle East leader of our time, whose refusal to countenance violence by his own supporters inevitably and sadly led to the demise of his 'civil society' at the hands of more ruthless clerical opponents. 'The death of even one Jew is a crime,' Khatami said, thus destroying in one sentence the lie that his successor was trying to propagate.

Indeed, his words symbolised something more crucial: that the importance and the evil of the Holocaust do not depend on the Jewish identity of the victims. The awesome wickedness of the Holocaust lies in the fact that the victims were human beings – just like you and me. How do we then persuade the Muslims of the Middle East of this simple truth? I thought that the letter which the head of the Iranian Jewish Committee, Haroun Yashayaie, wrote to Ahmadinejad provided part of the answer. 'The Holocaust is not a myth any more than the genocide imposed by Saddam [Hussein] on Halabja or the massacre by [Ariel] Sharon of Palestinians and Lebanese in the camps of Sabra and Chatila,' Yashayaie – who represents Iran's 25,000 Jews – said.

Note here how there is no attempt to enumerate the comparisons. Six million murdered Jews is a numerically far greater crime than the thousands of Kurds gassed at Halabja or the 1,700 Palestinians murdered by Israel's Lebanese Phalangist allies at Sabra and Chatila in 1982. But Yashayaie's letter was drawing a different kind of parallel: the pain that the denial of history causes to the survivors.

So what is there to learn from the second volume of Klemperer's diaries? Just after he received word from the Gestapo that he and Eva were to be transported east to their deaths, the RAF raided Dresden and, amid the tens of thousands of civilians which the February 1945 firestorm consumed, the Gestapo archives also went up in flames. All record of the Klemperers' existence was turned to ash, like the Jews who preceded them to Auschwitz. So the couple took off their Jewish stars and wandered Germany as refugees without papers until they found salvation after the Nazi surrender.

Just before their rescue, they showed compassion to three distraught German soldiers who were lost in the forests of their homeland. And even during their worst ordeals, as they waited for the doorbell to ring and the Gestapo to arrive to search their Dresden home and notify them of their fate, Klemperer was able to write in his diary a sentence which every journalist and historian should learn by heart: 'There is no remedy against the truth of language.'

The Independent, 1 April 2006

•

CHAPTER FOUR

Cinema begins to mirror
the world

Cinema has an unstoppable power to convince. Film's unique combination of sound, music and moving pictures combines radio, art, music and theatre. And I suspect, as the years go by, it will become the only medium with which we can influence the world. Yes, films lie. They always have. They will always represent a director's reality. Yet a whole new genre of film-making – especially in the United States – has opened up a different perspective for cinemagoers, especially on the Middle East. The creation of documentary features, pioneered most recently by Michael Moore (even if he still takes care to voice no criticism of Israel), has allowed millions the chance of watching political drama as it has never been seen before.

Feature films were a great influence on my early life. I lived movies, examined screenplays as vigorously as I would read books. For at least a year, I wanted to be a film critic rather than a foreign correspondent. Far from flying out of Beirut to report wars, I wanted to spend my life in the safety of a cinema seat, viewing a dangerous world without experiencing it. In the end, I spent my life watching real and terrible conflict first-hand, able to compare the tragedy of war with the film version. Oddly, I found that movies could show the obscenity of battle far more truthfully than television. The self-censoring executives of the big networks – and I include the BBC among them – will not allow their viewers to see the headless corpses, the eviscerated children, the desert dogs tearing apart the bodies of the dead. This would be in 'bad taste'. If you want to see what I see – what all of us journalists see in war – you have to watch *Saving Private Ryan* or the suicide bombing in *Rendition*.

And so, in the dog days between the crises of the Middle East, I settle into Beirut's remarkably luxurious cinemas to live that other life I once craved. I become a foreign correspondent turned film critic.

Applause from the Muslims of Beirut

Long live Ridley Scott. I never thought I'd say this. *Gladiator* had a screenplay that might have come from the *Boy's Own Paper*. *Black Hawk Down* showed the Arabs of Somalia as generically violent animals. But when I left the cinema after seeing Scott's extraordinary sand-and-sandals epic on the Crusades, *Kingdom of Heaven*, I was deeply moved – not so much by the film, but by the Muslim audience among whom I watched it in Beirut. I know what the critics have said. The screenplay isn't up to much and Orlando Bloom, playing the loss-of-faith Crusader Balian of Ibelin, does indeed look – as my own *Independent* mischievously observed – like a backpacker touring the Middle East in a gap year.

But there is an integrity about the film's portrayal of the Crusades which, while fitting neatly into our contemporary view of the Middle East – the moderate Crusaders are overtaken by crazed neo-conservative barons while Saladin is taunted by a dangerously al-Qaeda-like warrior – treats the Muslims as men of honour who can show generosity as well as ruthlessness to their enemies. And it was certainly a revelation to sit through *Kingdom of Heaven* not in London or New York but in Beirut, in the Middle East itself, among Muslims – most of them in their twenties – who were watching historical events that took place only a couple of hundred miles from us. How would the audience react when the Knights Templars went on their orgy of rape and head-chopping among the innocent Muslim villagers of the Holy Land, when they advanced, covered in gore, to murder Saladin's beautiful, chadored sister? I must admit, I held my breath a few times.

I need not have bothered. When the leprous King of Jerusalem – his face covered in a steel mask to spare his followers the ordeal of looking at his decomposition – falls fatally ill after honourably preventing a battle between Crusaders and Saracens, Saladin, played by that wonderful Syrian actor Ghassan Massoud – and thank God the Arabs in the film are played by Arabs – tells his deputies to send his own doctors to look after the Christian king. At this, there came from the Muslim audience a round of spontaneous applause. They admired this act of mercy from their warrior hero; they wanted to see his kindness to a Christian.

There are some things in the film which you have to be out here in the Middle East to appreciate. When Balian comes across a pile of Crusader heads lying on the sand after the Christian defeat at the 1187 battle of Hittin, everyone in the cinema thought of Iraq; here is the nightmare I face each time I travel to report in Iraq. Here is the horror that the many Lebanese who work in Iraq have to confront. Yet there was a wonderful moment of self-deprecation among the audience when Saladin, reflecting on one of his Crusader antagonists, says: 'Somebody tried to kill me once in Lebanon.' The house came down. Everyone believed that Massoud must have inserted this line to make fun of the Lebanese ability to destroy themselves and – having lived in Lebanon twenty-nine years and witnessed almost all its tragedy – I too found tears of laughter running down my face.

I suppose that living in Lebanon, among those Crusader castles, does also give an edge to *Kingdom of Heaven*. It's said that Scott originally wanted to film in Lebanon (rather than Spain and Morocco) and to call his movie *Tripoli* after the great Crusader keep I visited a few weeks ago. One of the big Christian political families in Lebanon, the Franjiehs, take their name from the 'Franj', which is what the Arabs called the Crusaders. The Douai family in Lebanon – with whom the Franjiehs fought a bitter battle, Knights Templars-style, in a church in 1957 – are the descendants of the French knights who came from the northern French city of Douai. Yet it is ironic that *Kingdom of Heaven* elicited so much cynical comment in the West. Here is a tale – unlike any other recent film – that has captured the admiration of Muslims. Yet we denigrated it. Because Orlando Bloom turns so improbably from blacksmith to Crusader to hydraulic engineer? Or because we felt uncomfortable at the way the film portrayed 'us', the Crusaders?

It didn't duck Muslim vengeance. When Guy de Lusignan hands the cup of iced water given him by Saladin to the murderous knight who slaughtered Saladin's sister, the Muslim warrior says menacingly: 'I did not give you the cup.' And then he puts his sword through the knight's throat. Which is, according to the archives, exactly what he said and exactly what he did. Massoud, who is a popular local actor in Arab films – he is known in the Middle East as the Syrian Al Pacino – in reality believes that George Bush is to blame for much of the crisis between the Muslim and Western worlds. 'George Bush is stupid and he loves blood more than the people and music,' he said in a recent interview. 'If Saladin were here he would have at least not allowed Bush to destroy the world, especially the feeling of humanity between people.'

Massoud agreed to play Saladin because he trusted Scott to be fair with history. I had to turn to that fine Lebanese writer Amin Maalouf to discover whether Massoud was right. Maalouf it was who wrote the seminal *The Crusades through Arab Eyes*, researching for his work among Arab rather than Crusader archives. 'Too fair,' was his judgement on *Kingdom of Heaven.* I see his point. But at the end of the film, after Balian has surrendered Jerusalem, Saladin enters the city and finds a crucifix lying on the floor of a church, knocked off the altar during the three-day siege. And he carefully picks up the cross and places it reverently back on the altar. And at this point the audience rose to their feet and clapped and shouted their appreciation. They loved that gesture of honour. They wanted Islam to be merciful as well as strong. And they roared their approval above the soundtrack of the film.

So I left the Dunes cinema in Beirut strangely uplifted by this extraordinary performance – of the audience as much as of the film. See it if you haven't. And if you do, remember how the Muslims of Beirut came to realise that even Hollywood can be fair. I came away realising why – despite the murder of Beirut's bravest journalist on Friday* – there probably will not be a civil war here again. So if you see *Kingdom of Heaven*, when Saladin sets the crucifix back on the altar, remember that deafening applause from the Muslims of Beirut.

The Independent, 4 June 2005

---

* Samir Kassir, a brilliant anti-Syrian academic, author and journalist, was blown up in his car outside his Beirut home on 3 June 2005.

Saladin's eyes

I met Gareth Peirce more than six years ago but am still embarrassed by our first rendezvous. I had arranged to meet this redoubtable lawyer – brilliantly played by Emma Thompson in the film *In the Name of the Father** – in the Sheraton Belgravia Hotel, the cosiest, almost the smallest and, I feel certain, the most expensive Sheraton in the whole world. And for more than fifteen minutes I prowled the lobby, looking in vain for Gareth, until a small woman with dark, rather straggly hair walked up to me and asked if I was Robert Fisk. That's when I realised I'd been looking for Emma Thompson.

So when I walked into the coffee shop of the Sham Palace Hotel in Damascus a few days ago, I was very definitely looking for Saladin, the twelfth-century Kurdish warrior portrayed by the Syrian actor Ghassan Massoud in Ridley Scott's *Kingdom of Heaven*. And there he was, looking just like Saladin, his beard turning white, his vast expressive hands moving around his head in fury at the wreckage of Iraq, demonstrating the same suppressed anger, the same humanity – and the same halting English – as he did in the movie. The Damascus waiters showed due deference to the celebrity in the corner of the coffee shop – not least because his politics are as fierce as

---

* A painful account of the imprisonment of eleven Irishmen wrongfully convicted of an IRA bombing in Guildford in 1974.

those of Saladin, whose real, green-shrouded wooden tomb lies scarcely half a mile from us, beside the majesty of the Ommayad mosque.

'I cannot imagine that what is happening in Iraq is true,' he says. 'I cannot believe this situation is better than the Saddam Hussein days. This great country of Iraq – it's not fair to see this. We have to prepare ourselves for a very bloody future in Iraq. I think it's now a civil war. Thank you, George Bush. You know, the Iranians are geniuses. They know George Bush needs them [in Iraq]. So now they are playing him along. I think Bush will make a deal with Iran – he would be foolish to make a strike on Iran. If he wants to destroy all this area – and all the oil that he wants – he will make a military strike.' Massoud leans back in his chair opposite me, recalling the 'civil society' and the friendship towards the West shown by former Iranian president Mohamed Khatami. 'Ah, what a mistake Bush made in not making a dialogue with Khatami. America wasn't interested in this man. And so they got [the new president] Ahmadinejad. And now what do we hear? "Look at the Iranians, they are fanatics – they elected Ahmadinejad!"' There are times when Ghassan Massoud reminds me of the defiant American journalist Seymour Hersh.

The thoughts and the anger bubble over as Massoud lights his third cigarette. You can see why he enjoyed playing the scourge of the Crusaders in Scott's movie, insisting on riding his own horse in preference to a stuntman – Massoud comes from the rugged countryside around Tartous – and taking the role of Saladin only when he was satisfied the script would respect his own culture. It's one reason why he turned down a part in the new film *Syriana*, a drama of oil, CIA skulduggery and Arab potentates. 'There are many attacks in the West against Islam these days. I met the director Stephen Gaghan in Dubai to discuss *Syriana*. I asked him: "Why Syriana? It is one of the historic names of my country, why the CIA? Why oil?" He said it was a point of view. I was frightened. When something frightens you, I say you shouldn't do it. Our profession is very, very, very sensitive. You cannot make a film if you have suspicion in a script. But when I met Sir Ridley Scott, from the first meeting in Spain, I trusted this man. He was a noble man, a knightly man, so I yielded myself to his film.'

Massoud's oddly courteous English – Chaucer's 'parfit gentil knyght' might have spoken like this – runs in tandem with the very Syrian way in which he expresses himself, thrusting his hands forward with thumbs upwards to express agreement, something he did in *Kingdom of Heaven* when the Crusader Balian surrenders Jerusalem to Saladin. How much is the city worth to the Muslim commander, Balian asks. 'Nothing,' Saladin replies. Then the Muslim warrior thrusts his thumbs in the air and cries: 'Everything.' Massoud grins when I recall this scene. 'Yes, this is how we talk and express ourselves – I am a man from the street.' Here he glances at the clogged traffic through the coffee shop window. 'This is my culture and you cannot make dialogue without respect between communities. We can say, "OK, there is no dialogue." We can use tanks, bombs, missiles – and have no dialogue. No one can tell me that George Bush makes dialogue. The American media that "holds" the world makes Syria into an image, a "terrorist state", a "terrorist people". Syria for us means ten thousand years of civilisation – this is not an accident of history! It is very difficult for Mr Bush to tell us what this means, to tell us about democracy. We watch his point of view about democracy with Hamas in Palestine. But the people in the streets, the restaurants, the cafés – I am sure they do not believe this man.'

Ridley Scott, according to Massoud, 'wanted to make a movie like he dreams. For him, it was a novel with Balian, Richard the Lionheart, Saladin. I can understand his film from this side. This does not mean it does not look like [Iraq] today. You know towards the end there is a scene when the Crusaders and the Muslim soldiers are fighting and their movements slow down until they stop altogether on the screen. In this way we find Balian and Saladin face to face and they had to make dialogue. Scott wanted to say, I think, that wars cannot give us good solutions. The only thing I put into the script was the scene where Saladin goes into Jerusalem and places a fallen crucifix back on a church altar. Scott said: "OK, let's do it." He wanted to show that side of Saladin's character.

'I last went to Saladin's tomb three weeks ago,' Massoud says. 'Before the making of the film, I read everything about him. Then I went to his tomb many times – to get the "spirit" of the man.'

The Independent, 27 May 2006

My challenge for Steven Spielberg

Steven Spielberg's *Munich* is absolutely brilliant. I can hear readers groaning already. It won't open in Britain until next Friday. But in the United States, Arabs have condemned the movie about the Israeli assassination of Palestinians after the 1972 massacre of Israeli athletes at the Munich Olympics as an anti-Arab diatribe that dehumanises an entire people suffering dispossession and occupation. Jewish groups have suggested that Spielberg has dishonoured his Jewish roots by portraying Mossad agents as criminal, self-doubting murderers who ultimately come to despise their own country. There must be something interesting here, I said to myself, as I sat down on the other side of the Atlantic to watch the director's blockbuster of murder and bloodshed.

There's plenty to be appalled by: the killing of the athletes interlocked with scenes of assassination leader 'Avner' copulating with his wife in a New York apartment, the Israeli murder of a Dutch call girl who has set up a Mossad killer for assassination – she walks naked and bleeding across the floor of her canal barge trying to breathe through the bullet wound in her breast – and the Middle East cliché of the year. It comes when Avner – in an entirely fictional scene – talks to an armed Palestinian refugee whom he will later kill. 'Tell me something, Ali,' he asks. 'Do you really miss your father's olive trees?' Well of course Ali does rather miss his father's olive trees. Ask any

Palestinian in the shithouse slums of the Ein el-Helwe, Nahr el-Bared or Sabra and Chatila refugee camps in Lebanon and you'll get the same reply. It's a staged, weird scene in which Avner's educated philosophical approach is contrasted with the harsh, uneducated Palestinian's anger.

And there's a lot else wrong. The same Mossad team's real-life murder of a perfectly innocent Moroccan waiter in Norway is deleted from the narrative of the film – thus avoiding, I suppose, the embarrassment of showing one of the murderers later hiding in the Oslo apartment of the Israeli defence attaché to Norway, a revelation that did not do a lot for Scandinavian–Israeli relations. But Spielberg's movie has crossed a fundamental roadway in Hollywood's treatment of the Middle East conflict. For the first time, we see Israel's top spies and killers not only questioning their role as avengers but actually deciding that 'an eye for an eye' does not work, is counter-productive, is just plain morally wrong. Murdering one Palestinian gunman – or one Palestinian who sympathises with the Munich killers – only produces six more to take their place. One by one, members of the Mossad assassination squad are themselves hunted down and murdered. Avner even calculates that it costs $1 m every time he liquidates a Palestinian.

And the film's ending – when Avner's Mossad minder comes to New York to persuade him to return to Israel, only to be rebuffed when he fails to supply evidence of the murdered Palestinians' guilt and to walk away in disgust from Avner's offer to break bread at his home – suggests for the first time on the big screen that Israel's policy of militarism and occupation is immoral. That the camera then moves to the left of the two men and picks up a digitalised, recreated image of the Twin Towers through the haze was what I call a 'groaner'. Yes, Steve, I said to myself, thank you – but we've got the message. Yet that's the point. This film deconstructs the whole myth of Israeli invincibility and moral superiority, its false alliances –

one of the most sympathetic characters is an elderly French mafia boss who helps Avner – and its arrogant assumption that it has the right to engage in state murder while others do not. Perhaps inevitably, the author of the book upon which *Munich* is based – George Jonas, who wrote *Vengeance* – has done his best to deconstruct Spielberg. 'One doesn't reach the moral high ground being neutral between good and evil,' he says. What turns audiences off the movie is 'treating terrorists as people . . . in their effort not to demonise humans, Spielberg and Kushner [Tony Kushner, the chief screenplay writer] end up humanising demons.' Yes, but that's the point isn't it? Calling humans terrorists does dehumanise them – whatever their background.

Presumably intended to coincide with the movie, Aaron Klein has come out with a new book on Munich, published by Random House. As one reviewer has pointed out, he writes of the same Mossad hoods as cold-blooded hit squads rather than self-doubting mercenaries. In quite another context, it's interesting to learn that Klein, a captain in the Israeli army's intelligence unit, also happens to be *Time* magazine's military affairs correspondent in Jerusalem. I assume that august pro-Israeli journal will soon appoint a Hamas member as its military affairs reporter on the West Bank. But again, all this misses the point. It's not whether Spielberg changes the characters of his killers – or whether Malta doubles for Beirut in the film and Budapest for Paris – but that Israel's whole structure of super-morality is brought under harsh, bitter self-examination. Towards the end, Avner even storms into the Israeli consulate in New York because he believes Mossad has decided to liquidate him too.

So now the real challenge for Spielberg. A Muslim friend once wrote to me to recommend *Schindler's List*, but asked if the director would continue the story with an epic about the Palestinian dispossession which followed the arrival of

Schindler's refugees in Palestine. Instead of that, Spielberg has jumped fourteen years to Munich, saying in an interview that the real enemy in the Middle East is 'intransigence'. It's not. The real enemy is taking other people's land away from them. So now I ask: will we get a Spielberg epic on the Palestinian catastrophe of 1948 and after? Or will we – like those refugees desperate for visas in the wartime movie *Casablanca* – wait and wait – and wait?

The Independent, 21 January 2007

Da Vinci shit

I once had to review a biography of that upstanding Palestinian academic and peace proponent Hanan Ashrawi, but admitted at the start of my article that it was almost impossible to write because the book was so unmitigatedly awful. Now I have forced myself to see *The Da Vinci Code*, I have reached a new literary crevasse, the near-inability to speak of this film, based – as we all know – on the novel by the exotically named Dan Brown.

God, it's awful! How His Holiness, the famous anti-gay, anti-divorce, anti-aircraft gunner Pope Benedict of Rome could have been so upset beats me, because the film makes the Roman Catholic Church even more boring than it actually is.* 'Roman mumbo-jumbo' is how my elderly dad used to talk about the rites of the Catholic Church, and it's not a bad description of this ghastly movie. Its popularity symbolises not our interest in Christ but our lack of faith, our desperate need for bunkum religion. It's actually about black magic. The film draws shamelessly from the work of others. The face masks and the ghostly siege of Jerusalem – complete with ballistas, although the Muslim armies have been replaced by Crusaders

* At the end of the Second World War, the future Pope was – 'briefly and unwillingly', according to the Vatican – a member of a German anti-aircraft guncrew.

– are cribs from Ridley Scott's *Kingdom of Heaven*. Some of the music sounds unnervingly close to the score from Scott's *Gladiator*. And as the actress Nelofer Pazira has pointed out, the flagellating murderer is almost identical – in character and physical likeness – to the figure of Death, played by Bengt Ekerot in Ingmar Bergman's *The Seventh Seal*. Remember the famous chess game between Ekerot and Max von Sydow's Crusader knight?

But it all raises an ancient question. How come this pap is so popular while great art and literature and music – and movies – are rarely if ever box office? How come the books and the films and the music which we are supposed to admire don't receive the world's admiration – or at least millions of dollars – while chick-lit and Paris Hilton and, yes, *The Da Vinci Code* pack them in from Singapore to Denver? Are we really just tools of the marketing boys who push this stuff like preachers or like the Wild West quack doctors who promised eternal youth in a bottle?

Let's start, though, on the side of the bad guys. *The Independent* once ran a review of James Cameron's *Titanic* under the headline: 'I've seen *Titanic* – and it stinks.' Now I liked *Titanic*, just as I admired Scott's snottily reviewed *Kingdom of Heaven*, and I still remember its best line, when the gorgeous Rose (Kate Winslet) asks Andrews, the ship's Irish designer, if the vessel will sink: 'Mr Andrews, I saw the iceberg – and I see it in your eyes.' And when the *Titanic* goes down, along with Andrews – the real-life brother, as it happens, of one of Northern Ireland's Protestant prime ministers – by heaven, you felt as if you were going to the bottom of the Atlantic with it.

And I remember with great fondness the long nights in Ireland when I was completing my PhD thesis (subject: Irish neutrality in the Second World War) at the window of a cottage immediately opposite another terraced home in which that most prolific of Irish writers, Maeve Binchy, was finishing her beautiful novel *Light a Penny Candle*. Like so much of Maeve's output, *Candle* was regarded as unworthy of serious critical attention, even though several scenes in the novel – the terrible moment, for example, when an Irish couple realise (while the reader does not) that their daughter has stolen from the local shop the Christmas present she is giving them – are Dickensian in their pathos. Yet Maeve is not placed alongside literary prizewinners like her much less read but near-neighbour novelist John Banville. Conversely, Banville – the man who once asked me to review the ghastly Ashrawi biography for the *Irish Times* – is not going to rake in the kind of profits that Maeve makes.

What, then, makes art popular? When I went to school, Charles Dickens was frowned upon as a fusty old Victorian who churned out pot-boilers for weekly newspapers (all true), even if his characters – Pip, Scrooge, Oliver Twist and the rest – were immensely popular with children. By the time I reached college, however, the very same Dickens appeared in every modern literature course – Dr David Craig, formerly of Lancaster University, please note – as a pseudo-leftist laying open the scandals of the Industrial Revolution (*Hard Times* and *Bleak House*). Equally, when I was at school, I developed a passion for largely ignored composers, boring my parents to tears with scratched but booming records of Bruckner and Shostakovich. Now they are flavour of the month all year round and the Leningrad is almost as overplayed as the masterpieces which the BBC's Your Hundred Best Tunes turned into clichés: Beethoven's Fifth, Tchaikovsky's 1812 Overture, Sibelius's *Finlandia*, Chopin's Preludes, Handel's Water Music, Vivaldi's *The Four Seasons* and the other 'pops' that have me reaching for the 'off' button as surely as if they were Carly Simon.

Clearly, there are no set rules for all this. Verdi was as popular in his time as he is among opera-goers today. *The Godfather* crossed the line between entertainment and art quite effortlessly. So has Hitchcock. *Casablanca* was as popular in 1941 as it is now, albeit for different reasons. David Lean's *Dr Zhivago* was immensely popular in the cinema; my dad loved it, but oddly regarded the original Pasternak novel – infinitely more moving and tragic – as the success of 'those damned publicists'. But my dilemma remains. I admire the poetry of Seamus Heaney, but regard *Bomber*, an account of an RAF fire raid on Nazi Germany, as one of the best novels of war – even though it was written by the distinctly unprized and overread author Len Deighton. John Le Carré's spy Smiley has clearly moved between art and mass appreciation (though not with me). Lean's *The Bridge on the River Kwai* made the same leap of imaginative and popular faith, though at the cost of relegating Pierre Boulle's original novel – with its much more painful ending, because the attack on the bridge is a failure – to an intellectual retreat.

Is it talent or genius that decides art's place in history? Or is it history itself? Must authors and directors and composers match their work to the age they live in? Must we wait for a 'War on Terror' symphony, a '9/11 Suite', an 'Iraqi Requiem' to match Shostakovich or Barber or Britten? As for *The Da Vinci Code*, we can only sympathise with Sophie, the French police cryptologist who turns out to be Jesus Christ's only direct blood relative left on earth. She ends the movie with a stigmata on her neck of the kind that the Holy Father was once trying to inflict – unwillingly, of course – on RAF crews over Nazi Germany. Popular movie? *Merde!*

The Independent, 17 June 2006

We've all been veiled from the truth

Yes, the film *O Jerusalem* – loosely based on the epic history of the birth of Israel by Dominique Lapierre and Larry Collins – has reached us and it is everything we have come to expect of the Hollywoodisation of Europe. It is dramatic – it stars the French singer Patrick Bruel as an Israeli commander – there is a flamboyant David Ben-Gurion, all white hair defying gravity – and Saïd Taghmaoui and J. J. Feild as that essential duo of all such movies, the honourable, moderate, kind-hearted Arab (Saïd Chahine) and Jew (Bobby Goldman) whose friendship outlives the war between them. We are used to this pair, of course. *Exodus*, based on Leon Uris's novel of the same 1948 events, contained a 'good' Arab who befriends Paul Newman's Jewish hero, just as Ben Hur introduced us to a 'good' Arab who lends Charlton Heston's Jehuda Ben Hur his horses to compete in the chariot race against the nastiest centurion in the history of the Roman Empire. Once we have established that there are 'good' Arabs with hearts of gold, we are, of course, free to concentrate on the rotten kind. They murder a young woman in *Exodus* and they also kill a brave young woman during the battle for Latroun in *O Jerusalem*. (She is seen being partially stripped by her aggressor before being killed by a shell.)

It is also a sign of the times that for 'security' reasons, *O Jerusalem* had to be made in Rhodes, just as the Beirut scenes in the infinitely better movie *Munich* had to be staged in Malta. *Exodus* was filmed on location in an earlier, much safer Israel. But it's not this routine bestialisation of Arabs and Muslims that concerns me. You only have to watch the Arab slave-trader film *Ashanti*, again filmed in Israel and starring Roger Moore and (of all people) Omar Sharif, to see Arabs portrayed, Nazi-style, as murderers, thieves and child-molesters. Anti-Semitism against Arabs – who are, of course, also Semites – is par for the course in movies. And I have to admit that in *O Jerusalem*, the confusion and plotting of the Arab leadership – only King Abdullah of Jordan is an honourable man – is all too realistic, not least the arrogance of the Grand Mufti of Jerusalem, Haj Amin al-Husseini (he who shook hands with Hitler).

No, what I object to is the deliberate distortion of history, the twisting of the narrative of events to present Jews as the victims of the Israeli war of independence (6,000 dead) when in fact they were the victors, and the Arabs of Palestine – or at least that part of Palestine that became Israel in 1948 – as the cause of this war and the apparent victors (because the Jews of East Jerusalem were forced from their homes after the ceasefire) rather than the principal victims. Take, for example, the 1948 massacre at Deir Yassin, where the Stern gang mur-dered the Arab villagers of what is now the Jerusalem suburb of Givat Shaul, disembowelled women and threw grenades into rooms full of civilians. In *O Jerusalem*, the Stern gang is represented as a gang of bloodthirsty men, a kind of Jewish al-Qaeda, hopelessly out of touch with the mainstream Israeli army of young, high-minded guerrilla fighters.

In the movie, you see the bodies of the dead Arabs – and a wounded woman later being treated by an Israeli – but at no point is it made clear that Deir Yassin was just one among many villages in which the inhabitants were butchered – this was particularly the case in Galilee – and the women raped by Jewish fighters. Israel's 'new' historians have already bravely disclosed these facts, along with the irrefutable evidence that they served Israel's purpose of dispossessing 750,000 Palestinian Arabs from their homes in what was to become Israel. Israeli historian Avi Shlaim has courageously referred to this period as one of 'ethnic cleansing'. But no such suggestion sullies the scene of slaughter at Deir Yassin in *O Jerusalem*.

Reality has to be separated from us. Thus a massacre that became part of a policy has been turned in the movie into an aberration by a few armed extremists. Indeed, after the film ends, a series of paragraphs on the screen bleakly record the dispossession of the Palestinians as a result of 'Arab propaganda'. This itself is a myth. Yet again, we must repeat: Israeli historians have already disproved the lie that the Arab regimes told Palestinian Arabs over the radio that they should leave their homes 'until the Jews have been thrown into the sea'. No such broadcasts were made. Most Palestinians fled because they were frightened of ending up like the people of Deir Yassin. The propaganda about radio broadcasts was Israeli, not Arab.

It's as if a blanket, a curtain, a veil has been thrown over history – so that the shadow of real events is just visible, but their meaning so distorted as to be incomprehensible. 'So this is why you wanted guns,' Bobby Goldman shouts at the Stern leader amid the dead of Deir Yassin. He's wrong. The guns enabled the Stern gang to murder the Arabs of Deir Yassin to produce the panic that sent three-quarters of a million Palestinians on the road to permanent exile.

But isn't this the world in which we live? Aren't we all veiled from the truth? I'm not talking about the remarks of Jack 'the Veil' Straw* but of his political master, Lord Blair of Kut

---

* Labour MP and now justice minister Jack Straw revealed in 2006 that he sometimes asked Muslim women to remove their veil during meetings in his parliamentary constituency so that they could more easily communicate.

al-Amara. For only a day after I watched *O Jerusalem*, I opened my newspaper to find that our prime minister was calling the Muslim women's *niqab* 'a mark of separation'. Yet can there be any man more guilty of 'separation', of separating British people from their own democratically elected government, than Blair? Can anyone have been more meretricious – could anyone have told more lies to the British people – to obscure, dissemble, distort and cover up the historical facts than Blair?

The weapons of mass destruction, the 45-minute warning, the links between Saddam and al-Qaeda, the whole wretched fiction of Iraq's post-invasion 'success' and Afghanistan's post-Taliban 'success' are attempts by Blair to make us wear the veil, a far more dangerous weapon than any Muslim female covering. We are supposed to look through the veil which Lord Blair placed in front of our eyes so that lies will become truth, so that what is true will become untrue. And thus we will be separated from the truth. Which is why Blair himself now represents that 'mark of separation'. O tempora! O mores! O Jerusalem!

The Independent, 21 October 2007

When art is incapable of matching life

Art and reality have a strange relationship. Take *Stuff Happens*, David Hare's account of the buildup to war in Iraq, its title taken from Donald Rumsfeld's reaction to the widespread looting and pillage on 11 April 2003. One of the most powerful scenes in the play is Colin Powell's appearance before the UN Security Council on 5 February. I was sitting in the UN chamber at the time and my notes of the meeting show considerable cynicism and a good deal of disbelief on my part. I was dumbfounded by the cheap pictures of a mobile chemical weapons laboratory – it was supposed to be in a train, of all places – and the nonsensical transcript of a conversation between two of Saddam's henchmen ('Consider it done, boss'). But only in the text of Hare's play do I realise what I missed.

'My colleagues, every statement I make today is backed up by sources, solid sources . . .' Powell says. 'These are not assertions. What we are giving you are facts and conclusions based on solid intelligence.' How come I didn't take this down in my notes? How come I missed the biggest whopper of them all? The source for the mobile weapons lab is 'an eyewitness, an Iraqi chemical engineer'. In fact, the 'source' was in Germany and had never been interviewed by the CIA. And so on and on. And the effect of Hare's play is devastating – far, far worse than the original Powell performance which I witnessed at first hand. Is that the effect of art or artifice? Maybe both, because it is now standard fare to watch our political world represented on the stage only weeks or days after the real thing.

It didn't use to be that way. Although Sassoon's and Owen's poetry were contemporary with the war they condemned, it was a long time before the stage caught up. R. C. Sherriff's *Journey's End* came a decade after 1918; and we had to wait the same amount of time for Graves and Blunden to tell it how it was. The film of Remarque's *All Quiet on the Western Front* took years to be made – I am still fond of the second version with Ernest Borgnine that was produced after the Second World War – and the 1939–45 conflict yielded few great movies at the time. Yes, I'll tip my hat to Leslie Howard and *The First of the Few* and to the forgotten 1942 David Lean film *One of Our Aircraft is Missing*. I used to watch them all on commercial television on Sunday afternoons, along with *Casablanca*, which was popular then more for the singing of the 'Marseillaise' than for 'Play it Sam'. I would watch Colonel Strasser arriving at Rick's café – he was played by a Jewish actor who might have died in Auschwitz had he not been in Hollywood (where he died on a golf course in 1943) – and always felt the best line was Bogey's half-drunken: 'Of all the gin joints in all the towns in all the world – and she has to walk into mine.'

Yet it took seventeen years after the event before we watched a movie called *Dunkirk* – John Mills's plucky infantryman is still strangely moving, although I never got over watching the blowing up of Teston bridge near Maidstone which was doubling at the time for the battlefields of northern France. By comparison, *The Longest Day* was a clunker. It was the 1960s before Britain's film-makers really got down to work on the Second World War.* Of course, there were some favourites

---

* A reader subsequently reprimanded me for excluding *The Cruel Sea*, in which Jack Hawkins plays the conscience-stricken commander of the corvette HMS *Compass Rose*. In the book by Nicholas Monsarrat and in the film, the captain depth-charges a German submarine while seamen from a sunken

made then – *The Great Escape* comes to mind, not least because it contains cinema's most pointless line. As Hilts (Steve McQueen) races his plundered German motorcycle towards the mountains of Switzerland, he pulls to a halt and stares at the Swiss snows and says – yes – he says: 'Switzerland!'

But I'm being unfair. *The Battle of Britain* – in which the music was almost as good as the Spitfires – didn't duck the horrors of air warfare and Lean's *The Bridge on the River Kwai* was probably the first cinema movie to show the terrible suffering of British PoWs in Asia. But I think I'd have to conclude that one of the finest postwar movies was *A Bridge Too Far*, the Arnhem epic which I now realise – on rewatching it only the other day – is about the end of empire and the tragedy its collapse imposes upon ordinary men and women. The battle of Arnhem was utterly worthless and the sheer waste in that film comes close to great art. It also gave Sean Connery one of his finest roles. There was, more than twenty years ago, a stunning three-hour television drama on the Suez crisis which I watched in Beirut during the civil war – and which comes close to Hare because the British government was in 1956 caught lying almost as outrageously as the American and British variety forty-seven years later.

So what comes next? Will we see new Hare works every time we go to war? Or is there a three-year gap – which is the time it took to put *Flight 93* on celluloid? My own suspicion is that it won't take that long – and that it will be our politicians who will be playing themselves; in other words, that reality and the world of movies (or stage plays) will become one. After all, who can deny that the international crimes against humanity of 11 September 2001 were more powerful images, more awesome in their effect, than *Flight 93*? Al-Qaeda Productions got

ship are struggling to swim in the water around him. All are killed by the explosions.

there first – by timing the second aircraft into the Twin Towers to coincide with real-time television coverage. This was why no claim of responsibility was ever made. There was no need for such a claim when the terrifying pictures told us all we needed to know. Which is why the video butchers of Baghdad have now slotted themselves on to the internet, showing near-live coverage of their decapitations.

Violence has now become so close to all our lives that art sometimes seems incapable of matching the reality. Indeed, actors might be losing their credibility. After all, wasn't the forty-third President of the United States all dolled up in a jumpsuit when he mouthed the greatest lie of all – Mission Accomplished?

The Independent, 1 July 2007

A policeman's lot is not a happy one

A frightening, inspiring film has just come from Germany. *Sophie Scholl – the Final Days*, directed by Marc Rothemund, recounts the last day of freedom – and the few short days before her guillotining – of the 21-year-old Munich University student who in 1943, together with her brother Hans, decided, as part of a tiny undergraduate movement called the White Rose, to start a student revolution against the Nazis.

They posted and distributed thousands of tracts accusing Hitler of the butchery of German troops at Stalingrad, the moral degradation of Germany and its future defeat. Julia Jentsch plays Sophie as an innocent who is given a choice by her Gestapo interrogator – denounce her brother, claim she was influenced by her admiration for him, and go free, or face the Nazi punishment for any German found guilty of trying to lower the morale of the Wehrmacht and aiding the 'enemy'.

The Gestapo interrogator is a certain Inspector Mohr, and he is one of the most fascinating, dreadful, sensitive figures in the film. His initial cross-questioning of Sophie – Why was she leaving her university with an empty suitcase seconds after the tracts were discovered across the floor of the vestibule? Why was she planning to take the 12.16 fast train to Ulm? Why did she need a suitcase just to collect laundry from her sister's flat – is devastating.

Of course, Inspector Mohr admires Sophie's courage – 'We

need people like her on our side,' he tells another prisoner – but Sophie also wants to be liked and trusted by Inspector Mohr, whose quivering left eyelid (and whose son – like Sophie's fiancé – is fighting on the eastern front) turns him into a human being whose power is almost as much a burden as it is a weapon. Perhaps there is something dark in all our souls that wants us to be liked by policemen.

I grew up with Jack Warner's *Dixon of Dock Green* on BBC television and Robert Beatty's Canadian cop in Britain in *Dial 999*. I was addicted to *No Hiding Place*, whose hero, Inspector Lockhart, was chided by my magistrate mother, who wanted to know why TV cops were always exhausted and working overtime. Her own experience in Maidstone court suggested that they didn't work as hard as the criminals, and often lied. After *Z Cars*, I tuned out. Too much realism.

My first brush with the lads in blue – or green-blue in this case – was in Northern Ireland. Three detectives turned up at my home outside Belfast in 1975 to ask if I'd seen a 'confidential' British government document found on my doormat (by my cleaning lady, who just happened to be married to an officer in the Royal Ulster Constabulary). I told the three detectives that I could not say if I had seen the document since they would only show me one inch of the first page of paper – though I was well aware that it recorded the minutes of a secret meeting between British security personnel and Labour Party executives at Stormont who were hatching a plot to blackmail Protestant politicians regarded as opponents of UK policy in the province. 'I'd like to help you,' I said at one point with supreme disingenuousness.

In Belgrade in 1998, where I was briefly the only British correspondent under Nato attack in the Serbian capital, I was called by my hotel receptionist early one morning. 'There are some policemen waiting for you in the lobby,' the voice said. 'Now!' I guessed they thought my visa had expired – and also guessed they didn't realise I had renewed it the previous day. The three men – all in leather jackets – were sitting in plastic armchairs. 'Passport!' Milosevic's inspector snapped at me, and I meekly handed it over. And I found myself, for a few seconds, standing in front of them. I was their victim, the guilty man. I even, for a millisecond, found myself lowering my head. Then I took a plastic armchair beside them and waited. Much conversation. Much producing of grubby notebooks and pencils (not unlike my own). And then: 'Everything seems to be in order – I'm sorry we bothered you.' And I heard my own voice – yes, it was definitely mine – replying: 'Oh, don't worry Inspector – you've got your job to do!'

It reminded me of the day my mum and dad and I got home to Bower Mount Lane in Maidstone and found there'd been a break-in and that some of my mum's jewellery had been taken and Dad called the police and an inspector eventually arrived – my father was, after all, the borough treasurer and this was 1955 – to take notes. 'Very grateful to you,' my father finished the conversation – they never found the brooches, of course – 'and all I can say is, I wouldn't have your job for all the tea in China.'

No indeed, when constabulary duty's to be done, a policeman's lot is not a happy one. They are the voice of our conscience, our own guilt – however honourably maintained that device may be. They are us. Look at Inspector Mohr. Just before Sophie is taken to the guillotine to have her head chopped off, he turns up to bow a goodbye – out of respect and, perhaps, guilt. But didn't the American who recruited the Nazi war criminal Klaus Barbie after the war make his excuses by saying that Barbie was 'a damned good detective'?

It reminds me of that scene in dozens of movies, referenced even in Cassell's *Dictionary of Clichés*, a wonderful volume which sits above my desk in Beirut. There is a knock on a middle-class front door and an equally middle-class woman answers. And she says, knowing the game is up: 'You'd better come in, Inspector.'

The Independent, 6 May 2006

Take a beautiful woman to the cinema

At university, we male students used to say that it was imposs-ible to take a beautiful young woman to the cinema and con-centrate on the film. But in Canada, I've at last proved this to be untrue. Familiar with the Middle East and its abuses – and with the vicious policies of George W. Bush – we both sat absorbed by *Rendition*, Gavin Hood's powerful, appalling testimony of the torture of a 'terrorist suspect' in an unidenti-fied Arab capital after he was shipped there by CIA thugs in Washington.

Why did an Arab 'terrorist' telephone an Egyptian chemical engineer – holder of a green card and living in Chicago with a pregnant American wife – while he was attending an inter-national conference in Johannesburg? Did he have knowledge of how to make bombs? (Unfortunately yes – he was a chemical engineer – but the phone calls were mistakenly made to his number.) He steps off his plane at Dulles International Airport and is immediately shipped off on a CIA jet to what looks suspiciously like Morocco – where, of course, the local cops don't pussyfoot about Queensberry rules during interrogation. A CIA operative from the local US embassy – played by a nervous Jake Gyllenhaal – has to witness the captive's torture while the prisoner's wife pleads with congressmen in Washing-ton to find him. A lovely touch is provided by the CIA's elimination of his name from the passenger manifest, a ploy that goes spectacularly wrong when the wife finds that her husband used his credit card to buy duty-free goods on board his flight home to America.

The Arab interrogator – who starts with muttered questions to the naked Egyptian in an underground prison – works his way up from beatings to a 'black hole', to the notorious 'waterboarding' and then to electricity charges through the captive's body. The senior 'mukhabarat' questioner is in fact played by an Israeli (who, like his Arab counterparts, knows how to make a prisoner wish he was never born) and was so good that when he demanded to know how the al-Jazeera channel got exclusive footage of a suicide bombing before his own cops, my companion and I burst into laughter.

Well, suffice it to say that the CIA guy turns soft, rightly believes the Egyptian to be innocent, forces his release by the local minister of the interior, while the senior interrogator loses his daughter in the suicide bombing – there is a mind-numbing reversal of time sequences so that the bomb explodes both at the start and at the end of the film – while Meryl Streep as the catty, uncaring CIA boss is exposed for her wrongdoing. Not very realistic?

Well, think again. For in Canada lives Maher Arar, a totally harmless software engineer – originally from Damascus – who was picked up at JFK Airport in New York and underwent an almost identical 'rendition' to the fictional Egyptian in the movie. Suspected of being a member of al-Qaeda – the Canadian Mounties had a hand in passing on this nonsense to the FBI – he was put on a CIA plane to Syria, where he was held in an underground prison and tortured. The Canadian government later awarded Arar $10 million in compensation and he received a public apology from Prime Minister Stephen Harper.

But Bush's thugs didn't get fazed like Streep's CIA boss. They still claim that Arar is a 'terrorist suspect'; which is why, when he testified to a special US congressional meeting on 18 October 2007, he had to appear on a giant video-screen in Washington. He's still, you see, not allowed to enter the US. Personally, I'd stay in Canada – in case the FBI decided to ship me back to Syria for another round of torture. But save for the US congressmen – 'Let me personally give you what our government has not: an apology,' Democrat Bill Delahunt said humbly – there hasn't been a whimper from the Bush administration.

Even worse, it refused to reveal the 'secret evidence' which it claimed to have on Arar – until the Canadian press got their claws on these 'secret' papers and discovered they were hearsay evidence of an Arar visit to Afghanistan from an Arab prisoner in Minneapolis, Mohamed Elzahabi, whose brother – according to Arar – once repaired Arar's car in Montreal. There was a lovely quote from America's Homeland Security secretary Michael Chertoff and Alberto Gonzales, the US attorney general at the time, that the evidence against Arar was 'supported by information developed by US law enforcement agencies'. Don't you just love that word 'developed'? Doesn't it smell rotten? Doesn't it mean 'fabricated'?

And what, one wonders, were Bush's toughs doing sending Arar off to Syria, a country that they themselves designate a 'terrorist' state which supports 'terrorist' organisations like the Hizballah? President Bush, it seems, wants to threaten Damascus, but is happy to rely on his brutal Syrian chums if they'll be obliging enough to plug in the electricity and attach the wires in an underground prison on Washington's behalf.

But then again, what can you expect of a president whose nominee for Alberto Gonzales's old job of attorney general, Michael Mukasey, tells senators that he doesn't 'know what is involved' in the near-drowning 'waterboarding' torture used by US forces during interrogations? 'If waterboarding is torture, torture is not constitutional,' the luckless Mukasey bleated. Yes, and I suppose if electric shocks to the body constitute torture – *if*, mind you – that would be unconstitutional. Right? *New York Times* readers at least spotted the immorality of Mukasey's remarks. A former US assistant attorney asked 'how the United States could hope to regain its position as a respected world leader on the great issues of human rights if its chief law enforcement officer cannot even bring himself to acknowledge the undeniable verity that waterboarding constitutes torture . . . ?' As another reader pointed out, 'Like pornography, torture doesn't require a definition.' Yet all is not lost for the torture-lovers in America. Here's what Republican senator Arlen Specter – a firm friend of Israel – had to say about Mukasey's shameful remarks: 'We're glad to see somebody who is strong with a strong record, take over this department.'

So is truth stranger than fiction? Or is Hollywood waking up – after *Syriana* and *Munich* – to the gross injustices of the Middle East and the shameless and illegal policies of the US in the region? Go and see *Rendition* – it will make you angry – and remember Arar. And you can take a beautiful woman along to share your fury.

The Independent, 3 November 2007

A river through time

Tampering with literature, with history, with films, has always seemed to me to be especially obscene. Someone, somewhere, wants us to be protected – or poisoned – by their views. I recall, some years ago, how a south London library wished to withdraw William Shirer's monumental *The Rise and Fall of the Third Reich* from its shelves because of his account of Hitler's 'Night of the Long Knives' massacre in 1934. The offending passage referred to one of Hitler's Stormtrooper victims as 'a notorious homosexual with a girlish face' and to Ernst Roehm, his Brownshirt leader and former friend and his comrades, as 'sexual perverts'. The problem, of course, was that when Shirer was writing his magnificent account of the Nazi era in 1959, 'gay' still meant 'happy' or 'blithe-spirited', and homosexuality was not only illegal but still provoked widespread public disgust among those not liberal or far-seeing enough to understand that society must accept it. But Shirer's work no longer conformed to our current social correctness or morality, and therefore had to be banned – or, I suppose, rewritten like a Soviet encyclopedia in Stalin's days.

Jewish friends still fear that *The Merchant of Venice* encourages anti-Semitism and I've heard it argued that Shakespeare's play should be banned, along with Marlowe's *The Jew of Malta*, who 'poisoned wells'. And then we have T. S. Eliot's 'Gerontion' in which '... the Jew squats on the window-sill, the owner,/

Spawned in some estaminet of Antwerp . . .' I cringe each time I read this. For yes, Eliot did betray in his work the anti-Semitism of his age and there is no point in trying to deny this. But history dictates that we must live with this fact, however unsavoury, rather than 'clean up' the prose and poetry of yesterday like Winston Smith in *Nineteen Eighty-Four*, who is constantly burning and rewriting news reports for Big Brother. Hitler's *Mein Kampf* is still on sale – though with eminently sensible prefaces which emphasise its evil – in order for us better to understand the wickedness of Nazism.

But cultural censorship has not disappeared. Shekhar Kapur's *Elizabeth* gave Cate Blanchett a unique moment to recreate the Virgin Queen in his 1998 film. But the sequel, *Elizabeth: The Golden Age*, is a lemon because – in the one vital scene where Elizabeth demonstrates to her soldiers that she is among them as their fighting sovereign – when she addresses her troops at Tilbury before the expected arrival of the Spanish armada in 1588, her most famous statement, learned by every schoolboy in Britain, has been ruthlessly expunged. My dad used to quote this to me and even took me to Tilbury to show me the fortress – still standing today – in which Elizabeth told her soldiers that 'I may have the body of a weak and feeble woman, but I have the heart and stomach of a king.'

Alas, this was too much for Mr Kapur. In the age of feminism, such statements are forbidden, unacceptable, inappropriate, provocative. How else can one account for the scene in which Ms Blanchett, prancing around on a silly white horse (in front of what looks more like a platoon than an army), simply does not utter these famous, historic words with which Elizabeth rallied her men. Millions of cinemagoers must have been waiting for that line – but it was taken from them. Elizabeth had to be a feminist queen, albeit a virgin, and had to represent today's womanhood in which women are not 'weak and feeble' – rather than the uniquely-placed lady who led her kingdom in an age of male domination. By saying that her heart was that of a man, she was not, of course, submitting herself to 'maledom'; in Tudor England, Elizabeth was saying that she was the equal of a man.*

But movies are capable of darker forms of manipulation. In the film of the award-winning *The English Patient*, for example, the spy David Caravaggio has his thumbs cut off by fascist troops. But a woman is ordered to perform this grisly task and a veiled Muslim indeed steps forward with a knife as Caravaggio's tormentor explains that a 'Muslim' understands this sort of thing. I could not comprehend, when I watched this gruesome, bloody scene, why Islam should have been brought into the film – whose cultural background is largely that of Renaissance Italy. Why did the screenplay – written by the director, Anthony Minghella – wish to associate Muslims with brutality? I bought Michael Ondaatje's novel upon which the film is based, only to find the following account of the amputation, in the words of 'Caravaggio': 'They found a woman to do it. They thought it was more trenchant. They brought in one of their nurses . . . She was an innocent, knew nothing about me, my name or nationality.' As I suspected, there was no reference to a Muslim. Indeed, the profoundly racist scene in the movie had no foundation whatever in the text of Ondaatje's book. So why was it there?†

A relief, then, in the past few days, to have watched Joe Wright's devastating film *Atonement*, a drama of betrayal and

* Tracy Martins, an *Independent* reader, was to point out that Elizabeth's 'heart and stomach of a king' speech first appeared 'only in a letter in 1623, 35 years after the Tilbury gathering . . . There is no evidence that Elizabeth I gave this speech . . .'

† The screenplay (Methuen Drama, 1997) reads as follows: 'The Nurse comes in. She is Arab . . . Her head is covered. Muller (the German): "I'll tell you what I'm going to do . . . She's Moslem, so she'll understand all of this. What's the punishment for adultery?" '

dishonesty and love among the upper classes in 1930s England, which moves from being almost low-budget domestic art house cinema into the epic of Dunkirk. The plot – to outline it for those who have not seen the film – is deeply prosaic. Briony falsely accuses her older sister Cecilia's lover Robbie – the son of a family servant who gained a scholarship to study medicine and is thus an honorary member of the middle classes – of raping her cousin Lola after an insufferably high dinner at the family manor house. Robbie is arrested – Cecilia believes in his innocence – and is inevitably convicted of rape and imprisoned. But when war is declared in 1939, he is given the opportunity of freedom if he enlists. As the second half of this dark film opens, he is concealing a chest wound from his two corporals as – lost amid the BEF's retreat to the Channel ports in 1940 – he leads them towards the northern French coast.

There is an uncanny familiarity to these scenes – in the 1957 movie *Dunkirk*, John Mills leads an equally lost platoon towards salvation – but when Robbie follows a canal, he tells his men that he can 'smell the sea'. As he climbs a sand-dune, we suddenly see before him 20,000 – perhaps 30,000 – British soldiers on the beaches. So sudden, so unexpected, is this sudden epic scene that in the cinema I muttered 'Fuck me!' under my breath and – a glorious marriage of audience and film – one of Robbie's corporals, confronted by the same scene, cries out, just after I did: 'Fuck me!'

The Dunkirk sequence lasts only just over five minutes but it penetrates the brain. French officers shoot their horses on the beach, drunken British soldiers lie in the gutters, cursing. No censorship here. But Robbie's black corporal walks further. In Ian McEwan's book, upon which the film is faithfully based, there is a mere reference to 'the feeble sound of a hymn being sung in unison, then fading'. But Joe Wright's film takes the corporal to a shattered seaside bandstand where British troops

– wounded, their uniforms bloodied – are singing that wonderful Quaker hymn 'Dear Lord and Father of Mankind, forgive
our foolish ways'. The camera encircles these brave men. It is
magnetic, a symbol of courage but also of futility in war that
gives this film a dignity it would otherwise not possess.*
Robbie, we are led to believe, makes it back to England in one
of the 'little ships' to be reunited with Cecilia. Briony turns up
at their south London slum to apologise, offering to go to
court to admit her lie. Lola's present-day husband, it transpires,
was the rapist. Only at the very end does the elderly and dying
Briony (now played by Vanessa Redgrave) admit that her novel
of the Robbie–Cecilia reunion does not represent the truth.
She wished them to be together but, in truth, Robbie died of
septicemia at Bray Dunes, Dunkirk, on 1 June 1940, and Cecilia
was killed in the bombing of Balham tube station four months
later. They were never reunited.

'The age of clear answers was over,' the elderly Briony says
of herself in the book. 'So was the age of characters and plots
. . . Plots were too like rusted machinery whose wheels would
no longer turn . . . It was thought, perception, sensations that
interested her, the conscious mind as a river through time . . .'
And it is this concept that informs the film of *Atonement*, as
honest an attempt as the world of movies has yet achieved in
portraying dishonesty, war and love.

The Independent, 19 January 2008

---

* I am indebted to *Independent* readers Peter Newton and Christina van
Melzen who correctly identified this hymn. In my original article I wrongly
gave its first line as 'For all the Saints, who from their labours rest' – proof
that my singing in the school choir was no guarantee of hymnal accuracy.

CHAPTER FIVE

The greatest crisis since the last greatest crisis

Death, so the cliché goes, is cheap. Personally, I find that *life* is cheap and that death is merely a price, paid according to relevent exchange rates. In our western newspapers, one American life equals 1,000 Iraqis or more, unless – like Rachel Corrie – you are an American 'martyr' on the 'wrong' side. Inverted commas are important here. A European 'crisis' is not the same as a 'crisis' in the Middle East; a rejection of the European Constitution is more important – for our press and television reporters – than a bombing in Baghdad. But when an Afghan refugee and his family are desperately seeking asylum in the Netherlands, does the crisis belong to him – because he faces deportation, even death at home – or to a new anti-immigrant, anti-Muslim Europe which has forgotten the Age of Enlightenment?

A long and honourable tradition of smearing the dead

Across the marble floor of the shrine of the Imam Hussein in Kerbala scampers Suheil with his plastic bag of metal. He points first to a red stain on the flagstones. 'This was a red smoke grenade that the Americans fired,' he tells me. 'And that was another grenade mark.' The Shia worshippers are kneeling amid these burn marks, eyes glistening at the gold façade of the mosque which marks the very place, behind silver bars kissed by the faithful, when – in an epic battle far more decisive in human history than any conflict fought by the United States – Imam al-Hussein was cut down in AD 680. There is a clink as, one by one, Suheil drops his souvenirs on to the marble.

US forces denied that any ordnance fell upon the shrine when they opened fire close to the Husseiniya mosque last month. Of course they denied it. Denial has become a disease in Iraq – as it has through most of the Middle East. The Americans deny that they kill innocent civilians in Iraq – but kill them all the same. The Israelis deny they kill innocent civilians in the occupied territories – indeed, they even deny the occupation – but kill them all the same. So folk like Suheil are valuable. They expose lies. The evidence, in this case, is his little souvenirs. On one of the grenades in his plastic bag are written the words 'Cartridge 44mm Red Smoke Ground Marker M713 PB-79G041–001'. Another is designated as a

'White Star Cluster M 585'. Yet another carries the code '40mm M195 KX090 [figure erased] 010–086'. They are strange things to read in a religious building whose scholars normally concentrate on the minutiae of Koranic sura rather than the globalised linguistics of the arms trade.

But one of the Kerbala shrine's guards, Ahmed Hanoun Hussein, was killed by the Americans when they arrived to assist Iraqi police in a confrontation with armed thieves near the shrine. Two more Shias were shot dead by the Americans during a protest demonstration the next day. Suheil insists that US troops wanted to enter the mosque – an unlikely scenario, since they are under orders to stay away from its vicinity – but four bullets did smash into an outer wall. 'We are peaceful people – so why do we need this?' Suheil asks me plaintively. 'Remember how we suffered under Saddam?' And here he points upwards to another sacrilegious assault on the shrine, this time amid the gold of one of the two principal minarets – a shrapnel gash from a shell fired by Saddam's legions during the great Shia revolt of 1991, the rebellion we encouraged and then betrayed after the last Gulf War.

So you'd think, wouldn't you, that the shootings at Kerbala were an established fact. But no. The US still insists it never fired into the shrine of the Imam Hussein and 'has no information' on the dead. Just as it had 'no information' about the massacre of at least six Iraqi civilians by its soldiers during a house raid in the Mansour district of Baghdad a month ago. Just as it has no information on the number of Iraqi civilian casualties during and after the illegal Anglo-American invasion, estimated at up to 5,223 by one reputable organisation and up to 2,700 in and around Baghdad alone according to the *Los Angeles Times*.

And I've no doubt there would have been 'no information' about the man shot dead by US troops outside Abu Ghraib prison last week had he not inconveniently turned out to be a prize-winning Reuters cameraman. Thus Mazen Dana's death became a 'terrible tragedy' – this from the same American authorities whose secretary of state Colin Powell thought that the tank fire which killed another Reuters cameraman and a Spanish journalist in April was 'appropriate'. Of course, the Americans didn't hesitate to peddle the old lie about how Dana's camera looked like a rocket-propelled grenade – the same cock-and-bull story the Israelis produced back in 1985 when they killed a two-man CBS crew, Tewfiq Ghazawi and Bahij Metni, in southern Lebanon.

But there's a far more hateful bit of denial and hypocrisy being played out now in the US over two young and beautiful women. The first, Private Jessica Lynch, is feted as an American heroine after being injured during the American invasion of Iraq and then 'rescued' from her Iraqi hospital bed by US Special Forces. Now it just happens that Private Lynch – far from firing at her Iraqi attackers until the last bullet, as the Pentagon would have had us believe – was injured in a road accident between two military trucks during an ambush and that Iraqi doctors had been giving her special care when Lynch's 'rescuers' burst into her unguarded hospital. But the second young American is a real heroine, a girl called Rachel Corrie who stood in front of an Israeli bulldozer that was about to demolish a Palestinian home and who was killed – wearing a clearly marked jacket and shouting through a loudhailer – when the Israeli driver crushed her beneath his bulldozer and then drove backwards over her body again. All this was filmed. As a Jewish writer, Naomi Klein, bravely pointed out in the *Guardian*, 'Unlike Lynch, Corrie did not go to Gaza to engage in combat; she went to try to thwart it.' Yet not a single American government official has praised Rachel Corrie's courage or condemned her killing by the Israeli driver. President Bush has been gutlessly silent. For their part, the Israeli government tried to smear the activist group to which Rachel Corrie belonged by claiming that two Britons later involved in a suicide bombing in Tel Aviv had attended a memorial service to her – as if the organisers could have known of the crime the two men had not yet committed.

But there's nothing new in smearing the dead, is there? Back in Northern Ireland in the early 1970s, I remember well how the British army's press office at Lisburn in Co. Antrim would respond to the mysterious death of British ex-soldiers or Englishmen who were inconveniently killed by British soldiers. The dead were always described as – and here, reader, draw in your breath – 'Walter Mitty characters'. I used to get sick of reading this smear in *Belfast Telegraph* headlines. Anonymous army officers would pass it along to the press. The guy was a Walter Mitty, a fantasist whose claims could not be believed. This was said of at least three dead men in Northern Ireland.

And I have a suspicion, of course, that this is where Tony Blair's adviser Tom Kelly first heard of Walter Mitty and the ease with which authority could libel the dead. Born and bred in Northern Ireland, he must have read the same lies in the Belfast papers as I did, uttered by the same anonymous army 'press spokesmen' with as little knowledge of Thurber as Mr Kelly himself when they spoke to journalists over the phone. So from that dark war in Northern Ireland, I think, came the outrageous smear against Dr David Kelly,* uttered by his namesake to a correspondent on *The Independent*.

So let us remember a few names this morning: Ahmed Hanoun Hussein, Mazen Dana, Tewfiq Ghazawi, Bahij Metni, Rachel Corrie and Dr David Kelly. All they have in common

---

* Dr David Kelly, an expert in biological warfare and former UN arms inspector in Iraq, told a BBC reporter that Downing Street's infamous 'dossier' on weapons of mass destruction contained gross exaggerations. He was found dead near his Oxfordshire home on 17 July 2003. A new book by Liberal Democrat MP Norman Baker suggests that Kelly was murdered.

is their mortality. And our ability to deny their deaths or lie about why we killed them or smear them when they can no longer speak for themselves. Walter Mitty indeed!

The Independent, 23 August 2003

Tricky stuff, evil

When George Bush sneaked into Baghdad airport for his two-hour 'warm meal' for Thanksgiving, he was in feisty form. Americans hadn't come to Baghdad 'to retreat before a bunch of thugs and assassins'. Evil is still around, it seems, ready to attack the forces of Good. And if only a handful of the insurgents in Iraq are ex-Baathists – and I suspect it is only a handful – then who would complain if Saddam's henchmen are called 'thugs'? But Evil's a tricky thing. Here one day, gone the next. Take Japan.

Now, I like the Japanese. Hard-working, sincere, cultured – just take a look at their collection of French Impressionists – they even had the good sense to pull out of George Bush's 'war on terror'. And Japan, remember, is one of the examples George always draws upon when he's promising democracy in Iraq. Didn't America turn emperor-obsessed Japan into a freedom-loving nation after the Second World War?

So, in Tokyo not so long ago, I took a walk down memory lane. Not my memory, but the cruelly cut-short memory of a teenage Royal Marine called Jim Feather. Jim was the son of my dad's sister Freda and he was on the *Repulse* when she was sunk by Japanese aircraft on 10 December 1941. Jim was saved and brought back to Singapore, only to be captured when the British surrendered. Starved and mistreated, he was set to work building the Burma railway. Anyone who

remembers David Lean's *Bridge on the River Kwai* will have a
good idea of what happened. One of his friends later told
Freda that in Jim's last days, he could lift the six-foot prisoner
over his shoulder as if he were a child. As light as a feather,
you might say. He died in a Japanese prisoner of war camp
sometime in 1942.

I wasn't thinking of Jim when I walked into the great Shinto
shrine in central Tokyo where Japan's war dead are honoured;
not just the 'banzai–banzai' poor bloody infantry variety, but
the kamikazes, the suicide pilots who crashed their Zero
fighter-bombers on to American aircraft carriers. Iraq's suiciders may not know much about Japan's 'divine wind', but
there's a historical narrative that starts in the Pacific and
stretches all the way through Sri Lanka's suicide bombers to
the Middle East. If President Bush's 'thugs and assassins' think
of Allah as they die, Japan's airmen thought of their emperor.
At the Shinto shrine, in the area containing photographs of
the Japanese campaign, there are some helpful captions in
English. But in the room with the portraits of the kamikazes
– including a devastating oil painting of a suicide attack on
a US carrier – the captions are only in Japanese. I wasn't
surprised.

What I was amazed to see, a few metres from the shrine,
was a stretch of railway with a big bright green *Boy's Own
Paper* steam locomotive standing on it. Japanese teenagers were
cleaning the piston rods and dabbing a last touch of green to
the boiler. As a boy, I of course wanted to be an engine driver,
so I climbed aboard. Anyone speak English? I asked. What is
this loco doing in a Shinto shrine? An intense young man
with thin-framed spectacles smiled at me. 'This was the first
locomotive to pull a Japanese military train along the Burma
railway,' he explained. And then I understood. Royal Marine
Jim Feather had died so this pretty little train could puff
through the jungles of Burma. In fact, this very same loco's

first duty was to haul the ashes of dead Japanese soldiers north from the battlefront.

The Japanese are our friends, of course. They are the fruit of our democracy. But what does this mean? Even now, the Japanese government will not acknowledge the full details of the crimes of rape and massacre against women in their conquered 'Greater South East Asia Co-Prosperity Sphere'. Since the postwar International Military Tribunal – twenty-seven Japanese war criminals were prosecuted and seven of them were hanged – not a single Japanese has been prosecuted for war crimes in Japanese courts. Men who have admitted taking part in the mass rape of Chinese girls – let alone the 'comfort women' from China and Korea forced to work in brothels – are still alive, safe from prosecution.

So didn't these men represent Evil? What is the difference between the young Japanese men honoured for blowing themselves up against American aircraft carriers and the equally young men blowing themselves up against American convoys in Iraq? Sure, the Iraqi insurgents don't respect the Red Cross. But nor did the Japanese.

I guess it's all a matter of who your friends are. Take that little exhibition of 'crimes against humanity' a year ago at the Imperial War Museum in London. Included was a section on the 1915 Armenian Holocaust. But the exhibition included a disclaimer from the Turkish government, which still fraudulently claims that the Armenians were not murdered in a genocide. Andy Kevorkian, whose father's entire family was murdered by the Turks in 1915, wrote a letter to Robert Crawford, the museum's director general. Nowhere in the exhibition is there a disclaimer of the Jewish Holocaust by the right-wing historian David Irving or by neo-Nazis, Kevorkian complained. Nor should there be. But 'for the IWM to bow to Turkish (or is it Foreign Office?) pressure to deny what the entire world accepts as the first genocide of the 20th century is an insult to the Armenians who survived ... For the IWM to allow the Turks to say that this didn't happen is a travesty of justice and truth.'

It's the same old problem. The steam loco in Tokyo and the disclaimer in the Imperial War Museum are lies to appease enemies who are now friends. Japan is a Western democracy. So Evil is ignored. Turkey is our secular ally, a democracy that wants to join the European Union. So Evil is ignored. But fear not. As the Americans try ever more desperately to escape from Iraq, the thugs and assassins will become the good guys again and the men of Evil in Iraq will be working for us.* The occupation authorities have already admitted rehiring some of Saddam's evil secret policemen to hunt down the evil Saddam.

Tricky stuff, evil.

The Independent, 29 November 2003

---

* In the summer of 2007, US officers persuaded and paid thousands of former Iraqi insurgents to change sides and fight alongside them. America's new collaborators then hunted down their former comrades, in many cases murdering them.

'Middle East hope!' – 'Europe in crisis!'

'What on earth are you Europeans on about? What is this nonsense about Europe breaking apart?' We were at lunch only a hundred metres from the crater of the bomb that killed Lebanon's former prime minister last February. The restaurant was almost destroyed in the explosion and the staff bear the scars. The head waiter at La Paillote has a very painful, deep slit down his right cheek. My host was still amazed. 'Do you people live on planet earth?' he asked.

Point taken. When I open the European papers here in Beirut, I read of European chaos, of constitution rejections in France and Holland, of the possible break-up of the EU, of the return of the lira (of all currencies, the most preposterous!), of shouting matches in Brussels (of all cities, the most preposterous!) about rebates. 'Blair tells Europe it must "renew"', the *International Herald Tribune* informs me. 'Brown in stark warning to EU,' my own paper headlines. Only the Eastern Europeans, it seems, like the European Union. And part of the answer to my Lebanese friend's question may lie among Eastern Europe's ghosts. But the Western press, when it reaches Beirut, has an awesome perversity about it.

Yesterday, for example, Lebanese newspapers – like others in the Arab world – published a picture that no Western publication would dare to show. At least a quarter of one front page here was given to this horror. It showed an Iraqi man amid the wreckage of a bomb explosion, trying to help a twelve-year-old boy to his feet. Well not quite; because the boy's left leg has been torn off just below the knee, and beneath his agonised face there is indeed, in colour, the bloody stump, a thing from a butcher's shop, a great piece of red bone and gristle and hanging flesh. Laith Falah, one of the lucky Iraqis to be 'liberated' by us in 2003, was bicycling to a Baghdad bakery to buy bread for his parents and three sisters. For him, for his parents and three sisters, for all Iraqis, for Arabs, for the Middle East, for my luncheon host, the EU's problems seem as preposterous as Brussels and the lira.

So why is it that we Europeans can no longer understand our own peace and contentment and safety and our extraordinary luxury and our futuristic living standards and our godlike good fortune and our long, wonderful lives? When I arrive in Paris on Air France and step aboard the RER train to the city, when I take the Eurostar to London and sip my coffee while the train hisses between the great military cemeteries of northern France where many of my father's friends lie buried, I see the glowering, sad faces of my fellow Europeans, heavy with the burden of living in the beautiful First World, broken down by minimum hours of work and human rights laws and protections the like of which are beyond the imagination of the people among whom I live.

And when the train eases towards Waterloo and I catch sight of the Thames and Big Ben, I call a friend on my mobile, an Iraqi who's trying to emigrate to Australia or Canada – he hasn't decided which yet but I've already told him that one can be quite hot, the other very cold – and he tells me that he can't cross the border to Jordan even to visit the Australian embassy. No Eurostars for him. Oddly – and this is part of the perversity that our newspapers accurately reflect – we want to believe that the Middle East is getting better. Iraq is the world's newest democracy; our soldiers are winning the war against the insurgents – at least we are now calling it a war – and Lebanon is free and Egypt will soon be more democratic and even the Saudis endured an election a couple of months ago. Israel will withdraw from Gaza and the 'road map' to peace will take off and there will be a Palestinian state and . . .

It's rubbish, of course. Iraq is a furnace of pain and fear, the insurrection grows bloodier by the day, Lebanon's people are under attack, Mubarak's Egypt is a pit of oppression and poverty and Saudi Arabia is – and will remain – an iconoclastic and absolute monarchy. 'Take the greatest care,' I say this week to a Lebanese lawyer friend whose political profile exactly matches the journalist and the ex-communist party leader who were assassinated in Beirut this month. 'You too,' he says. And I sit and think about that for a bit.

Maybe we Europeans need to believe that the Middle East is a spring of hope in order to concentrate on our own golden grief. Perhaps it helps us to feel bad about ourselves, to curse our privileges and hate our glorious life, if we persuade ourselves that the Middle East is a paradise of growing freedom and liberation from fear. But why? We lie to ourselves about the tragedy of the Middle East and then we lie to ourselves about the heaven of living in Europe. Maybe – a wilful notion now slides into this paragraph – maybe the Second World War was too long ago. Almost outside living memory, the real hell of Europe persuaded us to create a new continent of security and unity and wealth. And now, I suspect, we've forgotten. The world in which my father's chums died in northern France in 1918 and the world in which my mother repaired Spitfire radios in the Battle of Britain is being 'disappeared', permitted to pop up only when Prime Minister Blair wants to compare his horrible little war in Iraq to Britain's Finest Hour or when we want to enjoy an orgy of cinematic Nazi destruction in *The Downfall*. Only in the east, where the mass graves litter the cold earth, does memory linger amid the mists. Which might explain their love of the EU. Yet Laith Falah's terrible wound was more grisly than *Saving Private Ryan* – which is why you will not have seen it in Europe this week.

And yesterday, before lunch, I went down to Martyrs' Square in Beirut to watch the funeral of old Georges Hawi, the former communist party leader who was driving to the Gondole coffee shop on Tuesday when a bomb exploded beneath his car seat and tore into his abdomen. And there was his widow – who had swooned from grief and horror when she actually saw her husband's body lying on the road – weeping before the coffin. And 2,000 miles away, Europe was in crisis.

The Independent, 25 June 2005

A poet on the run in Fortress Europe

Mohamed Ziya sits on the chair beside me in Amsterdam and opens his little book of poetry. His verse slopes down the page in delicate Persian script, the Dari language of his native Afghanistan. 'God, why in the name of Islam is there all this killing, why all this anti-people killing . . . the only chairs left in my country are chairs for the government, those who want to destroy Afghanistan.' He reads his words of anger slowly, gently interrupted by an old chiming Dutch clock. Outside, the Herengracht canal slides gently beneath the rain. It would be difficult to find anywhere that less resembles Kabul.

'The donkeys came to Afghanistan, Massoud, Rahbani and the rest,' Mohamed reads on. 'All the people were waiting for the donkeys. Gulbuddin said these donkeys have no tails – "Only I have a tail, so I shall have a ministry," he said. The donkeys are now in the government.' Donkeys may be nice, friendly beasts to us, but to call anyone in the Muslim world a *khar* – a donkey – is as insulting as you can get. Mohamed was talking about the 'mujahedin' guerrilla fighters who moved into Kabul after the Russian withdrawal in 1990, an arrival that presaged years of civil war atrocities which left at least 65,000 Afghans dead. This was the conflict which so sickened the anti-Soviet fighter Osama bin Laden that he left Afghanistan for Sudan.

Mohamed looks at me – a small energetic man with dark,

sharp eyes. 'I wanted future generations to know what we went through, to understand our pain,' he says to me. 'I couldn't stop myself writing this poetry.' This was his mistake. Betrayed to the 'mujahedin', he was thrown into a foul prison in Kabul, rescued only by his father's intercession. The Taliban came next and Mohamed could not prevent his pen from betraying him again. 'I kept my poetry "under the table", as we say, but someone at my office found a poem I had written called "Out of Work" and told the boss, who was a mullah.' When he knew that he had been discovered, Mohamed ran in terror from his office to his father's home.

Mohamed seems to spend his life on the run. He and his wife and three children live in the north of Holland, desperate to stay in the land to which they fled six years ago, but the courts – in the new spirit of anti-immigrant, anti-Muslim Europe – have rejected their pleas to stay. Mohamed's papers have expired. Now he waited in fear for the policeman who would demand: 'Your papers please.' A family friend, Hoji Abdul-Rahman, originally arranged for Mohamed and his family to flee Kabul for Jalalabad and then across the Afghan border to Pakistan where 'Hoji' – an honorific title bestowed on those who have made the pilgrimage to Mecca – obtained fake visas and passports that enabled them to fly to Holland. 'I went straight to the police to tell them we were here,' Mohamed said. 'They were very good to us. They told us to register at Zevenaar as asylum-seekers, which we did.'

He was housed in a small Dutch village where the local people treated the Afghan family with great kindness. 'They always came to see us in our flat and gave us food and invited us to their homes,' Mohamed said, producing a sad poem entitled 'Thank You for Everything' in tribute to the Dutch people. But fate struck Mohamed again. Had the last of four court hearings into his case dated his refugee status from the day he arrived in Holland rather than from that of his first visit to Zevenaar in 2000 – which was delayed because the Dutch authorities were enjoying the week-long millennium celebrations – he would probably have qualified for permanent refugee status.

'But the court dated my arrival from the delayed registration at Zevenaar and told me my family had to leave Holland. They said that the Taliban had been defeated and that Afghanistan was now a "democracy". But they wouldn't accept that Karzai's government includes many of the 'mujahedin' warlords who locked me up in prison. They will do the same again.' Which is probably true. But now Mohamed, his wife and three children – one of them born in Holland – wait for the police to take them to Schiphol airport for the long journey back to their dangerous homeland.

The ferocious murder of film-maker Theo van Gogh and the callous behaviour of his Muslim murderer – who announced in court that he felt no compassion for van Gogh's family – has hardened Dutch government hearts, just as the rioting in Clichy-sous-Bois has hardened those of Messrs Sarkozy and Chirac. So what am I to say to Mohamed as he sits hunched in the deep, soft armchair of my hotel room, clutching his poetry book and his sack of expired refugee papers, a mechanical engineer with a foreign language degree from a Ukrainian university who must now clear garbage from Dutch apartment blocks to earn money? I can't help you, I say quietly. I will write about you. I will try to pump some compassion out of the authorities. But the days of such humanity have run out.

Next day, I am giving a lecture in the Belgian city of Antwerp when a man in the audience starts to berate me. 'Why should we help Afghans or Iraqis or other Muslims when their own governments treat them like shit?' he asked. 'Why should we have to save them from their own people? Why do we have to treat them better?' I explain that it was us – we, the West – who armed the 'mujahedin' to fight the Russians and then ignored Afghanistan when it collapsed into civil war, that we nurtured the Taliban via Saudi Arabia and Pakistan when we thought we could negotiate with them for a gas pipeline across Afghanistan, that the current US ambassador in Iraq – that other blood-drenched democratic success story – was once involved with the company Unocal, which negotiated with the Taliban over the pipeline route, that Karzai had also been working for Unocal. To no avail.

Our new morality, it seems, no longer revolves around 'Saddam was worse than us' but 'Why should we treat Muslims any better than they treat each other?' And now we know that the CIA is holding other Muslims in bunkers deep beneath the earth of democratic Romania and brave old democratic Poland for a little torture, what hope is there for Mohamed? For him – and for us in Britain soon if Prime Minister Blair gets his way – it will be a familiar story from Europe's dark past. *Vos papiers, Monsieur. Arbeitspapiere, bitte schön.* Your papers, please.

The Independent, 5 November 2005

Mohamed Ziya's story has a happy ending. In February 2007 he e-mailed relatives that the Dutch authorities had given permission for his family to stay in the Netherlands.

CHAPTER SIX

When I was a child . . .
I understood as a child

I remember my childhood by recalling memories of memories. True, I have my mother's early black-and-white movie film – the camera was a gift from my grandmother, Phyllis – which shows me to have been a blond-eyed, smiling baby, forever waving my fists in the air. I think I even remember the smell of my pram cover in the rain. Later film shows me, aged ten, holidaying in France and Germany with my parents. And looking back, of course, I like to think of these as glorious days, playing cowboys in my parents' apple orchard with primary school friends when I was twelve, passing my A-levels and arriving at Lancaster University to read English and Linguistics and Latin. I forget my father's incendiary temper, how he would reduce my mother to tears over some domestic misdemeanour, how he would beat me, over and over again on the hand if I interrupted him, how I failed my first A-level examinations. When I flew in an aircraft – from Kent to the city of Beauvais in the French department of Oise – I was terrified that we would fall out of the sky. If God had intended us to fly, I reasoned, he would have given us wings. The logic was faulty. If he had intended the short-sighted to see, he would have given them spectacles. But of course, it is we who create the products of science, whether or not our abilities to do so are God-given. Only when I was a foreign correspondent would I discover how to overcome my fear of flying – and then after an emergency landing in revolutionary Iran.

Another of Arthur's damned farthings

This is the story of Arthur's farthings. Arthur was my maternal grandfather, a small baker who married above his station – the family of my grandmother Phyllis strongly objected to the match – but who, with his new wife, bought up and ran a very profitable string of cafés across Kent in the 1920s. Arthur Rose was passionate about bowls – he was a member of the English bowls team (chief qualification: lots of money) – and was playing his favourite game in Australia when what our local Maidstone doctor had claimed was arthritis forced him to fly back to England. Wrong diagnosis. Arthur had cancer of the bone.

The farthing – about the size of a euro cent – was a quarter of an old penny. There were 12 pennies in a shilling and 20 shillings to the pound. The farthing was worth 1,000th of a pound. Old British coins seemed very warlike to me; they appeared to be obsessed with crowns and portcullises and warships. I always preferred the Irish equivalent; the currency of 'Eire' was embossed with birds and pigs and horses and harps. The Empire of Power versus the Empire of the Farmyard. But the friendly old British farthing – perhaps because it had so little value – carried the image of a diminutive wren.

Back to Arthur. Phyllis was 'Nana' to me but Arthur – through a two-year-old Robert's misunderstanding of 'Grandpa' – became 'Gabba'. He was a canny man, devoted to

Phyllis but reputedly stingy. After family lunch on Boxing Day, Phyllis would always secretly press a £20 note into my hand, an enormous amount of money for which I had to promise her that I would never tell 'Gabba'. Then Arthur would appear, flourish a £5 note in front of the entire family and with great publicity hand it to me. 'Gosh, thank you Gabba,' crafty little Robert would say loudly, ensuring a total of £25 next Christmas. Phyllis died of cancer when I was thirteen, but when Arthur died five years later my mother Peggy and her sister found dozens of cheques in Arthur's drawer, all signed by Phyllis as gifts to her husband, all uncashed. They thought this was a sign of his refusal to spend money. I suspected it was a gesture of love.

Only when he was dying did I really come to like Arthur. He encouraged me to be a journalist – my father was against it – and loved listening to my classical records as he lay sick in bed at our home in Maidstone. He would sing 'The Volga Boatmen' and, before he became too ill, he taught me to chop down trees. He treated me as a grown-up, which is what all small boys want. He loved his daughters and he admired my dad, Bill, and heard me many times telling Peggy that I was bored or saw me interrupting Bill's television viewing of the Test match. 'Robert needs something to do,' he said. So he ordered 3,000 farthings from the bank; they arrived at our home in Rectory Lane in currency sacks. Arthur walked into our large garden on his crutches and hurled them by the hundred on to the flower beds, behind bushes, around trees, over the long grass in the apple orchard. 'Now, if you find them all,' he announced to his acquisitive grandson, 'I'll give you three pound notes.' In heavy rain or blistering sun, I spent weeks during Arthur's dying months searching through the long grass and the flower beds for his farthings. At first, I collected them daily, by the cupful; then weekly, by the handful. A moment of boredom and Bill and Peggy would send me back into the garden to search again. I might find three or four a week.

But of course, as the years went by and the rains swept across Kent, some of the coins slipped deeper into the soil to poison the roots of my mother's flowers. Others were washed into the flower borders and then moved gently across the flooded lawns. Years after Arthur's death, my father would be pushing the hand-mower over the lawn and there would be a metallic crack and Peggy and I would arrive to find Bill standing beside the machine with its broken blade. 'It must have been another of Arthur's damned farthings,' he'd say. Peggy even found one, around 1996, buried in the thick branch of a tree, six feet above the ground. After her death, I sold Rectory Lane and when I passed by recently, I noticed that the new owners had built an extension over the lawn; I have no doubt that somewhere beneath its concrete foundations those little brass wrens are rotting quietly away.

But I wonder now whether those farthings don't symbolise the legacy of Tony Blair, the man who allowed New Labour to give Britain new dreams to occupy itself with. It all seemed quite harmless. Originally, many believed in him. Parliament even sanctioned the illegal war in Iraq because it trusted him, a decision that has cost more than half a million lives. No, unlike Blair, Arthur never lied. He once announced that he would refuse to pay his local taxes on the grounds that he would rather keep the money for himself (a decision he changed after discovering that Maidstone's borough treasurer – who happened to be my father Bill – would have to take him to court). But Arthur happily sowed his money around our garden, little realising that for years after his demise, his legacy would rise up to break our mower blades and blight my mother's flowers and embed itself in the bark of trees.

Lord Blair's legacy, I fear, will be the same. Long after he was written his self-serving memoirs – indeed, long after he has himself gone to the great White House in the sky – we will find that his political legacy continues to haunt and poison the Middle East and the governance of the United Kingdom.

I never did get to cash in Arthur's coins, of course. He died, in terrible agony, in Maidstone's West Kent Hospital – 'I wish I could drink something that would send me to sleep for ever,' he told a weeping Peggy – long before I had collected even 500 of his 'damned' farthings. I wouldn't wish such a fate on Lord Blair. But I wonder what *our* fate has to be.

The Independent, 17 February 2007

First mate Edward Fisk

A bit of the Fisk family went up in smoke last week. For when the *Cutty Sark* burned, the wooden deck upon which my grandfather Edward once walked – no doubt a little unsteadily in the great storms off the Cape of Good Hope – was turned to cinders.

Edward Fisk was a cantankerous, tough, recalcitrant old man: my father William refused to visit him when he was dying – just as I later refused, foolishly, to visit Bill on his deathbed – complaining that he 'didn't see the point in driving all the way from Maidstone to Birkenhead to see the old man through a glass window'. But when I showed a friend of mine around the *Cutty Sark* back in 1987 – the Thames mist cowling the old tea clipper, much as she must have been smothered when becalmed in the Pacific 100 years earlier – I found an extraordinary photograph on the lower decks. It showed a group of seamen gathered beneath the masts in Sydney Harbour, and one of them – about nineteen or twenty, I'd say – bore my own face as a young man. They say that a man resembles his grandfather more than his father and this was true in my case. Edward Fisk had my eyes, my large forehead; even his hair was combed with a parting on the left. He was smiling, standing to the right of the other seamen. He had been born in 1868, a year before the *Cutty Sark* was built – and long before it became synonymous with a well-known brand of whisky, a beverage with which my grandfather later became too familiar.

By the time Edward was sailing before the mast, the great vessel had abandoned the tea route from China and was carrying wool from Australia. I don't know whether he was aboard when the *Cutty Sark* made its record-breaking trip via the Cape – Bill rather thought he had been – but he ended up as first mate on the legendary clipper and I still possess his sailing manual, passed on to me by my father before he died. Capt. R. S. Cogle's *New Hand Book for Board Trade Examinations* says that a first mate 'must be nineteen years of age and must have served five years at sea.' It is a slim, leather-bound volume of ship's flags and sailing technology; how to turn a four-master around in a gale – it took about five miles minimum – and how to 'compute the latitude from the meridien altitude of a star,' and its very feel made young Robert decide that he would be a merchant seaman when he grew up. (This was not long before I resolved upon being the driver of a steam locomotive.) For what struck me were the ripples on the black leather cover that had almost washed off the gold lettering. They were made of salt, the very physical mark of the massive seas through which my grandfather sailed more than 120 years ago. When my father Bill applied to join the army in the First World War – his first, under-age effort was thwarted by his mother Margaret – his British service log noted that he was 'born 1899 at "Stone House", Leasowe, Wirral, Cheshire'. This was Edward's home and the document lists him as 'Master Mariner Born 1868'.

Margaret – referred to as 'Market Gardner's [*sic*] daughter' – was a year younger than her future husband. 'She was a wonderful, dear woman,' Bill once enthused about her and it was only many years later – in 2004 – that Bill's niece Jean sent me one of those sepia prints so beloved of the Victorian age. It showed Margaret in a very tight, over-flowered dress with a bun, a serious-faced woman – slightly suffering, I thought – who must have found it a fearful experience living with a hard-drinking ex-seaman, even though Edward did become deputy harbourmaster of Birkenhead. 'I came home once with a terrible wound on my head because I had been fighting with some other lads,' Bill told me once. 'My mother was cleaning the floor with a mop and a pail of water and when she saw me she just dipped the mop in the bucket and brought it down on my head. There was blood all over the floor.' Bill said sometimes that his father 'treated my mother terribly' and there were hints from time to time that Edward would return home drunk and beat poor Margaret in front of the children.

Either way, Edward clearly didn't save much money. Before the First World War, Bill was taken from his school 'because my father was no longer able to support me', and apprenticed as a bookkeeper to the borough treasurer's office in Birkenhead. This was his first step – interrupted by the Third Battle of the Somme – towards becoming borough treasurer of Maidstone, a post he held when I was born in 1946. Yet Edward's spirit – he was to die aged ninety-six after recovering from typhoid at ninety-two, and my own father managed to reach the age of ninety-three – lived on. In 1980, at the start of the Iran–Iraq war, I was in the Iraqi port city of Basra when Jon Snow (now of Channel 4 News) was asked to rescue the crew of a British ship trapped in the Shatt al-Arab river. Problem: the Iraqis had no maps of the Shatt al-Arab. But Edward's grandson remembered his father Bill once telling him that Edward said every merchant ship was required to carry charts of the waterways it sailed. And sure enough, the first ship I boarded in Basra provided me with a Royal Navy chart of the Shatt al-Arab. So Jon set off on his successful, crazed mission, courtesy of the *Cutty Sark*'s long-dead first mate.

Seamanship must have been in the family. Only at the end

of the First World War did Bill discover that his grandfather – Edward's dad and my great-grandfather – had fought at Zeebrugge in 1915 as a Royal Naval Reserve officer. The old boy must have been at least seventy. And as a little boy, my father would take me (as well as to the battlefields of the Great War) to Gravesend in Kent to watch the great liners steaming from Tilbury down the Thames for the faraway corners of what was still, in many cases, our empire. The big white P&O ships sailed for India, always chided down river by the red-funnelled 'Sun' tugs that stood alongside at Gravesend.

Edward finally earned Bill's contempt by remarrying within a few months of the generous Margaret's death. Jean went to see the old man in his nursing home some years later and found him deeply sad that he had lost Bill. Which is why his only physical reward to the world is that old, salt-encrusted seaman's manual that survived, safe on my own library shelf, the death of the great ship upon which he once sailed.

The Independent, 26 May 2007

'Come *on*, Sutton!'

When I was at school, I was once beaten by a prefect for reading a book on Czech history at a football match. Sutton Valence was – and remains – a minor public school whose straw boaters and long-distance runs along snow-covered roads and brutal punishments were supposed to mimic those wealthier but even more sadistic character-building sweatshops like Rugby and Eton. Sutton Valence has since moderated its ways, but back in 1960, screaming 'Come *on*, Sutton!' at a bunch of grunting, muddied idiots in blue, black and white shirts was deemed more important than the 1948 defenestration of Jan Masaryk in Prague. A prefect later lashed me with a cane on the orders of a spectacularly cruel housemaster whose unwillingness to prevent the most vicious beatings almost equalled his love of soccer and rugby football.

His memory returned to me as I read the first sports book of my life over Christmas, Franklin Foer's American bestseller *How Soccer Explains the World*.* It confirmed for me what I have always suspected: that football and violence are intimately linked in cause and effect and that – far from the first being an outlet to avoid the second – they are mutually interchangeable. Foer wades in at the deep end with a visit to Belgrade's

* Franklin Foer, *How Soccer Explains the World: An Unlikely Theory of Globalization* (New York, Harper Perennial, 2005).

top-scoring Red Star, a team nurtured by Serbia's equally top war criminal Arkan, who took his well-armed footballers down the Drina Valley in 1992 on an orgy of killing, plunder and mass rape. Arkan drove a pink Cadillac and sported a football wife – the gorgeous retro singer Ceca – whom he married in full Serb military uniform. Red Star's pre-war match against the Croatian Dinamo – beloved of its fascist president Franjo Tudjman – ended in a pitched battle.

It was Margaret Thatcher who famously described football hooligans as 'a disgrace to civilised society' – the very words we later used about the murderers of Serbia. In Glasgow, Protestant supporters of Rangers would sit in separate stands – 'We're up to our knees in Fenian blood,' they would roar in unison – from fans of the Catholic Celtic football club. I well remember, covering the beat in Belfast in the early Seventies, how during Rangers or Celtic matches I would see more RUC cops patrolling the bridge over the Lagan than I would ever come across in a weekday sectarian riot. Come to think of it, the first time I ever saw a uniformed British policeman in France was from the window of the Eurostar – he was patrolling the platform at Lille station before an England–France match.

Vandalism, assault and murder have now become so much a part of European football that it has become a habit. 'Football fan shot dead after racist mob attack,' read a headline as I passed through Paris the other day. Typically, the story – of an off-duty French cop who killed a white supporter of the Paris Saint-Germain team as he screamed anti-Semitic insults while trying to murder a French Jewish fan of Tel-Aviv's Hapoel – was printed on page 27. It is quite normal, you see, for racist football fans to try to kill their opponents – and for the police to open fire.

The connections between football and violence – and, by extension, sadism – are truly frightening. An Irish friend who was a member of the European Union monitoring team in the Balkans recounted to me during the Bosnian war how he witnessed an exchange of bodies between Serb and Croatian armies near the city of Mostar. 'Both sides brought their corpses in sacks on lorries and they backed them up to a small field. But when the Serbs emptied the sacks, it was evident that the heads of their Croatian bodies had been chopped off. I didn't believe what I would see. Right there, in front of the Croats who had brought along their Serbian corpses, the Serbs began playing football with the heads of the dead Croatians. They were laughing because they knew how much this would enrage the Croats.'

Odd, isn't it, how football gets muddied by armies. Whenever an Iraqi soldier or a Druze militiaman or an Egyptian Islamist wants to hold out the hand of friendship to me in the Middle East, he will always announce that he is a fan of Manchester United. In Lebanon, needless to say, teams represent the Shia, Sunni and Christian sects – murdered ex-prime minister Rafiq Hariri was the backer of one, just as Berlusconi became the owner of Milan and just as the Russian oligarchs branched out into football ownership – including British football ownership – as a symbol of their power. Individual players could disgrace themselves – George Best could sink into alcoholism, Zidane could headbutt his opponent for insulting his sister – but the team went on for ever. The immense wealth accrued by football's stars – £10 m in sponsorship reportedly picked up by the Brazilian Pelé – is regarded by the poorest of the poor as a tribute to the human worth of Edson Arantes do Nascimento (the future Pelé), who grew up in the dirt-poor town of Três Corações west of Rio.

It's not all bad, I know. I remember flying into Tehran with the Iranian soccer team in 1997 after they beat Australia in a World Cup qualifier and the outburst of joy that greeted them – the thousands of Iranian women who poured illegally into the Azadi stadium afterwards, the political support the team gave to the reforming but tragically impotent president, Mohamed Khatami – constituted what Franklin Foer calls the Middle East 'football revolution'.

Maybe. But I remember a more disturbing moment in the Middle East when I was investigating one of the many – and all too true – incidents of brutality by British soldiers against Iraqi prisoners. In a Basra hospital, I listened to a badly wounded ex-prisoner of the British army as he described how his tormentors had entered the room in which he and his friends were being held. 'Before they assaulted us, your soldiers gave us all names – the names of world-famous footballers,' he said. 'Then they started beating and kicking us until we screamed and begged for mercy. Why would they do that?'

I suspect I know.

The Independent, 30 December 2006

Cold war nights

In a country of political assassinations, Palestinian battles and constant political crisis, it seemed a romantic idea to send a sprig of lavender-coloured bougainvillea from my Beirut balcony to a friend abroad. The bush was covered in purple, so I snipped off a small bloom and swept it off to DHL for shipment. Nothing so simple, you may say. But that reckons without The State. Hours later, I was summoned to the shipper's office to be solemnly informed that there was a problem. If I took the individual petals off the bloom, I could stuff them into an envelope and off they would go. But if I left them on the stem, complete with twigs, I would need an export permit from the Lebanese Ministry of Agriculture. Aaarrgghhh!

The rationale was simple, of course. However disastrous or fanciful the reality, the machinery of power must continue to exert its baleful influence over our lives, the preservation of authority infinitely more important than us, its integrity supported by massive amounts of money and labour – even though provably worthless.

I am reminded of this by a hobby in which we Kentish schoolboys once indulged: the sending of reception reports – 'double-Rs', we inevitably called them – to Eastern European radio stations during the Cold War. It didn't matter to us that we were helping the communist serpent spread its venom into the living rooms of England. We would listen with rapt attention to the English-language service of Radio Moscow or Radio Prague or Radio Warsaw or Radio Sofia – occasionally, incredibly, even to Radio Tirana – and then send off a postcard to the Communist Beast to report on the audibility of some tedious programme about Bulgarian steelworking, Polish agronomy or Soviet collective farm production. Was there too much static? A little distortion perhaps? Or was this nonsense crossing the Iron Curtain with pristine clarity on Thursday night?

In return, the producers of these awful fictions would send us heaps of books and magazines, most of them groaning with statistics, or photographs of gaily smiling farmers and industrial slaves or beaming autocrats. Few were those of us who did not know the much loved features of Todor Zhivkov or Walter Ulbricht or, indeed, the entire central presidium of the Communist Party of the Soviet Union. Pity the postmen of the Warsaw Pact. The Polish literature came by the double whammy, volumes heavy with grainy wartime photographs of the destruction of Warsaw which linked the villainy of Nazism to the supposedly fascist government of Adenauer and other Western lackeys. The Czechs were by far the smartest; they sent out quite well-produced books on the masterpieces of Prague's art galleries.

Of course, we self-important schoolboys believed that our double-Rs were being discussed at the plenary session of every local party headquarters. Perhaps they were – and who knows what MI5 made of this mass conspiracy by the pupils of Kent's richest schools. I fondly imagined how – from Potsdam to the Urals – legions of Stakhanovite workers were clambering up massive transmitters under pale blue east European skies (copies of my double-Rs in hand, of course) to tamper with the giant cross-pylons and beacons that were sending their socialist message to the world.

I once even sent off a double-R to dear old Radio Eireann in Dublin – only to receive back a black-and-white postcard of De Valerian bleakness, informing me that I need send no more. The Irish, of course, had got the point: the whole fandango was a complete waste of time – just as the entire billion-dollar propaganda radio system of Eastern Europe converted not a single capitalist to the cause of world revolution. The entire thing was a sham, dreamed up by communist bureaucrats to keep other communist bureaucrats happy.

I guess we played the same tune in Britain. I recall how, driving up the A1 with my mum and dad, Peggy Fisk would use her new cine-camera to film the forests of white-painted – but totally unconcealed – anti-aircraft missiles that lay to the right of the highway. We would even picnic beside RAF stations in Lincolnshire while Mum happily filmed away at every creaking Vulcan bomber which soared into the air to threaten the Soviet monolith (and all those radio stations) with its nuclear might. And yes, I still have the film. But what would have happened to her today – a trip to Paddington Green, I imagine – now that we are fighting the 'war on terror'?

For as we all know, this particular spurious conflict is our latest version of the Cold War – as I discovered during an interview with a Spanish journalist and her photographer in London a few months ago. We had, by chance, met at Paddington and I was talking about my childhood delight in loco-spotting (the railway version of double-Rs, I suppose) and I suggested that the photographer might take a picture of me next to a locomotive. So we padded to a platform where a London–Oxford stopping train was about to leave. Yet after a couple of snaps, two members of the British Transport Police arrived in what appeared to be flak jackets and ordered us to stop filming. One of them said that it was 'not permitted' because of the 'terrorist campaign'. I had vivid images of a nest of ETA militants scissoring out our pictures of the Titfield Thunderbolt and packing their explosive equipment before heading for Paddington.

It's the kind of police tomfoolery which I enjoy most. And with reason. For only last month, advertising the brilliance of the new Eurostar terminal, almost every newspaper in Britain carried huge aerial pictures of St Pancras – which showed almost the entire network of rail tracks, switching points, signal gantries and marshalling yards outside the station. I felt sorry for the vulnerable Titfield Thunderbolt over at Paddington. Because, after all, no terrorist would ever dream of attacking the Eurostar, would they, or study the tracking system outside St Pancras from the air? The words 'not permitted' didn't cross the lips of the lads in blue when confronted by the commercial campaign to launch the new Eurostar terminal.

And that's it, I suspect. We create monsters, and then – in the interest of money or bureaucracy – we quietly dismantle them. In the face of evil and incipient civil war, we build transmitters by the thousand or rockets by the million. Our leaders are happy. They have power. And that's what matters. So remember this morning my double-Rs and that sprig of bougainvillea on my balcony.

The Independent, 6 October 2007

'All this talk of special trains . . .'

With a spare hour on my hands before lunch in Lebanon this week, I revisited the joys of my childhood, crunched my way across the old Beirut marshalling yards and climbed aboard a wonderful nineteenth-century rack-and-pinion railway locomotive. Although scarred by bullets, the green paint on the wonderful old Swiss loco still reflects the glories of steam and of the Ottoman Empire. For it was the Ottomans who decided to adorn their jewel of Beirut with the latest state-of-the-art locomotive, a train which once carried the German Kaiser up the mountains above the city where, at a small station called Sofar, the Christian community begged for his protection from the Muslims. 'We are a minority,' they cried, to which the Kaiser bellowed: 'Then become Muslims!'

All my life, I have been fascinated by trains. My mother used to take me down to Maidstone East station in Kent to watch the tank engines pull their local trains in from Ashford or the old Second World War Super Austerity class steamers – big, ugly beasts with a firebox the shape of a squashed toilet roll – with a mile of rusting trucks in tow. Sometimes she would take me one station down the line to Bearsted where my father would be playing golf, the compartment – we travelled first class – filling with smoke in the tunnel beneath Maidstone prison, the old black-out curtains banging against the windows. For days, I would stand on the platform of Tonbridge station and watch the Battle of Britain class locos and the Merchant Navy class and the Schools class (from which, I would later note, my own minor public school, Sutton Valence, was rigorously excluded) as they pummelled through with boat trains to Victoria or Dover. The Golden Arrow, in those pre-Eurostar days, was the joy of every loco-spotter, its cream and gold carriages hauled by an engine with the British and French flags snapping from the boiler. We all held that train lovers' bible in our hands, Ian Allen's loco-spotter's guide to engine numbers.

I used to think all this was a fetish until I realised how deeply the railway system had permeated art. Turner was obsessed with trains. Tolstoy's Anna Karenina falls in love on a train journey, decides to leave her husband on a railway platform and commits suicide by throwing herself in front of a goods train. 'And exactly at the moment when the space between the wheels drew level with her . . . and with a light movement, as though she would rise again at once, sank on to her knees . . . something huge and relentless struck her on the head and dragged her down on her back. "God forgive me everything!" she murmured.' Tolstoy even died in a railway station. Part of Pasternak's *Doctor Zhivago* revolves around his flight from Moscow by rail, his sight of Strelnikov's revolutionary locomotive and his subsequent trek back to Lara down a partially snow-covered track. The film's treatment of this is not as good as the book's, where a female barber warns Zhivago that he risks arrest with 'all this talk of special trains'.

The point was that all trains were 'special'. My mother took early colour film of ten-year-old Robert watching the big cream and red 'Trans Europe Express' – a diesel-hauled all-first-class train – sliding into Freiburg station in Germany in 1956. But equally special was a wind-up model 'O'-gauge steam loco which my father brought me back from Germany, where he had been aiding the postwar reconstruction of Hamburg. Being

German, it was so powerful that it once flew off its English Hornby tracks, raced across the front hall carpet, jumped the front door step of our home and struck out across the drive, coming to rest under my father's car. When the Lebanese authorities briefly restored the coastal line from east Beirut to the Crusader port of Byblos, I travelled its length in the driving cab of a big Polish diesel. It pulled just one wooden carriage – an import from the British Empire's Indian empire after the 1914–18 war – and travelled at no more than 15 miles per hour because the Lebanese, being Lebanese, insisted on parking their cars on the track when they went swimming.

Despite the great liners of the world and the growth of air power, leaders – especially dictators – loved trains. Hitler had his own luxurious train, complete with mobile flak batteries. So did Goering, and so did Himmler. And Tito. Soviet commissars loved trains. And trains, of course, became accessories to murder. Turkish railways carried thousands of Armenians to their places of massacre. European trains carried millions of Jews and gypsies to their annihilation. The steam train whistle which permeates D. H. Lawrence's *Sons and Lovers* had a quite different connotation as it drifted over the snowfields around Auschwitz.

Somehow, airports never captured the magic of railway stations. Name me an air version of Saint Pancras or the Gare du Nord or Grand Central. But it was years before I grasped – I think – just what the fascination of trains involves. It's about the track, the rails, the permanent way as much as the locomotives. At Edinburgh Waverley, you can look at the twin rails and know that, with points and unwelded track and occasional changes of width, those minutely shaped ramrods of iron stretch unbroken from Scotland via the Channel Tunnel to Turkey or Saint Petersburg or Vladivostok or – save for the Iraqi insurgents who keep blowing up the permanent way – to Baghdad.

I suspect this sense of continuity appeals to us. An airliner might fly a route, but never through the same stretch of air. Nor does a ship pass through exactly the same waters each voyage. But the train will always travel – to an inch – along precisely the same journey as it took yesterday or a hundred years ago, the same journey that it will take next week and in a hundred years from now.

In the overgrown Beirut marshalling yards, the tracks are still visible, maintaining a ghostly continuum with the past, reminding us of the permanence of history and power and – in its worst performance of industrialised murder – of death. Which is why, I suppose, trains capture our imagination and fear from childhood to old age.

The Independent, 12 February 2005

Fear of flying

I'm writing this in a strange hiatus known to all foreign correspondents. My plane never took off from Paris – en route to Beirut – because snow closed down Charles de Gaulle airport. It happens to all of us. When we should be heading to war or interviewing the participants of velvet, orange or cedar revolutions, we are queuing for the return of our checked baggage and taking the taxi home because that staple of our existence – the *sine qua non* of all travel, the most technologically sophisticated creature we will ever aspire to touch – can't land in ice. Or it doesn't have Cat-3 landing capability. Or maybe the reverse thrust of the Airbus A-320–400 series can't cope with the weather.

Yes, we journos fly so much that we pick up huge amounts of highly detailed and utterly useless information about aircraft. Want to know about the torque capability of a Bell/Agusta helicopter, the avionics of a Boeing 777, the seat configuration of the MD-111? Well, I'm your man. Along with heaps of appalling knowledge about injuries – I will not entertain you with the details of sucking wounds and emergency tracheotomies – reporters probably know more about aircraft than many of the cabin crews.

I'm sure this applies to the old Afghan Ariana airlines jets when they were flying under the Taliban. Back in 1997, I was on my way to Afghanistan – to see Osama bin Laden, no less

– and could only find a flight to Jalalabad from the old Trucial state of Sharjah, a home for pariah aircraft like the old Boeing 727 that was waiting for me on the runway. On boarding, however, I found that only the first row of seats remained in place. The rest of the aircraft was taken up by large wooden boxes containing 'mechanical imports', according to the crew, each heavy crate chained to the floor of the plane. Even more trouble was the forward lavatory. For only minutes after take-off, the door opened of its own accord and a dark tide of sewage slowly washed over our shoes and then surged down the cabin. I didn't feel like an in-flight meal. I was sitting next to two Afghans, the second of whom – vastly bearded to abide by the Taliban's tonsorial rules – was dressed only in jeans and open-necked shirt and who kept glaring at me while squeezing and resqueezing a large and very dirty oil rag in his left hand. Over Kandahar, we flew into heavy turbulence, the plane bucking about, the chains clanking as the wooden boxes tried to move across the cabin, the tide of sewage revisiting us from the forward lavatory. It was at this point that the purser arrived at my seat. 'Mr Fisk, you are our only passenger and you have no need to worry about your safety,' he said. 'You see, you have the honour to be sitting' – and here he pointed at the bearded, hostile figure to my left – 'next to our senior flight engineer.'

Ah, for the pleasures of Air France. This was the airline which once calculated that – if I included all my transatlantic lecture trips, my aerial treks for *The Independent* and a host of other appointments around the world – I travel more frequently than every Air France crew member. This also accounts for the fact that I almost always know some of the crew when I'm flying to Los Angeles or New York – and why, not long ago, one of their flight attendants met me with the sort of greeting that gives journalists a bad name. '*Ah, Monsieur Fisk, après le décollage, c'est un gin-tonic, oui?*' Oh *oui* indeed dear reader, for I have to explain at once that I am frightened of flying.

It began when I endured a crash landing at Tehran airport just after the Islamic revolution. The front wheel failed to emerge from its pod before landing – for aerobuffs, it was a Boeing 737, but Iran was now under UN sanctions – and the plane came down on grass with the biggest bang I have ever heard in my life. No lives were lost. But almost immediately afterwards, the fuselage filled with thick clouds of blue smoke, which – I realised after a few seconds – was every terrified passenger lighting cigarettes at the same moment. I returned to Lebanon with about the worst case of flying fear in the history of the world.

Fortunately, I knew every pilot then working for Lebanon's Middle East Airlines – they were flying the mighty old 707s in those civil war days – and one of them immediately told me to turn up next morning for a series of Boeing test flights out of Beirut airport in stormy weather. He sat me down behind his pilot seat on the flight deck, poured me a huge glass of champagne, strapped earphones on to my head and took off into the kind of turbulence seen only in the movie *The Day After Tomorrow*. He flew the empty airliner over the desolate, frothing Mediterranean, turned around, landed on runway 1-18, took off again into the storm, landed and went on and on – each take-off accompanied by another glass of champagne – until, after 14 take-offs and landings, I was giggling like a baby. I never lost my fear of flying – but I no longer believed I would die every time I boarded a plane.

Deep down, of course, like almost everyone I know, I don't believe in powered flight. I simply do not accept that it is natural to tie oneself to a seat in a metal tube and hurl oneself into the sky at 500 miles per hour for seven hours, with or without a gin and tonic. And I have come to realise that I employ my old friend, the willing suspension of disbelief.

The Independent, 5 March 2005

CHAPTER SEVEN

The old mandates

Under the 1919 Treaty of Versailles, Britain and France, the principal victors of the First World War, received mandates from the League of Nations – predecessor of today's United Nations – to govern most of the Levant. The British were given Palestine, Transjordan and Iraq; the French received Syria (and, initially, northern Iraq). The French government tore off the south-west corner of Syria and created the state of 'Greater Lebanon'.

God damn that democracy

Hamas won its Palestinian election victory on 26 January 2006 and has been ostracised ever since. Israeli prime minister Ehud Olmert said Israel would not negotiate with a Palestinian government that included Hamas. Sanctions were placed on Gaza and the West Bank by both Israel and the West. President Mahmoud Abbas's Fatah movement, which won only 43 of the 132 seats in the Palestinian parliament, threatened new elections – and is now regarded by the international community as the only 'legitimate' Palestinian authority.

Oh no, not more democracy again! Didn't we award this to those Algerians in 1990? And didn't they reward us with that nice gift of an Islamist government – and then they so benevolently cancelled the second round of elections? Thank goodness for that! True, the Afghans elected a round of representatives, albeit that they included warlords and murderers. But then the Iraqis last year elected the Dawa party to power in Baghdad, which was responsible – let us not speak this in Washington – for most of the kidnappings of Westerners in Beirut in the 1980s, the car bombing of the (late) Emir and the US and French embassies in Kuwait.

And now, horror of horrors, the Palestinians have elected the wrong party to power. They were supposed to give their support to the friendly, pro-Western, corrupt, absolutely pro-

American Fatah, which had promised to 'control' them, rather than to Hamas, which said they would represent them. And, bingo, they have chosen the wrong party again. Result: Hamas wins 76 out of 132 seats to Hamas. That just about does it. God damn that democracy. What are we to do with people who don't vote the way they should?

Way back in the 1930s, the British would lock up the Egyptians who turned against the government of King Farouk. Thus they began to set the structure of anti-democratic governance that was to follow. The French imprisoned the Lebanese government which demanded the same freedom. Then the French left Lebanon. But we have always expected the Arab governments to do what they are told. So today we are expecting the Syrians to behave, the Iranians to kowtow to our nuclear desires (though they have done nothing illegal), and the North Koreans to surrender their weapons (though they actually do have them, and therefore cannot be attacked).

Now let the burdens of power lie heavy on the shoulders of the party. Now let the responsibilities of people lie upon them. We British would never talk to the IRA, or to Eoka, or to the Mau Mau. But in due course Gerry Adams, Archbishop Makarios and Jomo Kenyatta came to take tea with the Queen. The Americans would never speak to their enemies in North Vietnam. But they did. In Paris. No, al-Qaeda will not do that. But the Iraqi leaders of the insurgency in Mesopotamia will. They talked to the British in 1920, and they will talk to the Americans. Back in 1983, Hamas talked to the Israelis. They spoke directly to them about the spread of mosques and religious teaching. The Israeli army boasted about this on the front page of the *Jerusalem Post*. At that time, it looked like the PLO was not going to abide by the Oslo resolutions. There seemed nothing wrong, therefore, with continuing talks with Hamas. So how come talks with Hamas now seem so impossible?

Not long after the Hamas leadership had been hurled into southern Lebanon, a leading member of its organisation heard me say that I was en route to Israel. 'You'd better call Shimon Peres,' he told me. 'Here's his home number.' The phone number was correct. Here was proof that members of the hierarchy of the most extremist movements among the Palestinians were talking to senior Israeli politicians.

The Israelis know well the Hamas leadership. And the Hamas leadership know well the Israelis. There is no point in journalists like us suggesting otherwise. Our enemies invariably turn out to be our greatest friends, and our friends turn out, sadly, to be our enemies. A terrible equation – except that we must understand our fathers' history. My father bequeathed to me a map in which the British and French ruled the Middle East. The Americans have tried, vainly, to rule that map since the Second World War. They have all failed. And it remains our curse to rule it since.

How terrible it is to speak with those who have killed our sons. How unspeakable it is to converse with those who have our brothers' blood on their hands. No doubt that is how Americans who believed in independence felt about the Englishmen who fired upon them. It will be for the Iraqis to deal with al-Qaeda. This is their burden. Not ours. Yet throughout history we have ended up talking to our enemies. We talked to the representatives of the emperor of Japan. In the end, we had to accept the surrender of the German Reich from the successor to Adolf Hitler. And today, we trade happily with the Japanese, the Germans and the Italians. The Middle East was never a successor to Nazi Germany or Fascist Italy, despite the rubbish talked by Messrs Bush and Blair. How long will it be before we can throw away the burden of this most titanic of wars and see our future, not as our past, but as a reality?

Surely, in an age when our governments no longer contain men or women who have experienced war, we must now lead a people with the understanding of what war means. Not Hollywood. Not documentary films. Democracy means real freedom, not just for the people we choose to have voted into power.

And that is the problem in the Middle East.

And now, horror of horrors, the Palestinians have elected the wrong party to power.

The Independent, 28 January 2006

Gold-plated taps

In a series of vicious street battles in June 2007, Hamas gunmen routed Fatah across the Gaza Strip. Hamas smothered all political dissent after 118 Palestinians were killed and 550 wounded in the fighting. Sporadic battles between the two Palestinian factions continued into 2008.

How troublesome the Muslims of the Middle East are. First, we demand that the Palestinians embrace democracy and then they elect the wrong party – Hamas – and then Hamas wins a mini civil war and presides over the Gaza Strip. And we Westerners still want to negotiate with the discredited President, Mahmoud Abbas. Today 'Palestine' – and let's keep those quotation marks in place – has two prime ministers. Welcome to the Middle East.

Who can we negotiate with? To whom do we talk? Well of course, we should have talked to Hamas months ago. But we didn't like the democratically elected government of the Palestinian people. They were supposed to vote for Fatah and its corrupt leadership. But they voted for Hamas, which declines to recognise Israel or abide by the totally discredited Oslo agreement. No one asked – on our side – which particular Israel Hamas was supposed to recognise. The Israel of 1948? The Israel of the post-1967 borders? The Israel that builds – and goes on building – vast settlements for Jews and Jews only on Arab land, gobbling up even more of the 22 per cent of 'Palestine' still left to negotiate over?

And so today we are supposed to talk to our faithful policeman, Mr Abbas, the 'moderate' (as the BBC, CNN and Fox News refer to him) Palestinian leader, a man who wrote a 600-page book about Oslo without once mentioning the word 'occupation', who always referred to Israeli 'redeployment' rather than 'withdrawal', a 'leader' we can trust because he wears a tie and goes to the White House and says all the right things. The Palestinians didn't vote for Hamas because they wanted an Islamic republic – which is how Hamas's bloody victory will be represented – but because they were tired of the corruption of Mr Abbas's Fatah and the rotten nature of the 'Palestinian Authority'.

I recall years ago being summoned to the home of a PA official whose walls had just been punctured by an Israeli tank shell. All true. But what struck me were the gold-plated taps in his bathroom. Those taps – or variations of them – were what cost Fatah its election. Palestinians wanted an end to corruption – the cancer of the Arab world – and so they voted for Hamas and thus we, the all-wise, all-good West, decided to sanction them and starve them and bully them for exercising their free vote. Maybe we should offer 'Palestine' EU membership if it would be gracious enough to vote for the right people? All over the Middle East, it is the same. We support Hamid Karzai in Afghanistan, even though he keeps warlords and drug barons in his government (and, by the way, we really are sorry about all those innocent Afghan civilians we are killing in our 'war on terror' in the wastelands of Helmand province).

We love Hosni Mubarak of Egypt, whose torturers have not yet finished with the Muslim Brotherhood politicians recently arrested outside Cairo, whose presidency received the warm support of Mrs – yes Mrs – George W. Bush, and whose succession will almost certainly pass to his son, Gamal.

We adore Muammar Ghadafi, the crazed dictator of Libya whose werewolves have murdered his opponents abroad, whose plot to murder King Abdullah of Saudi Arabia preceded Tony Blair's recent visit to Tripoli – Colonel Ghadafi, it should be remembered, was called a 'statesman' by Jack Straw for abandoning his non-existent nuclear ambitions – and whose 'democracy' is perfectly acceptable to us because he is on our side in the 'war on terror'.

Yes, and we love King Abdullah's unconstitutional monarchy in Jordan, and all the princes and emirs of the Gulf, especially those who are paid such vast bribes by our arms companies that even Scotland Yard has to close down its investigations on the orders of our prime minister – and yes, I can indeed see why he doesn't like *The Independent*'s coverage of what he quaintly calls 'the Middle East'. If only the Arabs – and the Iranians – would support our kings and shahs and princes whose sons and daughters are educated at Oxford and Harvard, how much easier the 'Middle East' would be to control.

For that is what it is about – control – and that is why we hold out, and withdraw, favours from their leaders. Now Gaza belongs to Hamas, what will our own elected leaders do? Will our pontificators in the EU, the UN, Washington and Moscow now have to talk to these wretched, ungrateful people (fear not, for they will not be able to shake hands) or will they have to acknowledge the West Bank version of Palestine (Abbas, the safe pair of hands) while ignoring the elected, militarily successful Hamas in Gaza? It's easy, of course, to call down a curse on both their houses. But that's what we say about the whole Middle East. If only Bashar al-Assad wasn't president of Syria (heaven knows what the alternative would be) or if the cracked President Mahmoud Ahmadinejad wasn't in control of Iran (even if he doesn't actually know one end of a nuclear missile from the other).

If only Lebanon was a home-grown democracy like our

own little back-lawn countries – Belgium, for example, or
Luxembourg. But no, those wretched Middle Easterners vote
for the wrong people, support the wrong people, love the
wrong people, don't behave like us civilised Westerners.

So what will we do? Support the reoccupation of Gaza perhaps? Certainly we will not criticise Israel. And we shall go on
giving our affection to the kings and princes and unlovely
presidents of the Middle East until the whole place blows up
in our faces and then we shall say – as we are already saying
of the Iraqis – that they don't deserve our sacrifice and our
love.

How do we deal with a coup d'état by an elected government?

The Independent, 16 June 2007

The man who will never apologise

I suppose that astonishment is not the word for it. Stupefaction comes to mind. I simply could not believe my ears in Beirut when a phone call told me that Lord Blair of Kut al-Amara was going to create 'Palestine'. I checked the date – no, it was not 1 April – but I remain overwhelmed that this vain, deceitful man, this proven liar, a trumped-up lawyer who has the blood of thousands of Arab men, women and children on his hands, is really contemplating being 'our' Middle East envoy.

Can this really be true? I had always assumed that Balfour, Sykes and Picot were the epitome of Middle Eastern hubris. But Blair? That this ex-prime minister, this man who took his country into the sands of Iraq, should actually believe that he has a role in the region – he whose own ridiculous envoy, Lord Levy, made so many secret trips there to absolutely no avail – is now going to sully his hands (and, I fear, our lives) in the world's last colonial war, is simply overwhelming.

Of course, he'll be in touch with Mahmoud Abbas, will try to marginalise Hamas, will talk endlessly about 'moderates'; and we'll have to listen to him pontificating about morality, how he's absolutely and completely confident that he's doing the right thing (and this, remember, is the same man who postponed a ceasefire in Lebanon last year in order to share George Bush's forlorn hope of an Israeli victory over Hizballah) in bringing peace to the Middle East . . .

Not once – ever – has he apologised. Not once has he said he was sorry for what he did in our name. Yet Blair actually believes – in what must be a record act of self-indulgence for a man who cooked up the fake evidence of Iraq's 'weapons of mass destruction' – that he can do good in the Middle East. For here is a man who is totally discredited in the region – a politician who has signally failed in everything he ever tried to do in the Middle East – now believing that he is the right man to lead the Quartet to patch up 'Palestine'. In the hunt for quislings to do our bidding – i.e. accept even less of Mandate Palestine than Arafat would stomach – I suppose Blair has his uses. His unique blend of ruthlessness and dishonesty will no doubt go down quite well with our local Arab dictators.

And I have a suspicion – always assuming this extraordinary story is not untrue – that Blair will be able to tour around Damascus, even Tehran, in his hunt for 'peace', thus paving the way for an American exit strategy in Iraq. But 'Palestine'? The Palestinians held elections – real, copper-bottomed ones, the democratic variety – and Hamas won. But Blair will presumably not be able to talk to Hamas. He'll need to talk only to Abbas's flunkies, to negotiate with an administration described so accurately this week by my old colleague Rami Khoury as a 'government of the imagination'.

The Americans are talking – and here I am quoting the State Department spokesman, Sean McCormack – about an envoy who can work 'with the Palestinians in the Palestinian system' to develop institutions for a 'well-governed state'. Oh yes, I can see how that would appeal to Lord Blair. He likes well-governed states, lots of 'terror laws', plenty of security – though I'm still a bit puzzled about what the 'Palestinian system' is meant to be. It was James Wolfensohn who was originally 'our' Middle East envoy, a former World Bank president who left in frustration because he could neither reconstruct Gaza nor work with a 'peace process' that was being eroded with every new Jewish settlement and every Qassam rocket fired into Israel. Does Blair think he can do better? What honeyed words will we hear?

I bet he doesn't mention the Israeli wall which is taking so much extra land from the Palestinians. It will be a 'security barrier' or a 'fence' (like the famous Berlin 'fence' which was actually called a 'security barrier' by those generous East German Vopo cops of the time). There will be appeals for restraint on all sides, endless calls for 'moderation', none at all for justice. And Israel likes Lord Blair. Indeed, Blair's slippery use of language is likely to appeal to Ehud Olmert, whose government continues to take Arab land as he waits to discover a Palestinian with whom he can 'negotiate', Mahmoud Abbas now having the prestige of a rabbit after his forces were crushed in Gaza. Which of 'Palestine's two prime ministers will Blair talk to? Why, the one with a collar and tie, of course, who works for Mr Abbas, who will demand more 'security', tougher laws, less democracy.

Once, our favourite trouble-shooter was James Baker – who worked for George W.'s father until the Israelis got tired of him – and before that we had a whole list of UN secretary generals who visited the region, frowned and warned of serious consequences if peace did not come soon. I recall another man with Blair's pomposity, a certain Kurt Waldheim, who – no longer the UN's boss – actually believed he could be an 'envoy' for peace in the Middle East, despite his wartime career as an intelligence officer for the Wehrmacht's Army Group 'E'. His visits – especially to the late King Hussein – came to nothing, of course. But Waldheim's ability to draw a curtain over his wartime past does have one thing in common with Blair. For Waldheim steadfastly, pointedly, repeatedly, refused to acknowledge – ever – that he had done anything wrong. Now who does that remind you of?

The Independent, 23 June 2007

The 'lady' in seat 1K

My seat on the Middle East Airlines 747 flying to Beirut was 1K, but Mstislav Rostropovich had put his 'wife' in it – a six-foot white plastic case containing the cello he would play in Baalbek, the casket neatly strapped in with a red safety belt. 'I call it my wife because a violin is feminine in the Russian language,' the great man announced. 'So you can sit on the other side of me.'

Offered a Beirut newspaper, the world's greatest cellist brandished a bundle of Russian papers. 'I don't think you have these on board,' he told the stewardess. And thus he avoided news of Israel's forty-seventh air raid on Lebanon this year, further ceasefire violations in the south of the country, the Israeli shelling of Habbouch and the Lebanese government's determination to prevent any further civil disobedience of the variety created by Shia Muslim clerics this month in Baalbek – the very city in which he, Rostropovich, would be playing Dvorak's Cello Concerto in A Major.

'Baalbek is so beautiful,' he enthused. 'It is the heart of beauty in the Middle East – I want to embrace these people with my music. I will try so hard for them. Their president is a Christian, their prime minister is a Muslim. Music is for everyone.' Rostropovich, it seemed, had adopted Lebanon's view of itself, a corner of paradise in which war, however unwisely, can be forgotten, in which religious coexistence –

whose breakdown cost 150,000 lives in Lebanon's 1975–90 civil war – can be held up as the cornerstone of the nation.

I had gloomily prepared myself for a diet of Perrier all the way to Beirut – musicians being parsimonious creatures – but Rostropovich knocked back a Black Label after take-off and launched eagerly into Lebanon's finest Ksara 1994 red wine over lunch. I had forgotten he was a Russian. When the stewardess handed him the first class menu, he gave it to me. 'Do you know why I'm choosing *langouste à la russe*?' he asked. 'No? Because in all the forty-seven years I lived in Russia before my exile, I never tasted *langouste à la russe* until I reached the West.' And he wolfed down the lobster like a starving man.

He had no worries about returning to Lebanon thirty years after his last performance at the Baalbek Festival. 'There is peace,' he said matter-of-factly. No wonder the Lebanese love this man; he reflects their dreams. Only two weeks ago, I had been sitting in the Beit Eddin palace in the Chouf mountains, watching the greatest dancers of the Bolshoi ballet perform Tchaikovsky and Khachaturian beneath a pageant of stars. Just 20 miles away, the Israelis were shelling the Hizballah.

Down the aisle of the 747 strode its pilot, Captain Ramzi Najjar. Would Rostropovich like to autograph his programme of that Baalbek performance thirty years ago? From the pages in front of the short, plump seventy-year-old musician stared a man from the past, slim and thin-faced, smiling into the camera, the columns of the Roman Temple of Jupiter behind, in his hand the very same cello that now sat beside him in seat 1K. 'When I came the last time, I had to travel from Belgrade to Rome on Yugoslav Airlines, to Athens on Alitalia and then to Beirut on MEA and when I landed it was only an hour before the concert was due to start in Baalbek,' he said. 'I knew it took two hours by road to Baalbek. But they had a helicopter waiting for me and they flew me right in among the Roman temples. The crowds were clapping and then they were all covered in a storm of dust and dirt from the rotor-blades and I stepped off the helicopter like someone from another planet. That was the night the first men landed on the moon.'

The inspiration for the festival came in 1922, when Henri Gouraud, the one-armed French general who tore Lebanon out of the body of Syria and created a new and dangerous nation for the Christians, stood amid the Roman temples one moonlit night and quoted Racine. By the time Rostropovich was planning his first visit, Ella Fitzgerald had sung at Baalbek. Jean Cocteau was there and Sviatoslav Richter, Herbert von Karajan and Joan Baez and the Egyptian singer beloved of President Nasser, Um Khaltum.

Rostropovich was nursing two passports in his jacket pocket for Lebanon's immigration men: a Swiss visitor's passport and a Monaco service passport, both of which require visas for the rest of Europe. 'I was told by friends in the West that I could have a British passport or an American or French one,' he told me. 'But I didn't want to legitimise my exile from Russia.' Continuity was what he was after, and the Lebanese would understand him. In Baalbek last night, along with the Radio France Philharmonic Orchestra, he was playing the Dvorak concerto again, just as he did thirty years ago.

A few hours earlier and only 200 miles further south, Jerusalem bombs had killed at least twelve innocent men and women. 'When the cannons speak, the music stops,' Rostropovich had told me on our flight to Beirut. And those cannons, I couldn't help thinking, may be speaking again very soon.

The Independent, 31 July 1997

Mstislav Rostropovich died, aged eighty, in April 2007. 'He gave Russian culture worldwide fame,' Alexander Solzhenitsyn said. 'Farewell, beloved friend.'

Whatever you do, don't mention the war

How on earth do you celebrate a civil war? This is no idle question because in Beirut the Lebanese – with remarkable candour but not a little trepidation – are preparing to remember that most terrible of conflicts in their lives, one that killed 150,000 and whose commemoration next week was originally in the hands of the former prime minister Rafiq Hariri, who was himself assassinated on 14 February. Is this something that should be contemplated? Is this the moment – when all Lebanon waits for a Syrian military withdrawal and when the Hizballah militia, itself a creature of that war, is being ordered to disarm by the United Nations – to remember the tide of blood that drowned so many innocents between 1975 and 1990?

On reflection, I think it probably is. The Lebanese have spent the past fifteen years in a political coma, refusing to acknowledge their violent past lest the ghosts arise from their mass graves and return to stir the embers of sectarianism and mutual suffering. 'Whatever you do, don't mention the war' had a special place in a country whose people stubbornly refused to learn the lessons of their fratricidal slaughter. For almost ten years, my own book on the civil war was banned by Lebanon's censors. Hariri himself told me he was powerless to put it back into the shops – ironically, it was a pro-Syrian security official whose resignation the Lebanese opposition is now demanding who lifted the ban last year – and none of Lebanon's television stations would touch the war. It remained the unspoken cancer in Lebanese society, the malaise which all feared might return to poison their lives.

There clearly was a need to understand how the conflict destroyed the old Lebanon. When al-Jazeera broadcast from Qatar a twelve-part documentary series about the war, the seaside Corniche outside my home in Beirut would empty of strollers every Thursday night; restaurants would close their doors. Everyone wanted to watch their own torment. So, I suppose, did I.

Everyone I knew lost friends in those awful fifteen years – I lost some very dear friends of my own. One was blown up in the US embassy on his first day of work in 1983; another was murdered with an ice-pick. One, a young woman, was killed by a shell in a shopping street. The brother of a colleague – a young man who helped to maintain my telex lines during the 1982 Israeli siege of Beirut – was shot in the head when he accidentally drove past a gun battle. He died a few days later.

And so this 13 April the centre of Beirut is to be filled with tens of thousands of Lebanese for a day of 'unity and memory'. There will be art exhibitions, concerts, photo exhibitions, a running and cycling marathon. Hariri's sister Bahia will be staging the events her murdered brother had planned. Nora Jumblatt, the wife of the Druze leader Walid Jumblatt – one of the warlords of those ghastly days – will be organising the musical concerts.

The original 13 April – in 1975 – marked the day when Phalangist gunmen ambushed a busload of Palestinians in Beirut. The bus still exists, the bullet holes still punctured through its rusting skin, but it will be left to rot in the field outside Nabatea where it lies to this day. The only bullet holes visible to the crowds next week will be the ones deliberately preserved in the statue of Lebanon's 1915 independence leaders, who were hanged in Martyrs' Square, where a 'garden of forgiveness' connects a church and a mosque and where Hariri's body now rests, along with his murdered bodyguards. The square itself was the front line for the entire war. Who knows how many ghosts still haunt its hundreds of square metres? Not far to the east is the infamous 'Ring' highway where Muslim and Christian gunmen stopped all traffic in 1975 and walked down the rows of stalled cars with knives, calmly slitting the throats of families of the wrong religion. Eight Christians had been found murdered outside the electricity headquarters and Bashir Gemayel directed that eighty Muslims must pay with their lives. The militias kept on multiplying the figures. When you are in a war, you feel it will never end. I felt like that, gradually coming to believe – like the Lebanese – that war was somehow a natural state of affairs.

And, like all wars, it acquired a kind of momentum *de la folie*. The Israelis invaded, twice; the American Marines came and were suicide-bombed in their base at the airport. So were the French. The United Nations arrived in 1978 with Dutch soldiers and more French soldiers and Irish soldiers and Norwegian soldiers and Fijians and Nepalese and Ghanaians and Finns. Everyone, it seemed, washed up in Lebanon to be bombed and sniped at. The Palestinians were slowly drawn into the war and suffered massacre after massacre at the hands of their enemies (who often turned out to be just about everybody). That the conflict was really between Christian Maronites and the rest somehow disappeared from the narrative. It was everyone else's fault. Not the Lebanese. Never the Lebanese. For years, they called the war *hawadess*, the 'events'. The conflict was then called the 'War of the Other' – of the foreigners, not of the Lebanese who were actually doing the killing.

A taxi-driver who gave me a lift several years ago turned to me as we were driving through the streets and said: 'Mr Robert, you are very lucky.' And he meant that I – like him – had survived the war. I remember the last day. The Syrians had bombed General Michel Aoun out of his palace at Baabda – in those days, the Americans were keen on Syrian domination of Lebanon because they wanted the soldiers of Damascus to face off Saddam's army of occupation in Kuwait – and I was walking behind tanks towards the Christian hills. Shells came crashing down around us and my companion shouted that we were going to die. And I shouted back to her that we mustn't die, that this was the last day of the war, that it would really now end. And when we got to Baabda, there were corpses and many people lying with terrible wounds, many in tears. And I remember how we, too, broke down and cried with the immense relief of living through the day and knowing that we would live tomorrow and the day after that and next week and next year.

But the silences remained, the constant fear that it could all reignite. No one would open the mass graves in case more blood was poured into them. It was in this sombre, ruined land that Hariri started to rebuild Beirut. It will be his new Beirut that will host next week's brave festivities, its smart shops and stores and restaurants and bars – despite Hariri's murder and the continuing crisis and the dark bombers who are still trying to re-provoke the civil war. That Lebanon's war did not restart with Hariri's murder is a sign of the people's maturity and of their wisdom, especially the vast sea of young Lebanese who were educated abroad during the conflict and who do not – and, I suspect, will not – tolerate another civil war. And so I think the Lebanese are right to confront their demons next week. Let them celebrate. Never mind the ghosts.

The Independent, 9 April 2005

Even after the murder of their ex-prime minister Rafiq Hariri in February 2005, the Lebanese continued to believe that their fifteen-year civil war would not return to destroy them again. The subsequent murder of at least seven prominent Lebanese journalists, writers and politicians in the following three years – and a series of bitter street confrontations between Muslims and Christians in early 2007 – however, suggested that the ghosts were still around.

'The best defender on earth of Lebanon's sovereignty'

I couldn't help a deep, unhealthy chuckle when I watched the French foreign minister, Philippe Douste-Blazy, arrive outside the wooden doors of Saint George's Maronite Cathedral in Beirut this week. A throb of applause drifted through the tens of thousands of Lebanese who had gathered for the funeral of murdered industry minister Pierre Gemayel.* Here, after all, was the representative of the nation which had supported the eviction of the Syrian army last year, whose president had been a friend of the likewise murdered ex-prime minister Rafiq Hariri, whose support in the UN Security Council was helping to set up the tribunal which will – will it, we ask ourselves in Beirut these days? – try the killers of both Hariri and Gemayel.

Douste-Blazy was aware of all this, of course, and uttered a statement of such self-serving exaggeration that even Lord Blair of Kut al-Amara would have felt jealous. 'President Jacques Chirac is the best defender on earth of Lebanon's sovereignty,' he proclaimed. 'France is determined . . . now more than ever [to] defend Lebanon's sovereignty and independence.' Now I'm not sure I would want the man who once embraced Saddam Hussein as a close friend to be my greatest defender, let alone

---

* Pierre Gemayel, grandson of the founder of the Phalange Party in Lebanon, was shot dead in his car in east Beirut on 21 November 2006. The culprits – in company with every other political assassin in Lebanon – have never been found.

my greatest defender 'on earth' – funny, isn't it, how the French can never shake off their Napoleonic self-regard – and like the doggy poo on Parisian streets, I'd certainly want to tread carefully around France's interest in Lebanon's 'independence'.

I hasten to add that – compared with the mendacious, utterly false, repulsively hypocritical and cancerous foreign policy of Dame Beckett of Basra* – Chirac's dealings with France's former colonies and mandates are positively Christlike in their integrity. But the Lebanon that France was to create after the First World War was to be based on the sectarian divisions which the infamous François Georges-Picot had observed earlier as a humble consul in this jewel of the old Ottoman Empire, divided as it was between Shia Muslims and Sunni Muslims and Druze and Christian Maronites – France's favourite community and the faith of the murdered Pierre Gemayel – and the Greek Orthodox and the Greek Catholics and the Chaldeans and the rest. At that time the Maronites represented a thin majority, but emigration and their propensity for smaller families than their Muslim neighbours steadily turned the Christians into a minority that may now number 29 per cent or less. But the French wanted the Maronites to run Lebanon and thus after independence bequeathed them the presidency. Sunni Muslims would hold the prime ministership and the Shias, who are today the largest community, would be compensated by holding the speakership of parliament. The French thus wanted Lebanon's 'independence' – but they wanted it to be in France's favour.

Two problems immediately presented themselves to the Lebanese. By claiming the largest area which it was possible to rule with the tiniest majority – the Maronite religious leader of the time, Patriarch Hayek, was responsible for this – the

---

* Margaret Beckett was briefly Tony Blair's submissive and deeply uninformed foreign secretary.

Christians ensured that they would soon be outnumbered and thus would rule their country from a position of minority power. After Irish partition, old James Craig, the founder of Northern Ireland, was a wiser bird than Hayek. From the historic province of Ulster, he ruthlessly dispensed with the three counties of Donegal, Monaghan and Cavan because their Protestant communities were too small to sustain – and created a new Ulster whose six counties ensured a Protestant majority for decades to come.

The other Lebanese problem – which the people of Northern Ireland will immediately spot – is that a sectarian state, where only a Maronite can be the president and only a Sunni the prime minister, cannot be a modern state. Yet if you take away the sectarianism France created, Lebanon will no longer be Lebanon. The French realised all this in the same way – I suspect – as the Americans have now realised the nature of their sectarian monster in Iraq. Listen to what that great Arab historian Albert Hourani wrote about the experience of being a Levantine in 1946 – and apply it to Iraq. To live in such a way, Hourani wrote:

> is to live in two worlds or more at once, without belonging to either – to be able to go through the external forms which indicate the possession of a certain nationality, religion or culture, without actually possessing it ... It is to belong to no community and to possess nothing of one's own. It reveals itself in lost-ness, cynicism and despair.*

Amid such geopolitical uncertainties, it is easy for Westerners to see these people in the borders and colours in which we have chosen to define them. Hence all those newspaper

---

* Albert Hourani, *Minorities in the Arab World* (Oxford University Press, 1947).

maps of Lebanon – Shias at the bottom and on the right, the Sunnis and Druze in the middle and at the top, and the Christians uneasily wedged between Beirut and the northern Mediterranean coast. We draw the same sectarian maps of Iraq – Shias at the bottom, Sunnis in the middle (the famous 'Sunni triangle', though it is not triangular at all) and Kurds at the top.*

The British army adopted the same cynical colonial attitude in its cartography of Belfast. I still possess their sectarian maps of the 1970s in which Protestant areas were coloured orange (of course) and Catholic districts green (of course) while the mixed, middle-class area around Malone Road appeared as a dull brown, the colour of a fine dry sherry. But we do not draw these maps of our own British cities. I could draw a map of Bradford's ethnic districts – but we would never print it. Thus we divide the 'other', while assiduously denying the 'other' in ourself. This is what the French did in Lebanon, what the British did in Northern Ireland and the Americans are now doing in Iraq. In this way we maintain our homogeneous power. Pierre Gemayel grew up in Bikfaya, firmly in that wedge of territory north of Beirut. Many Lebanese now fear a conflict between those who support the 'democracy' to which Gemayel belonged and the Shias, the people – in every sense of the word – at the 'bottom'. And the French are going to ensure that the country in which all these poor people are trapped remains 'independent'.

Quite so. And by the way, when did we ever see an ethnic map of Paris and its banlieus?

The Independent, 25 November 2006

* See also pp. 351–54.

Alphonse Bechir's spectacles

Something was strangely familiar when my Beirut optician put
me through my latest eye test. Antoine Bechir is a Chaldean
– yes, as in Ur of the Chaldees, that ancient Mesopotamian
race – and he must be the only Chaldean I know. His
family business was started by his dad, Alphonse, and it was
he who initiated the family eye test album. And it reads like
this: 'Waterloo–Staines–Reading Wednesdays – Afternoon.
Waterloo 1.20, Vauxhall 1.23, Queen's Road 1.26, Clapham
Junction 1.28 . . .' Yes, it really is a Southern Railways timetable,
circa 1948, and Antoine tells me he has many times stood
lovingly reading out the name of each station which – he
fondly imagines – must lie in the sleepy folds of rural England.
'One day I shall travel to your country and go to all these
places,' he says. 'Wandsworth, Clapham, Putney, Hounslow,
Ashford . . . Aren't they beautiful?'

Checking my vision is therefore a ramble down an imaginary
memory lane in which viewers are firmly recommended to
visit Theodore Hamblin, Dispensing Opticians at 15 Wigmore
Street (Phone: Langham 4343) and practise their eye capabili-
ties with this wonderful text: 'The streets of London are better
paved and better lighted than those of any metropolis in
Europe. There are lamps on both sides of every street, in the
mean proportion of one lamp to three doors . . .' Or try the
following extract for those with myopia: 'Water Cresses are

sold in small bunches, one penny each, or three bunches for twopence. The Crier of Water Cresses frequently travels seven or eight miles before the hour of breakfast to gather them fresh – but there is generally a pretty good supply of them in Covent Garden.' Was postwar London really so well lit? And how did you qualify as a Crier of Water Cresses? Old Alphonse Bechir, however, not only collected London railway timetables. He was also a buyer of spectacles in bulk, and this is how he came to have a little problem in the Second World War. Indeed, when Antoine produces his father's passport – issued by the 'High Commissioner of the French Republic in Syria and Lebanon' (under the terms of the old League of Nations French mandate) – I spot the snag at once: three bloody great German eagles on page 29, each clutching an evil little swastika in its claws. It's a real Nazi visa, issued by the German consulate in neutral Turkey in July of 1941, together with entry and exit stamps from Hitler's Reich.

Alphonse had decided to bulk-buy hundreds of pairs of new spectacles in wartime Germany – but he chose the wrong moment to travel and got caught up in a truly Lebanese mess. For when France fell in 1940, Lebanon became part of Vichy territory and the Bechir family, like every Lebanese at the time, found themselves allied with the Nazis. In theory, this should have made Alphonse's journey easy. Or so he must have thought. However, just a few days before he collected his visa in Istanbul, the British and Australian armies invaded Lebanon from Palestine and 'liberated' its people from the Vichy French after a bloody and costly campaign south of Beirut.

It was only a few days later that the luckless Alphonse Bechir headed back to Lebanon with his hundreds of pairs of brand-new German spectacles, only to find that things had changed while he was away. On the Syrian border, the new French authorities did not take kindly to page 29 of the passport and those governessy eagles with their swastikas. So along with up to a hundred fascist suspects he was bundled off to the Mieh Mieh prison camp above Sidon. By grim irony, Mieh Mieh is today a Palestinian refugee camp housing the descendants of those Arabs who fled northern Palestine in 1948, crossing the same Lebanese border that the Allies had traversed seven years earlier. Their fate was still unknown, of course, when Alphonse arrived behind the prison wire near Sidon.

It remains a mystery to me – and to Antoine – why his father should have risked a wartime trip to Nazi Germany, profitable though it was to be. The RAF was raiding Berlin by night and the Germans were preparing their vast armies for the invasion of the Soviet Union. Alphonse was lucky to have made it back to Lebanon. 'My father spent eight months in the camp before he could persuade the authorities that he was just an innocent optician,' Antoine says. 'Can you imagine being locked up for having the wrong visa in your passport?' Actually I could well imagine just such a scenario in wartime Lebanon. But like so few Lebanese tales, this one has a happy ending.

'While he was locked up, there was a huge spectacle shortage in the Middle East and when he eventually persuaded the military that he wasn't a Nazi spy, they gave him all his spectacles back – and they had increased in value by 800 per cent. That's the money he used to set up our optician's business.'

Which is why, every year, I study Alphonse's Southern Railways timetable, wonder at the Criers of Water Cresses and cringe at the sight of that wretched visa.

The Independent, 3 June 2006

The cat who ate missile wire for breakfast

Walter was a street cat, a *pusseini baladi* as they say in Beirut, brown and black with sharp ears and sharper teeth, the only creature of its kind to consume part of an Israeli wire-guided air-to-ground missile. On warm evenings, she would sit on the balcony and survey the seafront Corniche, the coffee stalls and the Mediterranean as it lapped idly against the green rocks below. She occasionally appeared in the pages of *The Independent*, not least when it seemed certain that our seafront highway was to be renamed Boulevard du Président Hafez al-Assad after the Syrian leader. This extraordinary honour eventually went to a road near the airport.

As a kitten, Walter liked the sofa, even at the height of General Aoun's lunatic bombardment of West Beirut. Where is Walter, we would ask every time the shells started to hiss over the house? I found her once, still sitting on the sofa, following with her eyes the lights of the tracers and targeting rounds as they flitted over the rooftop. One tough puss.

The missile wire? Well back in 1993, in Israel's week-long bombardment of southern Lebanon, I came across the guidance-wire of a missile that had exploded in a truck. The wire interested me because I suspected it might have been manufactured in Britain. So I took back about six feet of the brass cable and laid it on my desk, intending to send it off to *The Independent*'s defence correspondent for examination. Which is where Walter found it one afternoon. And ate it. 'Missile wire?' the vet's wife shrieked in terror. She is German.

Her husband, Dr Musri, saved Walter's life. Liquid paraffin was poured into the beast and – within hours – the wire emerged from the wrong end of Walter. I spared our defence correspondent what was left. Walter shrugged it off and returned to her favourite game – playing with toy mice. Indeed, she enjoyed this so much that when a real live mouse walked up the side of the balcony one day and trotted across the floor past Walter's feet, she merely yawned.

But she was a journalistic cat. She would snuggle down on winter evenings in my office, perched on top of copies of that venerable old Lebanese journal *L'Orient Le Jour*, the only newspaper to be written in Royalist French. Or sit like a teapot on the top of the UPS, the Uninterrupted Power Supply system that every computer in Lebanon needs as a back-up when Messrs Netanyahu or Barak bomb the country's power stations. On one occasion Walter walked across the telephone and pressed the automatic redial. I found her standing beside the machine with a puzzled look as journalist John Cooley's voice crackled down the line from Cyprus to demand why the caller was refusing to talk to him. Walter could strike anywhere. And the old telex machine – yes, I was still filing on telex until the Nineties – became a bed for Walter, its constantly running motor warming her underside night after night, the information from *The Independent* repeatedly garbled as the paper messages – unable to escape Walter's furry bulk – hopelessly overprinted. When I was punching on the telex, she would attack the tape, ripping the holes with her claws. She could not escape journalism. And journalism couldn't escape Walter.

She was even named after a newspaper editor: Walter Wells of the *International Herald Tribune* in Paris whose refusal to defend the journalist Lara Marlowe after the US military lied about an article she wrote for the paper prompted us to commemorate the event in style. Returning from a Gulf war or southern Lebanon or Ireland, Walter would always be there, waiting for her evening tin of Whiskas in the room where we stored the spare fuel for the generator. But when she went off her food last month, even the great Dr Musri could not find out what was wrong. Walter stopped purring and skulked under a chair in the living room.

After almost a week without food, I bundled her into her basket and flew to Paris, where two veterinarians were waiting for her. She sat meekly in her basket on the floor of Club Class. 'What a well-behaved cat,' the head of the Hariri Foundation charity remarked from the neighbouring seat. Neither of us knew that Walter was dying. She had an enlarged heart, myocardia they said, and water on the lungs was preventing her from eating. They drained the water and for a few days Walter was back munching roast chicken. Then she suffered a blood clot and the young female doctor said that she might go into convulsions. It was the end. It took a few seconds for Walter to go limp and an hour to cremate her. Under French law, her ashes had to remain unscattered for a year and a day.

But we broke the law and brought what was left of Walter back to Beirut. And where the waves lap the green rocks below the house, we threw her ashes, into the sea she watched so often and in which live the fish she ate so many times.

But I should have guessed that Walter's presence had not gone. This week, the UPS started smoking as the fan stopped at the back of the machine and everything I need as a correspondent – computer, phone recharger, fax machine, printer – abruptly stopped working. A Lebanese technician lugged the heavy iron box away, only to return hours later with a mass of brown and black fur in his hand. 'You have a cat?' he asked. 'There was about a ton of fur clogging the fan.' Walter had struck again.

The Independent, 10 June 2000

The torturer who lived near the theatre

Scorched is the right title for Wajdi Mouawad's play about Lebanon. The word 'Lebanon' doesn't occur in the script and 'the army invading from the south' – the Israeli army – remains needlessly anonymous. But any playwright who calls a town 'Nabatiyeh', or refers to a prominent Shia figure called 'Shamseddin' – the late Mehdi Shamseddin was the leader of the Shia clergy in Lebanon – hasn't tried very hard to hide the country in which his powerful, murderous scenario takes place. Suitably gory, *Scorched* is a story of love, family honour, civil war and barbarity.

Wajdi Mouawad, who is of Lebanese Christian Maronite origin but is now a French Canadian – his play was written in French and translated into English for its latest performance at the Tarragon Theatre in Toronto – has written a programme note in which he acknowledges his own background, even the devastating Israeli–Hizballah war last summer. But his play, he says, is 'anchored above all else by poetry, detached from its political context and instead anchored in the politic of human suffering, the poetry which unites us all'.

The plot is simple. Nawal, an old lady, dies in Canada, and her son and daughter try to discover – from two sealed envelopes left to them by their mother – why she had remained silent for years before her death. In her youth in Lebanon, it transpires, Nawal's lover made her pregnant and the child was taken from her to preserve her family's honour. So she sets off, amid the massacres of the Lebanese civil war – there is a terrifying moment when blood from the victims of a bus massacre sprays over the young Nawal's clothes – to find her missing child.

During the war, she poses as a schoolteacher to educate the children of a local militia commander – so that she can assassinate him once she has gained his trust. The militia leader is killed, but Nawal is caught and taken to a prison where she is regularly raped by the jail's chief torturer. An old man later recalls for Nawal's daughter – who has gone to Lebanon to find out why her mother endured those years of silence – that he was ordered by the jail authorities to throw two newborn babies into a nearby river. Instead, he takes the babies, covered in a cloth, to a local family who save their lives.

Nawal's secret – which turns her from being 'the woman who sings songs' into a silent old lady – is that the original child for whom she is searching, the child of her long-dead lover, is her torturer and rapist. The torturer is the father of the son and daughter in Canada. He is also their brother. It is a secret revealed to the daughter by the militia leader called 'Shamseddin' and it breaks the mind of her brother/father. He, too, lapses into eternal silence. An Oedipal drama if ever there was one.

And I can accept the play on that level. The duty of an artist, I have always thought, is to place imagination on a higher level than history, to frame real events – if he or she must – to fit the interpretation that an author or playwright chooses to reveal about life. But as a witness to the Lebanese civil war, I find Mouawad's work much more difficult to accept on the level of mere art. Shamseddin, as head of the country's Shia, was the first to call on the Lebanese to fight the Israeli occupation army in 1982. And there really was a girl who posed as a schoolteacher to murder a militia leader. Her name was Soad Bshara and she was a Christian leftist, not a Shia – I've even

met the man who gave her the gun to kill the militia leader –
and she did indeed attempt to assassinate him.

But General Antoine Lahd did not die. He showed me his
wounds – two bullet holes – not long after his return to
Lebanon from hospital in Israel. He was one of Israel's ruthless
proxy warlords in Lebanon and he was in charge of the same
brutal Israeli-controlled prison in which Bshara was subsequently locked up. She was not raped, but she was beaten
and endured years of solitary confinement until the French
government organised her release; she lives today in Paris while
Lahd, after the collapse of his cruel 'South Lebanon Army' in
2000, now lives in Tel Aviv where he runs – wait for it – a
nightclub.

However, there certainly were well-trained torturers in
Lahd's jail – its real name was Khiam prison and it was turned
by the Hizballah into a museum until being largely destroyed
in last summer's war. The sadists of Khiam used to electrocute
the penises of their prisoners and throw water over their bodies
before plunging electrodes into their chests and kept them in
pitch-black, solitary confinement for months. For many years,
the Israelis even banned the Red Cross from visiting their foul
prison. All the torturers fled across the border into Israel when
the Israeli army retreated under fire from Lebanon almost
seven years ago.

After watching *Scorched*, I went backstage to meet the actors
and actresses – one of them gives a frighteningly accurate
portrayal of a jazz-crazed sniper – only to find they had no
idea that they were, in some cases, playing real people. They
didn't even know that Israel had farmed out Khiam's torturers to Western countries as 'refugees' – on the grounds that
they would be killed if they returned to Lebanon. The Israelis,
of course, didn't mention their role in Khiam's horrors – which
is why, several years ago, two members of the Royal Canadian
Mounted Police turned up at my home to ask if I could identify

any torturers who might have been given asylum in Canada. I told them that their names were now written on the gates of Khiam prison.*

But I do know that one of the torturers – who appears in *Scorched* as Nawal's rapist – is believed to have found guilty sanctuary in Toronto, where he has set up in business. In other words, he probably lives less than three miles from the Tarragon Theatre in Bridgman Avenue. And who knows, maybe he will drop by for a ticket this month, just to enjoy the suffering he caused in a faraway land to which he will never dare return. Would that be history? Tragedy? Or art?

The Independent, 10 March 2007

---

* See also pp. 395–8.

The temple of truth

We used to call it the Temple of Truth. The ten-storey cube of brown and cream marble on the Mezze Boulevard in Damascus had vast, sand-covered windows that were never cleaned, a set of four battered silver elevators that took up to fifteen minutes to reach the dreaded top floor, and a bust of President Hafez al-Assad which appeared to be made of dark yellow margarine. Herein sat the cigarette-smoking priests of the temple whose sullen fate was to ensure that foreign journalists – alas for them, Fisk among their number – understood the avuncular, humanist, Arab nationalist values of Baathism.

In the days of Old Syria, this was a harsh task for any attendant lord. Iskander Ahmed Iskander was the minister of information when I first arrived in Damascus, a slim, musta-chioed helmsman whose title belied his proximity to the Great Man. He ruled from an office with a heavily bolted security door in a building which housed the Syrian Arab News Agency; its indigestible dispatches filled the pages of each day's *Syria Times*, a tabloid-sized journal invariably recording the com-pletion of five-year industrial plans and telegrams from deliri-ous agricultural workers congratulating the president on the anniversary of his corrective revolution.

Iskander it was whose task in 1982 was to berate me for daring to enter the forbidden city of Hama where the legions of Rifaat al-Assad – brother of the Great Man and now quietly enjoying forced retirement in the European Union (that scourge of war criminals) – butchered thousands of Islamist rebels. This occurred without a squeak of complaint from the same Americans who are currently trying to liquidate an equal number of insurgents in Iraq. Damascus Radio (one of Iskander's pets) had already denounced me as a liar for claiming to have wormed my way into Hama even though I had penetrated the burning city by offering a lift to two of Rifaat's officers.

Yet when he received me in the spring of 1982, Iskander was anxious to preserve good relations with my then employer, *The Times*. First he insisted I had not been to Hama – a charitable suggestion I swiftly disposed of – and then that he knew nothing of Damascus Radio's claim that I had lied. I had no doubt that Iskander had approved this very broadcast. But he beamed at me, thrust a cigar in my direction and said: 'Only true friends can have this kind of argument.'

Years later, Iskander would go for cancer surgery in London, where part of his brain was removed. When I asked him what it was like to wake up after the operation, he replied: 'Part of me did not exist.' Tough folk, Baathists. These were also difficult days for Zuhair Jenaan, Syria's 'director of foreign press', whose genial, kindly ability to wangle visas for ungrateful journalists – his 'minders' shadowed all of them – was rarely rewarded. Zuhair was eventually appointed press officer at his country's London embassy, a post swiftly abandoned when the Brits discovered that the would-be bomber of an El Al airliner had been hidden by Syrian diplomats – not Zuhair – in London. Back in Damascus, he approved a visa to an American journalist who failed to tell Zuhair that he was also an Israeli and who filed a number of reports to his paper in Tel Aviv.

Zuhair was then dispatched to the lower floors of the Temple of Truth, protected only by a new minister of information, Mohamed Salman, a shrewd Baathist whose fall from grace was inevitable after he unveiled yet another bust of the Great

Leader outside the Temple of Truth. The following morning, a squad of workmen was seen dismantling the statue. Next time I saw Mohamed he was under house arrest, freighted to a Baath Party Congress to vote for the leadership of Assad's son Bashar in 2000, nervously sipping coffee in a corner of the room while his Baathist colleagues showed their fear of contamination by creating a 20-ft radiation zone around him. Along with a colleague, I broke the radiation belt by approaching Mohamed to ask after his health. His look of relief was palpable. A few hitherto timid Baathists then followed our example.

I liked Ahmed Hariri, translator and 'minder' to Zuhair's successor. His chain-smoking detracted from his ascetic, cynical, literary approach to the world. Amid quotations from William Blake, Ahmed – who suffered from a weak heart – would explain Baathist teachings with a roll of the eyes and often prefaced his remarks with the words: 'You promise me, Robert, you will never repeat what I say.' There would then follow a transparently honest account of life under Hafez al-Assad and – once – a description of how his colleagues would behave on the day the Great Leader passed away. 'In my native Tadmor, the people will go to the mass graves of political prisoners and throw rose petals on the sand,' he said. 'And in our offices at what you call the Temple of Truth, we will sit with cigarettes in our mouths, each watching our comrades from the corner of our eyes to observe their reactions to the death of the Great Leader.'

On that day in 2000, the denizens of the Temple of Truth behaved in exactly this manner – though there were, unfortunately, no rose petals on the graves of Tadmor – but, once Bashar settled into office, a carefully modulated Baathist breeze stirred along the corridors of the temple. When I joked about the previous 'iron rule', there would be much back-slapping and praise for Bashar. Why only this week, the new minister, a cheerful, intellectual surgeon called Mohsen Bilal, recounted how he had often discussed my reports with General Ghazi Kenaan, the interior minister who last year unhappily blew his brains out at the height of the UN inquiry into the murder of former Lebanese prime minister Rafiq Hariri.

To my shock, I found that Ahmed had recently died of a heart attack. Iskander is long dead. Mohamed Salman currently 'lives at home', though no longer under house arrest, while Zuhair, whose neck was saved by Salman, now edits a newspaper about horses. Horses? I asked at the temple. Horses? 'Yes, his paper's called *The Thoroughbred.*' Big circulation? 'The people of Damascus, Mr Robert, do not all talk about horses.' Indeed. The *Syria Times* has gone broadsheet and is as boring as ever. 'Cabinet Stresses National Unity' was one of this week's headlines. But other papers are reporting Lebanese accusations that Syria was behind Hariri's murder. My hotel displays magazines recording the repression of Syrian Kurds. The windows are still covered in sand and the lift still takes fifteen minutes to reach the tenth floor. But this is New Syria and life has changed in the Temple of Truth.

And they call this place, I keep reminding myself, the Axis of Evil.

The Independent, 22 April 2006

We are all Rifaats now

Could Rifaat al-Assad's day in court be growing closer? Yes, Rifaat – or Uncle Rifaat to President Bashar al-Assad of Syria – the man whose brother Hafez hurled from Damascus after he tried to use his special forces troops to stage a coup. They were the same special forces who crushed the Islamist rebellion in Hama in February 1982, slaughtering up to – well, a few thousand, according to the regime, at least 10,000 according to Fisk (who was there) and up to 20,000 if you believe the *New York Times* (which I generally don't). Either way, I've always regarded it as a war crime, along with the massacre of Palestinians in the Sabra and Chatila camps in Beirut a few months later. Ariel Sharon, who was held personally responsible by Israel's own court of inquiry, is an unindicted war criminal. So is Rifaat.

That's why the faintest draught blew through my fax machine this week when I received a letter sent to the UN Secretary General by Anas al-Abdeh, head of the London-based Movement for Justice and Development in Syria. Abdeh left his Syrian town of Zabadani before the Hama massacres – he works now as an IT consultant for a multinational – so he's hardly able to breathe the air of Sister Syria. But then again nor can Rifaat, who languishes – complete with bodyguards – in that nice EU island of refuge called Marbella. And refuge he probably needs. Because Abdeh is asking the UN to institute an inquiry into the Hama bloodbath in the same way that it is powering along with its tribunal into the murder almost two years ago of Lebanese ex-prime minister Rafiq Hariri.

In his letter Abdeh describes how 'warplanes and tanks levelled whole districts of the city [of Hama] ... the evidence clearly suggests that government forces made no distinction between armed insurgents and unarmed civilians ... the assault on the city represents a clear act of war crimes and murder on a mass scale'. The letter has now been passed to the UN's legal head, Nicolas Michel, who is also involved in the Hariri murder case. The sacred name of Rifaat has not been mentioned in the letter but it specifically demands that 'those who are responsible should be held accountable and charged ...' Now there are a few discrepancies in the facts. The Syrians did not use poison gas in Hama, as Abdeh claims. They certainly did level whole areas of the city – they are still level today, although a hotel has been built over one devastated district – and when Rifaat's thugs combed through the ruins later, they executed any civilians who couldn't account for their presence.

But of course, the Hama uprising was also a Sunni Muslim insurrection and the insurgents had murdered entire families of Baath party officials, sometimes by chopping off their heads. In underground tunnels, Muslim girls had exploded themselves among Syrian troops – they were among the Middle East's first suicide bombers, although we didn't appreciate that then. And the Americans were not at all unhappy that this Islamist insurgency had been crushed by Uncle Rifaat. Readers will not need any allusion to modern and equally terrible events involving Sunni insurgents to the east of Syria. And since the Americans are getting pretty efficient at killing civilians along with gunmen, I have a dark suspicion that there won't be any great enthusiasm in Washington for a prosecution over Hama.

But still ... What strikes me is not so much the force of

Abdeh's letter but that it was written at all. When the Hama massacre occurred, neighbouring Arab states were silent. Although the Sunni prelates of the city called for a religious war, their fellow clerics in Damascus – and, indeed, in Beirut – were silent. Just as the imams and scholars of Islam were silent when the Algerians began to slaughter each other in a welter of head-chopping and security force executions in the 1990s.

Just as they are silent now over the mutual killings in Iraq. Sure, the mass murders in Iraq would not have occurred if we hadn't invaded the country. And I do suspect a few 'hidden hands' behind the civil conflict in a nation that never before broke apart. In Algeria, the French spent a lot of time in the early 1960s persuading – quite successfully – their FLN and ALN enemies to murder each other. But where are the sheikhs of Al-Azhar and the great Arabian kingdoms when the Iraqi dead are fished out of the Tigris and cut down in their thousands in Baghdad, Kerbala, Baquba? They, too, are silent.

Not a word of criticism. Not a hint of concern. Not a scintilla (an Enoch Powell word, this) of sympathy. An Israeli bombardment of Lebanon? Even an Israeli invasion? That's a war crime – and the Arabs are right, the Israelis do commit war crimes. I saw the evidence of quite a few last summer. But when does Arab blood become less sacred? Why, when it is shed by Arabs. It's not just a failure of self-criticism in the Arab world. In a landscape ruled by monsters whom we in the West have long supported, criticism of any kind is a dodgy undertaking. But can there not be one small sermon of reprobation for what Iraqi Muslims are doing to Iraqi Muslims?

Of course, but the real problem the Arabs now face is that their lands have been overrun and effectively occupied by Western armies. I worked out a few weeks ago that, per head of population – and the world was smaller in the twelfth century – there are now about 22 times more Western soldiers in Muslim lands than there were at the time of the Crusades. How do you strike back at these legions and drive them out? Brutally and most terribly, the Iraqis have shown how. I used to say the future of the Bush administration will be decided in Iraq, not in Washington. And this now appears to be true.

So what should we do? Allow the Rifaats of this world to go on enjoying Marbella? And the killers of Hariri go free? And the Arabs remain silent in the face of the shameful atrocities which their brother Muslims have also committed? I'll take a bet that Rifaat will be safe from the UN lads. In Iraq right now, he'd be on 'our' side, wouldn't he, battling the Islamic insurgency as he did in Hama? And that, I fear, is the problem. We are all Rifaats now.

The Independent, 10 February 2007

The ministry of fear

After the capture of three Israeli soldiers and the killing of two others by Hizballah gunmen who crossed the Lebanese–Israeli frontier on 12 July 2006, Israel launched a 34-day war against Lebanon, killing more than a thousand men, women and children and destroying much of the country's infrastructure. Only a handful of the Lebanese dead were gunmen. More than a hundred Israelis, most of them soldiers, died at the hands of the Hizballah. It was towards the end of this terrible conflict that Scotland Yard discovered another 'terror' plot in London.

When my electricity returned at around 3 a.m. yesterday, I turned on BBC World Service. There was a series of powerful explosions that shook the house – just as they vibrated across all of Beirut – as the latest Israeli air raids blasted over the city. And then up came the World Service headline: 'Terror Plot'. Terror what, I asked myself? And there was my favourite cop, Deputy Police Commissioner Paul Stephenson, explaining how my favourite police force – the ones who bravely executed an innocent young Brazilian on the London Tube, taking thirty seconds to fire six bullets into him – had saved the lives of hundreds of innocent civilians from suicide bombers on airliners.

I'm sure it's quite by chance that the lads in blue chose yesterday – with anger at Blair's shameful failure over Lebanon at its peak – to save the world. After all, it's scarcely three years since the other great Terror Plot had British armoured vehicles surrounding Heathrow on the very day – again quite by chance, of course – that hundreds of thousands of Britons were demonstrating against Lord Blair's intended invasion of Iraq. So I sat on the carpet in my living room and watched all these heavily armed chaps at Heathrow protecting the British people from annihilation and then on came President George Bush to tell us that we were all fighting 'Islamic fascism'. There were more thumps in the darkness across Beirut where an awful lot of people are suffering from terror – although I can assure George W. that while the pilots of the aircraft dropping bombs across the city in which I have lived for thirty years may or may not be fascists, they are definitely not Islamic.

And there, of course, was the same old conundrum. To protect the British people – and the American people – from 'Islamic terror', we must have lots and lots of heavily armed policemen and soldiers and plainclothes police and endless departments of anti-terrorism, homeland security and other more sordid folk like the American torturers – some of them sadistic women – at Abu Ghraib and Baghram and Guantanamo. Yet the only way to protect ourselves from the real violence which may – and probably will – be visited upon us, is to deal, morally, with courage and with justice, with the tragedy of Lebanon and 'Palestine' and Iraq and Afghanistan. And this we will not do.

I would, frankly, love to have Paul Stephenson out in Beirut to counter a little terror in my part of the world – Hizballah terror and Israeli terror. But this, of course, is something that Paul and his lads don't have the spittle for. It's one thing to sound off about the alleged iniquities of alleged suspects of an alleged plot to create alleged terror – quite another to deal with the causes of that terror and to do so in the face of great danger.

I was amused to see that Bush – just before my electricity was cut off again – still mendaciously tells us that the 'terrorists' hate us because of 'our freedoms'. Not because we support the Israelis who have massacred refugee columns, fired into Red Cross ambulances and slaughtered more than 1,000 Lebanese civilians – here indeed are crimes for Paul Stephenson to investigate – but because they hate our 'freedoms'.

And I notice with despair that our journalists again suck on the hind tit of authority, quoting endless (and anonymous) 'security sources' without once challenging their information or the timing of Paul's 'terror plot' discoveries or the nature of the details nor the reasons why, if this whole odd scenario is correct, anyone would want to carry out such atrocities. We are told that the arrested men are Muslims. Now isn't that interesting? Muslims. This means that many of them – or their families – originally come from south-west Asia and the Middle East, from the area that encompasses Afghanistan, Iraq, 'Palestine' and Lebanon.

In the old days, chaps like Paul used to pull out a map when faced with folk of different origins or religion or indeed different names. Indeed, if Paul Stephenson takes a school atlas he'll notice that there are an awful lot of violent problems and injustice and suffering and – a speciality, it seems, of the Metropolitan Police – of death in the area from which the families of these 'Muslims' come. Could there be a connection, I wonder? Dare we look for a motive for the crime, or rather the 'alleged crime'? The Met used to be pretty good at looking for motives. But not, of course, in the 'war on terror', where – if he really searched for real motives – my favourite policeman would swiftly be back on the beat as Constable Paul Stephenson.

Take yesterday morning. On day 31 of the Israeli version of the 'war on terror' – a conflict to which Paul and the lads in blue apparently subscribe by proxy – an Israeli aircraft blew up the only remaining bridge to the Syrian frontier in northern Lebanon, in the mountainous and beautiful Akka district above the Mediterranean. With their usual sensitivity, the pilots who bombed the bridge – no terrorists they, mark you – chose to destroy it when ordinary cars were crossing. So they massacred the twelve civilians who happened to be on the bridge. In the real world, we call that a war crime. Indeed, it's a crime worthy of the attention of Paul and his lads. But alas, Stephenson's job is to frighten the British people, not to stop the crimes that are the real reason for the British to be frightened.

Personally, I'm all for arresting criminals, be they of the 'Islamic fascist' variety or the bin Laden variety or the Israeli variety – their warriors of the air really should be arrested next time they drop into Heathrow – or the American variety (Abu Ghraib *cum laude*), and indeed of the kind that blow out the brains of Tube-train passengers. But I don't think Paul Stephenson is. I think he huffs and he puffs but I do not think he stands for law and order. He works for the Ministry of Fear which, by its very nature, is not interested in motives or injustice. And I have to say, watching his performance before the next power cut last night, I thought he was doing a pretty good job for his masters.

The Independent, 12 August 2006

A senior member of the British security services later sent me a four-page handwritten letter, complaining that I had been unfair to Paul Stephenson. Would I care to visit him next time I was in London? But when I turned up at his office some weeks later, he made no mention of Stephenson. Instead he explained that he was troubled by acting on intelligence information from Pakistan which may have been obtained through torture. 'I get information and we find the guns in London exactly where the Pakistanis said they would be. So what I am to do? Ignore what I'm told and place the lives of Londoners in danger? No, I have to act on this information.'

'We have all made our wills'

Secrecy, an intellectual said, is a powerful aphrodisiac. Secrecy is exciting. Danger is darker, more sinister. It drifts like a fog through the streets of Beirut these days, creeping down the laneways where policemen – who may or may not work for the forces of law and order – shout their instructions through loudhailers.

No parking. Is anyone fooled? When the Lebanese MP Antoine Ghanem was assassinated last week, the cops couldn't – or wouldn't – secure the crime scene. Why not? And so last Wednesday, the fog came creeping through the iron gateway of Druze leader Walid Jumblatt's town house in Beirut where he and a few brave MPs had gathered for dinner before parliament's useless vote on the presidential elections. There was much talk of majorities and quorums; 50 plus one appears to be the constitutional rule here, although the supporters of Syria would dispute that. I have to admit I still meet Lebanese MPs who don't understand their own parliamentary system; I suspect it needs several PhDs to get it right.

The food, as always, was impeccable. And why should those who face death by explosives or gunfire every day not eat well? Not for nothing has Nora Jumblatt been called the world's best hostess. I sat close to the Jumblatts while their guests – Ghazi Aridi, the minister of information, Marwan Hamade, minister of communications, and Tripoli MP Mosbah al-Ahdab and a

Beirut judge – joked and talked and showed insouciance for the fog of danger that shrouds their lives.

In 2004, 'they' almost got Hamade at his home near my apartment. Altogether, forty-six of Lebanon's MPs are now hiding in the Phoenicia Hotel, three to a suite. Jumblatt had heard rumours of another murder the day before Ghanem was blown apart. Who is next? That is the question we all ask. 'They' – the Syrians or their agents or gunmen working for mysterious governments – are out there, planning the next murder to cut Fouad Siniora's tiny majority down. 'There will be another two dead in the next three weeks,' Jumblatt said. And the dinner guests all looked at each other.

'We have all made our wills,' Nora said quietly. Even you, Nora? She didn't think she was a target. 'But I may be with Walid.' And I looked at these educated, brave men – their policies not always wise, perhaps, but their courage unmistakable – and pondered how little we Westerners now care for the life of Lebanon. There is no longer a sense of shock when MPs die in Beirut. I don't even feel the shock. A young Lebanese couple asked me at week's end how Lebanon has affected me after thirty-one years, and I said that when I saw Ghanem's corpse last week, I felt nothing. That is what Lebanon has done to me. That is what it has done to all the Lebanese.

Scarcely 1,000 Druze could be rounded up for Ghanem's funeral. And even now there is no security. My driver Abed was blithely permitted to park only 100 metres from Jumblatt's house without a single policeman checking the boot of his car. What if he worked for someone more dangerous than *The Independent*'s correspondent? And who were all those cops outside working for?

Yet at this little dinner party in Beirut, I could not help thinking of all our smug statesmen, the Browns and the Straws and the Sarkozys and the imperious Kouchners and Merkels and their equally arrogant belief that they are fighting a 'war on terror'

– do we still believe that, by the way? – and reflect that here in Beirut there are intellectual men and women who could run away to London or Paris if they chose, but prefer to stick it out, waiting to die for their democracy in a country smaller than Yorkshire. I don't think our Western statesmen are of this calibre.

Well, we talked about death and not long before midnight a man in a pony tail and an elegant woman in black (a suitable colour for our conversation) arrived with an advertisement hoarding that could be used in the next day's parliament sitting. Rafiq Hariri was at the top. And there was journalist Jibran Tueni and MP Pierre Gemayel and Hariri's colleague Basil Fleihan, and Ghanem of course. All stone-dead because they believed in Lebanon. What do you have to be to be famous in Lebanon, I asked Jumblatt, and he burst into laughter. Ghoulish humour is in fashion.

And at one point Jumblatt fetched Curzio Malaparte's hideous, brilliant account of the Second World War on the eastern front – *Kaputt* – and presented it to me with his personal inscription. 'To Robert Fisk,' he wrote. 'I hope I will not surrender, but this book is horribly cruel and somehow beautiful. W Joumblatt [*sic*].' And I wondered how cruelty and beauty can come together.

Maybe we should make a movie about these men and women. Alastair Sim would have to play the professorial Aridi, Clark Gable the MP al-Ahdab. (We all agreed that Gable would get the part.) I thought that perhaps Herbert Lom might play Hamade. (I imagine he is already Googling for Lom's name.) Nora? She'd have to be played by Vivien Leigh or – nowadays – Demi Moore. And who would play Walid Jumblatt? Well, Walid Jumblatt, of course.

But remember these Lebanese names. And think of them when the next explosion tears across this dangerous city.

The Independent, 29 September 2007

'Duty unto death' and the United Nations

There were bagpipers in Scottish tartan, hundreds of soldiers coming to attention with all the snap of Sandhurst and a banner proclaiming 'Duty Unto Death', which could have been a chapter title in the dreadful old G. A. Henty novels of empire that my dad once forced me to read. I had to pinch myself to remember yesterday that this corner of the British Empire was actually southern Lebanon. But there was nothing un-British about the Assam Regiment, whose battle honours go back to 1842 and whose regimental silver still bears the names of Victorian colonels of the Raj. It was Malcolm Muggeridge who once observed that the only Englishmen left were Indians. The Assam Regiment's 15th battalion is India's contribution to the United Nations' peacekeeping force along the Israeli border – Israel's listening posts were stitched across the brown snows of Golan high above us yesterday – and its soldiers, from the seven north-eastern states of India, have turned out to be among the most popular of UN units for two simple reasons. They help with much of the veterinary work among the poor farmers and – shades, here, I suppose, of the new hi-tech city of Hyderabad – they repair all the computers in local schools. But there was one salient feature of the battalion's UN medal parade yesterday; the other units which had sent their officers were almost all non-Western.

There were Fijians and Nepalese and Ghanaian soldiers but

only a smattering of French and the odd Australian UN observer. When the United Nations Interim Force in Lebanon – Unifil – was at its height during the Israeli occupation, its soldiers tended to come from richer countries, from Ireland, Norway, Finland and France. Now it is the poorer nations whose soldiers are spread across the hills between Tyre and Golan. India's army can also be found on duty in the Democratic Republic of Congo and, shortly, in the Sudan and Ethiopia. Almost all of them have fought in Kashmir – most of the 15th battalion's men were wearing the red and green medal of Kashmir on their chests yesterday, although this was not officially pointed out. After all, most Lebanese are Muslims.

The UN's global reach seems thus to be revolving more and more around non-Nato forces. Our superior Western armies, I suppose, are much happier in Bosnia or illegally invading Iraq. Prime Minister Blair is not going to waste his men on the Israeli border. Cyprus is quite enough for the British. But all this does raise an important question. Do nations that we once called 'Third World' make better peacekeepers? Would it not be more appropriate – if this is not already happening – to have soldiers who understand poverty keeping the peace in lands of poverty?

When the Irish first deployed to Lebanon in 1978, Ireland was still a comparatively poor nation, and its soldiers instantly formed great affection for the Shia Muslim farmers and their families who lived off their smallholdings in the stony hills and valleys. Ireland, I have to remind myself, now fields a full battalion in Liberia, and Irish troops can be found in Kabul, Pristina and Monrovia. And as the Indians were addressed by their commanders yesterday, there came the names of Somalia, Cambodia and Angola. I can remember now, amid the corruption and terrors of the Bosnian and Croatian wars, how the smartest and the most disciplined contingent turned out to be not the French or Canadians but the Jordanian battalion on the Serb border.

There was a time, back in 2002, when George W. Bush was threatening the United Nations – just as he still is with his idiotic choice of John Bolton as the next American ambassador to the UN – when I was asked in New York if I 'believed in the UN'. It was a bit like being asked if one believed in God or the Devil, which I'm sure George Bush does. But I have to admit that while I'm not at all sure about God – or at least Bush's version of him – I did reply that, yes, I believed in the UN. And I still do. It was in Bosnia that I had a long discussion with a Canadian UN officer about the worth of the United Nations. We were under quite a lot of shellfire, so this probably concentrated our minds. His theory was quite simple. If we'd had a United Nations in 1914, it might have stopped the First World War. 'I don't think there would have been a Somme or Verdun if the UN had been there,' he said. 'And despite everything that's gone wrong in Bosnia, it would have been far worse – much more like the Second World War – if the UN wasn't here.'

The débâcle in Somalia hardly supports this view, but have the Americans done any better in Iraq? Once the UN was discarded, in went the US army and Blair's lads and now they've got an insurgency on their hands which is growing in intensity and where no Westerner – or Iraqi for that matter – can walk or drive the streets of Baghdad without fear of instant death. Duty Unto Death might suit the Indian battalion in Lebanon but I doubt if many US troops would adopt this as their regimental motto. For some reason, we believe that our Western armies do the toughest fighting, but I'm not sure that's true. The Indian army served in Sri Lanka, whose suicide bombers would make even Iraq's killers look tame. 'You had to drive everywhere at a hundred miles an hour,' one of India's Sri Lanka veterans once told me. 'I don't think I've ever fought a force like theirs.'

So here's a satanic question. What if the UN had sent a

multinational force into Iraq in the early spring of 2003? What if we could have had Indian troops and Nepalese soldiers rather than the American First Infantry Division, moving up the Tigris and Euphrates under a blue banner? Could it have been a worse mess than we have in Iraq today? If Saddam Hussein could have his weapons of mass destruction destroyed by the UN – and they were destroyed by the UN, were they not, because we know that there weren't any there when we invaded? – might the UN not also have been able to insert military units after forcing Saddam to disband his regime? No? Well, in that case, how come Syria's regime in Lebanon is crumbling under UN Security Council Resolution 1559? Yesterday, even Jamil Sayyed – the pro-Syrian head of Lebanon's General Security, a figure more powerful and very definitely more sinister than the Lebanese president – stepped aside, along with one of his equally pro-Syrian underlings. True, it was the French and the Americans who pushed for Resolution 1559. But how many of us will stand up today and admit that the UN is doing in Lebanon what the United States has failed to do in Iraq?

The Independent, 23 April 2005

The United Nations Interim Force in Lebanon, Unifil, was greatly enlarged with armoured combat battalions from Nato powers under the new US-supported Security Council Resolution. A Spanish unit of the force was car-bombed in the first attack of its kind in southern Lebanon in the summer of 2007. Six 'blue berets' were killed.

CHAPTER EIGHT

The cult of cruelty

For millions of Muslims, torture and 'rendition' have become the new symbols of the 'liberal' West. Electrodes, 'waterboarding', beatings, anal rape and murder have now become so commonplace in Iraq and Afghanistan that we are no longer surprised by each new revelation. And although the photographs of humiliated, naked prisoners in Abu Ghraib are now a monument to our inhumanity, we easily forget that the pictures we have seen are a mere fraction of those acquired by the Pentagon, some of which show the rape of an Iraqi woman. It was George W. Bush who first announced that we must go on a 'Crusade' against the killers of 9/11. And now we are behaving in the Middle East with all the cruelty of the original Crusaders. Up to half a million Iraqi civilians may have been killed since the invasion. Every time I visit Baghdad, someone I know has died.

The age of the warrior

In the week that George Bush took to fantasising that his blood-soaked 'war on terror' would lead the twenty-first century into a 'shining age of human liberty', I went through my mailbag to find a frightening letter addressed to me by an American veteran whose son is serving as a lieutenant colonel and medical doctor with US forces in Baghdad. Put simply, my American friend believes the change of military creed under the Bush administration – from that of 'soldier' to that of 'warrior' – is encouraging American troops to commit atrocities.

From Abu Ghraib to Guantanamo to Bagram, to the battle-fields of Iraq and to the 'black' prisons of the CIA, humiliation and beatings, rape, anal rape and murder have now become so commonplace that each new outrage is creeping into the inside pages of our newspapers. My reporting notebooks are full of Afghan and Iraqi complaints of torture and beatings from August 2002, and then from 2003 to the present. How, I keep asking myself, did this happen? Obviously, the trail leads to the top. But where did this cult of cruelty begin?

So first, here's the official US Army 'Soldier's Creed', originally drawn up to prevent any more Vietnam atrocities:

> I am an American soldier. I am a member of the United States
> Army – a protector of the greatest nation on earth. Because I

am proud of the uniform I wear, I will always act in ways creditable to the military service and the nation that it is sworn to guard . . . No matter what situation I am in, I will never do anything for pleasure, profit or personal safety, which will disgrace my uniform, my unit or my country. I will use every means I have, even beyond the line of duty, to restrain my Army comrades from actions, disgraceful to themselves and the uniform. I am proud of my country and its flag. I will try to make the people of this nation proud of the service I represent for I am an American soldier.

And here's the new version of what is now called the 'Warrior Ethos':

I am an American soldier.

I am a warrior and a member of a team. I serve the people of the United States and live the Army values.

I will always place the mission first.

I will never accept defeat.

I will never quit.

I will never leave a fallen comrade.

I am disciplined, physically and mentally tough, trained and proficient in my warrior tasks and drills. I always maintain my arms, my equipment and myself.

I am an expert and I am a professional. I stand ready to deploy, engage and destroy the enemies of the United States of America in close combat. I am a guardian of freedom and the American way of life.

I am an American soldier.

Like most Europeans – and an awful lot of Americans – I was quite unaware of this new and ferocious 'code' for US armed forces, although it's not hard to see how it fits in with Bush's rantings. I'm tempted to point this out in detail, but my American veteran did so with such eloquence in his letter to me that the response should come in his words: 'The Warrior Creed,' he wrote:

> allows no end to any conflict except total destruction of the 'enemy'. It allows no defeat . . . and does not allow one ever to stop fighting (lending itself to the idea of 'the long war'). It says nothing about following orders, it says nothing about obeying laws or showing restraint. It says nothing about dishonourable actions . . .

Each day now, I come across new examples of American military cruelty in Iraq and Afghanistan. Here, for example, is Army Specialist Tony Lagouranis, part of an American mobile interrogation team working with US Marines, interviewed by Amy Goodman on the American *Democracy Now!* programme, describing a 2004 operation in Babel, outside Baghdad: 'Every time Force Recon went on a raid, they would bring back prisoners who were bruised, with broken bones, sometimes with burns. They were pretty brutal to these guys. And I would ask the prisoners what happened, how they received these wounds. And they would tell me that it was after their capture, while they were subdued, while they were handcuffed and they were being questioned by the Force Recon Marines . . . One guy was forced to sit on an exhaust pipe of a Humvee . . . he had a giant blister, third-degree burns on the back of his leg.' Lagouranis, whose story is powerfully recalled in Goodman's new book, *Static*, reported this brutality to a Marine major and a colonel-lawyer from the US Judge Advocate General's Office. 'But they just wouldn't listen, you know? They wanted numbers. They wanted numbers of terrorists apprehended . . . so they could brief that to the general.'

The stories of barbarity grow by the week, sometimes by the day. In Canada, an American military deserter appealed for refugee status and a serving comrade gave evidence that when US forces saw babies lying in the road in Fallujah – outrageously, it appears, insurgents sometimes placed them there to force the Americans to halt and face ambush – they were under orders to drive over the children without stopping. Which is what happens when you always 'place the mission first', when you are going to 'destroy' – rather than defeat – your enemies. As my American vet put it:

> the activities in American military prisons and the hundreds of reported incidents against civilians in Iraq, Afghanistan and elsewhere are not aberrations – they are part of what the US military, according to the ethos, is intended to be. Many other armies behave in a worse fashion than the US Army. But those armies don't claim to be the 'good guys' . . . I think we need . . . a military composed of soldiers, not warriors.

Winston Churchill understood military honour. 'In defeat, defiance,' he advised Britons in the Second World War. 'In victory, magnanimity.' Not any more. According to George W. Bush this week, 'the safety of America depends on the outcome of the battle in the streets of Baghdad' because we are only in the 'early hours of this struggle between tyranny and freedom'. I suppose, in the end, we are intended to lead the twenty-first century into a shining age of human liberty in the dungeons of 'black' prisons, under the fists of US Marines, on the exhaust pipes of Humvees. We are warriors, we are Samurai. We draw the sword. We will destroy. Which is exactly what Osama bin Laden said.

The Independent, 16 September 2006

Torture's out – abuse is in

'Prevail' is the 'in' word in America just now. We are not going to 'win' in Iraq – because we did that in 2003, didn't we, when we stormed up to Baghdad and toppled Saddam. Then George Bush declared 'Mission Accomplished'. So now we must 'prevail'. That's what F. J. 'Bing' West, ex-soldier and former assistant secretary for International Security Affairs in the Reagan administration, said this week. Plugging his new book *No True Glory: A Frontline Account of the Battle for Fallujah*, he gave a frightening outline of what lies in store for the Sunni Muslims of Iraq.

I was sitting a few feet from Bing – plugging my own book – as he explained to the people of New York how General Casey was imposing curfews on the Sunni cities of Iraq, one after the other, how if the Sunnis did not accept democracy they would be 'occupied' (he used that word) by Iraqi troops until they did accept democracy. He talked about the 'valour' of American troops – there was no word of Iraq's monstrous suffering – and insisted that America must 'prevail' because a 'Jihadist' victory was unthinkable. I applied the Duke of Wellington's Waterloo remark about his soldiers to Bing. I don't know if he frightened the enemy, I told the audience, but by God Bing frightened me.

Our appearance at the Council on Foreign Relations – housed in a 58th Street townhouse of deep sofas and fearfully strong air conditioning (it was early November for God's sake) – was part of a series entitled 'Iraq: The Way Forward'. Forward, I asked myself? Iraq is a catastrophe. The Bing might believe he was going to 'prevail' over his 'Jihadists', but all I could say was that the American project in Iraq was over, that it was a colossal tragedy for the Iraqis dying in Baghdad alone at the rate of 1,000 a month, that the Americans must leave if peace was to be restored and that the sooner they left the better.

Many in the audience were clearly of the same mind. One elderly gentleman quietly demolished Bing's presentation by describing the massive damage to Fallujah when it was 'liberated' by the Americans for the third time last November. I gently outlined the folk that Bing's soldiers and diplomats would have to talk to if they were to disentangle themselves from this mess – I included Iraqi ex-officers who were leaders of the non-suicidal part of the insurgency and to whom would fall the task of dealing with the 'Jihadists' once Bing's boys left Iraq. To get out, I said, the Americans would need the help of Iran and Syria, countries which the Bush administration is currently (and not without reason) vilifying. Silence greeted this observation.

It was a strange week to be in America. In Washington, Ahmed Chalabi, one of Iraq's three deputy prime ministers, turned up to show how clean his hands were. I had to remind myself constantly that Chalabi was convicted in absentia in Jordan of massive bank fraud. It was Chalabi who supplied *New York Times* reporter Judith Miller with all the false information about Saddam's weapons of mass destruction. It was Chalabi's fellow defectors who persuaded the Bush administration that these weapons existed. It was Chalabi who was accused only last year of giving American intelligence secrets to Iran. It is Chalabi who is still being investigated by the FBI. But Chalabi spoke to the right-wing American Enterprise Institute in Washington, refused to make the slightest apology to the United

States, and then went on to meetings with Secretary of State Condoleezza Rice and national security adviser Stephen Hadley. Vice President Cheney and Defense Secretary Donald Rumsfeld also agreed to see him.

By contrast, Chalabi's gullible conservative dupe was subjected to a truly vicious interview in the *Washington Post* after she resigned from her paper over the Libby 'Plame-Gate' leak. A 'parade of Judys' appeared at her interview, *Post* reporter Lynne Duke wrote. 'Outraged Judy. Saddened Judy. Charming Judy. Conspiratorial Judy. Judy, the star *New York Times* reporter turned beleaguered victim of the gossip-mongers . . .' proclaiming her intention to make no apologies for writing about threats to the United States, Miller did so 'emphatically almost frantically, her crusading eyes brimming with tears'. Ouch. I can only reflect on how strange the response of the American media has become to the folly and collapse and anarchy of Iraq. It's Judy's old mate Chalabi who should be getting this treatment but no, he's back to his old tricks of spinning and manipulating the Bush administration while the American press tears one of its reporters apart for compensation.

It's like living in a prism in New York and Washington these days. 'Torture' is out. No one tortures in Iraq or Afghanistan or Guantanamo. What Americans do to their prisoners is 'abuse', and there was a wonderful moment this week when Amy Goodman, who is every leftist's dream, showed a clip from Pontecorvo's wonderful 1965 movie *The Battle of Algiers* on her *Democracy Now* programme. 'Colonel Mathieu' – the film is semi-fictional – was shown explaining why torture was necessary to safeguard French lives. Then up popped Mr Bush's real spokesman, Scott McClellan, to say that while he would not discuss interrogation methods, the primary aim of the administration was to safeguard American lives.

American journalists now refer to 'abuse laws' rather than

torture laws. Yes, abuse sounds so much better, doesn't it? No screaming, no cries of agony when you're abused. No shrieks of pain. No discussion of the state of mind of the animals perpetrating this abuse on our behalf. And it's as well to remember that the government of Prime Minister Blair has decided it's quite all right to use information gleaned from this sadism. Even Jack Straw agrees with this.

So it was a relief to drive down to the US National Archives in Maryland to research America's attempts to produce an Arab democracy after the First World War, one giant modern Arab state from the Turkish border to the Atlantic coast of Morocco. US soldiers and diplomats tried to bring this about in one brief, shining moment of American history in the Middle East. Alas, President Woodrow Wilson died; America became isolationist, and the British and French victors chopped up the Middle East for their own ends and produced the tragedy with which we are confronted today. Prevail, indeed.

The Independent, 12 November 2005

'The truth, the truth!'

'Torture works,' an American Special Forces major – now, needless to say, a colonel – boasted to a colleague of mine a couple of years ago. It seems that the CIA and their hired thugs in Afghanistan and Iraq still believe this. There is no evidence that rendition and beatings and waterboarding and the insertion of metal pipes into men's anuses – and, of course, the occasional torturing to death of detainees – has ended. Why else would the CIA admit in January that they had destroyed videotapes of prisoners being almost drowned – the 'waterboarding' technique – before they could be seen by US investigators?

Yet only a few days ago, I came across a medieval print in which a prisoner has been strapped to a wooden chair, a leather hosepipe pushed down his throat and a primitive pump fitted at the top of the hose where an ill-clad torturer is hard at work squirting water down the hose. The prisoner's eyes bulge with terror as he feels himself drowning, all the while watched by Spanish inquisitors who betray not the slightest feelings of sympathy with the prisoner. Who said 'waterboarding' was new? The Americans are just aping their predecessors in the Inquisition. Another print I found in a Canadian newspaper in November shows a prisoner under interrogation in what I suspect is Spain. In this case, he has been strapped backwards to the outer edge of a wheel. Two hooded men are ministering to his agony. One is using a bellows to encourage a fire burning at the bottom of the wheel while the other is turning the wheel forwards so that the prisoner's feet are moving into the flames. The eyes of this poor man – naked save for a cloth over his lower torso – are tight shut in pain. Two priests stand beside him, one cowled, the other wearing a robe over his surplice, a paper and pen in hand to take down the prisoner's words.

Anthony Grafton, who has been working on a book about magic in Renaissance Europe,* says that in the sixteenth and seventeenth centuries, torture was systematically used against anyone suspected of witchcraft, his or her statements taken down by sworn notaries – the equivalent, I suppose, of the CIA's interrogation officers – and witnessed by officials who made no pretence that this was anything other than torture; no talk of 'enhanced interrogation' from the lads who turned the wheel to the fire. As Grafton recounts:

> the pioneering medievalist Henry Charles Lea ... wrote at length about the ways in which inquisitors had used torture to make prisoners confess heretical views and actions. An enlightened man writing in what he saw as an enlightened age, he looked back in horror at these barbarous practices and condemned them with a clarity that anyone reading public statements must now envy.

There were professionals in the Middle Ages who were trained to use pain as a method of inquiry as well as an ultimate punishment before death. Men who were to be 'hanged, drawn and quartered', in medieval London, for example, would be shown the 'instruments' before their final suffering began with the withdrawal of their intestines in front of vast crowds of

---

* His preliminary findings were published in *The New Republic* and reprinted in the *National Post* in Toronto on 15 November 2007.

onlookers. Readers who have seen *Braveheart* will recall that William Wallace is shown the 'instruments' before being racked – but is ultimately spared disembowelment before his beheading. Most of those tortured in medieval times were anyway executed after they had provided the necessary information to their interrogators. These inquisitions – with details of the torture that accompanied them – were published and disseminated widely so that the public should understand the threat which the prisoners had represented and the power of those who inflicted such pain upon them. No destroying of videotapes here. Illustrated pamphlets and songs, according to Grafton, were added to the repertory of publicity. Ronnie Po-chia Hsia and Italian scholars Diego Quaglioni and Anna Esposito have studied the fifteenth-century Trent Inquisition whose victims were usually Jews and who, in 1475, were three Jewish households in Trent accused of murdering a Christian boy called Simon to carry out the supposed Passover 'ritual' of using his blood to make 'matzo' bread. This 'blood libel' – it was, of course, a total falsity – is still, alas, believed in many parts of the Middle East, although it is frightening to discover that the idea was well established in fifteenth-century Europe.

As usual, the 'podestà' – a city official – was the interrogator, who regarded external evidence as providing mere clues of guilt. Europe was then still governed by Roman law which required confessions in order to convict. As Grafton describes horrifyingly, once the prisoner's answers no longer satisfied the 'podestà', the torturer tied the man's or woman's arms behind their back and the prisoner would then be lifted by a pulley, agonisingly, towards the ceiling. 'Then, at the "podestà's" orders, the torturer would make the accused "jump" or "dance" – pulling him or her up, then releasing the rope, dislocating limbs and inflicting stunning pain.' Other methods of torture included thrusting onions and sulphur under a prisoner's nose or holding hot eggs under the armpits. When a member of one of the Trent Jewish families, Samuel, asked the 'podestà' where he had heard that Jews needed Christian blood, the interrogator replied – and all this while, it should be remembered, Samuel was dangling in the air on the pulley – that he had heard it from other Jews. Samuel said that he was being tortured unjustly. 'The truth, the truth!' the 'podestà' shouted, and Samuel was made to 'jump' up to eight feet, telling his interrogator: 'God the Helper and truth help me.' After forty minutes, he was returned to prison.

Once broken, the Jewish prisoners, of course, confessed. After another torture session, Samuel named a fellow Jew. Further sessions of torture – including eggs under the armpit – finally broke him and he invented the Jewish ritual murder plot and named others guilty of this non-existent crime. Two tortured women managed to exonerate children but eventually, in Grafton's words, 'they implicated loved ones, friends and members of other Jewish communities'. Thus did torture force innocent civilians – craftsmen, housewives and teenagers – to confess to fantastical crimes, along with supposed witches, women who confessed under torture that they had flown through the air to worship the Devil, destroyed crops and killed babies. Oxford historian Lyndal Roper found that the tortured eventually accepted the view that they were guilty.

Grafton's conclusion is unanswerable. Torture does not obtain truth. It will make most ordinary people say anything the torturer wants. Why, who knows if the men under the CIA's 'waterboarding' did not confess that they could fly to meet the Devil? And who knows if the CIA did not end up by believing them?

The Independent, 2 January 2008

Crusaders of the 'Green Zone'

I drove Pat and Alice Carey up the coast of Lebanon this week to look at some castles. Pat is a builder from County Wicklow, brave enough to take a holiday with his wife in Beirut when all others are thinking of running away. But I wanted to know what he thought of twelfth-century construction work. How did he rate a Crusader keep? The most beautiful of Lebanon's castles is the smallest, a dinky-toy palisade on an outcrop of rock near the village of Batroun. You have to climb a set of well-polished steps – no handrails, for this is Lebanon – up the sheer side of Mseilha castle and then clamber over doorsills into the dark, damp interior. So we padded around the battlements for half an hour. 'Strongly made or they wouldn't be still here,' Pat remarked. 'But you wouldn't find any company ready to put up the insurance. And in winter, it must have been very, very cold.' And after some minutes, he looked at me with some intensity. 'It's like being in a prison,' he said. And he was right. The only view of the outside world was through the archers' loopholes in the walls. Inside was darkness. The bright world outside was cut off by the castle defences. I could just see the splashing river to the south of the castle and, on the distant horizon, a mountainside. That was all the defenders – Crusaders or Mamelukes – would have seen. It was the only contact they had with the land they were occupying.

Up at Tripoli is Lebanon's biggest keep, the massive Castle

of Saint Gilles that still towers ominously over the port city with its delicate minarets and mass of concrete hovels. Two shell holes – remnants of Lebanon's 1975–90 civil war – have been smashed into the walls, but the interior of the castle is a world of its own; a world, that is, of stables and eating halls and dungeons. It was empty – the tourists have almost all fled Lebanon – and we felt the oppressive isolation of this terrible place.

Pat knew his Crusader castles. 'When you besieged them, the only way to get inside was by pushing timber under the foundations and setting fire to the wood. When they turned to ash, the walls came tumbling down. The defenders didn't throw boiling oil from the ramparts. They threw sand on to the attackers. The sand would get inside their armour and start to burn them until they were in too much pain to fight. But it's the same thing here in Tripoli as in the little castle. You can hardly see the city through the arrow slits. It's another – bigger – prison.'

And so I sat on the cold stone floor and stared through a loophole and, sure enough, I could see only a single minaret and a few square metres of roadway. I was in darkness. Just as the Crusaders who built this fortress must have been in darkness. Indeed, Raymond de Saint-Gilles spent years besieging the city, looking down in anger from his great fortress, built on the 'Pilgrim's Mountain', at the stout burghers of Tripoli who were constantly resupplied by boat from Egypt. Raymond himself died in the castle, facing the city he dreamed of capturing but would not live to enter. And of course, far to the east, in the ancient land of Mesopotamia, there stand today equally stout if less aesthetic barricades around another great occupying army. The castles of the Americans are made of pre-stressed concrete and steel but they serve the same purpose and doom those who built them to live in prisons.

From the 'Green Zone' in the centre of Baghdad, the US

authorities and their Iraqi satellites can see little of the city and country they claim to govern. Sleeping around the gloomy republican palace of Saddam Hussein, they can stare over the parapets or peek through the machine-gun embrasures on the perimeter wall – but that is as much as most will ever see of Iraq. The Tigris river is almost as invisible as that stream sloshing past the castle of Mseilha. The British embassy inside the 'Green Zone' flies its diplomats into Baghdad airport, air-lifts them by helicopter into the fortress – and there they sit until recalled to London. Indeed, the Crusaders in Lebanon – men with thunderous names like Tancred and Bohemond and Baldwin – used a system of control remarkably similar to the US Marines and the 82nd Airborne. They positioned their castles at a day's ride – or a day's sailing down the coast in the case of Lebanon – from each other, venturing forth only to travel between their keeps.

And then out of the east, from Syria and also from the Caliphate of Baghdad and from Persia came the 'hashashin', the 'Assassins' – the Crusaders brought the word back to Europe – who turned the Shia faith into an extremist doctrine, regarding assassination of their enemies as a religious duty. Anyone who doubts the relevance of these 'foreign fighters' to present-day Iraq should read the history of ancient Tripoli by that redoubt-able Lebanese–Armenian historian Nina Jidejian, which covers the period of the Assassins and was published at the height of the Lebanese civil war. 'It was believed that the terrorists partook of hashish to induce ecstatic visions of paradise be-fore setting out to perform their sacred duty and to face martyrdom . . .' she writes. 'The arrival of the Crusaders had added to . . . latent discontent and created a favourable terrain for their activities.'

One of the Assassins' first victims was the Count of Montfer-rat, leader of the Third Crusade who in 1191 had besieged Acre – 'Saint Jean d'Acre' to the Christians – and who met his death at the hands of men sent by the Persian 'terrorist' leader, Hassan-i Sabbah. The Assassins treated Saladin's Muslim army with equal scorn – they made two attempts to murder him – and within a hundred years had set up their own castles around Tripoli. They established a 'mother fortress' from which – and here I quote a thirteenth-century Arab geographer – 'the Assassins chosen are sent out thence to all countries and lands to slay kings and great men'. And so it is not so hard, in the dank hallways of the Castle of Saint Gilles, to see the folly of America's occupation of Iraq. Cut off from the people they rule, squeezed into their fortresses, under constant attack from 'foreign fighters', the Crusaders' dreams were destroyed.

Sitting behind that loophole in the castle at Tripoli, I could even see new meaning in Osama bin Laden's constant reference to the Americans as 'the Crusader armies'. The Crusades, too, were founded on a neo-conservative theology. The knights were going to protect the Christians of the Holy Land; they were going to 'liberate' Jerusalem – 'Mission Accomplished' – and ended up taking the spoils of the Levant, creating petty kingdoms which they claimed to control, living fearfully behind their stone defences. Their Arab opponents of the time did indeed possess a weapon of mass destruction for the Crusaders. It was called Islam.

'You can see why the Crusaders couldn't last here,' Pat said as we walked out of the huge gateway of the Castle of Saint Gilles. 'I wonder if they even knew who they were fighting.' I just resisted asking him if he would come along on my next trip to Baghdad, so I could hear part two of the builder's wisdom.

The Independent, 2 April 2005

Paradise in Hell

During the 1975–90 civil war, a clammy joke made the rounds on both sides of the Beirut front line. God, the old saw went, created Lebanon as the most beautiful country on earth. But it looked so like Paradise that God became jealous – so He put the Lebanese there. Yet the Lebanese, amid all their suffering and destruction, continued to care for their cedar trees and to plant vines and wheat and apple orchards and jasmine. Even on my own Beirut balcony, there was saxifrage and a single bougainvillea and a couple of miserable palm trees. I remember wanting to feel the warmth of plants, but I cared for them in a half-hearted way because shells fell regularly around my apartment and I was never really sure if they – or I – would survive.

In Baghdad a couple of burning summers ago, I did the same thing, setting off through the dangerous streets to a market garden of fountains and pink flowers – run by an ex-Iraqi soldier who had seen the gassed and putrefying Kurdish bodies at Halabja – and bought three two-foot pot plants. These I ceremoniously put on the balcony of *The Independent*'s room at the Hamra Hotel in bleak memory of my Beirut flowers, the imaginary Mediterranean opposite, in reality occupied by a sinister, cracked apartment block. The plants consumed litres of dirty water each day, but eventually successive colleagues let them die, just as Baghdad was dying. And who could blame them? Flowers in war are a kind of beautiful obscenity, heaven amid disaster, an attempt to create Paradise in Hell.

Yet this month once more, we set off to the Beirut market garden called Exotica to renew the balcony flowers amid Lebanon's latest and dangerous crisis. And yes, the old bougainvillea, no longer flowering, has been replanted. But three more – blazing with orange and scarlet and pink – have taken its place. There are now African violets and chrysanthemums and clostridia on the balcony. And why? Well, by extraordinary coincidence my latest mail package from *The Independent* contains the 26 April issue of *The London Review of Books*, and as I sat reading it on our newly flowering balcony, there was Brian Dillon's review of a book by Kenneth Helphand, *Defiant Gardens: Making Gardens in Wartime*. I shall, of course, buy it. The extracts were enticing enough, for Helphand had discovered that French and British troops in the trenches of the First World War also created miniature gardens.

In May 1915, the *Illustrated London News* published a full-page drawing entitled 'Beauty Amid War'. As Dillon writes:

A sign that reads 'Regent Street' has been nailed to a blackened tree, and in the foreground, two soldiers tend a pair of perfectly rectangular beds of daffodils. A photograph taken the previous winter, in the Ypres salient, shows a soldier of the London Rifle Brigade posing in what is clearly intended . . . to be an approximation of a traditional English cottage garden.

Idealised gardens obviously did really exist – what Dillon calls 'an unlikely pelago of tidy plots that stretched across the front itself'.

And I began to wonder, reading this, if flowers did not soften war for us. Wasn't 'The Roses of Picardy' a wartime song? Don't we still immortalise the blood-red poppies of Flanders

Fields? Didn't Gracie Fields mock the Nazi Blitz with 'The Biggest Aspidistra in the World'? And for that matter, more gloomily, didn't the British codename Arnhem 'Operation Market Garden'?

Of course, Britons in wartime London cultivated kitchen gardens for food rather than flowers, and it's probably true, as Dillon suggests, that the wartime garden is as much a symbol of desperation as a spiritually sustaining stretch of earth. Helphand's book records how the Jews of the Warsaw Ghetto – long banned from public parks – could see from their windows 'young girls with bouquets of lilac walking on the "Aryan" part of the street'. Mary Berg recorded in the ghetto in 1941 how she could 'even smell the tender fragrance of the opening buds. But there is no sign of spring in the ghetto.' And for symbolism of America's collapse in Iraq, what could be more profound than the story of US Warrant Officer Brook Turner, at an army base north of Baghdad, trimming a tiny lawn less than a metre across and a couple of metres long with a pair of scissors? Turner was acting out of nostalgia for the grass of his native Oregon, but it was an 'artificially sustained territory', threatened from within by a tenacious enemy of insurgent ants.

I was originally inspired to place plants on my own balcony by my landlord Mustafa, who used to raise fig trees, olives and roses on the shell-smashed vacant lot next door. (Palestinians later buried rockets a few metres away.) Now a grim parking lot covers Mustafa's little orchard, but he dutifully rescued most of his flowers and now they hang from 24 white boxes on the front railing of his home. And after all, was it not the late Ryszard Kapuscinski, in his magnificent book on the Shah, who realised why Iranians made such beautiful carpets? They wove birds with splendidly coloured wings on to silken trees and rivers and blossom-covered branches. And they would throw their carpets to the ground, creating a garden in the desert.

An army of lovebirds now flocks past Mustafa's garden and hides in the palm trees of the Corniche. But there was one persistent, ratty bird with no sense of music that would wake us all before dawn each morning. 'Cheep–cheep–cheep–cheep–cheep,' it would go, monotonously, ruthlessly off key. Even the howl of shells would have been more musical, Wilfred Owen's 'choir' of artillery rounds. For months Mustafa would emerge in his pyjamas and dressing gown and storm on to the road with an ammunition pouch of stones. These he would fling into the trees in an attempt to hit the wretched bird which prevented our sleep. He always missed, and in the end he simply gave up, and now the same bird's descendants sound the same ghastly chorus at 4.30 a.m. There is nothing we can do. Nature has won over humanity.

The Independent, 12 May 2007

'Bush is a revelatory at bedtime'

Sy Hersh is an ornery, cussed sort of guy, not one to suffer fools gladly. As the man who broke the My Lai story and the atrocities at Abu Ghraib, I reckon he has a right to be ornery from time to time – and cussed. He's dealing with powerful folk in Washington, including one – George W. Bush – who would like to cut him down. And when Hersh wrote – as he did in the *New Yorker* this month – that 'current and former American military and intelligence officials' have said Bush has a target list to prevent Iran obtaining nuclear weapons and that Bush's 'ultimate goal' in the nuclear confrontation with Iran is regime change – again! – you can see why Bush was worried. 'Wild', he called the Hersh story. Which must mean it has some claim to truth.

So when I cornered Hersh at Columbia University in New York and dropped him a note during a Charles Glass presentation asking for an interview, I expected a stiff reply. 'Anything you ask,' he scribbled obligingly on a piece of paper. His own lecture was frightening. Bush has a messianic vision – and intends to go down in history (probably he has chosen the right direction) as the man who will have 'saved' Iran. 'So we're in a real American crisis ... we've had a collapse of Congress ... we have had a collapse of the military ... the good news is that when we wake up tomorrow morning, there will be one less day [of Bush]. But that is the only good news.'

Hersh might have said that we'd also had a 'collapse' of the media in the United States, a total disintegration of the Ed Murrow/Howard K. Smith/Daniel Ellsberg/Carl Bernstein and Bob Woodward school of journalism. The greying, bespectacled, obscenity-swearing Hersh is about all we have left to frighten the most powerful man in the world (save for the jibes of Maureen Dowd in the *New York Times*).

So it's good to know he's still doing some fighting, including other journalists on his target list. 'I know some serious generals,' he says. 'I can't urge them to go public. They'd be attacked by Fox [TV], and the [New York] *Times* and the *Washington Post* would wring their hands. It's a mechanism. You don't get rewarded in the newsroom for being a malcontent.' Journalists on the mainstream papers are largely middle-class college graduates – not reporters who came up the hard way like Hersh's street reporting in Chicago in his early days. They have largely no connection to the immigrants' society. 'They don't know what it's like to be on social welfare. Their families weren't in Vietnam and their families are not in Iraq.' The BBC, too, has 'fallen off the way'.

So what is the Hersh school of journalism?

'In my business, I get information, I check it out and I find it's not true – that's what my business is. Now there is [also] stuff in the military from people I don't know – I don't touch it . . . I was seeing [President] Bashar [Assad of Syria] at the time of the assassination of [former Lebanese prime minister Rafiq] Hariri. There was obviously bad blood between Bashar and Hariri. Bashar was saying that Hariri wanted to take over the cell-phone business in Damascus. To this day I don't know what happened. I saw Bashar from 11 a.m. until 1 p.m. [on 14 February 2005]. He talked about what a thief Hariri was. I didn't write it.'

And there goes a scoop about bad blood, I said to myself. But on Iran, it was something different for Hersh. He was talking to a contact. 'I brought up Iran. "It's really bad," he said. "You ought to get into it. You can go to Vienna and find out how far away [from nuclear weapons production] they are." Then he told me they were having trouble walking back the nuclear option with Bush. People don't want to speak out – they want the shit on *my* head.'

As Hersh said in his *New Yorker* report, nuclear planners routinely go through options – 'We're talking about mushroom clouds, radiation, mass casualties, and contamination over years,' he quotes one of them as saying – but once the planners try to argue against all this, they are shouted down. According to another intelligence officer quoted by Hersh, 'The White House said, "Why are you challenging this? The option came from you".' In other words, once the planners routinely put options on the table, the options become possibilities to be considered rather than technical reports.

'That whole Johns Hopkins speech,' Hersh goes on, referring to the address in which Bush attacked Hersh's own article, 'he talked about the wonderful progress in Iraq. This is halluci-natory – and there are people on a high level in the Pentagon and they can't get the President to give this up. Because it's crazy. In the UK, you might have some crazy view – but you knew it was. But these guys [in Washington] are talking in revelations. Bush is a revelatory at bedtime – he has to take a nap. It's so childish and simplistic. And don't think he's diminished. He's still got two years ... he's not diminished. We've still got a Congress that can't articulate opposition. This is a story where I profoundly hope, at every major point, that I'm wrong.'

Hersh has also been casting his wizened eye on the Brits. 'Your country is very worried about what Bush is going to do – your people' – Hersh means the Foreign Office – 'are really worried. There are no clearances ... no consultations.' In Washington, 'advocating humanity, peace, integrity is not a value in the power structure . . . my government are incapable of leaving [Iraq]. They don't know how to get out of Baghdad. We can't get out. In this war, the end is going to be very, very messy – because we don't know how to get out. We're going to get out body by body. I think that scares the hell out of me.' It's all put neatly by one of Hersh's sources in the Pentagon: 'The problem is that the Iranians realise that only by becoming a nuclear state can they defend themselves against the US. Something bad is going to happen.'

What was that line from Bogart in *Casablanca*, when he asked Sam, his pianist, what time it is in New York? Sam replies that his watch has stopped, and Bogart says, 'I bet they're asleep in New York. I'll bet they're asleep all over America.' Except for Hersh.

The Independent, 20 April 2006

The worse it gets, the bigger the lies

We are now in the greatest crisis since the last greatest crisis. That's how we run the Iraq War – or the Second Iraq War as Prime Minister Blair would now have us believe. Hostages are paraded in orange tracksuits to remind us of Guantanamo Bay. Kidnappers demand the release of women held prisoner by the Americans. Abu Ghraib is what they are talking about. Abu Ghraib? Anyone remember Abu Ghraib? Remember those dirty little snapshots? But don't worry. This wasn't the America George Bush recognised, and besides we're punishing the bad apples, aren't we? Women? Why, there are only a couple of dames left – and they are 'Dr Germ' and 'Dr Anthrax'. But Arabs do not forget so easily. It was a Lebanese woman, Samia Melki, who first understood the true semantics of those Abu Ghraib photographs for the Arab world. The naked Iraqi, his body smeared with excrement, back to the camera, arms stretched out before the butch and blond American with a stick, possessed, she wrote in *Counterpunch*, 'all the drama and contrasting colours of a Caravaggio painting'.

The best of Baroque art invites the viewer to be part of the artwork. 'Forced to walk in a straight line with his legs crossed, his torso slightly twisted and arms spread out for balance, the Iraqi prisoner's toned body, accentuated by the excrement and the bad lighting, stretches out in crucifix form. Exuding a dignity long denied, the Arab is suffering for the world's sins.'

And that, I fear, is the least of the suffering that has gone on at Abu Ghraib. For what happened to all those videos that members of Congress were allowed to watch in secret and that we – the public – were not permitted to see? Why have we suddenly forgotten about Abu Ghraib? Seymour Hersh, one of the few journalists in America who is doing his job – has spoken publicly about what else happened in that terrible jail. I'm indebted to a reader for the following extract from a recent Hersh lecture:

> Some of the worst things that happened that you don't know about. OK? Videos. There are women there. Some of you may have read that they were passing letters out, communications out to their men. This is at Abu Ghraib . . . The women were passing messages out saying please come and kill me because of what's happened. And basically what happened is that those women who were arrested with young boys, children, in cases that have been recorded, the boys were sodomised, with the cameras rolling, and the worst above all of them is the soundtrack of the boys shrieking . . .

Already, however, we have forgotten this. Just as we must no longer talk about weapons of mass destruction. For as the details slowly emerge of the desperate efforts of Bush and Blair to find these non-existent nasties, I don't know whether to laugh or cry. US mobile site survey teams managed, at one point, to smash into a former Iraqi secret police headquarters in Baghdad, only to find a padlocked inner door. Here, they believed, they would find the horrors that Bush and Blair were praying for. And what did they find behind the second door? A vast emporium of brand-new vacuum cleaners. At Baath party headquarters, another team – led by a Major Kenneth Deal – believed they had discovered secret documents which would reveal Saddam's weapons programme. The papers turned out to be an Arabic translation of A. J. P. Taylor's *The Struggle for Mastery in Europe*. Perhaps Bush and Blair should read it.

So as we continue to stagger down the crumbling stairway of our own ghastly making, we must listen to bigger and bigger whoppers. Iyad Allawi, the puppet prime minister – still deferentially called 'interim prime minister' by many of my reporter chums – insists that elections will be held in January even though he has less control of the Iraqi capital (let alone the rest of the country) than the mayor of Baghdad. The ex-CIA agent, who obediently refused to free the two women prisoners the moment Washington gave him instructions not to do so, dutifully trots over to London and on to Washington to shore up more of the Blair–Bush lies.

Second Iraq War indeed. How much more of this sophistry are we, the public, expected to stomach? We are fighting in 'the crucible of global terrorism', according to Blair. What are we to make of this nonsense? Of course, he didn't tell us we were going to have a Second Iraq War when he helped to start the First Iraq War, did he? And he didn't tell the Iraqis that, did he? No, we had come to 'liberate' them. So let's just remember the crisis before the crisis before the crisis. Let's go back to last November when our prime minister was addressing the Lord Mayor's banquet. The Iraq War, he informed us then – and presumably he was still referring to the First Iraq War – was 'the battle of seminal importance for the early twenty-first century'.

Well, he can say that again. But just listen to what else Lord Blair of Kut informed us about the war. 'It will define relations between the Muslim world and the West. It will influence profoundly the development of Arab states and the Middle East. It will have far-reaching implications for the future of American and Western diplomacy.' And he can say that again, can't he? For it is difficult to think of anything more profoundly dangerous for us, for the West, for the Middle East, for Christians and Muslims since the Second World War – the real second world war, that is – than Blair's war in Iraq. And Iraq, remember, was going to be the model for the whole Middle East. Every Arab state would want to be like Iraq. Iraq would be the catalyst – perhaps even the 'crucible' – of the new Middle East. Spare me the hollow laughter.

I have been struck these past few weeks how very many of the letters I've received from readers come from men and women who fought in the Second World War, who argue ferociously that Blair and Bush should never be allowed to compare this quagmire to the real struggle against evil which they waged more than half a century ago.

'I, now 90, remember the men maimed in body and mind who haunted the lanes in rural Wales where I grew up in the years after 1918,' Robert Parry wrote to me.

> For this reason, Owen's 'Dulce et decorum est'* remains for me the ultimate expression of the reality of death in war, made now more horrific by American 'targeted' bombing and the suicide bombers. We need a new Wilfred Owen to open our eyes and consciences, but until one appears this great poem must be given space to speak again.

It would be difficult to find a more eloquent rejoinder to the infantile stories now being peddled by our prime minister. Not for many years has there been such a gap – in America as well as Britain – between the people and the government they

---

* Wilfred Owen wrote the poem in August 1917. The closing lines tell the reader that if he knew the full horrors of war:

> My friend, you would not tell with such high zest
> To children ardent for some desperate glory,
> The old Lie: Dulce et decorum est
> Pro patria mori.

elected. Blair's most recent remarks are speeches made – to quote that Owen poem – 'to children ardent for some desperate glory'. Ken Bigley's blindfolded face is our latest greatest crisis.* But let's not forget what went before.

The Independent, 25 September 2004

---

* Civil engineer Ken Bigley was kidnapped in Baghdad on 16 September 2004 and – despite a desperate intervention by the Muslim Council of Britain – was beheaded by his captors on 7 October of that year. His captors had demanded the release of Iraqi women prisoners.

Let's have more martyrs!

I wonder sometimes if we have not entered a new age of what the French call *infantilisme*. I admit I am writing these words on the lecture circuit in Paris where pretty much every political statement – including those of Messrs Chirac, Sarkozy, de Villepin et al. – might fall under this same title. But the folk I am referring to, of course, are George W. Bush, Prime Minister Blair and – a newcomer to the Fisk Hall of Childishness – President Mahmoud Ahmadinejad of Iran.

For as someone who has to look at the eviscerated corpses of Palestine and Israel, the murdered bodies in the garbage heaps of Iraq, the young women shot through the head in the Baghdad morgue, I can only shake my head in disbelief at the sheer, unadulterated, lazy bullshit – let's call a spade a spade – which is currently emerging from our great leaders. There was a time when the Great and the Good spoke with a voice of authority, albeit mendacious, rather than mediocrity; when too many lies spelled a ministerial resignation or two. But today we seem to live on two levels: reality and myth.

Let's start with the reality of Iraq. It is, to quote Winston Churchill on Palestine in the late 1940s, a 'hell-disaster', a nation of anarchy from Mosul and Irbil down to Basra, where armed insurgents control streets scarcely half a mile from the Baghdad 'Green Zone' wherein American and British diplomats and their democratically elected Iraqi 'government' dream up optimism for a country whose people are burning with ferocious resentment against Western occupation. No wonder I'm more sure each day that I want to be away from conflict.

But for Bush, America is not anxious to withdraw from Iraq. Far from it. The United States is fighting enemies who want to establish a 'totalitarian empire', he says, a 'mortal danger to all humanity' which America will confront. Washington is fighting 'as brutal an enemy as we have ever faced'. But what about Hitler's Nazi Germany? Mussolini's fascist Italy? The expansionist Japanese empire which bombed Pearl Harbor in 1941? It's one thing, surely, for Bush and Lord Blair of Kut al-Amara to play Roosevelt and Churchill or to claim that Saddam is Hitler, but to exalt our grubby, torture-encrusted, illegal conflicts as being more important than the Second World War – or our turbaned enemies as more malicious than the Auschwitz SS killers – is surely a step on the road to the madhouse.

'By any standard of history,' my favourite American president declared this week, 'Iraq has made incredible progress.' Excuse me? By any standard of history, the Iraqi insurgents have made incredible inroads into the US military occupation of Iraq. 'We've lost some of our nation's finest men and women in the war on terror,' Bush tells us. '. . . The best way to honour the sacrifice of our fallen troops is to complete the mission.' In other words, we are going to prove the worth of the sacrifice by making more sacrifices. Truly, this is bin Laden-like in its naivety. We've suffered martyrs? Then let's have more martyrs!

Then we have President Ahmadinejad of Iran. Israel, he tells one of those infinitely dull and boring Tehran conferences on 'Zionism' this week, must be 'wiped off the map'. I'm old enough to remember this claptrap from Yasser Arafat's weary old cronies in Beirut in the late 1970s. Ahmadinejad's speech – before the obligatory 4,000 'students' who used to be a regular feature of Iran's revolution – was replete with all the antique claims. 'The establishment of the Zionist regime was a move by the world oppressor against the Islamic world. The skirmishes [*sic*] in the occupied land are part of the war of destiny.' Was this silly man, I ask myself, the scriptwriter for Ridley Scott's movie *Kingdom of Heaven*? Surely not, for the Hollywood epic is Homeric in its scope and literacy compared to Ahmadinejad's sterile prose. This, after all, is the sort of stuff I had to suffer during the original Iranian revolution when Ayatollah Khomeini set up his theocracy in Iran. Government for and by the dead is becoming a vision for both Bush and Ahmadinejad.

But hold on. We have not counted on the Churchillian vision of Lord Blair. 'I have never come across a situation of [*sic*] the president of a country stating they want to wipe out another country,' he told us on Thursday. Oh deary me. What can we do with this man? For Rome was rather keen, was it not, to wipe out Carthage. And then there is the little matter of Herr Hitler – a regular bogeyman for Blair when he stares across the desert wastes towards the Tigris – who insisted that Poland should be wiped out, who turned Czechoslovakia into the Nazi protectorate of Bohemia and Moravia, who allowed the Croatian Ustashe to try to destroy Serbia, who ended his days by declaring that his own German state should be wiped out because its people didn't deserve him.

But now let's listen to Lord Blair of Kut al-Amara again. 'If they [the Iranians] carry on like this, the question that people are going to be asking is: when are you going to do something about this? Can you imagine a state like that with an attitude like that having a nuclear weapon?' Well yes, of course we can. North Korea. Whoops! But they've already got nuclear weapons, haven't they? So we'll ask a different question. Exactly who are those 'people', Lord Blair, who might expect you to 'do something'? Could they have anything in common with the million people who told you not to invade Iraq? And if not, could we have some addresses, identities, some idea of their number? A million perhaps? I doubt it.

Is there to be any end of this? Not yet, I fear. In Australia a couple of weeks ago I found Muslims in Melbourne and Adelaide regaling me with stories of abuse and obscenities in the street. New laws are about to be introduced by Prime Minister John Howard to counter 'terror' which will not only allow detention without trial, but also the extension of 'sedition' laws which could be used against those (mainly Muslims, of course) who oppose Australia's pointless military involvement in Afghanistan and Iraq.

Well, count me in, John. I think you live in a great country with great people, but I'm planning to turn up in Adelaide again in the spring to argue against any Western involvement in those two countries, including yours. I look forward to a sedition charge. And to Lord Blair 'doing something' against North Korea. I hope Mr Bush never does discover enemies worse than the Wehrmacht and the SS. And I sincerely trust that the little satraps of the religious necrocracy that is Iran will grow up in the years to come. Alas. Like Peter Pan, our leaders wish to be for ever young, for ever childish, and for ever ready to play in their bloodless sandpits – at our expense.

The Independent, 29 October 2005

The flying carpet

I tried out the new Beirut–Baghdad air service this week. It's a sleek little 20-seater with two propellers, a Lebanese-Canadian pilot and a name to take you aback. It's called 'Flying Carpet Airlines'. As Commander Queeg said in *The Caine Mutiny*, I kid thee not. It says 'Flying Carpet' on the little blue boarding cards, below the captain's cabin and on the passenger headrest covers where the aircraft can be seen gliding through the sky on a high-pile carpet.

And it's an odd little flight, too. You arrive at Beirut's swish new glass and steel airport where you are told to meet your check-in desk handler in front of the post office in the arrivals lounge. There is a group of disconsolate Americans – 'contractors' who've been passing the weekend in the fleshpots – and fearful Lebanese businessmen and, well, you've guessed it, *The Independent*'s equally fearful correspondent.

It was a while before I realised that the whole thing was a kind of Iraqi metaphor. From the Beirut arrivals lounge, you pass through the metal detectors in Departures, breeze past the spanking new duty-free, pick up a cappuccino and then – here we go – head for the special Mecca pilgrimage departure gate. In a box-like room painted all white, you wait for a small blue bus which eventually chugs guiltily off round the side of the airport, past the shell-blasted freight cargo hangars from

Beirut's very own, pleased-to-be-forgotten war, to the steps of the only aircraft in Flying Carpet's fleet.

Only when I had clambered, half doubled up, down the tube to my seat did I realise that we were only a few hundred metres from the site of the old US Marine base, suicide-bombed back in 1983 at a cost of 241 American lives. I remember how the air pressure changed in my Beirut apartment when the bomb exploded and how, a couple of days later, I saw Vice President George Bush Snr standing amid the rubble, telling us: 'We will not let a bunch of insidious terrorist cowards change the foreign policy of the United States.' Then within months, President Reagan decided to 'redeploy' his US Marines to their ships offshore.

These, of course, were heretical thoughts as we climbed above the snow-frothed Lebanese mountains, crossed the Syrian border and then flew east across the ever-darkening, deep-brown deserts of Syria and Iraq. I opened my morning paper. And there was old George Bush's cantankerous son, wearing that silly smile of his, telling the world that while there may be a few problems in old 'Ayrak', the 30 January elections would go ahead; violence would be defeated; the bad guys would not be able to stop the forward march of democracy. In other words, he wasn't going to let a bunch of insidious terrorist cowards change the foreign policy of the United States.

Of course, the moment you arrive at the scene of Bush's great new experiment in democracy – and we are all looking forward to the elections in Baghdad with the same kind of enthusiasm that the people of Dresden showed when the first Lancasters flew down the Elbe – it all looks very different. Baghdad airport is crowded with heavily armed mercenaries and friendly, but equally armed, Gurkhas. And there's a big poster not far from the terminal with a massive colour photograph of the aftermath of a Baghdad car bombing, complete with the body of a half-naked woman in the lower right-hand corner.

The text beneath this obscenity is in Arabic:

> They want to destroy our country – they attack schools. These dogs want to keep our children in ignorance so they can teach them hatred. We need the help of the multinational forces to show them that we will do anything to get our country back and to root out the killers and looters on our roads who bear the full responsibility for these terrible crimes committed against our peaceful Iraqi people. The Iraqi people refuse to be victims because they are a strong community which will never die.

But while the Iraqis want security, an increasing number of them are coming to support the 'dogs' and ever fewer want the assistance of the 'multinational forces' which, in Baghdad and much of the Sunni provinces controlled by the insurgents, means Mr Bush's very own army. Now of course, opinion polls – an invention of the West, not the East – do show that a majority of Iraqis would like some of Mr Bush's democracy. Back in the days of the beastly Saddam, they surely wanted even more of it – though, at the time, we were busy supporting Saddam's regime so that he could root out all the killers in Iran, not to mention the Iraqi communists and Iraqi Shias and Kurds who were trying to destroy him.

Opinion polls would also show that a majority of Iraqis – an even larger majority, I suspect – would like some security from all the killers and looters whom the present-day multinational force doesn't seem able to catch. And the greatest majority of all Iraqis would, no doubt, like US passports. Indeed, I've often thought that the one sure way of closing down Iraq's war would be to give American citizenship to every Iraqi, in just the same way that the Romans made their conquered peoples citizens of Rome. But since this is not an idea that would commend itself to Mr Bush and his empire-builders, the Iraqis are just going to have to endure democracy in their violent, electricity-free, petrol-less towns and cities.

The Shias, of course, have been waiting impatiently for elections for almost two years. The American proconsul of the time, Paul Bremer, was too frightened to hold them soon after the invasion – when they might have taken place without much violence – in case Iraq turned into a Shia theocracy. The Kurds are also waiting to put their stamp on their emerging statelet in the north.

The problem is that without the participation of the Sunni Muslims, the results of these elections – while they will be free in the sense that Saddam's were not – will be as unrepresentative of the Iraqi nation as the polls which used to give The Beast 98.96 per cent of the vote. The Americans are now threatening to 'top up' the parliament with a few chosen Sunnis of their own. And we all know how representative they're going to be of the Sunni community which is the heart of the insurgency against American occupation.

All in all, then, a mighty mess to contemplate after the 30 January elections.* The brush fires are already being lit, but fear not, Bush and Blair will tell us that they always knew things would get violent on polling day – which will make it all right, I suppose – and that, if the violence gets worse, it all goes to show how successful those elections were because they made the killers and looters and 'dogs' angry. A bunch of insidious terrorist cowards are not going to change the foreign policy of the United States. Well, we shall see. Meanwhile, I'm checking the flight schedules to see if my magic carpet can take me back to Beirut after 30 January.

The Independent, 15 January 2005

* The main Shia parties won 140 of the 275 seats in the Iraqi National Assembly, the Kurdish bloc 75. Secular groups – supported by the Americans – picked up only 40. The Sunnis – representing about 20 per cent of the Iraqi population – largely boycotted the poll. On election day, nine suicide bombers killed 35 people.

The show must go on

It makes you want to scream. I have been driving the dingy, dangerous, ovenlike streets of Baghdad all week, ever more infested with insurgents and their informers, the American troops driving terrified over the traffic islands, turning their guns on all of us if we approach within 50 metres. In the spaceship isolation of Saddam's old republican palace, the Kurds and the Shia have been tearing Iraq apart, refusing to sign up for a constitution lest it fail to give them the federations – and the oil wealth – they want. They miss their deadline – though I found no one in 'real' Baghdad, no one outside the Green Zone bunker, who seemed to care. And that evening, I turn on my television to hear President Bush praise the 'courage' of the constitution negotiators whose deadline Bush himself had promised would be met.

Courage? So it's courageous, is it, to sit in a time capsule, sealed off from your people by miles of concrete walls, and argue about the future of a nation which is in anarchy? Then Condoleezza Rice steps forward to tell us this is all part of the 'road to democracy' in the Middle East.

I am back on the streets again, this time at the an-Nahda bus station – *nahda* means 'renaissance' for those who want the full irony of such situations – and around me is the wreckage of another bombing. Smashed police cars, burnt-out, pulverised buses (passengers all on board, of course), women screaming with fury, children taken to the al-Kindi hospital in bandages to be met by another bomb. And that night, I flip on the television again and find the local US military commander in the Sadr City district of Baghdad – close to the bus station – remarking blithely that while local people had been very angry, they supported the local 'security' forces (i.e. the Americans) and were giving them more help than ever and that we were – wait for it – 'on the path to democracy'.

Sometimes I wonder if there will be a moment when reality and myth, truth and lies, will actually collide. When will the detonation come? When the insurgents wipe out an entire US base? When they pour over the walls of the Green Zone and turn it into the same trashed blocks as the rest of Baghdad? Or will we then be told – as we have been in the past – that this just shows the 'desperation' of the insurgents, that these terrible acts (the bus station bombing this week, for example) only prove that the 'terrorists' know they are losing?

In a traffic jam, a boy walks past my car, trying to sell a magazine. Saddam's face – yet again – is on the cover. The ex-dictator's seedy, bewhiskered features are on the front pages, again and again, to remind the people of Baghdad how fortunate they are to be rid of the dictator. Saddam to go on trial next month, in two months' time, before the end of the year. Six deadlines for the ghastly old man's trial have come and gone – like so many other deadlines in Iraq – but the people are still supposed to be fascinated and appalled at Saddam's picture. You may sweat at home in powerless houses; you may have no fresh food because your freezer is hot; you may have to queue for hours to buy petrol; you may have to suffer constant death threats and armed robbery and your city may suffer 1,100 violent deaths in July alone (all true), but, just to take your mind off things, remember that Saddam is going on trial.

I have not met anyone in Iraq – save for those who lost their loved ones to his thugs – who cares any more about Saddam. He is yesterday's man, a thing of the past. To conjure up this monster again is an insult to the people of Baghdad – who have more fears, more anxieties and greater mourning to endure than any offer of bread and circuses by the Americans can assuage. Yet in the outside world – the further from Iraq, the more credible they sound – George Bush and Tony Blair will repeat that we really have got democracy on its feet in Iraq, that we overthrew the tyrant Saddam and that a great future awaits the country and that new investments are being planned at international conferences (held far away from Iraq, of course) and that the next bombings in Europe, like the last ones, will have nothing – absolutely nothing – to do with Iraq. The show must go on and I know, when I return to Beirut or fly to Europe, Iraq will not look so bad. The Mad Hatter will look quite sane and the Cheshire Cat will smile at me from the tree.

Democracy, democracy, democracy. Take Egypt. President Mubarak allows opponents to stand in the forthcoming elections. Bush holds this up as another sign of democracy in the Middle East. But Mubarak's opponents have to be approved by his own party members in parliament, and the Muslim Brotherhood – which ought to be the largest party in the country – is still officially illegal. Sitting in Baghdad, I watched Mubarak's first party rally, a mawkish affair in which he actually asked for support. So who will win this 'democratic' election? I'll take a risk: our old pal Mubarak. And I'll bet he gets more than 80 per cent of the votes. Watch this space.*

And of course, from my little Baghdad eyrie I've been watching the eviction of Israelis from their illegal settlements in the Palestinian Gaza Strip. The word 'illegal' doesn't pop up on

* In fact, Mubarak received 88 per cent of the votes in the 2005 presidential election, and less than 80 per cent in parliamentary elections the same year.

the BBC, of course; nor the notion that the settlers – for which read colonisers – were not being evicted from their land but from land they originally took from others. Nor is much attention paid to the continued building in the equally illegal colonies within the Palestinian West Bank which will – inevitably – make a 'viable' (Blair's favourite word) Palestine impossible. In Gaza, everyone waited for Israeli settler and Israeli soldier to open fire on each other. But when a settler did open fire, he did so to murder four Palestinian workers on the West Bank. The story passed through the television coverage like a brief, dark, embarrassing cloud and was forgotten. Settlements dismantled. Evacuation from Gaza. Peace in our time.

But in Baghdad, the Iraqis I talk to are not convinced. It is to their eternal credit that those who live in the hell of Iraq still care about the Palestinians, still understand what is really happening in the Middle East, are not fooled by the nonsense peddled by George Bush and Lord Blair of Kut al-Amara. 'What is this "evil ideology" that Blair keeps talking about?' an Iraqi friend asked me this week. 'What will be your next invention? When will you wake up?'

I couldn't put it better myself.

The Independent, 20 August 2005

'He was killed by the enemy' – but all is well in Iraq

Taking things for granted. Or, as a very dear friend of mine used to say to me, 'There you go.' I am sitting in Baghdad airport, waiting for my little Flying Carpet aircraft to take me home to Beirut, but the local Iraqi station manager, Mr Ghazwan, has not turned up like he used to. Without him, I can't enter Departures or check in.

Back in January, he was here, telling me he wouldn't forget to take me through security, talking to an Iraqi officer who looked remarkably like him, telling the officer to look after me. Ghazwan spoke careful, grammatical English and would laugh at himself when he made mistakes. So I call Ghazwan's mobile and an old man answers. I want to speak to Ghazwan, I say. 'Why?' Because I need to know when he'll be at the airport. There is a kind of groan from the other end of the line. 'He was killed.' I sit there on my plastic airport seat, unable to speak. What? What do you mean? 'He was killed by the enemy,' the old man says, and I hear the receiver taken from him.

A young woman now, with good English. 'Who are you?' A passenger. English. I start apologising. No one told me Ghazwan was dead. Even the Beirut travel agents still list his name as a Baghdad contact. The young woman – it is his wife, or rather his young widow – mutters something about him being killed on the way to the airport and I ask when this happened.

'On the 14th of March,' she says. I had last seen him exactly five weeks before his death. And the story comes out. His brother was a security guard at the airport – presumably the officer who looked like him whom I had met in February – and the two men were leaving home together to go to work in the same car when gunmen shot the brother dead and killed Ghazwan in the same burst of fire. I apologise again. I say how sorry I am. There is an acknowledgement from the young woman and the mobile is switched off.

Taking things for granted. I am back in Beirut, watching the new Pope visit his native Germany. He meets Cologne's Jewish community. He talks of the wickedness of the Jewish Holocaust. He should. He speaks warmly of Israel. Why not? Then he meets the Muslim community and I see them on the screen, heads slightly bowed, eyes glancing furtively towards the cameras. To them he lectures on the evils of terrorism. It all seems logical.

But then I sit up. In his first address, there is no word about Israel's occupation of the West Bank, its expanding settlements on other people's land, against all international law. And the Muslims, well, they do have to be reminded of their sins, of their duty to extirpate 'terrorism', to preach moderation at all times, to stop the scourge of suicide bombers. And suddenly I am shocked at this profound lack of judgement on the Pope's part. Yet meekly aware that I had myself gone along with it. It was the Pope's job, wasn't it, to apologise to the Jews of Europe. And it was his job, wasn't it, to warn the Muslims of Europe.

Thus do we fall in line. Yes, he should apologise for the Holocaust – to the end of time. But might not His Holiness, the former anti-aircraft gunner, have also apologised to the Muslims for the bloody and catastrophic invasion of Iraq – no, no, of course there's no parallel in evil, scale, etc. – but he might have at least shown the courage of his predecessor who stood up against George Bush and his ferocious war. Taking

things for granted. In Baghdad and then in Beirut, I read of
the latest 'anti-terror' laws of Prime Minister Blair. Of course,
of course. After suicide bombers on the London Underground,
what else do we expect? Our precious capital and its people
must be protected. Having been three or four trains in front
of the King's Cross Tube that exploded on 7 July, I take these
things seriously myself. And were I back on the London Tube
today, I'd probably be trying to avoid young men with backpacks – as well as armed members of the Metropolitan Police.*

And after all the panegyrics in the press about our wonderful
security forces, I'd also be taking a close look at these fine and
patriotic folk. These are the men (and women?) who lied to
us about weapons of mass destruction in Iraq. These are the
chaps who couldn't get a single advance trace of even one of
the four suicide bombings on 7 July (nor the non-lethal ones
a few days later). These are the lads who gunned down a
helpless civilian as he sat on a Tube train.

But hold on a moment, I say to myself again. The 7 July
bombings would be a comparatively quiet day in Baghdad.
Was I not at the site of the an-Nahda bus station bombings
after forty-three civilians – as innocent, their lives just as precious as those of Londoners – were torn to pieces last week?
At the al-Kindi hospital, relatives had a problem identifying
the dead. Heads were placed next to the wrong torsos, feet
next to the wrong legs. A problem there. But there came not
a groan from England. We were still locked into our 7 July
trauma. No detectives are snooping around the an-Nahda

* Four British 'anti-terrorist' police officers systematically fired bullets over
a 30-second period into the head of a totally innocent Brazilian, Jean Charles
de Menezes, a 27-year-old electrician, on a London Underground train on
22 July 2005, because they believed he was a suicide bomber. He was not.
Although an official report strongly criticised the police, none of the killers
were demoted or forced to resign. A senior officer was to say later: 'We did
our best.' Four British Muslim suicide bombers had killed 52 civilians and
wounded another 700 on the London Tube and bus system on 7 July 2005.

bomb site looking for clues. They're already four suicide bombs later. An-Nahda is history.

And it dawns on me, sitting on my balcony over the Mediterranean at the end of this week, that we take far too much for granted. We like to have little disconnects in our lives. Maybe this is the fault of daily journalism – where we encapsulate the world every twenty-four hours, then sleep on it and start a new history the next day in which we fail totally to realise that the narrative did not begin before last night's deadline but weeks, months, years ago. For it is a fact, is it not, that if 'we' had not invaded Iraq in 2003, those forty-three Iraqis would not have been pulverised by those three bombs last week. And it is surely a fact that, had we not invaded Iraq, the 7 July bombs would not have gone off. In which case the Pope would not last week have been lecturing German Muslims on the evils of 'terrorism'.

And of course, had we not invaded Iraq, Mr Ghazwan would be alive and his brother would be alive and his grieving widow would have been his young and happy wife and his broken father would have been a proud dad. But, as that friend of mine used to say, 'there you go'.

The Independent, 27 August 2005

CHAPTER NINE

We have lost our faith and they have not

I live in a Muslim district of Beirut, in the western half of the city. More precisely, I live in a Druze sector of the Lebanese capital – and in parliament, the Druze are counted as Muslims. My landlord, Mustafa, is a Druze. My driver Abed, however, is a Sunni Muslim, my classical Arabic translator Imad is a Shiite and my grocer, Patrick, a Christian. The odd thing is that we never think about this in any conscious way. During Ramadan, I do not eat when I am travelling with Abed or Imad. If I am with observant Muslims, I do not drink alcohol. If am with Christians, I often speak in French, the preferred language of Lebanon's Maronite community. But these are merely acts of respect. Verbal political correctness has no place in the Muslim world in which I live. Abed wishes me a happy Christmas and I say 'Eid Moubarak' – congratulations on the Eid – on the Muslim holiday that ends Ramadan. It was the Imam Ali who said that, if you see another man, he is either your brother in religion or your brother in humanity. Ali was right. Muslims have saved my life – many times – in the thirty-two years I have spent in the Middle East. How can I not regard them as my brothers in humanity?

I am not uncritical of Muslim society. I am appalled by the honour killing of young women which is still practised with virtual impunity across the Muslim world. I am sickened by the ritual head-chopping of the Wahhabi Saudis. I grow tired of the refusal of Muslims to undertake a spiritual renaissance, to question the nature of their society. I am angered and frustrated by the tribal nature of these people, how parents will ritually oppose the marriage of a Sunni daughter to the son of a Shiite or a Christian. Or vice versa. When the late President Elias Hrawi proposed civil marriage in Lebanon, families of all faiths expressed their support. Why should the Church control the union of souls, forcing the Lebanese to marry in civil ceremonies in Cyprus? But the moment Hrawi made his announcement, the priests and imams, the Patriarch and the Grand Mufti chorused their disapproval. Who says religion is a force for good, for tolerance, for compassion?

I weary at my own efforts – to Christians as well as Muslims, and to Jews in Israel – to correct the historical record, to force an acknowledgement of the other's suffering. When Muslims claim that they do not believe the facts of the Jewish Holocaust, when Turkish Muslims deny the reality of the 1915 Armenian Holocaust, when Zionist Christians give their uncritical support to Israel and talk of the Apocalypse to come, when Christians insist that Islam is an alien, violent religion which rules by the sword and wishes to overwhelm 'Christian' Europe, I am horrified. Just as I am when the bin Ladens of this world say so, and when the George W. Bushes provoke this very sentiment within Islam by their own arrogance and violence. We have still not understood the land from which the terrifying suicide bomber emerged to threaten us. Nor have we yet realised our role in producing this phenomenon. For if the words of bin Laden carry conviction for many millions of Muslims, be sure we are still Crusaders.

God and the devil

That fine French historian of the 1914–18 world conflict, Stéphane Audoin-Rouzeau, suggested not long ago that the West was the inheritor of a type of warfare of very great violence. 'Then, after 1945,' he wrote, '. . . the West externalised it, in Korea, in Algeria, in Vietnam, in Iraq . . . we stopped thinking about the experience of war and we do not understand its return [to us] in different forms like that of terrorism . . . We do not want to admit that there is now occurring a different type of confrontation . . .' He might have added that politicians – even Prime Ministers – would deliberately refuse to acknowledge this. We are fighting evil. Nothing to do with the occupation of Palestinian land, the occupation of Afghanistan, the occupation of Iraq, the torture at Abu Ghraib and Bagram and Guantanamo. Oh no, indeed. 'An evil ideology', a nebulous, unspecified, dark force. That's the problem.

There are two things wrong with this. The first is that once you start talking about 'evil', you are talking about religion. Good and evil, God and the Devil. The London suicide bombers were Muslims (or thought they were), so the entire Muslim community in Britain must stand to attention and – as Muslims – condemn them. We 'Christians' were not required to do that because we are not Muslims – nor were we required as 'Christians' to condemn the Christian Serb slaughter of 8,000 Muslims at Srebrenica just over ten years ago. All we had to do was say sorry for doing nothing at the time. But Muslims, because they are Muslims, must ritually condemn something they had nothing to do with. And that, I suspect, is the point. Deep down, I wonder if we do not think that their religion does have something to do with all this, that Islam is a backward religion, un-renaissanced, potentially violent. It's not true, but our heritage of orientalism suggests otherwise.

It's weird the way we both despise and envy the 'other'. Many of those early orientalists showed both disgust and fascination with the East. They loathed the punishments and the pashas, but they rather liked the women; they were obsessed with harems. Westerners found the idea of having more than one wife quite appealing. Similarly, I rather think there are aspects of our Western 'decadence' which are of interest to Muslims, even if they ritually condemn them. I was very struck some years ago when the son of a Lebanese friend of mine went off to study for three years at a university in the south of England. When I passed through London from Beirut, I would sometimes bring audio tapes or letters from his parents – these were the glorious days before the internet – and the student would usually meet me in a pub in Bloomsbury. He would invariably turn up with a girl and would drink several beers before setting off to her flat for the night. Then in his last term at college, he called home and asked his mother to find him a bride. The days of fun and games were over. He wanted Mummy to find him a virgin to marry.

I thought about this a lot at the time. He was – and is – a most respectful, honourable man who has passed up much wealthier job opportunities abroad to teach college kids in Beirut. But had he been a weaker man, I can imagine he might have quite a few problems with his life. What was he doing in Britain? Why was he enjoying himself like 'us', only to turn his back on that enjoyment for a more conservative life?

Take another example – though the two men have nothing

in common – that of Ziad Jarrah. He lived in Germany with a Turkish girlfriend – not just dating but living with her – and then on 11 September 2001 he called up the girl to say 'I love you'. What's wrong, the young woman asked? 'I love you,' he said simply again and hung up the phone. And then he went off to board an airliner and slash the throats of its passengers and fly it into the ground in Pennsylvania. What happened in his brain as he heard the voice of the girlfriend he said he loved? His father, whom I know quite well, was as stunned as the parents of the London suicide bombers. To this day, he still cannot believe what Ziad Jarrah did. He is even waiting for him to come home.

It's not difficult to be cynical about the way in which Arabs can both hate the West and love it. In Arab capitals, I can read the anti-Bush fury expressed in the pages of local newspapers and then drive past the American embassy where sometimes hundreds of Arabs are standing round the walls in the hope of acquiring visas to the US. The Koran is a document of inestimable value. So is a green card.

But from the many letters I receive from Muslims, especially in Britain, I think I can understand some of the anger generated among them. They come, many of them, from countries of great repression and from lands where the strictest family and religious rules govern their lives. You know the rest. So in Britain – and even Muslims who were born in the country often grow up in traditional families – there can be a fierce dichotomy between their lives and that of the society around them. The freedoms of Britain – social as well as political – can be very attractive. Knowing that its elected government sends its soldiers to invade Iraq and kill quite a lot of Muslims at the same time might turn the 'dichotomy' into something far more dangerous.

Here is a land – Britain – in which you could live a good life. Pretty girls to go out with (note, we are talking about men), or marry or just live with. Movies to watch – no snipping of the nude scenes in our films – and, if you like, a beer or two at the local. These things are *haram*, of course, wrong, but enjoyable, part of 'our' life. Most British Muslim men I know don't actually drink alcohol and they behave honourably to women of every religion (so please, no angry letters). Others enjoy our freedoms with complete ease. But those who cannot, those who have enjoyed our freedoms but feel guilty for doing so – who can be appalled by the pleasure they have taken in 'our' society but equally appalled by the way in which they themselves feel corrupted (especially after a trip to Pakistan for a dose of old-fashioned ritualised religion – have a special problem.

Palestine or Afghanistan or Iraq turn it incendiary. They want both to break out of this world and to express their moral fury and political impotence as they do so. They want, I think, to destroy themselves for their own feelings of guilt and others for the crime of 'corrupting' them. Even if that means murdering a few co-religionists and dozens of other innocents. So on go the backpacks – whoever supplied them is a different matter – and off go the bombs. Something happens, something that takes only a second, between saying 'I love you' and then hanging up the phone.

The Independent, 23 July 2005

The childishness of civilisations

*In January 2006, Muslims across the world expressed their out-
rage at a series of Danish newspaper cartoons, one of which
portrayed the Prophet Mohamed with a bomb in his turban.
Mobs burned the Danish embassy in Beirut.*

So now it's cartoons of the Prophet Mohamed with a bomb-
shaped turban. Ambassadors are withdrawn from Denmark,
Gulf nations clear their shelves of Danish produce, Gaza gunmen threaten the European Union. In Denmark, Fleming Rose,
the 'culture' editor of the pipsqueak newspaper which published these silly cartoons – last September – announces that we
are witnessing a 'clash of civilisations' between secular Western
democracies and Islamic societies. This does prove, I suppose,
that Danish journalists follow in the tradition of Hans Christian Andersen. Oh lordy, lordy. What we're witnessing is the
childishness of civilisations.

So let's start off with the Department of Home Truths. This
is not an issue of secularism versus Islam.

For Muslims, the Prophet is the man who received divine
words directly from God. We see our prophets as faintly historical figures, at odds with our high-tech human rights,
almost caricatures of themselves. The fact is that Muslims live
their religion. We do not. They have kept their faith through
innumerable historical vicissitudes. We have lost our faith ever

since Matthew Arnold wrote about the sea's 'long, withdrawing roar'. That's why we talk about 'the West versus Islam' rather than 'Christians versus Islam' – because there aren't an awful lot of Christians left in Europe. There is no way we can get round this by setting up all the other world religions and asking why we are not allowed to make fun of Mohamed.

Besides, we can exercise our own hypocrisy over religious feelings. I happen to remember how, more than a decade ago, a film called *The Last Temptation of Christ* showed Jesus making love to a woman. In Paris, someone set fire to the cinema that showed the movie, killing a young man. I also happen to remember a US university which invited me to give a lecture three years ago. I did. It was entitled 'September 11, 2001: ask who did it but, for God's sake, don't ask why'. When I arrived, I found that the university had deleted the phrase 'for God's sake' because 'we didn't want to offend certain sensibilities'. Ah-ha, so we have 'sensibilities' too!

In other words, while we claim that Muslims must be good secularists when it comes to free speech – or cheap cartoons – we can worry about adherents to our own precious religion just as much. I also enjoyed the pompous claims of European statesmen that they cannot control free speech or newspapers. This is also nonsense. Had that cartoon of the Prophet shown instead a chief rabbi with a bomb-shaped hat, we would have had 'anti-Semitism' screamed into our ears – and rightly so – just as we often hear the Israelis complain about anti-Semitic cartoons in Egyptian newspapers.

Furthermore, in some European nations – France is one, Germany and Austria are among the others – it is forbidden by law to deny acts of genocide. In France, for example, it is illegal to say that the Jewish Holocaust or the Armenian Holocaust did not happen. So it is, in fact, impermissible to make certain statements in European nations. I'm still uncertain whether these laws attain their objectives; however much you may proscribe Holocaust denial, anti-Semites will always try to find a way round. But we can hardly exercise our political restraints to prevent Holocaust deniers and then start screaming about secularism when we find that Muslims object to our provocative and insulting image of the Prophet.

For many Muslims, the 'Islamic' reaction to this affair is an embarrassment. There is good reason to believe that Muslims would like to see some element of reform introduced to their religion. If this cartoon had advanced the cause of those who want to debate this issue, no one would have minded. But it was clearly intended to be provocative. It was so outrageous that it only caused reaction. And this is not a great time to heat up the old Samuel Huntingdon garbage about a 'clash of civilisations'. Iran now has a clerical government again. So, to all intents and purposes, does Iraq (which was not supposed to end up with a democratically elected clerical administration, but that's what happens when you topple dictators). In Egypt, the Muslim Brotherhood won 20 per cent of the seats in the recent parliamentary elections. Now we have Hamas in charge of 'Palestine'. There's a message here, isn't there? That America's policies – 'regime change' in the Middle East – are not achieving their ends. These millions of voters were preferring Islam to the corrupt regimes which we imposed on them. For the Danish cartoon to be dumped on top of this fire is dangerous indeed.

In any event, it's not about whether the Prophet should be pictured. The Koran does not forbid images of the Prophet, even though millions of Muslims do. The problem is that these cartoons portrayed Mohamed as a bin Laden-type symbol of violence. They portrayed Islam as a violent religion. It is not. Or do we want to make it so?

The Independent, 4 February 2006

Look in the mirror

In an age when Prime Minister Blair can identify 'evil ideologies' and when al-Qaeda can call the suicide bombing of 156 Iraqi Shias 'good news' for the 'nation of Islam', thank heaven for our readers, in particular John Shepherd, principal lecturer in religious studies at St Martin's College, Lancaster. Responding to a comment of mine – to the effect that 'deep down' we do, however wrongly, suspect that religion has something to do with the London bombings – Mr Shepherd gently admonishes me. 'I wonder if there may be more to it than that,' he remarks. And I fear he is right and I am wrong. His arguments are contained in a brilliantly conceived article on the roots of violence and extremism in Judaism, Christianity and Islam – and the urgent need to render all religions safe for 'human consumption'.

Put very simply, Mr Shepherd takes a wander through some of the nastiest bits of the Bible and the Koran – those bits we prefer not to quote or not to think about – and finds that mass murder and ethnic cleansing get a pretty good bill of health if we take it all literally. The Jewish 'entry into the promised land' was clearly accompanied by bloody conquest and would-be genocide. The Christian tradition has absorbed this inheritance, entering its own 'promised land' with a ruthlessness that extends to cruel anti-Semitism. The New Testament, Mr Shepherd points out, 'contains passages that would . . . be actionable under British laws against incitement to racial hatred' were they to be published fresh today. The Muslim tradition – with its hatred of idolatry – includes, in the career of the Prophet, 'scenes of bloodshed and murder which are shocking to modern religious sensibilities'.

Thus, for example, Baruch Goldstein, the Israeli military doctor who massacred twenty-nine Palestinians in Hebron in 1994, committed his mass murder on Purim, a festival celebrating the deliverance of the Jewish communities from the Persian Empire, which was followed by large-scale killing 'to avenge themselves on their enemies' (Esther 8:13). The Palestinians, of course, were playing the role of the Persians, at other times that of the Amalekites ('". . . kill man and woman, babe and suckling, ox and sheep, camel and donkey"', 1 Samuel 15: 3). The original 'promised land' was largely on what is now the West Bank – hence the Jewish colonisation of Palestinian land – while the coastal plain was not (although suggestions that Israel should transplant itself further east, leaving Haifa, Tel Aviv and Ashkelon to the Palestinians of the West Bank, are unlikely to commend themselves to Israel's rulers).

The 'chosen people' theme, meanwhile, moved into Christianity – the Protestants of Northern Ireland, for example (remember the Ulster Covenant?), and apartheid South Africa and, in some respects, the United States. The New Testament is laced with virulent anti-Semitism, accusing the Jews of killing Christ. Read Martin Luther. The Koran demanded the forced submission of conquered peoples in the name of religion (the Koran 9: 29), and Mohamed's successor, the Caliph Abu Bakr, stated specifically that 'we will treat as an unbeliever whoever rejects Allah and Mohamed, and we will make holy war upon him . . . for such there is only the sword and fire and indiscriminate slaughter.'

So there you go. And how does Mr Shepherd deal with all this? Settlement policy should be rejected not because it is theologically questionable but because the dispossession of a people is morally wrong. Anti-Semitism must be rejected not because it is incompatible with the Gospels but because it is incompatible with any basic morality based on shared human values. If Muslim violence is to be condemned, it is not because Mohamed is misunderstood but because it violates basic human rights. 'West Bank settlements, Christian anti-Semitism and Muslim terrorism . . . are not morally wrong because theologically questionable – they are theologically questionable because morally wrong.'

And it is true that most Christians, Jews and Muslims draw on the tolerant, moderate aspects of their tradition. We prefer not to accept the fact that the religions of the children of Abraham are inherently flawed in respect of intolerance, discrimination, violence and hatred. Only – if I understand Mr Shepherd's thesis correctly – by putting respect for human rights above all else and by making religion submit to universal human values can we 'grasp the nettle'. Phew. I can hear the fundamentalists roaring already. And I have to say it will probably be the Islamic ones who will roar loudest. Reinterpretation of the Koran is such a quicksand, so dangerous to approach, so slippery a subject that most Muslims will not go near.

How can we suggest that a religion based on 'submission' to God must itself 'submit' to our happy-clappy, all-too-Western 'universal human rights'? I don't know. Especially when we 'Christians' have largely failed to condemn some of our own atrocities – indeed, have preferred to forget them. Take the Christians who massacred the Muslims of Srebrenica. Or take the Christians – Lebanese Phalangist allies of the Israelis – who entered the Sabra and Chatila refugee camps in Beirut and slaughtered up to 1,700 Palestinian Muslim civilians. Do we remember that? Do we recall that the massacres occurred between 16 and 18 September 1982? Yes, today is the 23rd anniversary of that little genocide – and I suspect *The Indepen-dent* will be one of the very few newspapers to remember it. I was in those camps in 1982. I climbed over the corpses. Some of the Christian Phalangists in Beirut even had illustrations of the Virgin Mary on their gun butts, just as the Christian Serbs did in Bosnia.

Are we therefore in a position to tell our Muslim neighbours to 'grasp the nettle'? I rather think not. Because the condition of human rights has been so eroded by our own folly, our illegal invasion of Iraq and the anarchy that we have allowed to take root there, our flagrant refusal to prevent further Israeli settlement expansion in the West Bank, our constant, whining demands that prominent Muslims must disown the killers who take their religious texts too literally, that we have long ago lost our courage.

A hundred years of Western interference in the Middle East has left the region so cracked with fault lines and artificial frontiers and heavy with injustices that we are in no position to lecture the Islamic world on human rights and values. Forget the Amalekites and the Persians and Martin Luther and the Caliph Abu Bakr. Just look at ourselves in the mirror and we will see the most frightening text of all.

The Independent, 17 September 2005

Smashing history

What is it about graven images? Why are we humanoids so prone to destroy our own faces, smash our own human history, erase the memory of language? I've covered the rape of Bosnian and Serb and Croatian culture in ex-Yugoslavia – the deliberate demolition of churches, libraries, graveyards, even the wonderful Ottoman Mostar Bridge – and I've heard the excuses. 'There's no place for these old things,' the Croat gunner reportedly said as he fired his artillery battery towards that graceful Ottoman arch over the Neretva. The videotape of its collapse was itself an image of cultural genocide – until the Taliban exploded the giant Buddhas of Bamiyan.

And yet there I was earlier this week, staring at another massive Buddha – this time in the Tajik capital of Dushanbe, only a few hundred miles from the Afghan border. So gently was it sleeping, giant head on spread right hand, that I tiptoed down its almost 40-ft length, talking in whispers in case I woke this creature with its Modigliani features, its firmly closed eyes and ski-slope nose. Saved from the ravages of iconoclasts, I thought, until I realised that this karma-inducing god had itself been assaulted.

The top of its head, eyes and nose are intact, but the lower half of its face has been subtly restored by a more modern hand, its long body perhaps three-quarters new, where the undamaged left hand, palm on hip, lies gently on its upper left leg above the pleats of its original robes. So what happened to this Buddha? Surely the Taliban never reached Dushanbe.

A young curator at Dushanbe's wonderful museum of antiquities explained in careful, bleak English. 'When the Arabs came, they smashed all these things as idolatrous,' she said. Ah yes, of course they did. The forces of Islam arrived in modern-day Tajikistan in around AD 645 – the Taliban of their day, as bearded as their twentieth-century successors, with no television sets to hang, but plenty of Buddhas to smash. How on earth did the Bamiyan Buddhas escape this original depredation?

The Buddhist temple at Vakhsh, east of Qurghonteppa, was itself new (given a hundred years or two) when the Arabs arrived, and the museum contains the 'work' of these idol-smashers in desperate, carefully preserved profusion. Buddha's throne appears to have been attacked with swords and the statue of Shiva and his wife Parvati (sixth to eighth centuries) has been so severely damaged by these ancient Talibans that only their feet and the sacred cow beneath them are left.

Originally discovered in 1969, 30 ft beneath the soil, the statue of 'Buddha in Nirvana' was brought up to Dushanbe as a direct result of the destruction of the Buddhas in Afghanistan. Taliban excess, in other words, inspired post-Soviet preservation. If we can no longer gaze at the faces of those mighty deities in Bamiyan because the Department for the Suppression of Vice and Preservation of Virtue in Kabul deemed them worthy of annihilation, we can still look upon this divinity in the posture of the 'sleeping lion' now that it has been freighted up to Dushanbe by the local inheritors of Stalin's monstrous empire. A sobering thought.

A certain B. A. Litvinsky was responsible for this first act of architectural mercy. Eventually the statue was brought to the Tajik capital in ninety-two parts. Not that long ago, a fratemal Chinese delegation arrived and asked to take the sleeping

Buddha home with them; they were told that they could only photograph this masterpiece – which may be the genesis of the 'new' Buddha in the People's Republic.

Needless to say, there are many other fragments – animals, birds, demons – that made their way from the monastery to the museum. And I had to reflect that the Arabs behaved no worse than Henry VIII's lads when they set to work on the great abbeys of England. Did not even the little church of East Sutton above the Kentish Weald have a few graven images desecrated during the great age of English history? Are our cathedrals not filled with hacked faces, the remaining witness to our very own brand of Protestant Talibans?

Besides, the arrival of the Arabic script allowed a new Tajik poetry to flourish – Ferdowsi was a Tajik and wrote the *Shah-nameh* in Arabic script – and in Dushanbe you can see the most exquisite tomb-markers from the era of King Babur, Arabic script verse carved with Koranic care into the smooth black surface of the stone. Yet when Stalin absorbed Tajikistan into the Soviet Empire – artfully handing the historic Tajik cities of Tashkent and Samarkand to the new republic of Uzbekistan, just to keep ethnic hatreds alive – his commissars banned Arabic script. All children would henceforth be taught Russian and, even if they were writing Tajik, it must be in Cyrillic, not in Arabic.

Mustafa Kemal Ataturk was similarly 'modernising' Turkey at this time by forcing Turks to move from Arabic to Latin script (which is one reason, I suspect, why modern Turkish scholars have such difficulty in studying vital Ottoman texts on the 1915 Armenian Holocaust). Get rid of the written language and history seems less dangerous. Didn't we try to do the same thing in Ireland, forcing the Catholic clergy to become hedge-preachers so that the Irish language would remain in spoken rather than written form? And so the Tajik couples and the children who come to look at their past in

Dushanbe cannot read the *Shahnameh* as it was written – and cannot decipher the elegant Persian poetry carved on those extraordinary tombstones. So here is a tiny victory against iconoclasm, perhaps the first English translation of one of those ancient stones which few Tajiks can now understand:

I heard that mighty Jamshed the King
Carved on a stone near a spring of water these words:
Many – like us – sat here by this spring
And left this life in the blink of an eye.
We captured the whole world through our courage and strength,
Yet could take nothing with us to our grave.

Beside that same East Sutton church in Kent, there still stands an English tombstone which I would read each time I panted past it in my Sutton Valence School running shorts on wintry Saturday afternoons. I don't remember whose body it immortalises, but I remember the carved verse above the name:

Remember me as you pass by,
As you are now, so once was I.
As I am now, so you will be.
Remember Death will follow thee.

And I do recall, exhausted and frozen into my thin running clothes, that I came to hate this eternal message so much that sometimes I wanted to take a hammer and smash the whole bloody thing to pieces. Yes, somewhere in our dark hearts, perhaps we are all Talibans.

The Independent, 8 September 2007

So now it's 'brown-skinned'

This has been a good week to be in Canada – or an awful week, depending on your point of view – to understand just how irretrievably biased and potentially racist the Canadian press has become. For, after the arrest of seventeen Canadian Muslims on 'terrorism' charges, the *Toronto Globe and Mail* and, to a slightly lesser extent, the *National Post* have indulged in an orgy of finger-pointing that must reduce the chances of any fair trial and, at the same time, sow fear in the hearts of the country's more than 700,000 Muslims. In fact, if I were a Canadian Muslim right now, I'd already be checking the airline timetables for a flight out of town. Or is that the purpose of this press campaign?

First, the charges. Even a lawyer for one of the accused has talked of a plot to storm the parliament in Ottawa, hold MPs hostage and chop off the head of Prime Minister Stephen Harper. Without challenging the 'facts' or casting any doubt on their sources – primarily the Royal Canadian Mounted Police or Canada's leak-dripping Canadian Security Intelligence Service (CSIS) – reporters have told their readers that the seventeen were variously planning to blow up parliament, CSIS's headquarters, the Canadian Broadcasting Corporation and sundry other targets. Every veiled and chadored Muslim woman relative of the accused has been photographed and their pictures printed, often on front pages. 'Home-grown terrorists' has become theme of the month – even though the 'terrorists' have yet to stand trial. They were in receipt of 'fertilisers', we were told, which could be turned into explosives. When it emerged that Canadian police officers had already switched the 'fertilisers' for a less harmful substance, nobody followed up the implications of this apparent 'sting'. A Buffalo radio station down in the US even announced that the accused had actually received 'explosives'. Bingo: guilty before trial.

Of course, the Muslim-bashers have laced this nonsense with the usual pious concern for the rights of the accused. 'Before I go on, one disclaimer,' purred the *Globe and Mail*'s Margaret Wente. 'Nothing has been proved and nobody should rush to judgement.' Which, needless to say, Wente then went on to do in the same paragraph. 'The exposure of our very own home-grown terrorists, if that's what the men aspired to be, was both predictably shocking and shockingly predictable.'

And just in case we missed the point of this hypocrisy, Wente ended her column by announcing that 'Canada is not exempt from home-grown terrorism'. Angry young men are the tinderbox and Islamism the match. The country will probably have better luck than most at 'putting out the fire', she adds. But who, I wonder, is really lighting the match?

For a very unpleasant – albeit initially innocuous – phrase has now found its way into the papers. The accused seventeen – and indeed their families and sometimes the country's entire Muslim community – are now referred to as 'Canadian-born'. Well, yes, they are Canadian-born. But there's a subtle difference between this and being described as a 'Canadian' – as other citizens of this vast country are in every other context. And the implications are obvious; there are now two types of Canadian citizen: the Canadian-born variety (Muslims) and Canadians (the rest).

If this seems finicky, try the following sentence from the

Globe and Mail's front page on Tuesday, supposedly an eyewitness account of the police arrest operation: 'Parked directly outside his ... office was a large, grey, cube-shaped truck and, on the ground nearby, he recognised one of the two brown-skinned young men who had taken possession of the next door rented unit . . .' Come again? Brown-skinned? What in God's name is this outrageous piece of racism doing on the front page of a major Canadian daily? What is 'brown-skinned' supposed to mean – if it is not just a revolting attempt to isolate Muslims as the 'other' in Canada's highly multicultural society? I notice, for example, that when the paper obsequiously refers to Toronto's police chief and his reportedly brilliant cops, he is not referred to as 'white-skinned' (which he most assuredly is).

So I put this question to Jonathan Kay, a *Post* columnist and a man not averse to a bit of fear-splashing in his own paper. Wasn't 'brown-skinned' pushing journalism into racism? Here is his astonishing reply: 'These things are heavily idiomatic in the sense that, you know, forty years ago, we would have said "coloured".' Idiomatic? My dictionary defines the word as follows: using, containing, denoting expressions that are natural to a native speaker. In other words, it's perfectly natural in Canada these days to refer to Muslims as 'brown-skinned'. Am I supposed to laugh or cry? Mr Kay believed that, if asked to describe Toronto's top cop by his racial origins, 'you'd say the "white police chief"'. Quite so.

Amid this swamp, Canada's journalists are managing to soften the realities of their country's new military involvement in Afghanistan. More than 2,000 troops are deployed around Kandahar in active military operations against Taliban insurgents. They are taking the place of US troops, who will be transferred to fight even more Muslim insurgents in Iraq. Canada is thus now involved in the Afghan war – those who doubt this should note the country has already shelled out

US$1.8 bn in 'defence spending' in Afghanistan and only $500 m in 'additional expenditures', including humanitarian assistance and democratic renewal (*sic*) – and, by extension, in Iraq. In other words, Canada has gone to war in the Middle East. None of this, according to the Canadian foreign minister, could be the cause of Muslim anger at home, although Jack Hooper – the CSIS chief who has a lot to learn about the Middle East but talks far too much – said a few days ago that 'we had a high threat profile [in Canada] before Afghanistan. In any event, the presence of Canadians and Canadian forces there has elevated that threat somewhat.'

I read all this on a flight from Calgary to Ottawa this week, sitting just a row behind Tim Goddard, his wife Sally and daughter Victoria, who were chatting gently and smiling bravely to the crew and fellow passengers. In the cargo hold of our aircraft lay the coffin of Mr Goddard's other daughter, Nichola, the first Canadian woman soldier to be killed in action in Afghanistan. The next day, he scattered sand on Nichola's coffin at Canada's national military cemetery. A heartrending photograph of him appeared in the *Post* – but buried away on page six. And on the front page? A picture of British policemen standing outside the Bradford home of a Muslim 'who may have links to Canada'. Allegedly, of course.

The Independent, 10 June 2006

The 'faith' question

First, the best Belfast joke in years, courtesy of my old mate David McKittrick, who in 1972 worked on the *Irish Times* in Northern Ireland when I was the London *Times* man there and whose dad once worked in Harland and Wolff, the shipyard that built the *Titanic*. 'You've got to hand it to Harland and Wolff,' David said. 'If it wasn't for them, the *Titanic* wouldn't be where it is today.' Maybe it was the skittles and beer of the Malmaison Hotel with its funereal decorations, but David's joke somehow represented a new Belfast. Northern Irelanders have always made fun of themselves, but it was usually a little self-conscious during the years of violence, even before.

When the first major *Titanic* movie was made in 1957 – the one with Kenneth More playing Second Officer Lightoller – Harland and Wolff, a Protestant fortress, was still ashamed of its most famous ship and refused the film-makers any assistance, even declining to permit access to the construction plans of the vessel. Today, Belfast advertises *Titanic* to tourists and Harland and Wolff proudly claims recognition of its extraordinary if doomed achievement. Belfast is Titanic Town and the original monument to the dead, freshly cleaned, stands outside City Hall and opposite the headquarters of the Ulster Bank (where my account must sometimes cause as much concern as the approaching iceberg in 1912).

Lecturing in Belfast last week, I was especially struck by the enormous knowledge that Northern Irelanders possess of the Middle East. Divided societies sometimes attract each other. The Bloody Sunday committee in Derry, commemorating the fourteen Catholics killed by British paratroopers in 1972, wanted to 'twin' with the Iraqi city of Fallujah in 2003 after fourteen Iraqi civilians were killed there by the US 82nd Airborne, the incident which provoked the insurgency that turned all of Iraq into a giant version of the original Bogside's 'no go' area.

It was back in 2000 that John Hume wrote an article for the *Jerusalem Post* in which he said that the Good Friday Agreement might be applied to the Palestinian–Israeli conflict. I disagreed. Other people's peace treaties don't travel well. The West Bank with its massive Jewish settlements is more like seventeenth-century Ireland after the Catholic dispossession, a point I made to an audience beside the river Lagan.

Audience questions. Could Israel be forced to abide by UN Security Council Resolution 242? Answer: No. Is Lebanon in greater danger now than before the latest war? Answer: Yes. Is Blair really the lapdog of Bush on the Middle East? Answer: Yes. How can 'faith' help to bring peace between the peoples of the Middle East and of the 'seed of Abraham' (John Paul II's initiative)? And, of course, what was the real effect of Pope Benedict's quotation from a medieval Byzantine emperor? Answer: Benedict – not my favourite Pope – is far too intelligent not to have anticipated the effect of this unpleasant and, in today's terms, provocative statement about violence and the Prophet Mohamed.

All this, I should add, came just a couple of days before Benedict decided to evacuate Limbo and send its occupants to more spacious accommodation in Heaven because – I suspect – the slow collapse of the Christian Church in the West means that it must itself move into Limbo. The 'faith' question came up at a large meeting – mainly of young people – in the

Clonard monastery in the Falls, a Redemptorist institution whose magnificent church has the acoustics of the Royal Albert Hall – it must have been built around the same time – and whose obvious religiosity should have intimidated a 'secularist' like me. I had been sounding forth on the evils of war and the immorality of 'armed humanitarian intervention' and the question came from Father Gerry Reynolds, himself a Belfast institution.

I was tempted to recall that my father, close to death, told me he did not fear 'going', but that I did 'because you have no faith', but I told the audience that we as Westerners (except for Father Reynolds) had largely lost our faith, whereas the Muslim world had not. The most frequent question in Belfast was: How can we force our leaders to stop their wars? I don't know the answer, but I like the remark of that highly original Canadian writer Margaret Atwood in *Moral Disorder*, her latest novel. 'You can't lead,' she wrote, 'if no one will follow.' Is that the way to deal with Lord Blair of Kut al-Amara and his chums?

Indeed, if only Jack Straw had said a little earlier in the week that he would like Muslim women to remove their veils in his parliamentary 'surgery', I could have put the knife of faith into him in the monastery. Heaven knows what he will next demand in his 'surgery'. The removal of the headpiece of all Catholic nuns? Or the wigs of Jewish Orthodox women? I can't escape the thought, though, that if it wasn't for Jack Straw, Islamophobia wouldn't be where it is today.

The Independent, 7 October 2006

Hatred on a map

Why are we trying to divide up the peoples of the Middle East? Why are we trying to chop them up, make them different, remind them – constantly, insidiously, viciously – of their divisions, their suspicions, their capacity for mutual hatred? Is this just our casual racism? Or is there something darker in our Western souls?

Take the maps. Am I the only one sickened by our journalistic propensity to publish sectarian maps of the Middle East? You know what I mean. We are now all familiar with the colour-coded map of Iraq. Shias at the bottom (of course), Sunnis in their middle 'triangle' – actually, it's more like an octagon (even a pentagon) – and the Kurds in the north. Or the map of Lebanon, where I live. Shias at the bottom (of course), Druze further north, Sunnis in Sidon and on the coastal strip south of Beirut, Shias in the southern suburbs of the capital, Sunnis and Christians in the city, Christian Maronites further north, Sunnis in Tripoli, more Shias to the east. How we love these maps. Hatred made easy.

Of course, it's not that simple. So do I tell my driver Abed, a Sunni, that our map shows he can no longer park outside my home? Or that the Muslim publisher of the Arabic edition of my book *The Great War for Civilisation* can no longer meet me at our favourite rendezvous, Paul's restaurant in east Beirut, for lunch because our map shows this to be a Maronite Christian area of Beirut?

In Tarek al-Jdeidi (Sunni), some Shia families have moved out of their homes – temporarily, you understand, a brief holiday, keys left with the neighbours, it's always that way – which means that our Beirut maps are now cleaner, easier to understand. The same is happening on a far larger scale in Baghdad. Now our colour-coding can be bolder. No more use for that confusing word 'mixed'.

We did the same in the Balkans. The Drina Valley of Bosnia was Muslim until the Serbs 'cleansed' it. Srebrenica? Delete 'safe area' and logo it 'Serb'. Krajina? Serb until the Croats took it. Did we call them 'Croats' or 'Catholics' or both on our maps?

Our guilt in this sectarian game is obvious. We want to divide the 'other', 'them', our potential enemies, from each other, while we – we civilised Westerners with our refined, unified, multicultural values – are unassailable. I could draw you a sectarian map of the English city of Birmingham, for example – marked 'Muslim' and 'non-Muslim' – but no newspaper would print it. I could draw an extremely accurate ethnic map of Washington, complete with front-line streets between 'black' and 'white' communities, but the *Washington Post* would never publish such a map.

Imagine the chromatic fun the *New York Times* could have with Brooklyn, Harlem, the East River, black, white, brown, Italian, Catholic, Jew, Wasp. Or the *Toronto Globe and Mail* with French and non-French Canadian Montreal (the front line at one point follows the city Metro) or with Toronto (where 'Little Italy' is now Ukrainian or Greek), and colour the suburb of Mississauga green for Muslim, of course. But we don't draw these Hitlerian maps for our societies. It would be unforgivable, bad taste, something 'we' don't do in our precious, carefully guarded civilisation.

Passing a book stall in New York this week, I spotted the iniquitous *Time* magazine, and there on the front – and this might truly have been a 1930s Nazi cover – were two cowled men, one in black, the other largely hidden by a chequered scarf. 'Sunnis vs Shi'ites,' the headline read. 'Why they hate each other.' This, naturally, was a 'take-out' on Iraq's civil war – a civil war, by the way, that America's spokesmen in Baghdad were talking about in August 2003 when not a single Iraqi in his worst nightmares dreamt of what has now come to pass.

Buy *Time* magazine, dear reader, turn to page 30, and what will you find? 'How to Tell Sunnis and Shi'ites Apart'. Helpful, uh? And after this are columns of useful, divisive information. 'Names', for example. 'Some names carry sectarian markers . . . Abu Bakr, Omar and Uthman . . . men with these names are almost certainly Sunni. Those called Abdel-Hussein and Abdel-Zahra' (I have never in my life met an 'Abdel-Zahra' by the way) 'are most likely Shi'ite.' Then there are columns headed 'Prayer', 'Mosques', 'Homes', 'Accents' and 'Dialects', even – heaven spare us – 'cars'. The last, for those readers not already reeling in disbelief, tells us which car stickers to look out for (spot a picture of Imam Ali and you know the driver is Shia) or which licence plate (Anbar province registrations, for instance, means a probable Sunni driver.)

Thanks again. I don't know why the American military doesn't just buy up this week's edition of *Time* and drop the lot over Baghdad to help any still ignorant local murderers with easy-to-identify targets. But will *Time* be helping us to identify America's deeply divided society (who has most rubbish in their gardens in Washington, which bumper stickers to look for in Dearborn, Michigan)? Will they hell.

I, too, am guilty of playing these little sectarian games in the Middle East. I ask a Lebanese where he or she comes from, not to remember the mountains or rivers near their home but to code them into my map. But I easily come unstuck. The man who tells me he comes from the Lebanese south (Shia) turns out to live in the southern Druze town of Hasbaya. The woman who tells me she's from Jbeil (Christian) turns out to be from the town's Shia minority. Oh, if only these pesky minorities would go and live in the right bit of our imperial, sectarian maps.

And we go on talking to our Sunni monarchs in the Middle East – we listen to their raving about the 'Shia crescent' – no wonder we hate Shia Iran so much. And we go on dividing and scissoring up the lands, and printing more and more of our racial maps and I do wonder most seriously if we wish to promote civil war across this part of the world. And you know what? I rather think we do.

The Independent, 3 March 2007

'If you bomb our cities, we will bomb yours'

On 7 July 2005 – on the day the G8 summit opened in Scotland – four British Muslim suicide bombers blew themselves up on the London Tube and bus system, killing 52 people and wounding another 700.

'If you bomb our cities,' Osama bin Laden said in one of his recent videotapes, 'we will bomb yours.' There you go, as they say. It was crystal-clear that Britain would be a target ever since Tony Blair decided to join George Bush's 'war on terror' and his invasion of Iraq. We had been warned. The G8 summit was obviously chosen, well in advance, as Attack Day.

And it's no use Mr Blair telling us yesterday that 'they will never succeed in destroying what we hold dear'. 'They' are not trying to destroy 'what we hold dear'. They are trying to get public opinion to force Blair to withdraw from Iraq, from his alliance with the United States, and from his adherence to Bush's policies in the Middle East. The Spanish paid the price for their support for Bush – and Spain's subsequent retreat from Iraq proved that the Madrid bombings achieved their objectives – while the Australians were made to suffer in Bali.

It is easy for Tony Blair to call yesterday's bombings 'barbaric' – of course they were – but what were the civilian deaths of the Anglo-American invasion of Iraq in 2003, the children torn apart by cluster bombs, the countless innocent Iraqis gunned down at American military checkpoints? When they die, it is 'collateral damage'; when 'we' die, it is 'barbaric terrorism'. If we are fighting insurgency in Iraq, what makes us believe insurgency won't come to us? One thing is certain: if Tony Blair really believes that by 'fighting terrorism' in Iraq we could more efficiently protect Britain – fight them there rather than let them come here, as Bush constantly says – this argument is no longer valid.

To time these bombs with the G8 summit, when the world was concentrating on Britain, was not a stroke of genius. You don't need a PhD to choose another Bush–Blair handshake to close down a capital city with explosives and massacre more than thirty of its citizens. The G8 summit was announced so far in advance as to give the bombers all the time they needed to prepare. A coordinated system of attacks of the kind we saw yesterday would have taken months to plan – to choose safe houses, prepare explosives, identify targets, ensure security, choose the bombers, the hour, the minute, to plan the communications (mobile phones are giveaways). Coordination and sophisticated planning – and the usual utter ruthlessness with regard to the lives of the innocent – are characteristic of al-Qaeda. And let us not use – as our television colleagues did yesterday – 'hallmarks', a word identified with quality silver rather than base metal.

And now let us reflect on the fact that yesterday the opening of the G8, so critical a day, so bloody a day, represented a total failure of our security services – the same intelligence 'experts' who claimed there were weapons of mass destruction in Iraq when there were none, but who utterly failed to uncover a months-long plot to kill Londoners. Trains, planes, buses, cars, metros. Transportation appears to be the science of al-Qaeda's dark arts. No one can search 3 million London commuters every day. No one can stop every tourist. Some thought the Eurostar might have been an al-Qaeda target – be sure they have studied it – but why go for prestige when your common or garden bus and Tube train are there for the taking?

And then come the Muslims of Britain, who have long been awaiting this nightmare. Now every one of our Muslims becomes the 'usual suspect', the man or woman with brown eyes, the man with the beard, the woman in the scarf, the boy with the worry beads, the girl who says she's been racially abused. And this is part of the point of yesterday's bombings: to divide British Muslims from British non-Muslims (let us not mention the name Christians), to encourage the very kind of racism that Tony Blair claims to resent.

But here's the problem. To go on pretending that Britain's enemies want to destroy 'what we hold dear' encourages racism; what we are confronting here is a specific, direct, centralised attack on London as a result of a 'war on terror' which Tony Blair has locked us into. Just before the US presidential elections, bin Laden asked: 'Why do we not attack Sweden?' Lucky Sweden. No Osama bin Laden there. And no Tony Blair.

The Independent, 8 July 2005

The lies of racists

Oh how – when it comes to the realities of history – the Muslims of the Middle East exhaust my patience. After years of explaining to Arab friends that the Jewish Holocaust – the systematic, planned murder of 6 million Jews by the Nazis – is an indisputable fact, I am still met with a state of willing disbelief. And now, this week, the preposterous President Mahmoud Ahmadinejad of Iran opens up his own country to obloquy and shame by holding a supposedly impartial 'conference' on the Jewish Holocaust to repeat the lies of the racists who, if they did not direct their hatred towards Jews, would most assuredly turn venomously against those other Semites, the Arabs of the Middle East.

How, I always ask, can you expect the West to understand and accept the ethnic cleansing of 750,000 men, women and children from Palestine in 1948 when you will not try to comprehend the enormity done to the Jews of Europe? And, here, of course, is the wretched irony of the whole affair. For what the Muslims of the Middle East should be doing is pointing out to the world that they were not responsible for the Jewish Holocaust, that, horrific and evil though it was, it is a shameful, outrageous injustice that they, the Palestinians, should suffer for something they had no part in and – even more disgusting – that they should be treated as if they have. But, no, Ahmadinejad has neither the brains nor the honesty to grasp this simple, vital equation.

True, the Palestinian Grand Mufti of Jerusalem shook hands with Hitler. But the downtrodden, crushed, occupied, slaughtered Palestinians of our time – of Sabra and Chatila, of Jenin and Beit Yanoun – were not even alive in the Second World War.

Yet it is to the eternal shame of Israel and its leaders that they should pretend that the Palestinians were participants in the Second World War. When the Israeli army was advancing on Beirut in 1982, the then Israeli prime minister, Menachem Begin, wrote a crazed letter to US president Ronald Reagan explaining that he felt he was marching on 'Berlin' to liquidate 'Hitler' (i.e. Yasser Arafat, who was busy comparing his own guerrillas to the defenders of Stalingrad).

That courageous Israeli writer Uri Avneri wrote an open letter to Begin. 'Mr Prime Minister,' he began, 'Hitler is dead.' But this did not stop Ariel Sharon from trying the same trick in 1989. By talking to the US State Department, Arafat was 'like Hitler, who also wanted so much to negotiate with the Allies in the second half of the Second World War,' Sharon told the *Wall Street Journal*. '. . . Arafat is the same kind of enemy.'

Needless to say, any comparison between the behaviour of German troops in the Second World War and Israeli soldiers today (with their constantly betrayed claim to 'purity of arms') is denounced as anti-Semitic. Generally, I believe that is the correct reaction. Israelis are not committing mass rape, murder or installing gas chambers for the Palestinians. But the acts of Israeli troops are not always so easy to divorce from such insane parallels. Israel sent its enraged Lebanese Christian Phalangist militias into the Sabra and Chatila camps after telling them that Palestinians had killed their beloved leader. Israeli troops watched the slaughter – and did nothing.

The Israeli novelist A. B. Yehoshua observed that, even if his country's soldiers had not known what was happening, 'then this would be the same lack of knowledge of the Germans who stood outside Buchenwald and Treblinka and did not know what was happening'.

After the killings of Jenin, an Israeli officer suggested to his men, according to the Israeli press, that with close-quarters fighting they might study the tactics of Nazi troops in Warsaw in 1944. And I have to ask – indeed, it needs to be asked – after the countless Lebanese civilian refugees ruthlessly cut down on the roads of Lebanon by the Israeli air force in 1978, 1982, 1993, 1996 and again this summer, how one can avoid being reminded of the Luftwaffe attacks on the equally helpless French refugees of 1940? Many thousands of Lebanese have been killed in this way over the past twenty-five years.

And please spare me the nonsense about 'human shields'. What about the marked ambulance of women and children rocketed by a low-flying Israeli helicopter in 1996? Or the refugee convoy whose women and children were torn to pieces by an equally low-flying Israeli air force helicopter as they fled along the roads after being ordered to leave their homes by the Israelis! No, Israelis are not Nazis. But it's time we talked of war crimes unless they stop these attacks on refugees. The Arabs are entitled to talk the same way. They should. But they must stop lying about Jewish history – and take a lesson, perhaps, from the Israeli historians who tell the truth about the savagery which attended Israel's birth.

As for the West's reaction to Ahmadinejad's antics, Prime Minister Blair was 'shocked' into disbelief while Israeli prime minister Ehud Olmert responded with more eloquent contempt. I've no doubt Ahmadinejad – equally conscious of Iran's precious relationship with Turkey – would gutlessly fail to honour the Armenian Holocaust in Tehran. Who would have thought that the governments of Britain, Israel and Iran had so much in common?

The Independent, 16 December 2006

Dreamology

As a little boy, I had only one recurring nightmare, and it always featured my grandfather's dog. Arthur Rose had a friendly Labrador called 'Sir Lancelot' – 'Lance' for short – and I adored this dog. I think he liked me too, because we raced around Arthur's great lawns together and when I tried to trip him up, he tried to trip me up and when I lay on the ground, he would sit with his back to me and bang his heavy, powerful tail into my face. But in my nightmares I would always be confronted by a hostile 'Lance' – no friendly 'Lab' now, but a biting, barking wolflike creature. His golden retriever's coat was the same, but his face was contorted with hatred for me and he would torment me until my cries of fear brought my father to my bed. He would shake me repeatedly until I freed myself from this fearsome phantom dog.

But we Westerners tend to regard dreams as a haphazard phenomenon wrought by the sleeping diminution of a still working brain, a coma of flotsam thrown up by our daily experiences or – in the one case where I ever previously dreamed a nightmare of war – by the shock of real terror. After the Sabra and Chatila camp massacre of 1982, I actually believed, in my sleep, that corpses were piled on the bed around me. The reason was simple: I had been climbing over decomposing bodies and my clothes smelt of death. But otherwise, my dreams have been pretty dull stuff; rough seas, an argument with a friend, a terrible fear that I should be preparing to file copy to *The Independent* on something I had just witnessed in a nightmare. Vietnam correspondents apparently went through the same thing.

But for many extreme Muslims, dreams are a far more serious affair. The Prophet Mohamed received his message from God – the Koran – after a series of dreams lasting six months, and there are those who believe that the entire text of the Koran was received by the Prophet in a dreamlike trance. Dreams, in other words, were no mere reflection of the idle human brain but could be a direct communication from God. Dr Iain Edgar of Durham University's Anthropology Department has sent me the results of his own investigation into this phenomenon,* the experience of the 'true dream' – 'ruya' in Arabic – which, he believes, 'is a fundamental, inspirational, and even strategic, part of the contemporary militant jihadist movement in the Middle East and elsewhere'. Describing Islam as 'probably the largest night dream culture in the world today', Edgar quotes a 'hadith' (saying of the Prophet) in which Mohamed's wife Aisha says that the 'commencement of the divine inspiration was in the form of good righteous dreams in his sleep . . . He never had a dream but that it came true like bright of day.'

An eighth-century dream writer from Basra in southern Iraq, Ibn Sirin, who wrote *Dreams and Their Interpretation*, divided dreams between the spiritual ('ruan'), those inspired by the Devil, and 'dreams emanating from the "nafs" [which means "running, hot blood"] – an earthly spirit that dwells in the dreamer's body and is distinct from the soul'. I fear that my grandfather's ferocious Labrador must be placed among the latter. But these ideas should not be trifled with. Mohamed

---

* 'The Inspirational Night Dream in the Motivation and Justification of Jihad' by Iain R. Edgar, University of Durham.

Amanullah presented a paper at Berkeley three years ago which stated that half of the twelve Muslim staff in the religious studies department at a Malaysian university reported 'true' dreams, fifty per cent of which revealed the Prophet. One 'hadith' quotes the Prophet as saying that 'whoever has seen me in a dream, then no doubt, he has seen me, for Satan cannot imitate my shape'.

Osama bin Laden certainly is a dream-believer. Not only did he once tell me that one of his 'brothers' had a dream that he had seen me in a Muslim gown, bearded and riding a horse, and that this must mean I was a 'true Muslim' – a possible attempt at recruitment which I swiftly turned down – but following the 11 September 2001 crimes against humanity, he is quoted as saying that 'Abul-Hassan al-Musri told me a year ago: "I saw in a dream, we were playing a soccer game against the Americans. When our team showed up in the field, they were all pilots!" He [al-Musri] didn't know anything about the [9/11] operation until he heard it on the radio. He said the game went on and we defeated them. That was a good omen for us.' Yosri Fouda, an al-Jazeera journalist who interviewed al-Qaeda planners Ramzi bin al-Shibh and Khalid Shaykh Mohamed in 2002, reported that al-Shibh spoke of experiencing many dreams about the brothers before the attacks. 'He would speak of the Prophet and his close companions as if he had actually met them.' Al-Shibh was to recall that 'Mohamed Atta [one of the leading 11 September hijackers] told me that Marwan [el-Shehdi] had a beautiful dream that he was flying high in the sky surrounded by green birds not from our world, and that he was crashing into things, and that he felt so happy.' Fouda notes that 'green birds' are often given significance in dreams; green is the colour of Islam and flying birds are a symbol of heaven. Edgar notes that bin Laden's recounting of the dream in which the luckless Fisk was seen as an imam has me mounted on a horse which – according to Iain Edgar –

symbolises a 'person's status, rank, honour, dignity, power and glory'. Well thanks, but no.

Richard Reid, the British would-be shoe bomber on a transatlantic American Airlines flight, referred to a dream in which he tried to hitch a ride in a pick-up truck which was full and was forced to travel in a smaller car. The truck presumably represented the four aircraft used on 11 September from which Reid was excluded, and the car was the American Airlines plane on which Reid was forced to try to 'catch up' with his nineteen comrades. Zacarias Moussawi, the Frenchman of Moroccan origin who may have been the intended twentieth hijacker, found his own dreams of flying a plane into a tall building became a significant issue in his 2006 trial in the US. Rahimullah Yusufzai, by far the wisest journalist reporting in Pakistan, was told by the Taliban that its founder, the one-eyed Mullah Omar, 'gets instructions in his dream and he follows them up'. A dream was the genesis of the Taliban's foundation. Mullah Omar once telehoned Yusufzai to ask for an interpretation of a dream in which a 'white palace' was on fire. He knew that Yusufzai had been to the White House. Did it look like the White Palace? This was before 11 September 2001.

Extraordinarily, Qari Badruzzaman Badr, a Guantanamo ex-prisoner, recounted to the *Daily Times* in Lahore how 'many Arabs had dreams in which the Holy Prophet personally gave them news of their freedom . . . One Arab saw Jesus who took his hand and told him that Christians were now misled. Later the other prisoners could smell the sweet smell of Jesus on his hand.' Jesus, in other words, a major prophet of Islam, is telling the Muslim prisoners that the Christians are misled. As Edgar comments: 'What a transcendence of their oppression this dream message must have seemed!'

But there are false dreams. A Peshawar imam recounted how a man told him that the Prophet said he could drink alcohol.

But when the man admitted that he himself drank alcohol, the imam said he had not seen the Prophet, only a self-justification for drinking. Alas, I fear there is no hope for us infidels!

The Independent, 26 January 2008

CHAPTER TEN

'A thing invulnerable'

History is not our responsibility, but it is our duty to study the past – not only to avoid its mournful repetition but to understand the present. In Lebanon, it is impossible to remain untouched by the great Roman monuments that litter the countryside, not to reflect on that vast and supposedly 'civilising' empire which made all its conquered peoples citizens of Rome. Fighting Muslims in the First World War, Gallipoli remains one of our greatest military defeats. Yet how we 'use' history for our own political ends; how we mourn only for the newly dead, how easily we feel able to step forward and claim a role for ourselves in history, how lost we are without the titans of yesterday . . . I'm not sure that foreign correspondents 'live' history. We certainly witness it. But without the past, we are watching only shadows on the wall.

What the Romans would have thought of Iraq

Professor Malcolm Willcock was, to be precise, the gentlest, finest of academics who taught the ghastly Fisk Latin and Roman history when I turned up in the second year of Lancaster University's life in 1965. He made the Roman Empire live and I think of him this morning – in the year of his death – as I walk the streets of ancient Rome and ponder the lessons of a later, even more dangerous empire. Professor Willcock, I should add, was primarily a Greek scholar – he introduced me to Achilles walking by 'the wine-dark sea' – and showed, according to one of his obituarists, 'how Homer's characters inventively tweaked standard myths into serving as persuasive paradigms of the way heroes should behave'.

Now who does that remind us of, I wonder? Indeed, what does the Roman Empire remind me of? I recall, back in 1997, taking bits of a US-made missile to Washington with the intention of placing the metal fragments in front of its manufacturers. I noted in my diary that the city 'that late spring day was beautiful – the Capitol and the great government buildings looked like ancient Rome . . .' and it is true that Washington's builders wanted their city to look like Malcolm Willcock's most famous capital. Several US soldiers serving in Iraq – including a young man who was killed there last year – compared their own lives to those of Roman centurions. And it's not difficult, watching the Americans in their combat kit – the Germanised helmets, the back-breaking Kevlar body armour, the soft brown boots – to see the centurions in their leather breastplates and plumed helmets.

We can go to Iraq, their uniforms tell us; we can march across the lands of Sumeria where civilisation supposedly began; we can bestride Baghdad; we are (was this not Antony, already a mere triumvir?) one of the 'triple pillars of the world'. For the Roman footfall, feel the vibration of an Abrams M1A1 tank. But is that how empires exist? I used to believe that they contained their own built-in fear system, that they struck out against those who would have to understand that *Carthago delenda est*. Carthage (for which read al-Qaeda) must be destroyed. But I'm not so sure. I think empires – Roman, British, American – expand because it is in their nature to project, constantly and fatally, military force. We can go to Baghdad, so we will go to Baghdad. Professor Willcock, I remember, drew my attention to Crassus, that great Roman billionaire who made his *sestertii* from Roman slum rents and whose personality was so persuasively captured by Laurence Olivier in the film *Spartacus*. Crassus took his legions into what we would today call the Syrian–Iraqi desert, where they were cut to pieces by the horse-borne Parthians (for whom, read our modern-day Syrian–Iraqi 'terrorists'). Crassus himself was invited to surrender talks in a tent where he was beheaded, his cranium filled with gold and sent back, Iraqi-style, to Rome as a tribute to his wealth.

When Howard Hayes Scullard wrote his monumental *From the Gracchi to Nero* in the 1930s, he clearly felt that Caesar Augustus was an early Mussolini. Many movie versions of Roman history – *Gladiator* would be Hollywood's most recent effort – depict imperial power as essentially fascistic, although that is a bit unfair on Rome. The Republic – the Rome of the triumvirs – was an attempt to divide power, and it is not Cicero's fault that Pompey, Caesar Augustus and Antony – who tried to retrieve Crassus's standards from the Parthian desert – failed to save democracy.

What Rome did project was the idea of 'belonging'. Every conquered people became Roman citizens. Think, for a moment, what would have happened in Baghdad if every Iraqi had been offered a US passport in 2003 – no insurgency, no war, no US casualties, only love and a desire on the part of every human being in south-west Asia to be invaded by George W. Bush! I once put this to a CIA official in Amara – yes, the same Amara which fell outside British rule last month and which Tony Blair will inherit as his lordship after his departure – and he scoffed at me. 'We're not here for their benefit,' he told me. Oh, but we were, weren't we?

Professor Willcock had a remarkable deputy commander in the Classics department at Lancaster University, a lecturer called David Shotter, whom I telephoned yesterday. Shotter used to compare the surging of the Roman legions to the German Wehrmacht in Second World War Russia, a parallel he now prefers to mute. He talks today of 'a Romanised place in time', the creation of 'a people with manic energy' and – I caught my breath when he said this down the phone to me as I stood scarcely 100 metres from the Roman forum – 'how conquest can be ferocious when it needs to be'. Virgil understood the need to profit from the benefits of peace. The Roman army, had its commanders viewed Iraq today, Shotter added slowly, 'would have found the place a pretty unacceptable situation'.

The Romans, of course, never retreated. They did not 'cut and run' and, when they were once visited by an al-Qaeda-like plague in Bithynia (in modern-day Turkey) in which every Roman man, woman and child was liquidated, they crucified their enemies to extinction. Human rights meant nothing in ancient Rome. The torture chamber was part of Roman civilisation. The crucifixion cross was the symbol of power.

So what brought it down? Corruption, of course. And well, in the end, the Goths, Ostrogoths and Visigoths arrived in Rome. Not far from where I'm writing this report, you can still find the green, burned coins – the *sestertii* – engraved in the stones of the Roman market when they were tipped into the fire at that moment when the 'other' – the 'alien' army, those who did not accept Roman 'values' – arrived in the forum so quickly that the merchants did not have time to shut up shop.

This morning, I shall go back and look at those burned coins again. But I must ask myself whether the 'terrorists' – the Goths, Ostrogoths and Visigoths – will be stopped in Iraq. Or whether, perhaps, they already live in Washington, tearing apart their empire from within. I suspect that Malcolm Willcock, the noblest Roman of them all, might have agreed.

The Independent, 4 November 2006

In memoriam

Wellington reminds me of Maidstone, Kent, when I was a little boy; the 1912 façades of so many New Zealand shops, the narrow streets, the trolley buses, the giant coins, the slightly old-fashioned English, the demand for doughnuts and hot-cross buns. Everyone in Maidstone used to call each other 'mate' – yes, I know this is an Australian expression as well – and older men in Wellington wear ties, just as my dad did back in the 1950s. My grandmother Phyllis used to run a string of cafés in Kent – my grandfather Arthur was her baker at the Bridge Café in Maidstone which was located inside a genuine Tudor house, torn down after they sold it, to be replaced with a concrete box insurance agency – but my first home in Bower Mount Road was built of lavatory brick, like so many houses in New Zealand.

True, there weren't many Maoris in Maidstone, but the cinemas were as art deco as Wellington's. In Maidstone, we had the Granada, which showed Hollywood films. I remember Kirk Douglas in *The Vikings* and Charlton Heston in the interminable *Ben Hur*. Then there was the Regal Cinema, a snogging fleapit showing B-movies with glimpses of bare breasts. When the Regal burned down one night, I went to watch the Maidstone fire brigade dousing the flames. Phyllis thought it must have been God's punishment for the bare breasts.

In Wellington there's an Embassy Cinema and a Paramount Cinema – both dead ringers for the old Regal – and they've shown *Munich* and *Shrek* and George Clooney's *Syriana*, which some younger New Zealand cinemagoers found too complicated to understand. And I have to admit that last weekend the Paramount was showing a thirteen-year-old, two-and-a-half-hour documentary film called *Beirut to Bosnia* in which a certain Robert Fisk walks into a burning Bosnian mosque – on 11 September 1993, for heaven's sake – and comments on the soundtrack that 'when I see things like this, I wonder what the Muslim world has in store for us'.

The trolley buses in Maidstone were vomit-coloured double-deckers whose wooden frames creaked each time the electric current clicked up to 30 miles an hour. The single-deckers in Wellington boast no wood, but at least one church, Old Saint Paul's, built in 1866, is constructed entirely of wood and contains the same brass plaques that I used to read along the aisles of All Saints Church in Maidstone. 'To the Glory of God and in Memory of Richard John Spotswood Seddon, Captain, New Zealand Expeditionary Force', says one. 'Killed in Action, Bapaume, France, 1918, aged 37. Faithful Unto Death.' Another carries the name of a more familiar battlefield. 'In Loving Memory of 2nd Lt S O'Carrol Smith, 9th Battalion Rifle Brigade. Fell at the Battle of the Somme, 25 August 1916, aged 25.'

And of course, I remember that 2nd Lt Bill Fisk of the 12th Battalion, the King's Liverpool Regiment, wore his regimental tie for the rest of his life to remind him of the Somme. He arrived there in August of 1918 to fight across the same mud in which 2nd Lt O'Carrol Smith was killed, and just three months after Captain Seddon died at Bapaume, which was in turn close to the village of Louvencourt where nineteen-year-old Bill Fisk spent the night of 11 November 1918. Bill Fisk used to attend the Maidstone cenotaph ceremonies each year, his blood-red poppy in the buttonhole of his huge best black coat, although he later refused to wear his Great War campaign medal, the one with 'The Great War for Civilisation' engraved on the back.

And then in Wellington's Old Saint Paul's Church, I come across the name of the Turkish bloodbath I have all along been waiting for: a brass plaque with a cross on the top and these words: 'In Memory of Sgt W R Richardson, Killed at Gallipoli, 5 December 1915, Aged 31.' He died only days before Winston Churchill's military adventure ended in ignominious withdrawal. A short walk to the state-of-the-art and decidedly un-Maidstone-like city museum establishes that William Richardson, service number 13/2243, was the son of Charles Thomas and Charlotte Richardson of Wellington and is buried at Gallipoli's Embarkation Pier Cemetery.

Gallipoli was the West's greatest twentieth-century battle with a Muslim army. You must have a heart of stone not to be moved by New Zealand's casualties. Out of 8,450 soldiers sent to fight in Turkey, 2,721 were killed and 4,752 wounded. What other nation can claim an 88 per cent casualty rate in battle? While I'm looking at the plaques in Saint Paul's, an elderly lady walks up to me, Joy McClean, and, out of the blue, says: 'My father was at Gallipoli. Yes, he was fighting Muslims but to him I think they were just the "enemy". He was fighting for his country, wasn't he, for what he thought was right.' And I ponder the remark of this gentle old lady until her mood changes. 'There used to be 300 Muslims here,' she says. 'Now there are 3,000.' And then I feel the darkness of these last words: 11 September 2001 has begun to shadow even this faraway wooden church.

I drive out to the south coast of New Zealand's North Island to escape that shadow. For on a cliff face remarkably similar to the hillside upon which the Anzacs landed is a memorial to Mustafa Kemal Ataturk. Yes, he was a secularist, a chain-smoker who banned Arabic script and the veil, a man who closed down the last caliphate but was a Muslim nonetheless. And there on a marble plaque is his address to the grieving New Zealand and Australian families who first went to Gallipoli to mourn their loved ones in the 1930s, the most compassionate words ever uttered by a Muslim leader in modern times:

> Those heroes that shed their blood and lost their lives . . . you are now lying in the soil of a friendly country. Therefore rest in peace. There is no difference between the Johnnies and the Mehmets to us, where they lie, side by side here in this country of ours. You, the mothers who sent their sons from faraway countries wipe away your tears. Your sons are now lying in our bosom and are in peace. After having lost their lives on this land, they have become our sons as well.

And I find myself wondering what Osama bin Laden would think of that.

The Independent, 25 March 2006

Read Lawrence of Arabia

Back in 1929, Lawrence of Arabia wrote the entry for 'Guerrilla' in the 14th edition of the *Encyclopaedia Britannica*. It is a chilling read – and here I thank one of my favourite readers, Peter Metcalfe of Stevenage, for sending me TE's remarkable article – because it contains so ghastly a message to the American armies in Iraq.

Writing of the Arab resistance to Turkish occupation in the 1914–18 war, Lawrence asks of the insurgents (in Iraq and elsewhere): '. . . suppose they were an influence, a thing invulnerable, intangible, without front or back, drifting about like a gas? Armies were like plants, immobile as a whole, firm-rooted, nourished through long stems to the head. The Arabs might be a vapour . . .' How typical of Lawrence to use the horror of gas warfare as a metaphor for insurgency. To control the land they occupied, he continued, the Turks 'would have need of a fortified post every four square miles, and a post could not be less than 20 men. The Turks would need 600,000 men to meet the combined ill wills of all the local Arab people. They had 100,000 men available.'

Now who does that remind you of? The 'fortified post every four square miles' is the ghostly future echo of George W. Bush's absurd 'surge'. The Americans need 600,000 men to meet the combined ill will of the Iraqi people, and they have only 150,000 available. Donald Rumsfeld, the architect of 'war lite', is responsible for that. Yet still these rascals get away with it.

Hands up those readers who know that Canada's defence minister, Gordon O'Connor, actually sent a letter to Rumsfeld two days before his departure in disgrace from the Pentagon, praising this disreputable man's 'leadership'. Yes, O'Connor wanted 'to take this opportunity to congratulate you on your many achievements [sic] as Secretary of Defence, and to recognise the significant contribution you have made in the fight against terrorism'. The world, gushed the ridiculous O'Connor, had benefited from Rumsfeld's 'leadership in addressing the complex issues in play'. O'Connor tried to shrug off this grovelling note, acquired through the Canadian Access to Information Act, by claiming he merely wanted to thank Rumsfeld for the use of US medical facilities in Germany to ferry wounded Canadian soldiers home from Afghanistan. But he made no mention of this in his preposterous letter. O'Connor, it seems, is just another of the world's illusionists who believe they can ignore the facts – and laud fools – by stating the opposite of the truth.

Oh, how we miss Lawrence. 'The printing press is the greatest weapon in the armoury of the modern [guerrilla] commander,' he wrote seventy-eight years ago, accurately predicting al-Qaeda's modern-day use of the internet. For insurgents, 'battles were a mistake . . . Napoleon had spoken in angry reaction against the excessive finesse of the 18th century, when men almost forgot that war gave licence to murder'. True, the First World War Arab Revolt was not identical to today's Iraqi insurgency. In 1917 the Turks had manpower but too few weapons. Today the Americans have the weapons but too few men. But listen to Lawrence again.

Rebellion must have an unassailable base . . .

In the minds of men converted to its creed, it must have a sophisticated alien enemy, in the form of a disciplined army of

occupation too small to fulfil the doctrine of acreage: too few
to adjust number to space, in order to dominate the whole
area effectively from fortified posts.

It must have a friendly population, not actively friendly, but
sympathetic to the point of not betraying rebel movements to
the enemy. Rebellions can be made by 2 per cent active in a
striking force, and 98 per cent passively sympathetic ...
Granted mobility, security ... time, and doctrine ... victory
will rest with the insurgents, for the algebraical factors are in
the end decisive, and against them perfections of means and
spirit struggle quite in vain.

Has US General David Petraeus read this? Has Bush? Have
any of the tired American columnists whose anti-Arab bias is
wobbling close to racism bothered to study this wisdom? I
remember how Daniel Pipes – one of the great illusionists of
modern American journalism – announced in the summer of
2003 that what the Iraqis needed was (no smirking here,
please), a 'democratically-minded strongman'.

They had already had one, of course, our old chum Saddam
Hussein, whom we did indeed call a 'strongman' when he
was our friend and when he was busy using our gas against
Iran. And I do wonder whether Bush – defeated, as he is, in
Iraq – may not soon sanction an Iraqi military coup d'état to
overthrow the ridiculous Maliki 'Green Zone' government in
Baghdad.

But wait, Pipes is at it again. The director of the 'Middle
East Forum' has been writing in Canada's *National Post* about
'Palestine'. His piece is filled with the usual bile. Palestinian
anarchy had 'spewed forth' warlords. Arafat was an 'evil' figure.
Israeli withdrawal from Gaza had deprived Palestinians of the
one 'stabilising element' in the region. Phew! 'Palestinianism'
(whatever that is) is 'superficial'. Palestinian 'victimisation' is
a 'supreme myth of modern politics'. Gaza is now an '[Islamist]

beachhead at the heart of the Middle East from which to infiltrate Egypt, Israel and the West Bank'. One of these days, Pipes concludes, 'maybe the idiot savant "peace processors" will note the trail of disasters their handiwork has achieved'. He notes with approval that 'Ehud Barak, Israel's brand new Defence Minister, reportedly plans to attack Hamas within weeks' and condemns the prime minister, Ehud Olmert, for buoying Mahmoud Abbas's 'corrupt and irredentist Fatah'.

So we are going to have yet another war in the Middle East, this time against Hamas – democratically elected, of course, but only as a result of what Pipes calls 'the Bush administration's heedless rush to Palestinian elections'? It's good to see that the late Tony Blair is already being dubbed a 'savant'. But shouldn't Pipes, too, read Lawrence? For insurgency is a more powerful 'vapour' than that which comes from the mouths of illusionists.

The Independent, 14 July 2007

A peek into the Fascist era

Sciuscia, in Neapolitan Italian, means 'Shoeshine'. It is the most controversial, provocative, irritating programme on the second channel of Italy's state television, RAI. Silvio Berlusconi, the prime minister of Italy, would like to make sure that last week's 33rd edition of *Sciuscia* – pronounced 'shiewsha' – is the last. Only last April, Mr Berlusconi claimed that Michele Santoro, the anchorman of this crazy mix of brilliant documentaries and *That Was The Week That Was* scorn, had 'made a criminal use of public television'. Italian journalists are waiting for blood to flow.

Last week's 'final' programme of the season – in which I was invited to participate – included a devastating documentary by reporter Corrado Formigli on the West's failure to help Afghanistan. It also featured a long, angry and sometimes hilarious studio debate on the folly of our involvement in the country between NGOs, defence specialists, an American actress, a leftist Italian reporter, a pro-Israeli journalist and Signor Fisk. If only the BBC could put this kind of harsh, real-time argument on air! At one point, I even managed to get the other guests to talk about why the crimes against humanity of 11 September had been committed.

But this is not the point. *Sciuscia* has been a plague on Mr Berlusconi's administration, at one point investigating the mafia-like background of one of the prime minister's closest

colleagues. In presenting the plight of Palestinians under occupation, Mr Santoro was accused by the Italian Jewish community – like so many journalists who dare to criticise Israel
– of 'anti-Semitism'. Mr Leone Paserman, the president of the
Jewish community in Rome, also asked the RAI administration
to fire Mr Santoro. Mr Paserman was subsequently ordered by
an Italian court to pay €50,000 to the journalist.

Like many leftist reporters in Italy, Mr Santoro was a communist – he began his career as a journalist on the then
communist party newspaper *L'Unità*, but today he is the perfect anchorman, as provocative as Jeremy Paxman and as theatrical as Brian Rix, the perfect David Frost before the latter
went to seed. He goads his guests into anger and generosity.
RAI's board of five administrators are not amused. Three of
them, appointed in February, are allies of Mr Berlusconi's
'Forza Italia' and the president of RAI, Antonio Baldassarre, is
close to the Berlusconi coalition. *Sciuscia* staff have not been
told if they will be allowed another series – by now, they should
already be planning next autumn's schedule. In addition to the
influence he holds over the RAI board, Mr Berlusconi has a
near monopoly on private sector television in Italy: he controls
three private channels – Channel Five, Italy 1 and Network 4
– and controls through his brother the daily newspaper *Il
Giornale*, with a circulation of 200,000. He effectively controls
the weekly newsmagazine *Panorama*, and also the gossip magazine *Chi*, with a circulation of about 1 million.

Is this, therefore, just another little fracas between the right-
wing *papivor* of Italian politics and the subversive, electorally
defeated forces of the left? It would be pleasant to think so.
But a few hours after the last programme of the series, I came
upon an exhibition in the basement of that Vittorio Emanuele
monument, the notorious ice-cream cake of concrete and
marble which houses Italy's First World War unknown warrior.
The exhibition, a plaque at the entrance announced, was the

inspiration of none other than Mr Berlusconi, a demonstration of 150 years of Italian unity.

Inside were dozens of military flags, indeed hundreds – in fact, far too many military flags – from the 1914–18 war and before. There was a piece of Garibaldi's leg bone, extracted after he was wounded at the 1862 battle of Aspromonte, and even the great man's right, fur-lined boot, complete with bullet hole. Far more impressive was a long documentary on the Italian army's campaign against the Austro-Hungarian Empire in the First World War, when Italy was, of course, on 'our' side. It includes incredible archive footage of the Alpine front lines – real film, not re-enacted like so much British film of the time – and of the sinking of a massive battleship which, *Titanic*-like, turns over on top of hundreds of crew.

Much more worrying, however, is the written commentary, appearing on screen as it must have done when the film was originally put together – presumably in the early years of Mussolini's rule. Over and over again, war is referred to as 'glorious'. The 600,000 Italian casualties of the war are even referred to, in Italian, as a 'holocaust'. The last great battle of the war – at Piave – is treated as a blood sacrifice. Nothing inaccurate from a factual point of view, perhaps, but what did this mean? Is blood really the unifying cement of Italy? I thought I might find an antidote across the square at the Palazzo Valentini, where another exhibition – 'Portrait of an Era: Art and Architecture in the Fascist Era' – was arranged in what were once the baths of the Emperor Trajan. The purpose of the exhibition, Rossana Bossaglia's introduction informed me, was 'to show how Italian art of the Fascist era developed an expressive language of its own, able to deal with different themes in a completely independent way . . .' This sounded a little dodgy. No condemnation of the Fascist era.

Rather, a peek into what might have been good about it. And sure enough, while the paintings and sculptures are fascinating enough there was an oil painting of Mussolini and then a sculpture of Mussolini, alongside a photograph of the Duce himself looking at the very same sculpture. Silvano Moffa, president of the Rome province, offers us, in the same introduction, the thought that 'Fascism as it was in the 1920s – that is to say a movement characterised by the need to celebrate itself – was not the same movement it would become in the 1930s. From the very beginning of his dictatorship, Mussolini stated that the relationship between politics and art was an important one, and promoted several exhibitions . . .' What did this mean?

I slunk through the afternoon sun for a late lunch and opened my Italian newspaper. And what did I find? President Carlo Ciampi of Italy wants to honour Garibaldi, the Italian soldiers who bravely fought the Nazis on the island of Cephalonia in the Second World War and – wait for it – the soldiers who fought in the battle of El Alamein in 1942. But the latter soldiers were fighting for Mussolini and his Nazi allies. Had Rommel won the battle with Italian help, the Axis powers would have reached Cairo and Palestine – whose Jewish population would then have been included in the Holocaust. I wondered, briefly, whether Mr Paserman wouldn't have done better to complain about this sinister plan of Mr Ciampi rather than slandering Mr Santoro.

Is this something to be worried about? Italian journalists like to ameliorate the situation. Mr Berlusconi is a businessman first, they told me. So is Mr Ciampi. Mr Santoro is an artist who likes to play the martyr. And if *Sciuscia* comes back on the air, it will be another Italian tempest. If it does not, however, a lot of Europeans might do well to think more seriously about Mr Berlusconi, to ask themselves whether he really is the president of a united Italy. Or a scoundrel.*

The Independent, 5 June 2002

---

* *Sciuscia* never returned to the screen. Berlusconi was at last defeated in Italian elections in 2007. But he might still return.

Who now cries for the dead of Waterloo?

'About suffering', Auden famously wrote in 1938, 'they were never wrong,/The Old Masters: how well they understood/Its human position; how it takes place/While someone else is eating or opening a window/Or just walking dully along.' Yet the great crucifixion paintings of Caravaggio or Bellini, or Michelangelo's *Pietà* in the Vatican – though they were not what Auden had in mind – have God on their side. We may feel the power of suffering in the context of religion but, outside this spiritual setting, I'm not sure how compassionate we really are.

The atrocities of yesterday – the Beslan school massacre, the Bali bombings, the crimes against humanity of 11 September 2001, the gassings of Halabja – can still fill us with horror and pity, although that sensitivity is heavily conditioned by the nature of the perpetrators. In an age where war has become a policy option rather than a last resort, where its legitimacy rather than its morality can be summed up on a sheet of A4 paper,[*] we prefer to concentrate on the suffering caused by 'them' rather than 'us'. Hence the tens of thousands of Iraqis who were killed in the 2003 Anglo-American invasion and

[*] Equivocal 13-page advice by the British Attorney-General, Lord Goldsmith, on the legitimacy of an invasion of Iraq was famously reduced to unequivocal advice to Mr Blair on a single sheet of A4 paper.

subsequent occupation, the hundreds of thousands of Vietnamese killed in the Vietnam War, the hundreds of Egyptians cut down by our 1956 invasion of Suez are not part of our burden of guilt. About 1,700 Palestinian civilians – equal to more than half the dead of the World Trade Center – were massacred in Lebanon in 1982.

But how many readers can remember the exact date? September 16–18, 1982. 'Our' dates are thus sacrosanct, 'theirs' are not; though I notice how 'they' must learn 'ours'. How many times are Arabs pointedly asked for their reaction to 11 September 2001, with the specific purpose of discovering whether they show the correct degree of shock and horror? And how many Westerners would even know what happened in September 1982?

It's also about living memory – and also, I suspect, about photographic records. The catastrophes of our generation – or of our parents' or even our grandparents' generation – have a poignancy that earlier bloodbaths lack. Hence we can be moved to tears by the epic tragedy of the Second World War and its 60 million dead, by the murder of 6 million Jews, by our families' memories of this conflict – a cousin on my father's side died on the Burma Road – and also by the poets of the First World War. Owen and Sassoon created the ever-living verbal museum of that conflict. But I can well understand why the Israelis have restructured their Holocaust museum at Yad Vashem. The last survivors of Hitler's death camps will be dead soon. So they must be kept alive in their taped interviews, along with the records and clothes of those who were slaughtered by the Nazis.

And here the compassion begins to wobble. Before the 1914–18 war there were massacres enough for the world's tears; the Balkan War of 1912 was of such carnage that eyewitnesses feared their accounts would never be believed. The Boer War turned into a moral disgrace for the British because we herded our enemies' families into disease-ridden concentration camps. The Franco-Prussian War of 1870–1 – though French suffering was portrayed by Daumier with stunning accuracy, and photos survive of the Paris Commune – leaves us cold. So, despite the record of still photographs, does the American Civil War. We can still be appalled – we should be appalled – by the million dead of the Irish famine, although it is painfully significant that, although photography had been invented by the mid-nineteenth century, not a single photograph was taken of its victims. We have to rely on the *Illustrated London News* sketches to show the grief and horror which the Irish famine produced.

Yet who cries now for the dead of Waterloo or Malplaquet, of the first Afghan War, of the Hundred Years War – whose rural effects were still being felt in 1914 – or for the English Civil War, for the dead of Flodden Field or Naseby or for the world slaughter brought about by the Black Death? True, movies can briefly provoke some feeling in us for these ghosts. Hence the *Titanic* remains a real tragedy for us, even though it sank in 1912 when the Balkan War was taking so many more innocent lives. *Braveheart* can move us. But in the end we know that the execution of William Wallace is just Mel Gibson faking death. By the time we reach the slaughters of antiquity, we simply don't care a damn. Genghis Khan? Tamerlane? The sack of Rome? The destruction of Carthage? Forget it. Their victims have turned to dust and we do not care about them. They have no memorial. We even demonstrate our fascination with long-ago cruelty. Do we not queue for hours to look at the room in London in which two children were brutally murdered? The Princes in the Tower?

If, of course, the dead have a spiritual value, then their death must become real to us. Rome's most famous crucifixion victim was not Spartacus – although Kirk Douglas did his best to win the role in Kubrick's fine film – but a carpenter from

Nazareth. And compassion remains as fresh among Muslims for the martyrs of early Islam as it does for the present-day dead of Iraq. Anyone who has watched the Shia Muslims of Iraq or Lebanon or Iran honouring the killing of Imams Ali and Hussein – like Jesus, they were betrayed – has watched real tears running down their faces, tears no less fresh than those of the Christian pilgrims in Jerusalem this Easter week. You can butcher a whole city of innocents in the Punic War, but nail the son of Mary to a cross or murder the son-in-law of the Prophet and you'll have them weeping for generations.

What worries me, I suppose, is that so many millions of innocents have suffered terrible deaths because their killers have wept over their religious martyrs. The Crusaders slaughtered the entire population of Beirut and Jerusalem in 1099 because of their desire to 'free' the Holy Land, and between 1980 and 1988 the followers of the Prophet killed a million and a half of their own co-religionists after a Sunni Muslim leader invaded a Shia Muslim country. Most of the Iraqi soldiers were Shia – and almost all the Iranian soldiers were Shia – so this was an act of virtual mass suicide by the followers of Ali and Hussein.

Passion and redemption were probably essential parts of our parents' religious experience. But I believe it would be wiser and more human in our twenty-first century to reflect upon the sins of our little human gods, those evangelicals who also claim we are fighting for 'good' against 'evil', who can ignore history and the oceans of blood humanity has shed – and get away with it on a sheet of A4 paper.

The Independent, 26 March 2005

Witnesses to genocide: a dark tale from Switzerland

So there I was in Locarno this week, attacking Carla del Ponte – the Judge Jeffreys of The Hague – for daring to threaten journalists who would not give evidence against Serb war criminals. Why wouldn't she, along with her little 'interrogators', try some of my local war criminals in the Middle East; Rifaat al-Assad, for example, or Ariel Sharon? Then, just down the road at a cramped little cinema, the Swiss provided a lesson in what war crimes were really about. Or how the knowledge of war crimes – and the failure to give witness to them – was a crime in itself. *Mission in Hell* is a terrifying film which recounts a hitherto secret, shameful chapter of the Second World War, as unknown in Britain as it still is in Switzerland.

All praise, therefore, to the tiny Locarno Film Festival for showing Frédéric Gonseth's two-and-a-half-hour exposé of the Swiss Red Cross missions to the Nazi Eastern Front between 1941 and 1944. We all know, of course, how the International Committee of the Red Cross was conned by the Germans, how it wrote glowing reports of the humanitarian treatment of Jews in Theresienstadt and other concentration camps. I am still prepared to accept the word of the Swiss historian of the Red Cross in the Second World War – when I interviewed him sixteen years ago – that 'Hitler's evil was on a level that left the Red Cross in a different moral world' – but I'm a lot less convinced that there's any excuse for what happened to the four Red Cross missions to Nazi-occupied Russia. For what Gonseth's film shows us is something unique: a group of moral, neutral, non-German surgeons and doctors and nurses who set off to care for the Russian as well as the German victims of Hitler's Operation Barbarossa – but who then slowly fell victim themselves to Nazi propaganda, moral cowardice and, most painful of all for Switzerland, the threats of a Swiss government desperate to conceal from the world their evidence of mass murder and genocide.

In all, 200 Swiss medical personnel took part in four missions to occupied eastern Europe. There is even film of these starry-eyed liberals setting off from Zurich station (all had affirmed in writing that they were 100 per cent 'Aryans') and there is documentation aplenty to prove that – unknown to the Swiss doctors – they were under the direct control of the Wehrmacht. Elderly survivors of the missions talk about their horror at the death of young German soldiers around Smolensk, of amputations without anaesthetic – there is grisly footage of just such an operation – and of the Red Cross doctor who turned out to be a friend of Himmler and who later recommended that the Swiss missions should work alongside the Waffen SS.

Throughout this catalogue of evidence, the ageing Swiss medical personnel recall how they understood – all too slowly, one has to add – that they would not be permitted to help the Russian wounded. A Swiss was ordered out of a hospital for Russian prisoners; another remembers the Russian POW trains carrying up to 3,000 prisoners, 'faces hidden by hair and dirt', fighting each other for bread, of their growing realisation that 200,000 Russian prisoners had been reduced to 20,000 during the winter of 1941–2. One Swiss female nurse keeps repeating that 'we looked at them [the Russians] through the window . . . some of them didn't even have shoes'. A male doctor tells how he saw a Russian prisoner, carried by two comrades, collapse between their arms. 'I did not fulfil my duty as a doctor, as a human being, for fear of troubles with our [German] hosts.'

There are a few heroes. There is a doctor, dismissively referred to as 'Rintelen' – his family name – by one of his surviving colleagues, who could no longer be a witness to such evil. 'When he saw what was going on, he couldn't take it mentally and was sent home, alone I think.' Then there were the Swiss who managed to get inside – actually to enter – the Warsaw Ghetto and witness at first hand the Jewish Holocaust. Charlotte Bisregger-Breno, a nurse, for example: 'There were people stretched out on the ground – everyone was dressed in rags.' And Charles Waldeberger: 'There were people on the ground, more or less unconscious, maybe already dead, I don't know.' Or Therese Buhler: 'There was a shed, a wooden shed. And the guardian of the cemetery, he came to us and said: "Come with me, come with me." He led us to a kind of shed and opened the door. I felt I have to vomit. The smell was so bad. There were piles of dead bodies, old, young, all types.'

As Gonseth's film makes clear, the Swiss were among the first neutral witnesses of the genocide of the Russians – it was Hitler's intention to kill off his millions of Soviet prisoners – as well as of the Jewish Holocaust. But when the last Swiss mission returned to Switzerland in 1944 – their personnel narrowly escaping capture by the advancing Red Army – they chose discretion rather than valour, locking up their daily logbooks of recorded horror for the next sixty years rather than damage the supposed neutrality of their native land. One of them – Rudolf Bucher – deserves to be a Swiss hero. He lectured in Zurich, told the Swiss public what he had seen, showed ferocious photographs of the butchery on the Eastern Front and condemned the persecution of the Jews.

True to form, a Swiss secret policeman was present at the lecture to take notes and Bucher was threatened with arrest, forbidden to lecture and warned – horror of horrors, I thought as I heard this – that he might not be permitted to serve in the Swiss army. Bucher's daughter was later to refer to the 'opaqueness of the political games', a gentle way, perhaps, of referring to the extraordinary statement of the Swiss foreign minister, Marcel Pilet-Golaz, who in 1941 wrote that 'we [the Swiss] must continue to demonstrate the unflagging support that the German effort warrants'.

No, I don't want to bash the Swiss. All praise to the Swiss who made this remarkable documentary. All praise to the elderly doctors who, albeit far too late, have given their testimony. 'What could we do?' one of them miserably asks. Nor am I convinced that Ms Del Ponte has the right to coerce journalists to give evidence of war crimes today. I still want the Middle East's war criminals on trial if journalists are going to have to give evidence to her court.

But I do remember, twenty years ago, writing a long report for my then employers, *The Times*, about Saddam Hussein's use of gas warfare against the Iranians – I had seen the young Iranian soldiers coughing their lungs into towels on a military hospital train moving up to Tehran from the front – and I also recall how a Foreign Office official that same week told my then editor that my story was 'not helpful' – because, of course, we were supporting Saddam at the time, and because Donald Rumsfeld was meeting Saddam just then, trying to persuade him to allow the US to reopen its embassy in Baghdad.

'Not helpful', of course, is exactly what the Swiss thought of their doctors' evidence from the Eastern Front.

The Independent, 16 August 2003

'You can tell a soldier to burn a village . . .'

Not far from my balcony overlooking the Mediterranean lies a sunken French submarine. It sits on the bottom of the sea just to the left of the blossoming purple jacaranda tree that stands opposite my bedroom window. It was sunk in 1941 when a disguised Royal Navy vessel slunk up the coast of Lebanon from Palestine and discovered two U-boats of the Vichy French fleet trying to make it home after the Anglo-Free French invasion of Lebanon. The French embassy in Beirut regularly reminds divers that this is a war grave, but the Lebanese still swim inside the hull. The gentle Mediterranean tides rock the vessel from time to time, and the skeletons inside – still in the remnants of their uniforms – rock with it. The Second World War will never go away.

There are war cemeteries in Sidon and Beirut – British and French dead from this extraordinary, largely unknown exploit of the war – and I often drive through the village of Damour where a Jewish Palestinian soldier, a certain Moshe Dayan, was hit in the eye by a French sniper. At home, I have an album of Lebanese Second World War photographs which depict the choice made by the French army in Lebanon when told that they could either sail home to Vichy France or stay in the Middle East and fight for de Gaulle. Almost all chose to return to Marseille, and a two-page spread in my photographic book shows thousands of French troops sailing out of Beirut port with a huge French flag upon which are embroidered the words 'Vive Pétain'.

Well, there you go. Nineteen forty-one was a bad year to back the Allies and Stalingrad was still eighteen months away, final proof that Hitler's power could be broken. But I am reminded of that French submarine every time I see a Lebanese diver friend of mine who sails out of the Riviera hotel and regularly visits the wreck. For the Second World War, I believe, remains the foundation of our modern history, the bedrock upon which all our narrative rests – the United Nations, the International Red Cross protocols, international humanitarian law.

I am outraged by the way in which the midgets Blair and Bush try to dress up in the waistcoats of Churchill and Roosevelt. I look at Blair poncing about in Basra and remember that Josip Broz Tito, the only man to liberate his country from Nazi tyranny from within an occupied nation, was the only Allied leader to be wounded in action during the war. What wounds has Blair sustained? A few months ago, I had the delight of participating in the BBC's *Desert Island Discs*, in which you can select eight records to bore – or entertain – the listener. One of my records was Winston Churchill's address to the British people (hardly music, I acknowledge) on 18 June 1940. I chose it because I wanted to prove that Blair and Bush were no Winston Churchills.

'Hitler knows that he must break us in this island or lose the war,' Churchill began. What a wondrous feat of words. Bush would have said 'defeat'. Blair would have said 'beat'. But Churchill said 'break'. If we stood up to Hitler, Churchill said, 'all Europe may be free and the life of the world may move forward into broad, sunlit uplands'. Compare that with the 'I am absolutely and totally convinced that I was right' of Lord Blair of Kut al-Amara when pontificating on Iraq.

Two days ago, I had lunch at the Spaghetteria restaurant in

Beirut with Adrien Jaulmes of *Le Figaro* newspaper, an immensely well-read French journalist who even knew the fate of my great hero Georges Guynemer, a French pilot who was blasted down over Ypres in 1917 after destroying a total of fifty-three German aircraft. So ferocious was the German bombardment at the time of his crash that when the *poilus* – the French infantry – reached the scene, there was nothing left of Guynemer or his plane. Guynemer gave his name to a beautiful street that runs up one side of the Jardin du Luxembourg in Paris, and Jaulmes and I talked of Verdun and the Somme and, of course, the second great conflict of 'our' generation in which 60 million souls perished. So how come our midgets still pretend they are fighting the Second World War? Is there not some way of switching this nonsense off?

Adrien and I talked of the fall of Berlin (watch the movie *Downfall* if you have not done so – you will sit in silence for minutes afterwards) and he made a remarkable comment towards the end of our meal. Adrien was a French foreign legionnaire – based in Corsica – before he (wisely) became a journalist. 'You know, there is something extraordinary, Robert,' he said. 'You can tell a soldier to burn a village and he will do it and commit a war crime. Or you can tell him to rescue people and he will do that and he is a humanitarian hero. Isn't that extraordinary?'

The Independent, 2 June 2007

Should journalists testify at war crimes trials?

Three Canadian war crimes investigators turned up to see me in Beirut last week. No, they didn't come to talk about the Bosnian war. They wanted to know about torture at Israel's notorious Khiam jail in southern Lebanon, about beatings and imprisonment in cupboard-size cells and electrodes applied to the toes and penises of inmates under interrogation. Most of the torturers were Lebanese members of Israel's proxy 'South Lebanon Army' militia, and they performed their vile work for the Israelis – on women as well as men – from the late Seventies until Israel's withdrawal in 2000: almost a quarter of a century of torture. Khiam prison is still there, open to the public, a living testament to brutality and Israeli shame.*

The problem is that Israel is now trying to dump its Lebanese torturers on Western countries. Sweden, Canada, Norway, France, Germany and other nations are being asked to give citizenship to these repulsive men in the interests of 'peace' – and also because the Israeli government would prefer they left Israel. The three investigators – two cops and a justice ministry official – had come to Beirut to make sure that their government wasn't about to give citizenship to Israel's war criminals. And they knew what they were talking about. We both knew

---

* No longer. It was seriously damaged by Israeli fire during the 2006 Israel–Hizballah war in Lebanon.

that one former torturer was living in Sweden with his two sons, and that another had opened two restaurants in America. And I was happy to chat to them. But chatting is one thing. Testifying is quite another. I make this point because the BBC told me last week that their Belgrade correspondent, Jacky Rowland, was planning to testify against Slobodan Milosevic at The Hague war crimes tribunal. I was invited this week to participate in a BBC radio interview with yet another BBC man who had given evidence at The Hague, Dan Damon.

And, in fact, I received a phone call from one of The Hague investigators a few weeks ago, wanting to know if I had accompanied a European Union delegation to a Bosnian concentration camp in 1992. I had travelled with the EU men to two camps – not the one that The Hague investigator was interested in. But this was not the first call I've heard from The Hague and I pointed out this time – as I had before – that I didn't believe journalists should be policemen. My articles could be used by anyone at The Hague and I was more than ready to sign a letter to the effect that they were accurate. But that was all.

So when Dan Damon of the BBC argued on air this week that the written or spoken report might not be 'believed' if a reporter wasn't ready to testify in a court, I was taken aback. In many cases, The Hague has commenced proceedings against war criminals on the basis of newspaper articles and television programmes. No one, so far as I know, has ever questioned our reports on Serbian, Croatian – and, yes, Muslim Bosnian – war crimes. In fact, I suspect Dan's argument was a bit of a smokescreen to cover his own concern about the boundaries of journalism.

I know, of course, how the arguments go. I may be a journalist, says the reporter as he or she turns up to the court, but I am also a human being. A time must come when a journalist's rules are outweighed by moral conscience. I don't like this argument. Firstly, because the implication is that journalists who don't intend to testify are not human beings; and secondly, because it suggests that reporters in general don't normally work with a moral conscience. Jonathan Randal, who worked for the *Washington Post* in Bosnia and has told The Hague tribunal that he will not testify against a Serb defendant, understands this all too well.

What worries me, though, is that journalism includes an element of masquerade if we cover wars as reporters and then participate in the prosecution of the bad guys at the request of a court whose writ extends only to those war crimes which it sees fit – or which the West sees fit – to investigate. Jacky Rowland of the BBC, for example, did not – while reporting the Balkan atrocities – turn up on Serbian assignments with the words: 'I'm from the BBC and – if your lot lose – I'm ready to help in your prosecution.' Indeed, if she had said that, she wouldn't have had the chance to undertake many more reporting assignments. Nor would any of us. But – if it's now going to be the habit for BBC reporters to turn up as prosecution witnesses at The Hague – heaven spare any of us in the future.

Now I have nothing against Jacky Rowland's reports. And if she feels her testimony is vital to convicting Mr Milosevic, that's up to her. But this story has another side. For Ms Rowland is not planning to attend The Hague court because she has chosen to give evidence against the former Serb leader. She is travelling to The Hague because the Western powers have decided that she should be permitted to testify against Mr Milosevic – though not, of course, against alleged war criminals of equal awfulness in other parts of the world.

Let me explain. Over twenty-six years, I've seen many war crimes in the Middle East. I was in Hama when Syrian Special Forces were killing up to 20,000 civilians during a Muslim revolt in 1982. I was at the Sabra and Chatila camps the same year when Israel's Phalangist thugs were butchering Palestinian civilians. I was with Iranian soldiers when Iraqi troops fired gas shells into them. I was in Algeria after the throat-slitting bloodbath of Bentalha, in which Algerian soldiers have since been implicated. And I believe that those responsible for these atrocities should be put before a court. Ariel Sharon – held 'personally responsible' by his own country's inquiry into Sabra and Chatila – is now the prime minister of Israel. The Iraqi army is safe from prosecution – indeed, we are inviting it to overthrow Saddam Hussein. So if any reporter wants to testify against the above gentlemen, they can forget it. Ms Rowland will not be invited to put Mr Assad or Mr Sharon behind bars. In fact, Belgium has just done its best to stop the survivors of Sabra and Chatila from ever testifying against Mr Sharon in Brussels.

And there you have it in a nutshell. We journalists are not being asked to testify in the interests of international justice. Ms Rowland is going to testify against a criminal whom we now wish to try; and we should remember that back in 1995, when we needed Mr Milosevic to sign the Dayton agreement, Ms Rowland was not required to testify by The Hague or anyone else.

As far as I'm concerned, I'm always ready to meet war crimes investigators. I admire most of those I have met. And if we ever have an international court to try all the villains, I might change my mind. But until then, a reporter's job does not include joining the prosecution. We are witnesses and we write our testimony and we name, if we can, the bad guys. Then it is for the world to act. Not us.

The Independent, 24 August 2002

Where are the great men of today?

Before Egyptian President Anwar Sadat set off for his journey to Jerusalem in 1977, he announced to the world that he did not intend to live 'among the pygmies'. This was tough on pygmies but there was no doubt what it revealed about Sadat. He thought he was a Great Man. History suggests he was wrong. His 1978 Camp David agreement with Menachem Begin of Israel brought the Sinai back under Egyptian control, but it locked Sadat's country into a cold peace and near-bankrupt isolation. He was finally called 'Pharaoh', a description Sadat might have appreciated had it not been shouted by his murderers as they stormed his military reviewing stand in 1981.

The Middle East, of course, is awash with kings and dictators who are called – or like to imagine themselves – Great Men. Saddam Hussein thought he was Stalin – barbarity, unfortunately, is also for some a quality of greatness – while George Bush Senior thought Saddam was Hitler. Eden claimed that Nasser, when he nationalised the Suez Canal in 1956, was the Mussolini of the Nile (though Mussolini was not Great, he thought he was). Yasser Arafat claimed that Hashemite King Hussein of Jordan, when he died, was Saladin, the warrior who drove the Crusaders out of Palestine. The truth was that the Israelis had driven the Hashemites from Palestine. But Hussein was on 'our' side and the Plucky Little King, when he died of cancer in 1999, was immortalised by President Clinton who said he was 'already in heaven', a feat that went unequalled until Pope John Paul II made it to the same location before his funeral this month.

I listened to much of the verbiage uttered about this hopelessly right-wing pontiff when he was dying, and read a good deal of the vitriol that was splashed on him a few days later. I agree with much of the latter. But he was the one prominent world figure – being of 'world' importance is not necessarily a quality for greatness, but it helps – who stood up to President Bush's insane invasion of Iraq. With absolute resolution, he condemned and re-condemned the illegality of the assault on Iraq in a way that no other prominent churchman did. Good on yer, Pope, I remember saying at the time – and it would be churlish of me to forget this now. But a Great Man? In truth, our world seems full of Little Men. Not just Sadat's 'pygmies'. Ghadafi may be a 'statesman' in the eyes of our Trot of a foreign secretary – this was around the time the Libyan dictator was found to be plotting the assassination of Crown Prince Abdullah of Saudi Arabia – but anyone who can seriously suggest that a joint Israeli–Palestinian state might be called 'Israeltine' is clearly a candidate for the men in white coats.*

Indeed, it raises the question: are there any Great Men in the Middle East? And, are there any Great Men in the world today? Where – this is a question I've been asked by several readers recently – are the Churchills, the Roosevelts, the Trumans, the Eisenhowers, the Titos, the Lloyd Georges, the Woodrow Wilsons, the de Gaulles and Clemenceaus? Our present band of poseur presidents and prime ministers cannot come close. Bush may think he is Churchill – but he cannot really compare himself to his dad, let alone our Winston. Bush

---

* Jack Straw, British foreign secretary in 2005, praised Ghadafi's surrender of nuclear technology (if indeed it was genuine) as an 'act of statesmanship'.

Junior looks like a nerd, while his friends – Cheney, Rumsfeld, Wolfowitz and the rest – actually look disreputable. Chirac would like to be a Great Man but his problem is that he can be mocked – see France's equivalent of *Spitting Image*. Blair has a worse impediment. He has become a mockery of himself, slowly assuming the role of his clergyman namesake in *Private Eye* – to the point where the latter simply became no longer funny.

Sacrifice obviously has something to do with it. To get bumped off for your good deeds – preferably 'making peace', although many of those at work on the 'peace' project seem to have spent a lot of time making war – is clearly a possible path to Greatness. Thus Sadat does have a chance. So does Yitzhak Rabin of Israel. And so, through sickness, King Hussein and – in more theatrical form – the last Pope, although my mum died of the same illness with much less drama and pomp. Those who successfully fight their countries' occupiers get a look in; de Gaulle again, Tito again, maybe Ho Chi Minh but not, apparently, the leaders of the Algerian FLN and most definitely not the lads from the Lebanese Hizballah. And we all know how Arafat went from being Superterrorist to Superstatesman and back to Superterrorist again. In the Middle East, I do have a soft spot for President Khatami of Iran. A truly decent, philosophical, morally good man, he was crushed by the political power of his clerical enemies set up by Ayatollah Khomeini. Khatami's 'civil society' never materialised; had it blossomed, he might have been a Great Man. Instead, his life seems to be a tragedy of withered hope. I mention Khomeini and I fear we have to put him on the list. He lived the poverty of Gandhi, overthrew a vicious dictatorship and changed the history of the Middle East. That his country is now a necrocracy – government ruled by and for the dead – does not, sadly, change this. Yet this raises another dark question. Why do we stop only a generation or two ago? Why stop at the First World

War? Where now, we might ask, are the Duke of Wellingtons and the Napoleons, the Queen Elizabeths, the Richard the Lionhearts, and yes, the Saladins and the Caesars and the Genghis Khans?

Oddly, the list of Great Men doesn't usually include Gandhi, whom I would think an obvious candidate for all the right reasons. He was palpably a good man, a peaceful man, and freed his country from imperial rule and was assassinated. Nelson Mandela would be among my candidates for all the obvious reasons (his objections to Bush not being the least of them). Nurse Edith Cavell – 'patriotism is not enough' – who was shot by the Germans in the First World War, and Margaret Hassan, the supremely brave and selfless charity worker butchered in Iraq, must be in my list – proving, of course, that we should also ask: where are the Great Women of our age? Rachel Corrie, I'd say, the American girl who was crushed by an Israeli bulldozer as she stood in its path to protect Palestinian homes in Gaza. And, on the list of men, how about Mordechai Vanunu, the Israeli nuclear whistle-blower? And yes, all the humble folk – little people, if you like – who did what they did, whatever the cost, not because they sought Greatness, but because they believed it was the right thing to do.

The Independent, 16 April 2005

CHAPTER ELEVEN

America, America

Americans visit great injustice on their real or imagined enemies, but the Muslim population of the United States – and the millions of non-Muslims in the US who refuse to be silenced by the conformity and pseudo-patriotism of conservative America – are perhaps the nation's greatest hope. I travel to the States from the Middle East almost every three weeks to lecture at American universities, a tough, often rancorous but rewarding experience. If you are going to condemn US policy in the Middle East, you might as well go and take the heat in the 'Land of the Free'.

Free speech

Laila al-Arian was wearing her headscarf at her desk at Nation Books, one of my New York publishers. No, she told me, it would be difficult to telephone her father. At the medical facility of his North Carolina prison, he can only make a few calls – monitored, of course – and he was growing steadily weaker. Sami al-Arian is forty-nine but he stayed on hunger strike for sixty days to protest the government outrage committed against him, a burlesque of justice which has largely failed to rouse the sleeping dogs of American journalism in New York, Washington and Los Angeles. All praise, then, to the reporter John Sugg from Tampa, Florida, who has been cataloguing al-Arian's little Golgotha for months, along with Alexander Cockburn of *CounterPunch*.

The story so far: Sami al-Arian, a Kuwaiti-born Palestinian, was a respected computer professor at the university of South Florida who tried, however vainly, to communicate the real tragedy of Palestinian Arabs to the US government. But according to Sugg, Israel's lobbyists were enraged by his lessons – al-Arian's family was driven from Palestine in 1948 – and in 2003, at the instigation of Attorney General Ashcroft, he was arrested and charged with conspiring 'to murder and maim' outside the United States and with raising money for Islamic Jihad in 'Palestine'. He was held for two and a half years in solitary confinement, hobbling half a mile, his hands and feet shackled, merely to talk to his lawyers. Al-Arian's $50 m (£25 m) Tampa trial lasted six months; the government called 80 witnesses (21 from Israel) and used 400 intercepted phone calls along with evidence of a conversation that a co-defendant had with al-Arian in – wait for it – a dream. The local judge, a certain James Moody, vetoed any remarks about Israeli military occupation or about UN Security Council Resolution 242, on the grounds that they would endanger the impartiality of the jurors.

In December 2005, al-Arian was acquitted on the most serious charges and on those remaining, the jurors voted ten to two for acquittal. Because the FBI wanted to make further charges, al-Arian's lawyers told him to make a plea that would end any further prosecution. Arriving for his sentence, however, al-Arian – who assumed time served would be his punishment, followed by deportation – found Moody talking about 'blood' on the defendant's hands. He would have to spend another eleven months in jail. Then prosecutor Gordon Kromberg insisted that the Palestinian prisoner should testify against an Islamic think tank. Al-Arian believed his plea bargain had been dishonoured and refused to testify. He was held in contempt. And continues to languish in prison.

Not so, of course, most of America's torturers in Iraq. One of them turns out to rejoice in the name of Ric Fair, a 'contract interrogator', who has bared his soul in the *Washington Post* – all praise, here, by the way to the *Post* – about his escapades in the Fallujah interrogation 'facility' of the 82nd Airborne Division. Fair has been having nightmares about an Iraqi whom he deprived of sleep during questioning 'by forcing him to stand in a corner and stripping him of his clothes'. Now it is Fair who is deprived of sleep. 'A man with no face stares at me . . . pleads for help, but I'm afraid to move. He begins to cry. It's a pitiful sound, and it sickens me. He screams, but as I awaken, I realise the screams are mine.'

Thank God, Fair didn't write a play about his experiences

and offer it to Channel 4, who got cold feet about *The Mark of Cain*, the drama about British army abuse in Basra. It quickly bought into the line that transmission of Tony Marchant's play might affect the now happy outcome of the far less riveting Iranian prison production of the Famous 15 'Servicepersons' – by angering the Muslim world with tales of how our boys in Basra beat up on the local Iraqis. As the reporter who first revealed the death of hotel worker Baha Mousa in British custody in Basra – I suppose we must always refer to his demise as 'death' now that the soldiers present at his savage beating have been acquitted of murder. Arab Muslims know all too well how our prisoners are treated during interrogation. It is we, the British at home, who are not supposed to believe in torture. The Iraqis know all about it, and knew all about Mousa's fate long before I reported it for *The Independent on Sunday*.

Because it's really all about shutting the reality of the Middle East off from us. It's to prevent the British and American people from questioning the immoral and cruel and internationally illegal occupation of Muslim lands. And in the Land of the Free, this systematic censorship of Middle East reality continues even in the country's schools. Now the principal of a Connecticut high school has banned a play by pupils, based on the letters and words of US soldiers serving in Iraq. Under the title *Voices in Conflict*, Natalie Kropf, Seth Koproski, James Presson and their fellow pupils at Wilton High School compiled the reflections of soldiers and others – including a nineteen-year-old Wilton High graduate killed in Iraq – to create their own play. To no avail. The drama might hurt those 'who had lost loved ones or who had individuals serving as we speak', proclaimed Timothy Canty, Wilton High's principal. And – my favourite line – Canty believed there was not enough rehearsal time to ensure that the play would provide 'a legitimate instructional experience for our students'.

And of course, I can quite see Mr Canty's point. Students who have produced Arthur Miller's *The Crucible* were told by Mr Canty – whose own war experiences, if any, have gone unrecorded – that it wasn't their place to tell audiences what soldiers were thinking. The pupils of Wilton High are now being inundated with offers to perform at other venues. Personally, I think Mr Canty may have a point. He would do much better to encourage his students to perform Shakespeare's *Titus Andronicus*, a drama of massive violence, torture, rape, mutilation and honour killing. It would make Iraq perfectly explicable to the good people of Connecticut. A 'legitimate instructional experience' if ever there was one.

The Independent, 7 April 2007

Al-Arian was cleared of contempt in mid-December 2007 and was to remain in prison for three or four more months. But his family feared he might then be charged with criminal contempt for not testifying before a grand jury. They hoped he would be deported to Egypt, where three of his five children live – even though Egypt practises systematic torture of all 'terror suspects'.

It's a draw!

I call it the Alice in Wonderland effect. Each time I tour the United States, I stare through the looking glass at the faraway region in which I live and work for *The Independent* – the Middle East – and see a landscape that I do not recognise, a distant tragedy turned, here in America, into a farce of hypocrisy and banality and barefaced lies. Am I the Cheshire Cat? Or the Mad Hatter?

I picked up Jimmy Carter's new book, *Palestine: Peace Not Apartheid*, at San Francisco airport, and zipped through it in a day. It's a good, strong read by the only American president approaching sainthood. Carter lists the outrageous treatment meted out to the Palestinians, the Israeli occupation, the dispossession of Palestinian land by Israel, the brutality visited upon this denuded, subject population, and what he calls 'a system of apartheid, with two peoples occupying the same land but completely separated from each other, with Israelis totally dominant and suppressing violence by depriving Palestinians of their basic human rights'. Carter quotes an Israeli as saying he is 'afraid that we are moving towards a government like that of South Africa, with a dual society of Jewish rulers and Arab subjects with few rights of citizenship . . .' A proposed but unacceptable modification of this choice, Carter adds, 'is the taking of substantial portions of the occupied territory, with the remaining Palestinians completely surrounded by walls, fences, and Israeli checkpoints, living as prisoners within the small portion of land left to them'.

Needless to say, the American press and television largely ignored the appearance of this eminently sensible book – until the usual Israeli lobbyists began to scream abuse at poor old Jimmy Carter, albeit that he was the architect of the longest-lasting peace treaty between Israel and an Arab neighbour, Egypt, secured with the famous 1978 Camp David accords. The *New York Times* ('All the News That's Fit to Print' of course) then felt free to tell its readers that Carter had stirred 'furore among Jews' with his use of the word 'apartheid'. The ex-president replied by mildly (and rightly) pointing out that Israeli lobbyists had produced among US editorial boards a 'reluctance to criticise the Israeli government'. Typical of the dirt thrown at Carter was the comment by Michael Kinsley in the *New York Times* (of course) that Carter 'is comparing Israel to the former white racist government of South Africa'. This was followed by a vicious statement from Abe Foxman of the Anti-Defamation League, who said that the reason Carter gave for writing this book 'is this shameless, shameful canard that the Jews control the debate in this country, especially when it comes to the media. What makes this serious is that he's not just another pundit, and he's not just another analyst. He is a former president of the United States'. But well, yes, that's the point, isn't it? This is no tract by a Harvard professor on the power of the lobby. It's an honourable, honest account by a friend of Israel as well as of the Arabs who just happens to be a fine American ex-statesman. Which is why Carter's book is now a bestseller – and applause here, by the way, for the great American public that bought the book instead of believing Mr Foxman.

But in this context, why, I wonder, didn't the *New York Times* and the other gutless mainstream newspapers in the United States mention Israel's cosy relationship with that very racist apartheid regime in South Africa which Carter is not supposed to mention in his book? Didn't Israel have a wealthy diamond trade with sanctioned, racist South Africa? Didn't Israel have a deep and fruitful military relationship with that racist regime? Am I dreaming, looking-glass-like, when I recall that in April of 1976, Prime Minister John Vorster of South Africa – one of the architects of this vile Nazi-like system of apartheid – paid a state visit to Israel and was honoured with an official reception from Israeli prime minister Menachem Begin, war hero Moshe Dayan and future Nobel prize-winner Yitzhak Rabin? This, of course, certainly did not become part of the great American debate on Carter's book.

At Detroit airport, I picked up an even slimmer volume, the Baker–Hamilton Iraq Study Group Report – which doesn't really study Iraq at all but offers a few bleak ways in which George Bush can run away from this disaster without too much blood on his shirt. After chatting to the Iraqis in the Green Zone of Baghdad – dream zone would be a more accurate title – there are a few worthy suggestions (already predictably rejected by the Israelis): a resumption of serious Israeli–Palestinian peace talks, an Israeli withdrawal from Golan, etc. But it's written in the same tired semantics of right-wing think tanks – the language, in fact, of the discredited Brookings Institution and of my old mate, the messianic *New York Times* columnist Tom Friedman – full of 'porous' borders and admonitions that 'time is running out'. The clue to all this nonsense, I discovered, comes at the back of the report where it lists the 'experts' consulted by Messrs Baker, Hamilton and the rest. Many of them are pillars of the Brookings Institution, and there is Thomas Friedman of the *New York Times*.

But for sheer folly, it was impossible to beat the post-Baker debate among the philosophers who dragged the United States into the Iraq catastrophe. General Peter Pace, the extremely odd chairman of the US joint chiefs of staff, said of the American war in Iraq that 'we are not winning, but we are not losing'. Bush's new defence secretary, Robert Gates, announced that he agreed with General Pace that 'we are not winning, but we are not losing'. Baker himself jumped into the same nonsense pool by asserting: 'I don't think you can say we're losing. By the same token [*sic*], I'm not sure we're winning.' At which point, Bush proclaimed this week that – yes – 'we're not winning, we're not losing'. Pity about the Iraqis.

I pondered this madness during a bout of severe turbulence at 37,000 feet over Colorado. And that's when it hit me, the whole final score in this unique round of the Iraq war between the United States of America and the forces of evil. It's a draw!

The Independent, 23 December 2006

Fear and loathing on an American campus

On the night of 11 September 2001, Al Dershowitz of Harvard law school exploded in anger. Robert Fisk, he roared over Irish radio, was a dangerous man. I was 'pro-terrorist'. I was 'anti-American' and that, Dershowitz announced to the people of County Mayo, 'is the same as anti-Semitism'. Of course I had dared to ask the 'Why' question. Why had nineteen Arabs flown aircraft into the World Trade Center, the Pentagon and Pennsylvania? How very odd. The nineteen murderers came from a place called the Middle East. Was there a problem out there?

I'm recalling all this nonsense because Al has been back at work attacking his old nemesis Norm Finkelstein, who has just applied for tenure at DePaul University in the US where he is an assistant professor of politics. Norm's department has supported him but Al has bombarded faculty members with a blistering attack on Norm and all his works. Let me just explain what these works are. Finkelstein, who is Jewish and the son of Holocaust survivors, has published a number of works highly critical of Israel's occupation of the Palestinian West Bank and the use Israel's supporters make of the Holocaust of 6 million Jews to suppress criticism of Israel's policies. Finkelstein's book, *The Holocaust Industry*, earned Dershowitz's continued fury.

Now, I've known Norm for years and he is a tough, no-holds-barred polemicist, angry against all the traditional supporters of Israel, especially those who turn a blind eye to torture. Personally, I find Norm's arguments sometimes a little overwrought. In radio discussions, his voice will take on a slightly whingeing tone that must infuriate his antagonists. But Al is clearly trying to destroy Norm's career, adding that the 'dossier' he sent to DePaul academics – we remember that word 'dossier' rather too well in Britain and, I should add, Al has absolutely no connection to DePaul University – contains details of 'Norman Finkelstein's . . . outright lies, misquotations and distortion'. It will be a disgrace, says Al, for DePaul to give tenure to Norm. 'His scholarship is no more than ad hominem attacks on his ideological enemies.' As if this is not enough, Al – who is also Jewish – takes a crack at philosopher and linguistic academic Noam Chomsky, who has supported Norm and whom Al refers to as 'the high priest of the radical anti-Israeli left'.

Enough, I hear readers shout. I agree. But Norm's politics department gives him top marks for scholarship and says he 'offers a detailed argument that suggests that Dershowitz plagiarised or inappropriately appropriated large sections of others' work in his book *The Case for Israel*'. Norm has a 'substantial and serious record of scholarly production and achievement' and has lectured at the university of Chicago, Harvard, Georgetown and Northwestern universities. So far so good. But now up pops 'Chuck' Suchar, the dean of DePaul's College of Liberal (*sic*) Arts and Sciences, with an extraordinary recommendation that Norm should not be granted tenure. While acknowledging that 'he is a skilled teacher' with 'consistently high course evaluations', Chuck has decided 'that a considerable amount of [his work] is inconsistent with DePaul's Vincentian values, most particularly our institutional commitment to respect the dignity of the individual and to respect the rights of others to hold and express different intellectual positions'. Norm's books, according to Chuck, 'border on character assassination and . . . embody a strategy clearly aimed at destroying the reputation of many who oppose his views'.

Now I have to say that scholars who read this column will be interested to know of Chuck's own work. I gather it has absolutely nothing to do with the Middle East, though I'm sure his study of *Gentrification and Urban Change: Research in Urban Society* (1992) had American readers queuing round the block of their major bookstores in search of first editions. All I do ask is how a college dean could involve himself in the same kind of ad hominem attacks against one of his own colleagues that he has accused that same colleague of being guilty of. I loved too, that bit about 'Vincentian values'. That really does warrant a chortle or two. St Vincent de Paul – the real de Paul who lived from 1581 to 1660, not the de Paul of Chuck's soft imagination – was a no-nonsense theologian who was captured by Muslim Turkish pirates and taken to Tunis as a slave. Here, however, he argued his religious values so well that he converted his owner to Christianity and earned his freedom. His charitable organisations – he also created a home for foundlings in Paris – became a legend which Chuck Suchar simply dishonours.

All over the United States, however, Norm's academic chums have been condemning Suchar's mean-spirited performance; even in Beirut, where Norm has lectured, academics of the American University have insisted that he be granted tenure in his department, Arabs supporting a Jewish professor and son of Holocaust survivors. Of course, I grant that all this is a little heavy for the real world and I do have a secret desire to take Norm, Chuck and Al and bang their bloody heads together. But what is happening at DePaul University is a very serious matter in the anodyne, frightened academic world that now exists in the US. Norm's moment of truth comes up in May. As they say, watch this space.

The Independent, 14 April 2007

Norman Finkelstein was denied tenure in June 2007, and placed on 'administrative leave' until 2008. But on 5 September 2007 he announced his resignation after coming to a settlement with DePaul University on undisclosed terms. The university described Finkelstein as 'a prolific scholar and outstanding teacher' – which obviously begs the question of his departure. Dershowitz condemned the university's statement as a 'compromise'. What the good Saint Vincent would have thought of it all doesn't bear thinking about.

How Muslim middle America made
me feel safer

Every time I enter the United States, I wonder what the lads in Homeland Security have in store for me. But last week, Chicago was a piece of cake. I was arriving from Lebanon, I told the young man at the desk, and I was to address a Muslim conference. 'Gee, you must have had a bad time out there in Lebanon,' he commiserated, stamping my passport in less than thirty seconds and handing it back to me with a scriptwriter's greeting: 'There you go, partner.' And so I passed through the barrier, saddled up my white Palomino in the parking lot, and rode off towards the crescent Islamic moon that hung over Chicago. Hi Ho Fisk, away!

I had forgotten how many American Muslims were south-west Asian rather than Middle Eastern in origin, Pakistani and Indian by family rather than Syrian or Egyptian or Lebanese or Saudi. But the largely Sunni congregation of 32,000 gathered for the Islamic Society of North America's annual gig were not the hotdog-sellers, bellhops and taxi-drivers of New York. They were part of the backbone of middle America, corporate lawyers, real estate developers, construction engineers, and owners of chain-store outlets. Nor were these the docile, hang-dog, frightened Muslims we have grown used to writing about in the aftermath of the international crimes against humanity of 11 September 2001. To about 12,000 of these Muslims in a vast auditorium, I said the Middle East had never been so dangerous. I condemned the Hizballah leader, Sayed Hassan Nasrallah, for saying he had no idea the Israelis would have responded so savagely to the capture of two Israeli soldiers and the killing of three others on 12 July 2006. Later, a worthy imam told me: 'I thought what you said about Sheikh Hassan [sic] was almost an insult.' But that clearly wasn't what the audience believed.

When I told them that as American Muslims, they could demand a right of reply when lobby groups maliciously claimed that a network of suicide bombers was plotting within their totally law-abiding community, they roared. But I warned them that I would listen carefully to their response to my next sentence. And then I said that they must feel free to condemn – and should condemn – the Muslim regimes that used torture and oppression, even if these dictators lived in the lands from which their families came. And those thousands of Muslims rose to their feet and clapped and yelled their agreement with more emotion and fervour than any rabble-rousing non-Muslim yelling about 'Arab terrorism'. This was not what I had expected.

While I was signing copies of the American edition of my book on the Middle East some hours later – the real reason, of course, for going to Chicago – these same people came up to me to explain they were not American Muslims but Muslim Americans, that Islam was not incompatible with life, liberty and the pursuit of happiness. Some had stories of great tragedy. One young man had written out a short sentence for me to inscribe in the front of his copy of my book. 'To my parents and siblings,' he had written on a pink slip, 'who perished in the hands of the Pol Pot Khmer Rouge in Cambodia. Yousos Adam.' I looked up to find the young man crying. 'I am against war, you see,' he said, and vanished into the crowd. There were other more ingratiating folk around: the Pakistani broadcaster, for example, who wanted me to talk about his country's peace-loving principles – until I began describing the continued secret relationship between Pakistan's intelligence service and the Taliban, at which the interview was swiftly concluded.

Then there was the young man with Asiatic features who said softly that he was 'Mr Yee, the Guantanamo imam' – who turned out to be the same Mr Yee foully and falsely accused by the US authorities of passing al-Qaeda-type messages while ministering to the supposed al-Qaeda prisoners at America's most luxurious prison camp. But there was no bitterness among any of these people. Only a kind of growing pain at the way the press and television in America continued to paint them – and all other Muslims in the world – as an alien, cruel, sadistic race. One woman produced an article of June this year from the *Toronto Star* about the Israeli town of Sderot, the target of hundreds of Palestinian missiles from Gaza. 'Under fire at Israel's Ground Zero,' ran the headline. 'Do you believe in this kind of journalism, Mr Fisk?' the woman demanded to know. And I was about to give her the 'both sides of the picture' lecture when I noticed from the article that just five Israelis had been killed in Sderot in five years. Yes, every life is equal. But who at the *Star* had decided that an Israeli town with one dead every year equalled the Ground Zero of Manhattan's 3,000 dead in two hours? All dead are equal in the Canadian press it seems, but some are more equal than others.

And I couldn't help noticing the degree to which the *New York Times*'s Thomas Friedman is stoking the fires. This is the same man who wrote a few years ago that the Palestinians believed in 'child sacrifice' – because they allowed their kids to throw stones at Israeli soldiers who then obligingly gunned them down. Most egregiously for the Muslims I spoke to, Friedman was now 'animalising' – as one girl put it beautifully – the Iraqis, and she presented me with a Friedman clipping which ended with these words: 'It will be a global tragedy if they [the insurgent Iraqi enemy] succeed, but … the US government can't keep asking Americans to sacrifice their children for people who hate each other more than they love their own children.'

So there we go again, I thought. Muslims sacrifice their children. Muslims feel hate more than they love their children. No wonder, I suppose, that their kiddies keep getting Israeli bullets through their hearts in Gaza and American bullets through their hearts in Iraq and Israeli bombs smashing them to death in Lebanon. It's all the Arabs' fault. And yet here in Chicago were Muslims dismissing all the calumnies and sophistries and lies and saying they were proud to be Americans. And I guess – for a man who wakes each morning in his Beirut apartment, wondering where the next explosion will be – that I felt a little safer in this world.

The Independent, 9 September 2006

Will the media boys and girls catch up?

Watching the pathetic old lie-on-its-back frightened Labrador of the American media changing overnight into a vicious Rottweiler is one of the enduring pleasures of society in the United States. I have been experiencing this phenomenon over the past two weeks, as both victim and beneficiary. In New York and Los Angeles, my condemnation of the George W. Bush presidency and Israel's continued settlement-building in the West Bank was originally treated with the disdain all great papers reserve for those who dare to question proud and democratic projects of state. In the *New York Times*, that ancient luminary Ethan Bonner managed to chide me for attacking American journalists who – he furiously quoted my own words – 'report in so craven a fashion from the Middle East, so fearful of Israeli criticism that they turn Israeli murder into "targeted attacks" and illegal settlements into "Jewish neighbourhoods"'.

It was remarkable that Bonner should be so out of touch with his readers that he did not know that 'craven' is the very word so many Americans apply to their grovelling newspapers (and quite probably one reason why newspaper circulations are falling so disastrously). But the moment that a respected Democratic congressman and Vietnam veteran in Washington dared to suggest that the war in Iraq was lost, that US troops should be brought home now – and when the Republican response was so brutal it had to be disowned – the old media dog sniffed the air, realised that power was moving away from the White House, and began to drool.

On live television in San Francisco, I could continue my critique of America's folly in Iraq uninterrupted. Ex-Mayor Willie Brown – who allowed me to have my picture taken in his brand-new pale blue Stetson – exuded warmth towards this 'ornery' Brit (though he claimed on air that I was an American) who tore into his country's policies in the Middle East. It was enough to make you feel the teeniest bit sorry – though only for a millisecond, mark you – for the guy in the White House. All this wasn't caused by that familiar transition from Newark to Los Angeles International, where the terror of al-Qaeda attacks is replaced by fear of the ozone layer. On the east coast, too, the editorials thundered away at the Bush administration. Seymour Hersh, that blessing to American journalism who broke the Abu Ghraib torture story, produced another black rabbit out of his Iraqi hat with revelations that US commanders in Iraq believe the insurgency is now out of control.

When those same Iraqi gunmen this week again took over the entire city of Ramadi (already 'liberated' four times by US troops since 2003), the story shared equal billing on prime-time television with Bush's latest and infinitely wearying insistence that Iraqi forces – who in reality are so infiltrated by insurgents that they are a knife in America's back – will soon be able to take over security duties from the occupation forces. Even in Hollywood – and here production schedules prove that the rot must have set in more than a year ago – hitherto taboo subjects are being dredged to the surface of the political mire. *Jarhead*, produced by Universal Pictures, depicts a bitter, traumatised Marine unit during the 1991 Gulf War. George Clooney's production of *Good Night, and Good Luck*, a devastating black-and-white account of Second World War correspondent Ed Murrow's heroic battle with Senator McCarthy in the 1950s – its theme is the management and crushing of all dissent – has already paid for its production costs twice over. Murrow is played by an actor but McCarthy appears only in real archive footage. Incredibly, a test audience in New York complained that the man 'playing' McCarthy was 'overacting'. Will we say this about Messrs Bush and Cheney and Rumsfeld in years to come? I suspect so.

And then there's *Syriana*, Clooney's epic of the oil trade which combines suicide bombers, maverick CIA agents (one of them played by Clooney himself), feuding Middle East Arab potentates – one of whom wants real democracy and wealth for his people and control of his own country's resources – along with a slew of disreputable businessmen and east coast lawyers. The CIA eventually assassinates the Arab prince who wants to possess his own country's oil (so much for democracy) – this is accomplished with a pilotless aerial bomb guided by men in a room in Virginia – while a Pakistani, fired from his job in the oil fields because an American conglomerate has downsized for its shareholders' profits, destroys one of the company's tankers in a suicide attack.

'People seem less afraid now,' Clooney told an interviewer in *Entertainment* magazine. 'Lots of people are starting to ask questions. It's becoming hard to avoid the questions.' Of course, these questions are being asked because of America's more than 2,000 fatalities in Iraq rather than out of compassion for Iraq's tens of thousands of dead. They are being pondered because the whole illegal invasion of Iraq is ending in calamity rather than success.

Yet still they avoid the 'Israel' question. The Arab princes in *Syriana* – who in real life would be obsessed with the occupation of the West Bank – do not murmur a word about Israel. The Arab al-Qaeda operative who persuades the young Pakistani to attack an oil tanker makes no reference to Israel – as every one of bin Laden's acolytes assuredly would. It was instructive that Michael Moore's *Fahrenheit 9/11* did not mention Israel once.

So one key issue of the Middle East remains to be confronted. Amy Goodman, whom I used to enrage by claiming that her *Democracy Now!* programme – broadcast from a former Brooklyn fire station – had only three listeners (one of whom was Amy Goodman), is bravely raising this unmentionable subject. Partly as a result, her 'alternative' radio and television station – how I hate that prissy word 'alternative' – is slowly moving into the mainstream. Americans are ready to discuss the United States' relationship with Israel. And America's injustices towards the Arabs. As usual, ordinary Americans are way out in front of their largely tamed press and television reporters. Now we have to wait and see if the media boys and girls will catch up with their own people.

The Independent, 3 December 2005

Brazil, America and the
Seven Pillars of Wisdom

Strange things happen when a reporter strays off his beat. Vast regions of the earth turn out to have different priorities. The latest conspiracy theory for the murder of ex-Lebanese prime minister Rafiq Hariri – that criminals involved in a bankrupt Beirut bank may have been involved – doesn't make it into the New Zealand *Dominion Post*. And last week, arriving in the vast, messy, unplanned city of São Paulo, it was a Brazilian MP's political corruption scandal, the bankruptcy of the country's awful airline Varig – worse, let me warn you, than any East European airline under the Soviet Union – and Brazil's newly nationalised oil concessions in Bolivia that made up the front pages.

Sure, there was Iranian president Ahmadinejad's long letter to President Bush – 'rambling', the local *International Herald Tribune* edition called it, a description the paper's headline writers would never apply to Mr Bush himself – and a whole page of Middle East reports in the *Folha de São Paulo* daily about the EU's outrageous sanctions against the democratically elected government of 'Palestine' – all, alas, written from wire agencies.

But then in steps Brazil with its geographical immensity, its extraordinary story of colonialism and democracy, the mixture of races in São Paulo's streets – which outdoes the ethnic origins of the occupants of any Toronto tram – and its cocktail version of Portuguese, and then suddenly the Middle East seems a very long way away. Brazil? Sure, the Amazon, tropical forests, coffee and the beaches of Rio. And then there's Brasilia, the make-believe capital designed – like the equally fake Canberra in Australia and the fraudulent Islamabad in Pakistan – so that the country's politicians can hide themselves away from their people. One thing the country shares with the Arab world, it turned out, is the ever-constant presence and influence and pressure of the US – never more so than when Brazil's right-wing rulers were searching for commies in the 1940s and 50s. They weren't hard to find.

In 1941, a newly belligerent America – plunged into a world war by an attack every bit as ruthless as that of 11 September 2001 – had become so worried about the big bit of Brazil that juts far out into the Atlantic that it set up military bases in the north of the country without waiting for the authorisation of the Brazilian government. Well, Washington needn't have worried. The sinking of five Brazilian merchant ships by German U-boats provoked huge public demonstrations that forced the right-wing and undemocratic Getúlio Vargas government to declare war on the Nazis. Hands up those readers who know that more than 20,000 Brazilian troops fought on our side in the Italian campaign right up to the end of the Second World War. Even fewer hands will be raised, I suspect, if I ask how many Brazilian troops were killed. According to Boris Fausto's excellent history of Brazil, 454 died in combat against the Wehrmacht. The return of the Brazilian Expeditionary Force helped to bring democracy to Brazil. Vargas shot himself nine years later, leaving a dramatic suicide note which suggested that 'foreign forces' had caused his country's latest economic crisis. Crowds attacked the US embassy in Rio.

Well, it all looks very different today when a left-wing Brazilian leader, Luiz Inacio Lula da Silva – who also found himself threatened by 'foreign forces' after his popular election

– is trying to make sense of the Bolivian nationalisation of Brazil's oil conglomerates, an act carried out by Lula's equally left-wing chum up in La Paz, Evo Morales. I have to say that the explosion inside Latin America's fashionable leftist governments does have something in common with meetings of the Arab League – where Arab promises of unity are always undermined by hateful arguments. No wonder one of *Folha*'s writers this week headlined his story 'The Arabias'.

But can I let that place leave me? Or does the Middle East have a grasp over its victims, a way of jerking their heads around just when you think it might be safe to immerse yourself in a city a world away from Arabia? After two days in Brazil, my office mail arrives from the foreign desk in London and I curl up on my bed to go through the letters. First out of the bag comes Peter Metcalfe of Stevenage with a photocopied page from Lawrence of Arabia's *Seven Pillars of Wisdom*. Lawrence is writing about Iraq in the 1920s, and about oil and colonialism. 'We pay for these things too much in honour and innocent lives,' he says.

> I went up the Tigris with one hundred Devon Territorials . . .
> delightful fellows, full of the power of happiness and of making
> women and children glad. By them one saw vividly how great
> it was to be their kin, and English. And we were casting them
> by thousands into the fire to the worst of deaths, not to win
> the war but that the corn and rice and oil of Mesopotamia
> might be ours.

My next day's Brazilian newspaper shows an American soldier lying on his back in a Baghdad street, blasted to death by a roadside bomb. Thrown into the fire to the worst of deaths, indeed.

Then in my mailbag comes an enclosure from Antony Loewenstein, my old journalistic friend in Sydney. It's an editorial from *The Australian*, not my favourite paper since it's still beating the drum for George W. on Iraq. But listen to this:

> Three years ago ... elite Australian troops were fighting in Iraq's western desert to neutralise Scud missile sites. Now, three years later, we know that at the same moment members of our SAS were risking their lives and engaging with Saddam Hussein's troops, boatloads of Australian wheat were steaming towards ports in the Persian Gulf, where their cargo was to be offloaded and driven to Iraq by a Jordanian shipping company paying kickbacks to – Saddam Hussein.

And I remember that one of the reasons Australia's Prime Minister John Howard gave for going to war against Iraq – he's never once told Australians that we didn't find any weapons of mass destruction, by the way – was that Saddam Hussein's regime was 'corrupt'. So who was doing the corrupting?

I prepare to check out of the São Paulo Maksoud Plaza hotel. Maksoud? In Arabic, this means 'the place you come back to'. And of course, the owner turns out to be a Brazilian-Lebanese. I check my flying times. 'São Paulo/Frankfurt/Beirut', it says on my ticket. Back on the inescapable beat.

The Independent, 13 May 2006

From Cairo to Valdosta

There's a helluva difference between Cairo University and the campus of Valdosta in the Deep South of the United States. I visited both this week and I feel like I've been travelling on a gloomy spaceship – or maybe a time machine – with just two distant constellations to guide my journey. One is clearly named Iraq; the other is Fear. They have a lot in common.

The politics department at Cairo's vast campus is run by Dr Mona El-Baradei – yes, she is indeed the sister of the head of the International Atomic Energy Agency – and her students, most of them young women, almost all scarved, duly wrote out their questions at the end of the turgid Fisk lecture on the failings of journalism in the Middle East. 'Why did you invade Iraq?' was one. I didn't like the 'you' bit, but the answer was 'oil'. 'What do you think of the Egyptian government?' At this, I looked at my watch. I reckon, I told the students, that I just had time to reach Cairo airport for my flight before Hosni Mubarak's intelligence lads heard of my reply.

Much nervous laughter. Well, I said, new constitutional amendments to enshrine Egypt's emergency legislation into common law and the arrest of Muslim Brotherhood supporters were not a path to democracy. And I ran through the US State Department's list of Egyptian arbitrary detentions, routine torture and unfair trials. I didn't see how the local constabulary could do much about condemnation from Mubarak's Ameri-

can friends. But it was purely a symbolic moment. These cheerful, intelligent students wanted to see if they would hear the
truth or get palmed off with another bromide about Egypt's
steady march to democracy, its stability – versus the disaster
of Iraq – and its supposed economic success. No one doubts
that Mubarak's boys keep a close eye on his country's students.

But the questions I was asked after class told it all. Why
didn't 'we' leave Iraq? Are 'we' going to attack Iran? Did 'we'
really believe in democracy in the Middle East? In fact 'our'
shadow clearly hung over these young people. Thirty hours
later, I flicked on the television in my Valdosta, Georgia, hotel
room and there was a bejewelled lady on Fox TV telling American viewers that if 'we' left Iraq, the 'jihadists' would come
after us. 'They want a Caliphate that will take over the world,'
she shrieked about a report that two children had deliberately
been placed in an Iraqi car bomb which then exploded. She
ranted on about how Muslim 'jihadists' had been doing this
'since the 1970s in Lebanon'. It was tosh, of course. Children
were never locked into car bombs in Beirut – and there weren't
any 'jihadists' around in the Lebanese civil war of the 1970s.
But fear had been sown. Now that the House of Representatives
is talking about a US withdrawal by August 2008, fear seems
to drip off the trees in America.

Up in the town of Tiger, Georgia, Kathy Barnes is reported
to be looking for omens as she fears for the life of her son,
Captain Edward Berg of the 4th Brigade, US 3rd Infantry
Division, off to Iraq for a second tour of duty, this time in
George Bush's infamous 'surge'. Last time he was there, Mrs
Barnes saw a dead snake and took it as a bad sign. Then she
saw two Canadian geese, soaring over the treetops. That was a
good sign. 'A rational mind plays this game in war time,'
as the *Atlanta Journal-Constitution* eloquently pointed out. 'A
thunderclap becomes a herald, a bird's song a prophecy.'

Dr Michael Noll's students at Valdosta are as smart and

bright-eyed as Dr El-Baradei's in Cairo. They packed into the
same lecture I had given in Egypt and seemed to share a lot of
the same fears about Iraq. But a sullen seminar that same
morning was a miserable affair in which a young woman broke
down in anger. If 'we' left Iraq, she said in a quavering voice,
the jihadists, the 'terrorists', could come here to America. They
would attack us right here. I sighed with frustration. I was
listening to her voice but it was also the voice of the woman
on Fox TV, the repeated, hopeless fantasy of Bush and Blair:
that if we fail in Iraq, 'they', the monstrous enemy, will arrive
on our shores. Every day in the American papers now, I read
the same 'fear' transformed into irrationality. Luke Boggs –
God, how I'd love that byline – announces in his local paper:
'I say let the terrorists rot in Guantanamo. And let the Europeans . . . howl. We are a serious nation, engaged in the serious
business of trying to kill or capture the bad guys before they
can do us more harm.' He calls Guantanamo's inmates 'hard-
core jihadists'.

And I realise that the girl in Dr Noll's seminar isn't spouting
this stuff about 'jihadists' travelling from Iraq to America
because she supports Bush. She is frightened. She is genuinely
afraid of all the 'terror' warnings, the supposed 'jihadist'
threats, the red 'terror' alerts and the purple alerts and all
the other colour-coded instruments of fear. She believes her
president, and her president has done Osama bin Laden's job
for him: he has crushed this young woman's spirit and courage.
But America is not at war. There are no electricity cuts on
Valdosta's warm green campus, with its Spanish-style department blocks and its narrow, beautiful church. There is no food
rationing. There are no air-raid shelters or bombs or 'jihadists'
stalking these God-fearing folk. It is the US military that is at
war, engaged in an Iraqi conflict that is doing damage of a far
more subtle kind to America's social fabric.

Off campus, I meet a gentle, sensitive man, a Vietnam veteran with two doctor sons. One is a lieutenant colonel, an army medical officer heading back to Baghdad this week for Bush's 'surge', bravely doing his duty in the face of great danger. The other is a civilian doctor who hates the war. And now the two boys – divided by Iraq – can hardly bring themselves to speak to each other.

The soldier son called this week from his transit camp in Kuwait. 'I think he is frightened,' his father told me. A middle-aged lady asked me to sign a copy of my book, which she intends to send to her Marine Corps son in Baghdad. She palpably shakes with concern as she speaks of him. 'Take the greatest care,' I find myself writing on the flyleaf to her Marine son. 'And come safe home.'

The Independent, 24 March 2007

Trying to get into America

This is the story of the internet, a passport and a chocolate mousse. The first told lies, the second was useless and the third never eaten.

It started when I set off for Santa Fe to read from my new book on the Middle East. There was to be an interview with that infamous radio host Amy Goodman, and an awful lot of people booked to listen to Bob of Arabia. US immigration cheerfully ran my little red passport through their computer scanner. It's full of visas from pariah countries, but this didn't seem to trouble the lady from Homeland Security. What worried her was something different. 'It doesn't scan,' she said. No, I said nonchalantly. I was sent into a large room full of angry would-be visitors to the United States. A tall man scanned my irises and took my fingerprints. So that's that, I thought. Not so. Forty-five minutes later, another lady from Homeland Security – I still don't like that word 'homeland', with its dodgy echo of the German *Heimat*. I only needed thirty-six hours in the States, I said. To give a lecture without a fee. Hundreds of people would be present.

'I'll see my supervisor to see if we can get you in,' she cheerfully announced. Long live America, I breathed. Until she came back and told me her supervisor would not let me travel. The lads and lassies who are supposed to stop Osama bin Laden attacking America were now making sure I couldn't read from a book in Santa Fe. Much deft technical work allowed me to give the talk and the reading by satellite, right into the Santa Fe lecture theatre. Then came the blow. One of the organisers had told the *New Mexican* – a newspaper I would now like to buy and close down – that the US authorities had refused me entry because my 'papers were not in order'. Which was true enough, up to a point. But within hours, the internet – a vile institution which I do not use – was awash with stories that the United States had banned my entry to America because of my critical articles about the Bush administration or because I had long ago interviewed bin Laden or because I was so horrible that no democracy would ever let me stain its front doormat.

This twaddle followed me round the world. In Australia to launch my book, I was asked – on ten radio and television shows and in four lectures – how it felt to be banned from the United States. I must have spent a total of two hours collectively explaining that this was untrue. I had simply travelled on an old passport that was no longer valid for entry to the US. It was useless. In Scotland, a university academic introduced me to his audience by announcing that my articles 'must at last have got up the nose of the Bush administration' because I had been banned. The internet bullshit followed me to Dublin and then to Cork and then to Belfast. Nothing, it seemed, could switch off the message.

Robin Harvie, the publicist for Fourth Estate, my publishers, called the passport office in London and secured an interview with an 'examiner' – a word that seems to reek of *Heimat* – to secure me the new computer-coded passport that the Americans now demand. I have, after all, to be in New York for the American launching of my book on 8 November. To the passport office I travelled. They were polite, humorous, cheerful and understood the problem. Ah, but I had two passports, didn't I? That would require a letter from *The Independent* explaining that I worked in the Middle East and that Israeli visa stamps were 'incompatible' – I liked that bit – with entry to Arab countries, and that two passports were necessary. A call to the foreign desk of the paper and a fax arrived at the passport office in three minutes. All well and good, my examiner said. But the set of passport pictures I had brought didn't fit. Would I like to take a new set in the photo machine at the end of the corridor? I did. 'See you again soon,' the machine jauntily told me as I left.

No good, my 'examiner' told me. My spectacles had reflected light on to the lower half of my eyes. Why not take the pictures without your glasses on, he suggested. I knew what this would mean. In future, every Arab visa officer would now demand that I take my glasses off when I approached their desks. And I no longer had the right £3.50 in change for the machine. So I ran round to Victoria Station, barged into Marks and Spencer and asked them to break a £10 note for me. No luck. I would have to buy something to get the change. I went round the shelves like an animal to find the smallest and cheapest item, seized a chocolate mousse and headed back to the cash desk.

I pounded back to the photo machine at the passport office, chucked the chocolate mousse at Harvie (he doesn't eat chocolate), shoved another £3.50 into the slot, tore off my glasses and stared sightlessly at the screen. 'See you again soon,' the voice announced again, just a little bit nastier in tone. Back to the examiner – a woman this time – who promised me a new passport one hour before I had to set off for Oxford and then to Heathrow for the European part of my book launch. It was around midday that *The Independent* phoned me. 'The passport office need new pictures again.'

Now for a word I don't usually use on the comment page. Aaaaaagh! Back to the passport office. The earlier pictures were too blurry, something my examiner had failed to spot when she accepted them. Of course they were too blurry. Because without my spectacles I couldn't see the bloody screen. And with my spectacles, of course, the glass would reflect on my eyes again. I grabbed Harvie. 'Put your head in the bloody doorway and tell me what my image looks like on the screen before I throw the money in,' I pleaded. Four more flashes. 'See you again soon,' the machine snarled at me. I kicked it.

Back to the examiner. Yes, all's well. But the passport would not now be ready for another four hours. And I had to be in Oxford for a lecture in three hours. I told Harvie he could DHL the new passport to me in Ireland. 'You're not allowed by law to do that,' another examiner snapped. Harvie was muttering under his breath, the way an anarchist does when plotting crimes. 'Tell you what,' he said. 'I'll pick it up first thing in the morning and try to reach you before you leave for Heathrow.' And at 8 a.m., there he was in his bicycle clips, holding out a brand-new passport. I raced for the airport. I snapped open the cover of the passport and looked at those glorious imperial words on page one. 'Her Britannic Majesty's Secretary of State requests and requires in the Name of Her Majesty all those whom it may concern to allow the bearer to pass freely without let or hindrance . . .' I could just see the Homeland Security boys cringing at this admonition from our foreign secretary. That will sail me into the United States on 8 November. Or will it?*

The Independent, 22 October 2005

---

* It did.

CHAPTER TWELVE

Unanswered questions

Journalists like to 'solve' mysteries, to uncover the 'truth', to scoop the world. But there are some stories that always elude us. The exact science of global warming, for example; few now deny that it is a fact, but the devil is indeed in the detail, and on this news reports will never agree. I am still sceptical of what really did happen on 11 September 2001 – though I do not belong to the 'ravers' who believe in massive conspiracies – and even more doubtful that we have heard the truth about the Lockerbie bombing. I don't know who killed Benazir Bhutto – though I have my suspicions. And I will never know exactly who my father was supposed to have executed in 1919 . . .

Is the problem weather? Or is it war?

Back in the Sixties, a great movie was released called *The Day the Earth Caught Fire*. Leo McKern, I recall, played a *Daily Express* reporter along with the then real-life editor of the paper, Arthur Christiansen. What the *Express* discovered was that the British government was erecting showers in Hyde Park to keep people cool when in fact it was still winter. Investigative reporting eventually revealed – and this, remember, was fiction – that the US and Soviet powers had, without knowing of the other's activities, tested nuclear weapons at exactly the same moment at opposite sides of the earth. I'm not sure that our present-day colleagues on the *Express* would discover any of this, but that's not the point. In the movie, our planet had been blasted off course – and was now heading towards the sun. The governments, of course, tried to cover this up.

Now I remembered this creaky old film early this week when I woke up at my home in Beirut shivering with cold. This is mid-February in Lebanon and early spring should have warmed the air. But it hasn't. Up in the Christian mountain town of Jezzine, it was snowing fiercely. I walked to my balcony over the Mediterranean and a sharp, freezing wind was coming off the sea. Well, poor old Bob, you might say. Better install central heating. (Most Lebanese exist like me with a series of dangerous and cheaply made gas heaters.) But right now, I'm finding a lot of odd parallels. In Melbourne last autumn, for example, the Australian spring turned out to be much colder than expected. Yet in Toronto at Christmas, all the snow melted. I padded round the streets of the city and had to take my pullover off because of the sun. It was the warmest winter in the records of a country whose tundra wastes are known for their frozen desolation.

I should add that those Canadians who welcomed this dangerous thaw seem at odds with reality – it's a bit like being cold and then expressing pleasure that your house is burning down on the grounds that you now feel warmer. Then there are the air crews. Out here in the Middle East, for instance, pilots have told me that head winds can now be so fierce at great heights that they are being forced to request lower altitudes from air traffic control. As a flyer who knows how to be afraid on a bumpy flight – I am – I can tell you that I haven't encountered as much turbulence as I have in the past twenty-four months.

Now a deviation – but an important one. A British scientist, Chris Busby, has been digging through statistics from the Aldermaston Atomic Weapons Establishment which measures uranium in high-volume air samples. His suspicion was that depleted uranium particles from the two Gulf wars – DU is used in the anti-armour warheads of the ordnance of American and British tanks and planes – may have spread across Europe. I'm not a conspiracy theorist, but here's something very odd. When Busby applied for the information from Aldermaston in 2004, they told him to get lost. When he demanded the information under the 2005 Freedom of Information Act, Aldermaston coughed up the figures. But wait. The only statistic missing from the data they gave him was for the early months of 2003. Remember what was happening then? A little dust-up in Iraq, a massive American–British invasion of Saddam's dictatorship in which tons of DU shells were used by American troops. Eventually Busby, who worked out all the high-altitude wind movements over Europe, received the data from the Defence Procurement Agency in Bristol – which showed an increase in uranium in high-volume air sampling over Britain during this period.

Well, we aren't dead yet – though readers in Reading will not be happy to learn that the filter system samplings around Aldermaston showed that even they got an increase. Shock and awe indeed.

Back to our main story. I'm tired of hearing about 'global warming' – it's become such a cliché that it's a turn-off, a no-read, a yawn. As perhaps our governments wish it to be. Melting ice caps and disappearing icebergs have become *de rigueur* for all reporting. After Unesco put the Ilulissat ice fjord on the World Heritage List, it was discovered to have receded three miles. And there's a lovely irony in the fact that the Canadians are now having a row with the United States about shipping lanes in the far north – because the Americans would like to use a melted North West Passage which comes partly under Canadian sovereignty. But I have a hunch that something more serious is happening to our planet which we are not being told about.

So let me remind you how *The Day the Earth Caught Fire* ended. Russian and American scientists were planning a new and joint explosion to set the world back on course. The last shot in the movie was set in the basement printing rooms (the real ones) of the *Daily Express*. The printers were standing by their machines with two headlines plated up to run, depending on the results of the detonation. One said 'World Doomed', the other 'World Saved'. As that great populist columnist John Gordon of the *Sunday Express* used to write: Makes you sit up a bit, doesn't it?

The Independent, 25 January 2006

Fear climate change, not our enemies

It was a warning. Scratched, of course, after more than fifty years, a home movie, shot by my mother in colour. But most of the colour is white. Fifty-seven-year-old Bill Fisk is standing in the garden of our home in his long black office coat, throwing snow balls at his son. I am ten years old, in short trousers but up to my waist in snow. There must have been two feet of it in the garden. You can even see the condensation from my mouth. My mother doesn't appear on the film. She is standing in the snow behind my father, thirty-six years old, the daughter of café proprietors who every Boxing Day would host my own and my aunt's family with a huge lunch and a roaring log fire. It really was cold then.

I think it was Andrew Marr, when editor of *The Independent*, who first made me think about what was happening. It was a stiflingly hot summer and I had just arrived in London from Beirut and commented that there wasn't much difference in temperature. And Andrew turned round and pointed across the city. 'Something's gone wrong with the bloody weather!' he roared. And of course, he was right.

Now I acknowledge it silently: the great storms that sweep across Europe, the weird turbulence that my passenger jet pilots experience high over the Atlantic. Because I have never travelled so far or so frequently, I notice that at year's end it's 15 degrees in Toronto and Montreal – a 'springtime Christmas', the Canadian papers announce. In Denver, the airport is blocked by snowfalls. I return to Lebanon to find so little snow has fallen that much of Mount Sannine above my home is the colour of grey rock, just a dressing of white on the top. The snow is deep in Jerusalem. There is a water shortage in Beirut.

How casually these warnings come to us. How casually we treat them. I suspect that most people feel so detached from political power – so hopeless when faced with a world tragedy – that they can do nothing but watch in growing anger and distress. Water levels in the world's oceans may rise 20 feet higher, we are told. And I calculate that in Beirut, the Mediterranean – in rough weather – will be splashing over my second-floor balcony wall.

I curl down deep in my bed, because the nights are strangely damp, and read by the bedside light Hans von Sponeck's gripping, painful account of his years as the UN's Humanitarian Coordinator for Iraq, *A Different Kind of War*, an analysis of the vicious, criminal sanctions regime levelled against the Iraqi people between 1990 and 2003. Here, for example, is what Sergei Lavrov, the Russian ambassador to the UN, wrote in March 2000: '. . . the scale of the humanitarian catastrophe in Iraq is inexorably leading to the disintegration of the very fabric of civil society.' It was 'a situation where an entire generation of Iraqis has been physically and morally crippled'. The French ambassador to the UN, Alain Dejammet, spoke similarly of 'the very serious humanitarian crisis in Iraq', a crime that would eventually persuade von Sponeck to resign. Another warning. I remember how von Sponeck said the very same words to me in Baghdad. So did Denis Halliday, his predecessor. But when Peter Hain – now so desperately anxious to distance himself from US policies in Iraq – was asked to comment, he said that von Sponeck and Halliday were 'obviously not the right men for the job'. James Rubin, then earning his keep as Madeleine Albright's spokesman, said that von Sponeck 'is paid to work, not to speak'.

Yet there are all the warnings. Did we really think that after we had impoverished them and destroyed so many of their children, after a generation of Iraqis had been 'physically and morally crippled', they were going to welcome our 'liberation'? From this wreckage of Iraq was bound to come the insurgencies and the hatreds now tearing its people apart and destroying the presidency of George W. Bush and the prime ministership of Tony Blair. Yet what do they tell us? They still want us to be frightened. Terror, terror, terror. Now we have Dr Death, our UK home secretary,* telling us that the War on Terror could last as long as the Cold War. Recently, it was the Dowager of Fear† in charge of our intelligence services who said that the War on Terror could last 'a generation'. So that's thirty years? Or sixty like Dr Death claimed? Bush claimed it might last 'forever', surely an ambitious goal for an ex-governor-executioner.

What these men know, of course – while waffling about our 'values' – is that the only way to lessen the risk of attack in London or Washington is to adopt a moral, just policy towards the Middle East. Failure to do this – and the Blairs and the Bushes clearly have no intention of doing so – means that we will be bombed again. And the words of Dr Death were not a warning to us. They were not intended to prepare us for the future. They were intended to allow him to say 'told you so' when the next backpacker murders the innocent on a London Tube train. And then we will be told that we need even harsher legislation. And we will have to be afraid.

Yes, we must fear. We must wake every morning in fear.

* John Reid, a family doctor, who was obsessed with the need for British citizens to hold identity cards.
† Dame Elizabeth Manningham-Buller was Director General of the UK's Security Service, MI5, from October 2002 till April 2007.

We must bend our entire political system into a machine of fear. Organised society must revolve around our fear. Like the terrorologists of old – the Claire Sterlings and Brian Croziers of this world, who told us of thousands of terrorists, 'bands of professional practitioners dispensing violent death', all trained in Cuba, North Korea, the Soviet Union or Eastern Europe – Dr Death and Lord Blair of Kut al-Amara and former foreign secretary Jack 'the Veil' Straw (remember him?) – want us to live in fear. They want us to be afraid.

I think we should be afraid – of what we are doing to our planet. But we should not fear our enemies in the world. They will return. Our Western occupation of so many Muslim lands has assured us of this fate. But if we can now end our injustice in the Middle East, Dr Death's sixty years could be over before he leaves his high office. Now there's a thought.

Meanwhile, watch the world and the weather and the turbulence at high altitude. And remember the snow in Maidstone.

The Independent, 20 January 2007

Just who creates reality?

Each time I lecture abroad on the Middle East, there is always someone in the audience – just one – whom I call the 'raver'. Apologies here to all the men and women who come to my talks with bright and pertinent questions – often quite humbling ones for me – and which show that they understand the Middle East tragedy a lot better than the journalists who report it. But the 'raver' is real. He has turned up in corporeal form in Stockholm and in Oxford, in São Paulo and in Yerevan, in Cairo, in Los Angeles and, in female form, in Barcelona. No matter the country, there will always be a 'raver'.

His – or her – question goes like this. Why, if you believe you're a free journalist, don't you report what you really know about 9/11? Why don't you tell the truth – that the Bush administration (or the CIA or Mossad, you name it) blew up the Twin Towers? Why don't you reveal the secrets behind 9/11? The assumption in each case is that Fisk knows – that Fisk has an absolute concrete, copper-bottomed fact-filled desk containing final proof of what 'all the world knows' (that usually is the phrase) – who destroyed the Twin Towers. Sometimes the 'raver' is clearly distressed. One man in Cork screamed his question at me, and then – the moment I suggested that his version of the plot was a bit odd – left the hall, shouting abuse and kicking over chairs.

Usually, I have tried to tell the 'truth'; that while there

are unanswered questions about 9/11, I am the Middle East correspondent of *The Independent*, not the conspiracy correspondent; that I have quite enough real plots on my hands in Lebanon, Iraq, Syria, Iran, the Gulf, etc., to worry about imaginary ones in Manhattan. My final argument – a clincher, in my view – is that the Bush administration has screwed up everything – militarily, politically, diplomatically – it has tried to do in the Middle East; so how on earth could it successfully bring off the international crimes against humanity in the United States on 11 September 2001?

Well, I still hold to that view. Any military which can claim – as the Americans did two days ago – that al-Qaeda is on the run is not capable of carrying out anything on the scale of 9/11. 'We disrupted al-Qaeda, causing them to run,' Colonel David Sutherland said of the childishly code-named 'Operation Lightning Hammer' in Iraq's Diyala province. 'Their fear of facing our forces proves the terrorists know there is no safe haven for them.' And more of the same, all of it untrue. Within hours, al-Qaeda attacked Baquba in battalion strength and slaughtered all the local sheikhs who had thrown in their hand with the Americans. It reminds me of Vietnam, the war that George Bush watched from the skies over Texas – which may account for why he this week mixed up the end of the Vietnam War with the genocide in a different country called Cambodia, whose population was eventually rescued by the same Vietnamese whom Mr Bush's more courageous colleagues had been fighting all along.

But – here we go. I am increasingly troubled at the inconsistencies in the official narrative of 9/11. It's not just the obvious *non sequiturs*: where are the aircraft parts (engines, etc.) from the attack on the Pentagon? Why have the officials involved in the United 93 flight (which crashed in Pennsylvania) been muzzled? Why did Flight 93's debris spread over miles when it was supposed to have crashed in one piece in a field? Again,

I'm not talking about the crazed 'research' of David Icke's *Alice in Wonderland and the World Trade Center Disaster* – which should send any sane man or woman back to reading the telephone directory.

I am talking about scientific issues. If it is true, for example, that kerosene burns at 820°C under optimum conditions, how come the steel beams of the Twin Towers – whose melting point is supposed to be about 1,480°C – would snap through at the same time? (They collapsed in 8.1 and 10 seconds.) What about the third tower – the so-called World Trade Center Building 7 (or the Salmon Brothers Building) – which collapsed in 6.6 seconds in its own footprint at 5.20 p.m. on 11 September? Why did it so neatly fall to the ground when no aircraft had hit it? The American National Institute of Standards and Technology was instructed to analyse the cause of the destruction of all three buildings. They have not yet reported on WTC 7. Two prominent American professors of mechanical engineering – very definitely not in the 'raver' bracket – are now legally challenging the terms of reference of this final report on the grounds that it could be 'fraudulent or deceptive'.

Journalistically, there were many odd things about 9/11. Initial reports of reporters that they heard 'explosions' in the towers – which could well have been the beams cracking – are easy to dismiss. Less so the report that the body of a female air crew member was found in a Manhattan street with her hands bound. OK, so let's claim that was just hearsay reporting at the time, just as the CIA's list of Arab suicide-hijackers, which included three men who were – and still are – very much alive and living in the Middle East, was an initial intelligence error.

But what about the weird letter allegedly written by Mohamed Atta, the Egyptian hijacker–murderer with the spooky face, whose 'Islamic' advice to his gruesome comrades

– released by the CIA – mystified every Muslim friend I know in the Middle East? Atta mentioned his family – which no Muslim, however ill-taught, would be likely to include in such a prayer. He reminds his comrades-in-murder to say the first Muslim prayer of the day and then goes on to quote from it. But no Muslim would need such a reminder – let alone expect the text of the 'Fajr' prayer to be included in Atta's letter.

Let me repeat. I am not a conspiracy theorist. Spare me the ravers. Spare me the plots. But like everyone else, I would like to know the full story of 9/11, not least because it was the trigger for the whole lunatic, meretricious 'war on terror' which has led us to disaster in Iraq and Afghanistan and in much of the Middle East. Bush's happily departed adviser Karl Rove once said that 'We're an empire now – we create our own reality.' True? At least tell us. It would stop people kicking over chairs.

The Independent, 25 August 2007

In January of 2008 it was disclosed that the CIA had destroyed videotapes of the interrogation of al-Qaeda suspects who may have been involved in the 9/11 atrocities. The existence of these tapes was never disclosed to the official commission inquiring into the attacks. In the New York Times *on 2 January 2008, Thomas H. Kean and Lee H. Hamilton, chairman and vice chairman of the commission, complained that George Tenet refused them access to detainees. They concluded that 'government officials decided not to inform a lawfully constituted body, created by Congress and the president, to investigate one of the greatest tragedies to confront this country. We call that obstruction.'*

A letter from Mrs Irvine

After writing about the 'ravers' who regularly turn up at lectures to claim that President Bush/the CIA/the Pentagon/ Mossad etc. perpetrated the crimes of 11 September, I received a letter this week from Marion Irvine, who feared that members of her family run the risk of being just such 'ravers' and 'voices heard in the wilderness'. Far from it. For Mrs Irvine was writing about Lockerbie, and, like her, I believe there are many dark and sinister corners to this atrocity. I'm not at all certain that the CIA did not have a scam drugs heist on board and I am not at all sure that the diminutive Libyan agent Megrahi – ultimately convicted on the evidence of the memory of a Maltese tailor – really arranged to plant the bomb on board Pan Am Flight 103 in December 1988.

But I take Mrs Irvine's letter doubly seriously because her brother, Bill Cadman, was on board 103 and died in the night over Lockerbie nineteen years ago. He was a sound engineer in London and Paris, travelling with his girlfriend Sophie – who, of course, was also killed – to spend Christmas with Sophie's aunt in the United States. Nothing, therefore, could be more eloquent than Mrs Irvine's own letter, which I must quote to you. She strongly doubts, she says, Libya's involvement in the bombing.

'We have felt since the first days in December 1988,' she writes, 'that something was being hidden from us':

... the discrediting of the Helsinki [US embassy] warning, the
presence of the CIA on Scottish soil before the work of identifying bodies was properly undertaken, the Teflon behaviour
of ministers and government all contributed to a deep feeling
of unease. This reached a peak when my father was told by a
member of the American Presidential Commission on Aviation
Security and Terrorism that our government knew what had
happened but that the truth would not come out. In the truth
vacuum, the worst-case scenario – that lives were sacrificed in
expiation for the Iranian lives lost in June 1988 – takes on a
certain degree of credibility. The plane was brought down in
the last dangerous moments of the Reagan presidency.

Now I should explain here that the Iranian lives to which
Mrs Irvine refers were the Iranian passengers of an Airbus
civilian airliner shot down over the Gulf by a US warship a
few months before Lockerbie, and just before the end of the
eight-year Iran–Iraq war. The USS *Vincennes* – nicknamed
Robocruiser by the crews of other American vessels – blasted
its missiles at the Airbus on the assumption that it was a diving
Iranian air force jet. It wasn't – the Airbus was climbing – but
Reagan, after a few cursory apologies, blamed Iran for the
slaughter, because it had refused to accept a UN ceasefire in
the war with Iraq in which we were backing our old friend
Saddam Hussein (yes, the same!). The US navy also awarded
medals – God spare us – to the captain of the *Vincennes* and
to his gunnery crew. Some weeks later the boss of the Popular
Front for the Liberation of Palestine General Command – a
pro-Iranian Palestinian outfit in Lebanon – suddenly called a
press conference in Beirut to deny to astonished reporters that
he was involved in Lockerbie.

Why? Was he being fingered? Was Iran? Only later did those
familiar 'official sources' who had initially pointed the finger
at Iran start blaming Libya. By then we needed the support of

Iran's ally Syria and Iranian quiescence in our attempt to liberate Kuwait after Saddam's 1990 invasion. Personally, I always thought that Lockerbie was revenge for the Airbus destruction – the PFLP's strange press conference lends credence to this – which makes sense of Mrs Irvine's courageous letter. Her parents, Martin and Rita Cadman, have, she says, had countless meetings with MPs, including Tam Dalyell and Henry Bellingham, Cecil Parkinson, Robin Cook and Tony Blair, and with Nelson Mandela (whose appeal for Megrahi to be transferred to a Libyan prison was supported by the Cadmans).

In a deeply moving sentence, Mrs Irvine adds that her parents 'are ageing and in their anxiety that they will die with no one having taken real responsibility for their son's death are in danger of losing focus and feeling that they themselves are "raving". The [1980–88] war in Iraq meant that no lessons were being learned, and because my brother chanced to be on that plane we all now feel a heightened sense of responsibility for the world situation.' Then Mrs Irvine comes to the point:

> What can we do? Now that my father is older it is up to us, the next generation, to try to needle the government, but is there any hope? I am writing to ask if you think there is any reasonable action that we can take that has a slight prospect of success . . . a refusal to understand and admit to the past is dangerous for the future.

I couldn't put it better myself – and I do have a very direct idea. If official untruths were told about Lockerbie – if skulduggery was covered up by the British and US governments and lies were told by those responsible for our security – then many in authority know about this. I urge all those who may know of any such lies to write to me (snail mail or hand-delivered) at *The Independent*. They can address their letters to Mrs Irvine in an envelope with my name on it. In other words, this is an appeal for honest whistle-blowers to tell the truth.

I can hear already the rustle of the lads in blue. Are we encouraging civil servants to break the Official Secrets Act? Certainly not. If lies were told, then officials should let us know, since the Official Secrets Act – in this case – would have been shamefully misused to keep them silent. If the truth has indeed been told, then no one is going to break the Official Secrets Act.

So I await news. Ravers need not apply. But those who know truths which cannot be told can have the honour of revealing them all. It's the least Martin and Rita Cadman and Mrs Irvine – and Bill and Sophie – deserve. As for a constabulary which just might be tempted to threaten me – or Mrs Irvine – in a quest for truth, to hell with them.

The Independent, 13 October 2007

Who killed Benazir?

Weird, isn't it, how swiftly the narrative is laid down for us. Benazir Bhutto the courageous leader of the Pakistan People's Party is assassinated in Rawalpindi – attached to the very capital of Islamabad wherein ex-General Pervez Musharraf lives – and we are told by George W. Bush that her murderers were 'extremists' and 'terrorists'. Well, you can't dispute that. The killer shot Ms Bhutto twice, it seems, before blowing himself up. But Bush's implication – faithfully supported by other world 'statesmen' and (here I pause for a chuckle) a 'Pakistan security analyst' on Canadian television – was that Islamists were behind the assassination. It was the Taliban madmen again, the al-Qaeda spider which struck at this lone and brave woman who had dared to call for democracy in her country.

There was even a truly laughable moment when Bush and his spokesman demanded that the culprits be 'brought to justice'. Let me repeat that. 'Brought to justice'. This, ladies and gentlemen, in a nation so corrupted that there has been no justice for decades and where General Musharraf, George W.'s friend, actually fired the chief justice and effectively ended any free court system in Pakistan. There may be plenty of 'justice' in the underground torture chambers of the Pakistani police – but we're not going to see any in public.

Of course, given the childish coverage of this appalling

tragedy – and however corrupt Ms Bhutto may have been, let us be under no illusions that this brave lady is indeed a true martyr – it's not surprising that the 'good versus evil' donkey can be trotted out to explain the carnage in Rawalpindi. Who would have imagined, watching the BBC or CNN on Thursday, that her two brothers, Murtaza and Shahnawaz, hijacked a Pakistani airliner in 1981 and flew it to Kabul, where Murtaza demanded the release of political prisoners in Pakistan? A military officer on the plane was murdered. There were Americans aboard the flight – which is probably why the prisoners were indeed released. No mention of this in our media coverage of the Bhutto murder.

Only a few days ago – in one of the most remarkable (but typically unrecognised) scoops of the year – Tariq Ali published a brilliant dissection of Pakistani (and Bhutto) corruption in the *London Review of Books*, focusing on Benazir Bhutto, and headlined 'Daughter of the West'. In fact, the article was on my desk to photocopy as its subject was being murdered in Rawalpindi. Towards the end of this extraordinary report, Tariq Ali dwelt at length on the subsequent murder of Murtaza Bhutto by police officers close to his home at a time when Benazir was prime minister – and at a time when Benazir was enraged at Murtaza for demanding a return to PPP values and for condemning Benazir's appointment of her own husband as minister for industry, a highly lucrative post in the administration.

In a passage that may yet be applied to the aftermath of Benazir's murder, the report continues: 'The fatal bullet had been fired at close range. The trap had been carefully laid, but as is the way in Pakistan, the crudeness of the operation – false entries in police logbooks, lost evidence, witnesses arrested and intimidated . . . a policeman killed who they feared might talk – made it obvious that the decision to execute the prime minister's brother had been taken at a

very high level.' When Murtaza's fourteen-year-old daughter
Fatima rang her aunt Benazir to ask why witnesses were being
arrested – rather than her father's killers – she says that Benazir
told her: 'Look, you're very young. You don't understand
things.'

Or so Tariq Ali's exposé would have us believe. Over all
this, however, looms the shocking power of Pakistan's ISI, the
Interservices Intelligence. This vast institution – corrupt, venal
and brutal – works for Musharraf. But it also worked – and
still works – for the Taliban. It also works for the Americans.
In fact, it works for everybody. But it is the key that Musharraf
can use to open talks with America's enemies when he feels
threatened or wants to put pressure on Afghanistan or wants
to appease the 'extremists' and 'terrorists' who so oppress
George W. Bush. And let us remember, by the way, that Daniel
Pearl, the *Wall Street Journal* reporter beheaded by his Islamist
captors in Karachi, actually made his fatal appointment with
his future murderers from an ISI commander's office. Ahmed
Rashid's wonderful book *Taliban* provides riveting proof of the
ISI's web of corruption and violence. Read it, and all of the
above makes more sense.

But back to the official narrative. George Bush announced
on Thursday that he was 'looking forward' to talking to his
old friend Musharraf. Of course, they would talk about Benazir.
They certainly would not talk about the fact that Musharraf
continues to protect his old acquaintance – a certain Mr Khan
– who supplied all Pakistan's nuclear secrets to Libya and Iran.
No, let's not bring the 'axis of evil' into this.

So of course, we were asked to concentrate once more on
all those 'extremists' and 'terrorists', not on the logic of questioning which many Pakistanis were feeling their way through
in the aftermath of Benazir's assassination. It doesn't, after all,
take much to comprehend that the hated elections looming
over Musharraf would probably be postponed indefinitely if

his principal political opponent happened to be liquidated before polling day.*

So let's run through this logic in the way that Inspector Ian Blair might have done in his policeman's notebook before he became top cop in London. Question: Who forced Benazir Bhutto to stay in London and tried to prevent her return to Pakistan? Answer: General Musharraf. Question: Who ordered the arrest of thousands of Benazir' supporters this month? Answer: General Musharraf. Question: Who placed Benazir under temporary house arrest this month? Answer: General Musharraf. Question: Who declared emergency rule this month? Answer: General Musharraf. Question: who killed Benazir Bhutto? Er. Yes. Well quite.

You see the problem? Yesterday, our television warriors informed us that the PPP members shouting that Musharraf was a 'murderer' were complaining that he had not provided sufficient security for Benazir. Wrong. They were shouting this because they believe he killed her.

The Independent, 29 December 2007

---

* Musharraf postponed elections until February, 2008. His supporters lost their majority in parliament; Benazir Bhutto's PPP – now nominally led by her student son but run by her widower, Asif Zardari – began coalition talks with Nawaz Sharif's surprisingly successful Pakistan Muslim League to form a government. But Musharraf insisted on remaining president – receiving, of course, American and British support.

The strange case of Gunner Wills

All wars, like the ways into a human heart, are mysteries. Even A. J. P. Taylor couldn't explain the origins of the First World War in his book of the same name. My dad couldn't either, and he was in it. But there's a mystery developing about the man whom 2nd Lieutenant Bill Fisk of the King's Liverpool Regiment was supposed to execute for the murder of a British military policeman in Paris. Bill knew him as Frank Wills. I've even seen Wills's signature at the end of his last appeal to the military court which sentenced him to death. It did no good. Wills was shot at Le Havre in May of 1919 – though not by my dad who, in the noblest act of his life, refused to command the firing party and probably destroyed his own military career. Frank Oswald Wills lies in the Sainte Marie cemetery (grave plot: Division 64/VI/F/5) near the place of his dawn execution. But the man buried there may not be Frank Wills at all. Indeed, Frank Wills may never have existed.

So here I have to thank the tireless work of the Great War Forum and military researchers Bob Doneley and Beppo Sapone and Sandra and Tim and other e-mailers, most of them apparently Australian (their hard copy sent to me by Gerard Holuigue, since I remain a Luddite non-e-mailer). Great War sleuths may send me their own conclusions to this tale. I will begin with my own copy of Wills's last words, vainly written to the court that ordered his execution in an attempt to spare his life:

I am 20 years of age. I joined the Australian Army in 1915
when I was 16 years of age. I went to Egypt and the Dardanelles.
I have been in a considerable number of engagements there, &
in France. I joined the British Army in April 1918 and came
to France in June 1918. I was discharged from the Australian
Army on account of fever which affected my head contracted
in Egypt. I was persuaded to leave my unit by my friends and
got into bad company. I began to drink and gamble heavily. I
had no intention whatever of committing the offences for
which I am now before the Court . . . I ask the Court to take
into consideration my youth and to give me a chance of leading
an upright and straightforward life in the future.

Wills's appeal – rejected by the court – can be found in the
Public Record Office (or the 'National Archives' as its Blairite
title now reads) at Kew. His signature, in slightly shaky hand,
is at the end.

And now to the first paragraph of Holuigue's 18-page file to
me:

1709 Private Richard Mellor left Australia (in 1915) as a
reinforcement for the 1st Light Horse Regiment. His mother
stated that he enlisted under his brother's name and falsified
his age. After less than salubrious service in Egypt and France,
he deserted in May 1918 and was never apprehended. In 1939
his mother Elizabeth was still writing to the [Australian]
Defence Department seeking information as to his fate.

Mellor's 213-page service record is in the Australian National
Archives.

And now to the jaw-dropper.

In May 1919, 253617 Gunner Frank O. Wills, Royal Field Artillery, was awaiting execution for the military policeman he shot

while being apprehended for desertion. He asked to speak to an Australian officer prior to his execution. Major Burford Sampson, Officer Commanding Australian Infantry Force troops in Paris, visited Wills in prison. There, Wills told him that he was actually Richard Mellor, an Australian deserter. He had been apprehended in a sweep for deserters and joined the British Army under the name of Wills. He outlined his past to Sampson and asked him to write to his mother and tell her what had happened to him ... On the 27th May he was executed by firing squad and buried in the Ste. Marie Cemetery, Le Havre.

Although Mellor's file contains Sampson's statement – which exactly matches the service record of Richard Mellor – and British Expeditionary Force orders recording Wills's execution, Mrs Mellor was never officially informed of her son's fate. Nor did the Australian army ever officially record that Mellor and Wills were the same man. Indeed, even today Mellor is still listed by the Australians as a deserter, whereabouts unknown. In 1933, parts of his official file were marked 'Secret'. One page, dated 26 August 1920, asks if Mellor has yet been apprehended – well over a year after Wills/Mellor had been executed.

Yet Wills's story to Sampson appears watertight because he was able to give the Australian major details of Mellor with great accuracy – place of birth, mother's details, home address in Wigram Road in the Forest Lodge area of Sydney, dates of enlistment – and was apparently the same age as Mellor, who officially enlisted in 1915 aged twenty-one, although Elizabeth says he was using his brother Richard's name and was actually only sixteen at the time. If this is true, then Richard Mellor was in fact the younger brother – whose name was Samuel Mellor.

But why did Mellor – drawing the obvious conclusions from 'Wills's statement to Sampson – reinvent himself? Did he join the British army in 1918 to avoid an Australian prison for desertion? Why didn't he provide his true identity to the court martial? And why wasn't poor Mrs Mellor told that her son had been executed? Sampson mentions his prison conversation with 'Wills' in his diary, later published privately by his son. Sandra, in one of her e-mails, wonders whether Mellor married an English girl and was forced to enlist in the British army. Did Wills 'fess up because he thought this would prevent his execution?

Mrs Mellor started her inquiries into her son's fate in 1920, and in 1939 she was telling the Australian authorities, stating that she was now elderly and wanted to know what happened to her son before she died. Her hopeless appeals for information about her son are a testament to official cruelty. 'The despair shown by his mother does deserve an answer,' one of the Great War Forum's investigators accurately points out today.

But the real fate of Frank Wills – if he existed – remains a mystery. I suspect Bill Fisk would rise from the grave (if he had one – he was cremated) to demand an explanation from the authorities for all this obfuscation. But alas, the authorities – like 'Frank Wills' and Richard Mellor or, probably, Samuel Mellor and Bill Fisk himself – are all now dead. Should the Commonwealth War Graves Commission think about a change of name on grave 64/VI/F/5 at Le Havre? A last intriguing clue: there's a W. Mellor listed today in the Sydney phone book, living only a short distance from Wigram Road, Forest Lodge. Had he been alive, Bill would have been tempted to ring the doorbell.

The Independent, 20 October 2007

CHAPTER THIRTEEN

The last enemy

When we are young, death seems impossible. Discussing the forbidden subject with my mother when I was about twelve, she said – and my mum was always an impossible optimist – that 'they' might have found a cure for it by the time I grew up. 'They' being the superior folk who control our lives, from scientists to BBC producers. Some hope. Death is, alas, as necessary as birth. And, as we grow older, our horror of it is tempered, I think, by fascination. Richard Hillary, the RAF fighter pilot whose memoirs of the Battle of Britain are perhaps the most literary work published in the early part of the Second World War, gave his book the title *The Last Enemy*, inspired by Corinthians 15: 33, 'The last enemy that shall be destroyed is death.'

I am not sure I believe this. I think that the last enemy is probably fear, though I am not sure how you destroy it. I recall, in 1978, driving through the Palestinian-held town of Damour south of Beirut during a ferocious Israeli air raid. Empty anti-aircraft shell cases were bouncing off the roof of my car and houses were exploding on both sides of the road, and I remember thinking that 'the worst thing that can happen to me is that I will be killed.' I reflected on this with resignation. It was the only way to conquer fear – though a dangerous one, since journalists can only survive wars if they convince themselves that they are there to report conflict, not to die in it.

I suppose that I have now seen so much death – by violence, of course, not through that wonderful policeman's formula, 'natural causes' – that I have grown resigned to its existence, even indifferent. Yet the tragedy of death – and this chapter includes a particularly distressing example of a young man who came to Lebanon as a photographer, only to die in a car accident after returning home to Germany – cannot be avoided. The unexpectedness of most deaths – save for the condemned prisoner or for the incurably ill – is part of the terror that afflicts all humanity. The British popular press has always been obsessed with life beyond the grave. Not me. As an institution, I have no fear of death. But a few years ago, travelling through the snow-covered Sannine Heights in Lebanon, I was discussing the afterlife with my driver Abed and my classical Arabic translator Imad, one a Sunni Muslim, the other a Shiite. Such are the subjects we talk about after thirty-two years of reporting Lebanon. 'All we know,' Abed said to me sadly, 'is that we go, and the world carries on without us.' I remonstrated with him. Surely the beauty of the mountain snows around us, the frost-covered, leafless branches of the trees, the pale blue sky – surely this could not have come about because two gas clouds bumped into each other billions of years ago. There must be 'something else'. But then I realised that this was as far as Fisk's faith could go. And Abed and Imad – in the kindest way, but not without a dark humour – laughed at me. They wanted to live in the present, not after death. Which is why, I suppose, the greatest courage we will ever have to show comes at the end of our lives.

In the Colosseum, thoughts turn to death

At midnight on Thursday, I lay on my back in the Colosseum and looked at a pageant of stars above Rome. Where the lions tore into gladiators, and only a few metres from the cross marking the place of Saint Paul's supposed crucifixion* – 'martyrdom' has become an uneasy word in this age of the suicide bomber – I could only reflect on how a centre of bestiality could become one of the greatest tourist attractions of our time. An Italian television station had asked me to talk about capital punishment in the Middle East for a series on American executions and death row prisoners. Two generators had melted down in an attempt to flood the ancient arena with light. Hence, the moment of reflection.

Readers with serious money may also like to know that it costs £75,000 to hire the Colosseum for twenty-four hours, a cool £10,500 just for our little night under the stars. Yet who could not think of capital punishment in the Colosseum? Watching the first episode of the Italian television series – which recounted the visits of an Italian man and woman to two Americans who had spent years on death row in Texas – I was struck by how both prisoners, who may or may not have remembered amid their drug-induced comas whether or not they murdered anyone, had clearly 'reformed'. Both deeply

* Saint Paul was in fact executed more than a mile from the Colosseum.

regretted their crimes, both prayed that one day they could return to live good lives, to care for their children, to go shopping, walk the dog. In other words, they were no longer the criminals they were when they were sentenced.

Given their predicament, I guess anyone would reform. But I suspect that guilt or innocence is not what the death sentence is about. Capital punishment, for those who believe in it, is almost a passion. I rather think it is close to an addiction, something – like smoking or alcohol – which can be cured only by total abstinence. And no excuses for secret Japanese executions or lethal injections in Texas or head-chopping out-side Saudi Arabian mosques. But how do you reach this stage when humanity is so obsessed with death in so barbaric a form?

Whenever the Iranians string up drug-dealers or rapists – and who knows their guilt or innocence? – the cranes that hoist these unfortunates into the sky like dead thrushes are always surrounded by thousands of men and women, often chanting 'God is Great'. They did this even when a young woman was hanged. Surely some of these people are against such terrible punishment. But there is, it seems, something primal in our desire for judicial killings. George Bernard Shaw once wrote that if Christians were thrown to the lions in the Royal Albert Hall, there would be a packed house every night. I'm sure he was right. Did not those thousands of Romans pack this very same, sinister Colosseum in which I was lying to watch just such carnage? Was not Saddam Hussein's execution part of our own attempt to distract the Iraqis with bread and circuses, the shrieking executioners on the mobile phone video the Baghdad equivalent of the gladiators putting their enemies to the sword? Nor, let us remember, is execution the prerogative only of states and presidents. The IRA practised capital punishment. The Taliban practises execution and so does al-Qaeda. Osama bin Laden – and I heard this from him in person – believes in the 'Islamic' punishment of head-chopping.

I remember the crowds who lynched three Palestinian collaborators in Hebron in 2001, their near-naked bodies later swinging from electric pylons while small children threw stones at their torsos, the thousands who cheered when their carcasses were tossed with a roar of laughter into a garbage truck. I was so appalled that I could not write in my notebook and instead drew pictures of this obscenity. They are still in the pages of my notebook today, hanging upside down like Saint Paul, legs askew above their heads, their bodies punctured by cigarette burns.

The leading antagonists in the 'war on terror' that we are all supposed to be fighting – Messrs Bush and bin Laden – are always talking about death and sacrifice, although, in his latest videotape, the latter showed a touching faith in American democracy when he claimed the American people had voted for Bush's first presidency. For bin Laden, 11 September 2001 was 'punishment' for America's bloodshed in the Muslim world; indeed, more and more attacks by both guerrillas and orthodox soldiers are turning into revenge operations. Was not the first siege of Fallujah revenge for the killing and desecration of the bodies of American mercenaries? Wasn't Abu Ghraib part of 'our' revenge for 11 September and for our failures in Iraq? Many of the suicide attacks in the Middle East – in 'Palestine', in Afghanistan, in Iraq – are specifically named after 'martyrs' killed in previous operations. Al-Qaeda in Iraq stated quite explicitly that it had 'executed' US troops in retaliation for the rape and murder of an Iraqi girl by an American soldier.

Yet I fear the real problem goes beyond the individual act of killing, judicial or otherwise. In a frightening way, we believe in violent death. We regard it as a policy option, as much to do with self-preservation on a national scale as punishment for named and individual wrongdoers. We believe in war. For what is aggression – the invasion of Iraq in 2003, for example – except capital punishment on a mass scale? We 'civilised' nations – like the dark armies we believe we are fighting – are convinced that the infliction of death on an awesome scale can be morally justified.

And that's the problem, I'm afraid. When we go to war, we are all putting on hoods and pulling the hangman's lever. And as long as we send our armies on the rampage – whatever the justification – we will go on stringing up and shooting and chopping off the heads of our 'criminals' and 'murderers' with the same enthusiasm as the Romans who cheered on the men of blood in the Colosseum two thousand years ago.

The Independent, 15 September 2007

Dead heroes and living memories

Let us now praise famous men. I'm talking about the dead variety, of course, because I suspect we are defined as a people by the way we honour our dead as much as the way we treat the living. My dad, old Bill Fisk, used to force me to walk round the aisles of All Saints Church in Maidstone to look at the inscriptions, pointing to the moth-eaten battle honours of the Royal West Kent Regiment over our heads. I rather liked the way we Brits did things in so haphazard a way. Churchill lies under a simple stone in Bladon in Oxfordshire. Our poets cluster together in Westminster Abbey. Under the nave are the remains of Isaac Newton. 'Mortals rejoice that there has existed so great an ornament of the human race,' it says in Latin above his grave. Three miles away, the Iron Duke commands heaven alone in his black iron catafalque in Saint Paul's. My favourite epitaph remains that of Dean Swift – he wrote it himself, again in Latin – in Saint Patrick's Cathedral in Dublin, the translation of which I owe to reader Stephen Williams:

> Here lies the body of
> Jonathan Swift
> Of this cathedral church
> The Dean
> Where savage indignation

Can no more lacerate his heart.
Traveller, go,
And imitate if you can
His strenuous vindication of
Man's liberty

So I was struck recently, wandering the Panthéon in Paris, by the sinister white conformity of Catholic France's semi-revolutionary house of the dead. '*Aux grands hommes, la patrie reconnaissante,*' it says along the frieze. 'To great men, from their grateful nation.' The French sometimes translate *patrie* as 'fatherland', which, for all the usual reasons, I find rather disturbing. Indeed, ever since *patrie* got mixed up with *famille* and *travail* during the Occupation – in place of liberty, equality and fraternity – I'm surprised even *patrie* has kept its integrity. But it's inside the Panthéon that I find things very odd. True, the feuding pair of Rousseau and Voltaire face each other in their original caskets. Voltaire arrived in London in time to see the funeral of Newton, whom he compared to Descartes. 'In Paris,' he wrote, 'you see the earth shaped like a melon, in London it is flattened on two sides. For a Cartesian light exists in the air, for a Newtonian it comes from the sun in six and a half minutes.'

But there is no natural light in the crypt of the Panthéon because, by God, there is conformity. All the *grands hommes* – plus a few women – are sealed inside identical stone sarcophagi. Alexandre Dumas's tomb is the same as that of Resistance hero Jean Moulin. So are those of Marie and Pierre Curie. And Zola. And André Malraux. And Victor Hugo and Jean Jaurès (like Moulin, one of my heroes) and Jean Monnet. *Egalité* here means what it says. Like the dead of Verdun, France's elite are allowed no extra favours, no extra flowers, no poems, no special concessions. Just those long white tombs which re-mind me of the hibernation cabinets in which the crew of the space craft in *2001: a Space Odyssey* are murdered by Hal the computer. 'Life functions critical,' the computer read-out announced as Hal put them to death. And then: 'Life functions terminated.' In the Panthéon, their life functions have also been terminated, mostly by God although, in the case of Jean Moulin, by Klaus Barbie.

And so of course I was moved to find out how little Lebanon – the child of France – treated her honoured dead, the Muslims and Christians hanged by the Turks in 1915 and 1916 for demanding independence from the Ottoman Empire. They went to the gallows in what is now called Martyrs' Square less than a mile from where my home stands, shouting their defiance at Turkish occupation as the hangman set about his work. The Turks threw their corpses into a common grave on the Beirut beach. But when the French liberated Beirut in 1918, they were dug up. Surely they should be given an honoured reburial. Ah yes, but it turned out that the Christian Church would not let the Muslim martyrs lie in their cemeteries. And the Muslim clergy would not contemplate allowing Christian martyrs to be interred in their cemeteries. So the mystical Druze allowed them to find their resting place on land they owned in central Beirut.

And that's where I found them last week, beside a ravine of traffic, locked away behind an iron gate, their graves covered with tree branches and surrounded by nettles, a cockerel croaking away between them. The Mahmessani brothers lie together in one concrete tomb, the others – there are nineteen in all – have graves on which their names and places of birth can just be identified. Omar Mustafa Hamad, born Beirut 1892, Prince Said al-Chehabi, born Hasbaya 1889 . . . 'The cemetery of the Lebanese martyrs', it says on a plaque beside the rusting gate, 'was renovated under the auspices of Prime Minister Rafiq Hariri, March 6, 1994.' But since 14 February last year, the murdered Hariri, too, has been a Lebanese martyr. And about

10 metres from the cemetery is the spot where President René Mouawad was vaporised by another massive bomb in 1989. Savage indignation indeed.

The Independent, 4 March 2006

The ship that stands upright at the bottom of the sea

We journalists are students of human folly. Palestine, Iraq, the Gulf, Persia; for more than a hundred years, our Western meddling in the Middle East falls under that label 'folly'. A 'foolish . . . and expensive undertaking that ends in disaster' is how one dictionary defines this. I suspect it also contains an unhealthy mix of vanity and hubris.

A few days ago, standing on the wave-thrashed rocks above the old Lebanese Crusader port of Enfeh – yes, Richard the Lionheart (he who spoke French, not English) spent a night here to escape the storms – I was able to contemplate that the most sublime as well as the most ridiculous folly always seems to occur at sea. For just as Captain Smith insisted on steering the *Titanic* at full speed into the North Atlantic ice in 1912 because he wanted to impress the Americans with her speed, so – nineteen years earlier – Vice Admiral Sir George Tryon of HMS *Victoria*, not far from where I was standing, decided to put the Royal Navy's Mediterranean fleet through the fastest and most dangerous naval manoeuvres known to man in order to impress the Ottoman Turks.

Off Enfeh today, the wind cracks off the sea – I've noticed how the treacherous tides here always make the sea heave in small mountains down the coast – but Christian Francis, a Lebanese–Austrian diver, still sets off daily from a semi-derelict hotel to look at the wreck he has discovered 480 feet beneath the surface. His enthusiasm – for history as much as for diving – is infectious and he happily printed off for me the one thing I more and more come to love in journalism: archives, papers, the official records that the 'centres of power' produce to justify their folly – or to pass the buck. In this case, the whole sorry story was contained in the Royal Navy's court-martial proceedings of 1893 'to enquire into the loss of Her Majesty's Ship *Victoria*'. Tryon, it appears, was a Smith in the making.

A stern disciplinarian – 'taciturn' and 'difficult' were among the lesser characteristics that his subordinates identified in him – he also had, like Smith, a reputation as a fine seafarer; he was, in fact, every schoolboy's nightmare, an impressive man who wanted obedience rather than initiative. So when on 22 June 1893 – with the Ottomans watching from the ancient city of Tripoli to the east – Tryon ordered his two fleets of eleven ships to turn 16 points and sail at speed towards each other, none of his subordinates said a word. At the last moment, the ships were supposed to turn again and sail alongside each other in the opposite direction. Tryon's men were too fearful to question this insanity. One who hesitated was his deputy, Rear Admiral Albert Markham, aboard HMS *Camperdown*; he received a testy flag message from his commander: 'What are you waiting for?' With Aeschylean inevitability, the 14,000-horsepower, 11,000-ton *Victoria* – one of the first British ironclads and the first naval vessel to be built with a steam turbine – collided with *Camperdown*, which tore into Tryon's ship 12 feet below the waterline, opening a 28-foot gash in her hull.

Last words are a journalist's favourite weapon against the dead, and the Admiralty provides us with a couple of classics to run alongside Smith's alleged remark to the *Titanic*'s owner after colliding with the iceberg: 'Well, you'll get your headlines now, Mr Ismay.' In Tryon's case, surrounded by his appalled but silent junior officers as the *Camperdown* bore down upon him, the Vice Admiral shouted: 'Go astern, go astern.' And then, as his great ship shuddered with the impact and began to turn over, his boilermen doomed as they vainly tried to keep the *Victoria* heading back to the coast, and his deck crew drowning as the vessel rolled over on top of them, Tryon announced – and you can imagine the Blair-like relief of the Admiralty – 'It's all my fault.' He thus doomed himself for ever as the man who took his flagship to the bottom. Watching from the shore, the Ottomans were indeed impressed. In all, 358 British seamen were killed, including Tryon, who was held entirely responsible for the greatest peacetime disaster in the history of the Royal Navy.

Disgrace in a land battle or in the air is somehow mitigated by time. Grass, as the American poet Carl Sandburg observed, always covers the graves. Aircraft fragments disintegrate in the air. But beneath the seas, like the *Titanic*, our folly remains sacrosanct and eternal. For young Christian Francis, provoked by old fishermen's stories and the Admiralty documents he read in the National Maritime Museum at Greenwich, has found Tryon's flagship 480 feet down, remarkably intact and – even more extraordinary – standing vertical, its bows buried deep in the Mediterranean seabed, its huge twin propellers pointing upwards and illuminated by the faint Mediterranean sunlight. Francis works with two British divers and three Poles, and they all produced their amateur videos for me. Shoals of fish sweep past the propellers. I could read the *Victoria*'s name on the stern.

There is Tryon's cabin, the iron landing from which he saw the *Camperdown* approaching, the *Victoria*'s ten-inch rear gun still in place, her twelve side-cannons still mounted to repel the Germans she would never fight in the First World War. For *Victoria* – how we love the 'might-have-beens' of history – would surely have fought in the Royal Navy's greatest battle of the conflict. Incredibly, Tryon's deputy was none other than

John Jellicoe. His escape that day off Lebanon probably did for the German High Seas fleet, when Jellicoe met them off Jutland in 1916. Francis treats the wreck as a British maritime grave and merely looks through the cabin windows – there is a silver salver visible through one of them – but presumes there are still bones, Tryon's included, in the buried part of the *Victoria*. Poor Tryon. His flagship stands up like a tombstone and it is the only vertical wreck in the world – nose in the mud, rear in the air for ever. But do we learn from it?

Oh do we indeed? I had been talking to the Poles who were diving on the *Victoria* for an hour before I realised that they were the men who had prowled through the Baltic wrecks of the world's greatest sea tragedies: the *Goya*, the *Wilhelm Gustloff* and the *General von Steuben*. As many as 18,000 Germans, most of them civilians, went down on these ships – compare this with the 1,500 on the *Titanic* – in the frozen winter of 1945 as the Nazis tried to evacuate their people from Danzig before the Soviet advance into Germany. The Russians sank all of them. One of the Poles punched at his laptop, and there in front of me were real skulls and bones, a German helmet, a belt, the remains of a shirt. 'The Polish authorities wanted to examine a skull and we brought one back to shore,' the Pole told me. 'It was identified as that of a woman in her thirties.'

Hubris again. The helmet was proof that the Wehrmacht was also aboard those vessels. But the majority were civilians and the Russians still idolise the submariners who killed so many civilians at sea between 30 January and 16 April 1945. It puts Admiral Tryon in the shade. A 'foolish . . . and expensive undertaking which ends in disaster' might as well define the human practice of war. The sea can no longer hide its secrets. Our folly is enshrined there – if we want to examine what it means.

The Independent, 19 February 2005

'Thanks, Bruce'

It comes as a shock to walk through the *Titanic* cemetery. Of course, we all knew that a Canadian cable ship brought back dozens of bodies from the Atlantic. But to walk past the headstones in Halifax, Nova Scotia, is a moving experience, albeit that they were 'restored' some years ago and don't look as old as they should. I didn't intend to write about the *Titanic* again, although it has been a fascination of mine ever since I discovered that many of the dead came from a village called Kfar Mishki in Lebanon. The village inhabitants still mourn their long-dead ancestors who fled what was then Syria because of a famine that was laying waste to the land. Many of the *Titanic* dead in Halifax have no name. Others do.

Take Ernest Waldron King of Currin Rectory, Clones, in Ireland. 'Died on duty, SS *Titanic*,' it says on his headstone. 'April 15, 1912, aged 28 years. Nothing in my hand I bring, simply to thy cross I cling.' And then I glance at the lowest writing on the stone 'Erected by Mr J Bruce Ismay to commemorate a long and faithful service.' And who can forget that this very same Mr Ismay was the manager of the White Star Line, who famously said in James Cameron's epic: 'This ship can't sink – it's unsinkable.' And indeed this is the same Bruce Ismay who climbed into one of the last lifeboats in the early hours of 15 April and made his getaway as hundreds of his fellow passengers on the maiden voyage died in the freezing waters of the Atlantic. How did he dare to erect such a headstone? I looked at my host in Halifax, a local Canadian librarian with a vast smile on his face. 'Thanks, Bruce,' he said.

How is it, though, that these graves move us so much? Many millions of other innocents have died infinitely more terrible deaths – they say that freezing to death isn't as bad as being torn to pieces by a shell, though I shall wait for confirmation of this – in two horrific world wars and in my own neck of the woods, the Middle East. And yet I walk around the sixty-one graves in the Fairview Lawn Cemetery – and yes, there is a rail yard beside it, as there seems to be beside every cemetery – and wonder at these poor people's fates. So do others. There is one headstone upon which is written the following words: 'Erected to the memory of an unknown child whose remains were recovered after the disaster to the *Titanic*, April 15, 1912.' (The *Titanic* was struck by the iceberg – which had been floating in the Atlantic before the ship was built in Belfast – late on the 14th, and foundered on the 15th.) And piled beside this solitary stone are two teddy bears, a child's tool kit, a wreath, a toy duck and two rings. What moved these unknown mourners, well over ninety years after this unknown child's death, to place these things beside its grave? Why am I so moved to see them here in this distant Canadian cemetery, with the wind off the sea and the long grass shuffling in the summer heat?

We are selective in our mourning. Why no tears every day for the millions of Russians, Poles, Jews and others murdered, done to death, gassed and cremated in the Second World War? So I prowl around this windswept cemetery so far from British shores. 'In loving memory of our dear son Harold Reynolds, April 15,1912, aged 21 years.

Out in that bitter waste.
Alone with thee,
Thou didst each hero saint
From sorrow free.
No human help around thy sea
Nearer to thee,
See angel faces beckon me,
Nearer to thee.

Both in Cameron's *Titanic* and in the 1958 film based on Walter Lord's *A Night to Remember* (and who now remembers there was a Broadway production in musical form?) the band played 'Nearer, My God to Thee'. However, it seems that this story was born when the rescue ship *Carpathia* (sunk in the First World War off Ireland) reached New York and the hymn was never actually performed. Titanicologists – for they exist, believe me – suspect that the band, all of whose members drowned, played 'Alexander's Ragtime Band', tunes from *The Merry Widow* or 'Songe d'Automne'. Most cynical of all was Cameron's decision to have his *Titanic* band play 'Nearer, My God to Thee' to the American score – which would never have been done on any British ship.

And yet those headstones carry a clarity all their own. 'Alma Paulson, aged 29, lost with her four children, Torburg Danna, aged eight, Paul Folke, aged six, Steina Viola, aged four, Costa Leonard, aged two.' Is it because these people represented the end of the age of innocence? Is it because we all know that in just over two years the first of the twentieth century's titanic wars would begin after the Archduke Ferdinand left the town hall in Sarajevo? I have a photograph of the said Archduke and his wife leaving the building just five minutes before their death. It is a postcard I bought in Paris thirteen years ago, written by a young man to a relative on the Marne in France on 5 July 1914, and it hangs beside the entrance to my apartment in Beirut to remind visitors (and myself) how dangerous life can be outside the front door. And I look at these graves yet again. What was their world like, when my dad was thirteen years old and had not yet been sent to the Somme? 'Everett Edward Elliott of the heroic crew, aged 24 years.

> Each man stood at his post
> While all the weaker ones
> Went by, and showed once
> More to all the world
> How Englishmen should die.

And here is Herbert Cave, aged 39.

> There let my way appear
> Steps unto heaven
> All thou sends't to me
> In mercy given
> Angels to beckon me
> Nearer My God to thee
> Nearer to thee.

Have we lost something over the years since 1912?

The Independent, 24 June 2006

Those who went before us

Sutton Valence School was an awful, misogynous place. Its one moment of glory was the annual dance with Benenden School for girls (Princess Anne, breathe it heavily) but the rest of the year was one of pea-soup fogs, humid lakes over the Weald and hopes for higher academic advancement. I laboured for my A-levels under a lunatic headmaster who insisted that we spend more time on our Latin grammar (especially Livy), as he also insisted on our pernicious study of Gilbert and Sullivan. Initially, I was his prize performer on the percussion in *Iolanthe*. Later, I learned – with schoolboy malice – to destroy *The Pirates of Penzance* on the violin.

But one thing I did learn from Sutton Valence: the dawning of early morning over the Weald of Kent. Even in Beirut, where I now walk out to that beautiful dawn which only the Mediterranean can give us, do I understand this. I dispute – and hate – much of what my old school used to tell me. But each year there flops on to my desk, in my mail bag from London, my annual copy of *The Suttonian*. It shows Westminster House wherein I was once a prefect – I waited there, one night, for Soviet missiles to arrive after the Cuban Missile Crisis was revealed – and I left that extraordinary red-brick building with untold feelings that 'we' had left many minefields in the world which I would have, as a journalist, to walk through. I was right. Yet I do remember how wonderful it was those summer evenings to read Chaucer and Shakespeare and Donne and Milton and to feel that there was something about their work that would enlighten me for all my life. Little did I realise how strongly I would later come to believe that it was the very breath of the air of the Weald of Kent that would overwhelm me. Did it give us long life?

I say this when I open my latest issue (volume 37) of *The Suttonian*. For example, I find that John Henry Ablitt, a scholar of our school in 1926, has just died aged ninety-four and I notice in the magazine that: 'We have been notified of the death in 1992 of Gavin William Carpenter . . . aged 79. He was the brother of the late Professor Garth Carpenter and the late Drew Carpenter . . . He worked in the timber trade for his career after war service in the RAFC.' And I note also that: 'We have been notified of the death in December 1993 of Edward William Pain (1929, St Margaret's House), aged 81. Edward was the elder brother of Geoffrey Sholto Pain and Dennison Bishop Pain and uncle of Timothy Bishop Pain.' And so my eye slips down the names of those old Suttonians who have passed us by. 'In January 2006, Alfred Brann Catt (1930, St Margaret's) aged 92. Alfred was the father of Anthony Catt [1963, Westminster House – my old house] who sadly died a month after his father and grandfather of Piers Catt (1996, Westminster House). Alfred farmed on the Romney Marshes for his whole life.'

I love these memorials to my long-dead and unknown school friends. Here, for example, we have, 'at the beginning of June 2006', Roy Hart Dunstan, aged eighty-nine.

Roy left school 'at the headmaster's request' after a series of boisterous escapades. However, he always had great affection for Sutton Valence. He went on to Dulwich College where he was a school prefect and captain of athletics. He qualified as a dentist at King's College Hospital in London before serving as a surgeon lieutenant in the Royal Naval Volunteer Reserve during the Second World War. Thereafter, he was in dental practice until his retirement in 1974.

How much I love these 'thereafters', and if only the stupid headmaster's request had been rescinded, what a fine man Mr Dunstan would have made to have been an old boy of my school. But let me continue, for the interest of readers, his CV after the Second World War:

> He was mayor of Warminster in 1985–86. He was closely involved with the International Order of Anysetiers (Commanderie of Great Britain). This was originally a guild of producers and traders in aniseed formed in France in the 13th century under the patrony of the kings of France. The Guild died in the 17th century but was revived in the Order of Anysetiers formed in 1955, opening its ranks to lovers of anis, gastronomy and convivial company.

In 1977 the Commanderie of Great Britain was established and Roy Dunstan was elected chamberlain at the first meeting held at Vintner's Hall, the headquarters of the Worshipful Company of Vintners.

Where do we go from here? On 2 December 2005, 'suddenly but peacefully' in Guernsey, I'm informed that Geoffrey Austin Nops (St Margaret's, 1932) passed away aged ninety-two. 'On leaving school Geoffrey went to Magdalen College, Oxford, to read law, he qualified as a barrister in 1937. He served in the Royal Artillery during the Second World War and was a prisoner of war from 1942 to 1945.' And so it goes on. Guy Goble died aged eighty-three and Peter Brill died aged seventy-seven. 'As a major, he served in Sicily and Italy during the Second World War and later served in the Middle East, Germany and spent some time in the Ministry of Defence.'

What did all these young men learn at Sutton Valence? Did they really understand that there was some kind of way in which we would all learn to live longer? Did we all appreciate something that, at the time, we didn't understand? And I look now, today, at the names in their old memoriam. Dunstan, Nops, Crowhurst, Lewis, Goble, Coleman, Butler, Molyneux-Berry, Scoble-Hodgins, Cresswell, Catt, Gorman, Hills, and I admire these long-dead men from a past I did not know.

We can admire those who went before us, from fathers whose names we never knew, but what was it that kept them alive? That wonderful view over the Weald of Kent, now so sadly curtailed (I went to have a look the other day and it is cynically cut back by council housing), or was there something of their belief in life which we don't have or cannot have? I do not know. I do remember in the great pea-soupers of the 1950s – and how we have all forgotten the smoke and fumes of old smog – how I would go to check the door locks on the chapel and the rooms wherein these great names were locked. I don't think I cared for them. I don't think we do. But now I do remember as I look through the old boys' list of deaths how there were good men (this was before women came to Sutton Valence School!) who believed in things which I hope I now also believe in.

The Independent, 18 August 2007

Farewell, Ane-Karine

Ane-Karine knew all about bombs. And she would have had strong views on the London atrocities.* 'There's no point in banging on about security,' she used to tell me in Beirut during the Lebanese civil war. 'You've got to find out why people do this – and what we might have done to prevent it. You're not going to stop it by talking about "terrorism".' Ane-Karine Arvesen, one of Norway's best diplomats and a good friend for more than two decades, would have understood the irony of my last journey to be with her: that because I travelled back to Beirut via London from her funeral in Oslo, I was on the Piccadilly Line heading for Heathrow just three or four trains in front of the one that exploded at King's Cross.

She was a tough lady, was Ane-Karine. Born in 1941 when Norway was under German occupation, war seemed to determine her life. She was a striking, tall, blonde lady who drank like the proverbial trooper – though never showing the least effect – and smoked cigarettes on a long holder in the hope that this would protect her from cancer.

It didn't, and she died in pain, trying to breathe air into her lungs, alone in a Norwegian hospital. She was always

* The Tube and bus suicide bombings of 7 July 2005, in which 52 people were killed, along with the four bombers. Another 700 were wounded, 22 of them seriously.

'recovering' but found herself at home, unable to walk, unable even to use e-mail any longer. I called her a few days before her death. She had sent a message that she wanted to talk and her high, wheezing voice down the line asked about Lebanon and what would happen in Iraq and whether I would return to Iraq. But we both knew that she wanted to talk to me so we could say goodbye. I tried to cheer Ane-Karine up by reminding her of the unwise, foolish, ridiculous, dangerous, necessary adventures we used to share in Lebanon, how in 1982 when Israel invaded and was attacking Syrian forces in the mountains near Bhamdoun, she drove up into the hills with me as Israeli aircraft destroyed the Syrian armour around us.

'It's neat, neat, Bob, that we could get this far,' she said as huge explosions ripped across the mountains. 'Neat' was one of her favourite words – 'neat' as in 'mission accomplished'.

'Ane-Karine,' I told her, 'this is bloody dangerous.' And she gave me a withering look. 'Bob, we have the Norwegian flag on the car. I am a diplomat.' And I looked at the 16-inch-long flag and reflected that the Israeli F-16s were flying at 10,000 feet and I stared at Ane-Karine and she was laughing.

I told this story at her funeral. The mourners, some of whom had been producing sumptuous tears, burst into parallel laughter. Ane-Karine, locked in her white coffin to my left, smothered in white roses, had come back to life. Yet she was one of the few people whom I could never imagine dead. Her love of life – and her love of adventure – gave her that superhuman quality which only those who have never feared the institution of death can possess. She was in Serbia and was stationed in Iran, a cowled, chadored Norwegian chargé d'affaires in a country that sometimes drove her crazy but who served devastating gin and tonics in the garden of her Tehran residence. One day, she turned up in Beirut with a defence ministry diplomat, who was deeply offended at my analysis of the Middle East because it did not coincide with his own. 'Shut up,' she snapped at him. 'You're here to listen, not try out your silly theories.' No, Ane-Karine didn't suffer fools – I could also feel the lash of her tongue from time to time if she thought I hadn't grasped some self-evident fact of Middle East life; to people here in the Arab world, she said, justice could sometimes be more important than democracy.

On the phone in her last days, she told me that she thought that in Iraq, security and electricity might be more important than democracy. And she may have been right. She felt that the Norwegian foreign ministry was too US-oriented, looking only through Washington's spectacles at 'peace processes' and 'road maps'. And she could be indiscreet. She once emerged from the Norwegian embassy in Beirut in the 1980s – she was an attaché then – with tears streaming down her face; tears of laughter, that is. 'I've just read a dispatch from our ambassador in Washington,' she said. 'He'd gone to meet Reagan and the President had a set of briefing cards so he could say all the right answers. But he got the cards all muddled up and when our ambassador asked about trade relations between Washington and Oslo, Reagan said there would be peace in the Middle East!'

I admired Ane-Karine because she always went to look, to see for herself, to be a witness to the events she would describe in her nightly dispatches to the foreign ministry in Oslo. While other Western diplomats cowered in their Beirut embassies – and a few Western journalists did much the same in their Beirut hotels – she was up there in the hills, working in danger and at first hand. No wonder, years later, she would be sent to Beirut to negotiate, cost-free, the release of a hostage. She succeeded. How I would one day love to read her reports to Oslo – and the anger they apparently contained.

Never was this so obvious as when she walked into the Sabra and Chatila refugee camp on 18 September 1982. She looked with fury – her face so taut that I thought it had lost all its beauty – at the piles of dead men and the eviscerated women and the dead babies, the work of Israel's Phalangist allies. 'Disgusting! Revolting! Obscene!' she shouted. 'One day, we're going to have to pay for this!' Perhaps we still are.

We said our last goodbyes to Ane-Karine in a former chapel not far from a row of British war graves containing the bodies of RAF crews lost over Norway around the time she was born. It was a big oval building with rather a lot of what I thought were runes on the walls, but it was somehow fitting that two Hanukkah candles stood on each side of her coffin. Ane-Karine was not Jewish, but she loved all the people of the Middle East.

The last music was a Swedish song about the third-class passengers on the *Titanic*, how they went from disbelief to conviction that they would die, and at last concluded – as the song claims – that they would go down bravely with the ship's flag still flying. It was entirely in keeping with Ane-Karine's character that she insisted that with money from her estate, her best friends should be taken into Oslo fjord that same afternoon on a boat stocked with forty bottles of Bollinger champagne. Given her courage in war, she was, I think, as much a reporter as a diplomat. She was a creature of our dangerous times. She knew how to live and she knew how to die.

The Independent, 16 July 2005

They told Andrea that Chris had not suffered

Death is generic. But not for me. Yes, I see the photographs of the Iraqis who were crushed, squeezed, plunged, thrown to death in Baghdad. I see the old man dead in the chair in New Orleans. But it is always those we know – those we can identify with as ourselves – who make the impact. Death seems to have followed me this year. On 14 February, the body of the former Lebanese prime minister Rafiq Hariri lay in front of me, his socks on fire. I thought at first he was a *kaak* seller on the Beirut Corniche, one of the men who sell toasted bread. Now four of Lebanon's most senior – and most frightening – security bosses have been arrested as suspects by the United Nations.

Then Ane-Karine Arvesen, my old Norwegian diplomat friend, died of cancer in June. And then, unbelievably, Christian Kleinert died. He was not a close colleague. I only met him in July when he came to Beirut with his friend and lover Andrea Bistrich. She is a journalist, he a photographer. 'Was' a photographer I keep saying to myself as I write this. She came to interview me for a German paper. He took the pictures. We sat on my balcony over the sea and chatted about the Middle East, the West's supercilious, lying coverage of wars, the future of poor old Lebanon. The couple had that special complicity that always attaches itself to people in love. She is thirty-six, he is – goddamit, was – thirty-seven. They had known each other for thirteen years. Then they left for southern Lebanon.

Later she told me of a museum near Tyre, recording the Palestinian exodus of 1948, and I followed up her tip and that is how *Independent* readers came to know a few days later of this extraordinary room full of documents, farm implements, photographs and books of the 'nakba', the Palestinian Arab 'catastrophe' of fifty-seven years ago.

Then this week, the *Independent* foreign desk sent me my usual weekly mail packet. Inside was a thick brown envelope containing coloured photos (Bob of Arabia looking far too serious) and two pictures of Andrea and Christian. He had laid his head on her shoulder. A black-and-white snapshot of him was captioned '26.7.1968–29.7.2005.' What in God's name did this mean, I asked myself? There was a letter from Andrea. Here is what she wrote, in full, complete with a few errors in her otherwise exemplary English:

Dear Robert,

It is sad to say: my dearest friend and partner died on 29 July in a car accident near Munich. Only two weeks after our Lebanon journey and three days after his 37th birthday. On his birthday he said to me that for the first time he felt 'like finally being arrived in life.'

Our journey to Beirut was very important for him. We had a wonderful time, met a lot of people and working together as a team was great. He prepared the photos for you, that was the first thing he did after our arrival. He was so happy that you gave us the chance to meet you. It was special for him and he liked you a lot.

We had plans to leave Munich next year and travel more and also to live in Beirut for a while. We applied at Goethe Institute for a three-months-project in autumn. Now, more than ever, I would like to leave Munich. Everything reminds me of him, I remember every walk we did, and it's terrible painful.

On Friday 29, he hurried to his work – and never came back. He was in a car with two other colleagues and sat next to the driver. Chris talked enthusiastically about Beirut and how he liked it. And he talked about me and how wonderful we worked together.

Perhaps the driver was so engaged with listening that she made a mistake and crashed into a BMW which came towards them at 100 miles/hour. Chris was immediately unconscious with heavy breathing. He had too many inner injuries and died two hours later in a Munich hospital. His colleague on the back seat survived but is still in hospital, the driver had nothing.

Now, three weeks after his death, I still cannot comprehend it. My life changed radically and I have no idea about the future nor about the next day. I reached a kind of 'valium point'. I am alive, but what next?

I was a freelancer, but always had some editorial projects going in order to pay the rent and to earn a living. I lost them all. And it's difficult to find work at newspapers at the moment. I hope something new is coming up. The only thing I know is that I want to keep on writing. More than ever I would like to leave Munich and go to the 'Orient'.

Dear Robert, thanks again from us both, that you were able to take time for meeting us. Enclosed please find some photos. We have more of you, but these we liked most. Let me know if you want them all.

Regards and best wishes from Munich,
Andrea.

I was stunned. Goddamit, I said out loud. GODDAMIT. I called Andrea.

'I had run to the window to wave goodbye that morning,' she said. 'He turned and waved at me.' The German cop who first reached the scene told Andrea that Chris had not suffered.

It will take a year for the post-mortem. I reread the letter, trying to understand its pathos and sorrow and courage. That special line at the end – 'thanks again from both of us' – in which Andrea had recreated, reborn her dead man, made Christian come alive again to send his wishes to Beirut – was heartbreaking.

But what was the message here? I kept asking myself this question. A murdered man, a child crushed on a Baghdad bridge, an old man dead in a chair because his president did not care about global warming, a prime minister who refuses to acknowledge that his citizens die on a London Tube train because of his folly in Iraq. All this has a meaning. But Munich?

Oddly, it was not the first time I had received heartbreaking news from that city. But this death had no meaning. Christian Kleinert should be alive today and he is dead and, as a journalist, I add him to the list of our 'martyrs', those of us who die in road accidents and storms and air crashes as well as from bombs and trigger-happy soldiers and occupation troops and gunmen. And still, I wake each morning in Beirut and hear the wind in the palm trees outside my bedroom window and ask myself what we all ask ourselves these days – or should ask ourselves: what horror waits for us today?

The Independent, 3 September 2005

The dilution of memory

A street named Pétain and the woman he sent to Auschwitz

I still possess a 1930s photograph of a cosy old Beirut street, its Ottoman houses draped with flowers, an ageing Citroën just visible at the end of the cobbled roadway, trees shading the narrow pavements on each side. 'Rue Pétain', it says on the caption. My old *poilu* – Dad – he of the Third Battle of the Somme – would teach me Pétain's pledge at Verdun. '*Ils ne passeront pas.*' They shall not pass. But of course, Pétain's patriotism in 1916 – his refusal to permit the Kaiser's army to advance beyond the Meuse – became France's shame in 1940. When it reached Beirut in 1941, the Anglo-Australian invasion force that drove Vichy France from Lebanon, stripped Pétain's name from the wall of that Ottoman street and Bill Fisk thereafter spoke of him with ambiguity. Bill, like most Englishmen and women – and many, though by no means all, Frenchmen and women – could not forgive the man who collaborated with Hitler's Germany.

I'm reticent about the French for three reasons. Firstly, because some years ago, driven by a sense of outrage and dark curiosity, I attended a mass for the dead in central Paris. It was celebrated by an American priest and was held for – well, yes, Marshal Philippe Pétain. With a dear friend and colleague, I sat in the nave and watched more than 100 mostly elderly middle-class ladies and gentlemen – faces set and grave, sinister and secretive amid the darkness of the church – come to remember the leader of Vichy France who replaced Liberty, Equality and Fraternity with Work, Family, Fatherland, and sent his country's Jews, along with thousands of foreign Jewish refugees, to Auschwitz with an enthusiasm that surprised even the Nazis.

Secondly, because I have just finished reading Irène Némirovsky's brilliant – no, let me speak frankly – transformative account of the Fall of France, *Suite Française*,* a novel which was intended by its young Jewish author to be her modern-day version of Tolstoy's *War and Peace*. *Suite Française* is one of those rare books that you can put down at night and wake up dreaming about, desperate to discover if the revolting Monsieur Corbin reaches his bank in Tours after the flight from Paris, whether the courageous Michaud couple will survive the Nazi onslaught, or if the beautiful Cécile – her unfaithful, unloved husband a French prisoner-of-war – will succumb to the educated, sometimes childlike, sometimes desperately loving German officer billeted in her home.

Némirovsky was born in Kiev in 1903, the daughter of a prominent banker, a refugee from the Russian Revolution, then a refugee from Paris in 1940, whose earlier novels were wildly successful but who could no longer be published under Nazi decrees. She fled Paris with her Jewish husband Michel Epstein to the village of Issy l'Evêque in the German-occupied zone, both marked out for extermination, but all the while writing in tiny, spider-like handwriting in small notebooks her epic of betrayal and heroism and the steady, sad slippage into collaboration which all occupied people must suffer. Her bank account is blocked. 'You must know that if this money must be held in a blocked bank account,' she pleads with her French publisher, 'it would be of no use to me whatsoever.'

---

* Irène Némirovsky, *Suite Française*, translated from the French by Sandra Smith (London, Chatto and Windus, 2006).

Suite Française was to be composed of five books. Némirovsky completed only two – *Storm in June* (the 1940 flight from Paris) and *Dolce*, the first year of occupation in a small French village. Incredibly, the German soldiers living there are treated with a sensitivity bordering on gentleness, although with great cynicism. 'Since the Germans [in the village] mistrusted their tendency to be tactless,' Némirovsky writes, 'they were particularly careful of what they said to the locals – they were therefore accused of being hypocrites.'

There is a wonderful scene in which Lucille and her would-be German lover are viewed through the eyes of a little girl:

> The German and the lady were talking quietly. He had turned white as a sheet too. Now and again, she could hear him holding back his loud voice, as if he wanted to shout or cry but didn't dare . . . She vaguely thought he might be talking about his wife and the lady's husband. She heard him say several times: 'If you were happy . . .'

After Hitler's invasion of Russia, the German unit in Némirovsky's village leaves for the Eastern Front. 'The men began singing, a grave, slow song that drifted away into the night. Soon the road was empty. All that remained of the German regiment was a little cloud of dust.' This is Borodino-like in its magnificence, Tolstoyan indeed.

But Némirovsky did not complete her epic – three books are still unwritten, although we have her notes for them. (Their titles were to be 'Captivity', 'Battles', 'Peace'.) She was arrested and sent to Auschwitz, where she died in the atrocious Birkenau infirmary on 17 August 1942. Believing her still alive, her brave husband Michel appealed to her publishers for help, to the Red Cross, to the German ambassador to Paris, to Pétain himself. The direct result of his letter to the old man was his own arrest and dispatch to Auschwitz. He was sent straight to the gas chamber.

In all, 100,000 Jews were sent from France to the death camps, 20,000 through the transit camp at Drancy outside Paris, almost 2,000 of them children. Four hundred of these children were handed over by the French authorities. All this was recalled at the 14th Jewish Film Festival in Vienna this week when Thomas Draschen introduced his film *Children's Memories*. But imagine Mr Draschen's rage – and here is my third reason for reticence about the French – when he discovered that the French embassy in Vienna, which hosted the film's premiere, deleted the following sentence from its programme: '11,400 Jewish children from France were handed over to the Nazis by the French authorities and murdered at Auschwitz.'

Why, in God's name, was this act of censorship permitted? President Jacques Chirac recognised in 1995 that the French state was responsible for the deportation of the Jews, but somehow the Quai d'Orsay seems to have missed out on this. Certainly the staff of the French Institute in Vienna didn't get the message. Should they be sent a complimentary copy of Némirovsky's agonisingly tragic novel? Or just an invitation to the next mass for the late Marshal Philippe Pétain of France?

The Independent, 2 December 2006

'I am the girl of Irène Némirovsky'

Maurice Papon, lowered into his grave along with his precious Légion d'honneur last week, proved what many Arabs have long suspected but generally refuse to acknowledge: that bureaucrats and racists and others who worked for Hitler regarded all Semitic people as their enemies and that – had Hitler's armies reached the Middle East – they would ultimately have found a 'final solution' to the 'Arab question', just as they did for the Jews of Europe. Papon's responsibility for the 1942 arrest and deportation of 1,600 Jews in and around Bordeaux – 223 children among them, all shipped off to the Drancy camp and then to Auschwitz – was proved without the proverbial shadow of a doubt at his 1998 trial.

Less clear was the exact number of Algerians murdered by his police force in Paris and hurled into the Seine in 1961. Of course, he was not tried for this lesser but equally unscrupulous crime. He organised the police repression of the independence demonstration by 40,000 Algerians; in the cities of Algiers and Oran and Blida and other areas of modern-day Algeria where this atrocity festers on among elderly relatives, they say that up to 400 Algerians were massacred by Papon's *flics*. Some historians suggest 250. Papon preferred to claim that only two were killed – in much the same way as he later insisted at his trial that he did not know the fate of the Jews he dispatched so efficiently to Drancy and onwards to Poland.

The same was always claimed of Haj Amin al-Husseini, the Grand Mufti of Jerusalem. He it was who fled to Iraq during the Second World War, escaped again after the British crushed the pro-Axis government that had taken power in Baghdad, and who ended up in Nazi Berlin, shaking hands with Hitler and working enthusiastically for the Third Reich's propaganda machine.

All this came back to me last week when I received a remarkable letter from Toulouse in my Beirut mailbag. It was a response to my article about Irène Némirovsky, which had earned a stiff call of complaint from the press attaché at the French embassy in London. But the letter from Toulouse, in slightly ungrammatical English, was written by Némirovsky's only surviving daughter, Denise Epstein, and I hope she will not mind if I quote from it:

> Allow me to present myself: I am the girl of Irène Némirovsky ... and I wanted to thank you for having spoken so well about my mother. This book caused a certain awakening of the consciences undoubtedly but according to what you teach me from the attitude of the French embassy when one evokes the memory of the Jewish children assassinated with the complicity of the authorities of the time, I realize that the memory is really diluted very easily and which that opens the door with other massacres innocent whatever their origin. It is thus with emotion and gratitude that I want to send this small message to you. I am now 77 years old and I nevertheless live the every day with the weight of this past on the shoulders, softened by happiness to see reviving my parents, and at the same time as them, I hope to make revive all those of which nobody any more speaks. PS: Sorry for my very bad English!*

* Letter from Denise Epstein to the author, 3 December 2006.

It would be hard to find more moving words than these, a conscious belief that the dead can be recalled in their own words along with that immensely generous remembrance of other innocents who have died in other massacres. And that extraordinary image of the 'dilution of memory' carries its own message. This, of course, is what Haj Amin suffered from. Papon, too, I imagine, before they buried the terrible old man last week.

The Independent, 24 February 2007

INDEX